94

4

i

95

12 APR 2002

Hosts, Immigrants and Minorities

Hosts, Immigrants and Minorities

Historical Responses to Newcomers in British Society 1870–1914

Edited by **KENNETH LUNN**
Department of Historical and Literary
Studies, Portsmouth Polytechnic

DAWSON

Wm Dawson & Sons Ltd, Cannon House
Folkestone, Kent, England

British Library Cataloguing in Publication Data

Hosts, immigrants and minorities.
1. Great Britain—Race relations
I. Lunn, Kenneth   II. Society for the Study of Labour History
301.45'1'0941   DA125.A1

ISBN 0-7129-0949-4

Printed litho in Great Britain
by W & J Mackay Ltd, Chatham

Contents

Contributors

John Rex is Director of the Social Science Research Council's Research Unit on Ethnic Relations and Professor of Sociology in Aston University. Among his many publications are Race, Community and Politics (1967) (with Robert Moore), Race Relations in Sociological Theory (1970), Race, Colonialism and the City (1970) and Colonial Immigrants in Great Britain (1979) (with Sally Tomlinson).

Richard C. Thurlow is Lecturer in Economic and Social History at Sheffield University. He has been a regular contributor to Patterns of Prejudice since 1974 and is co-editor of British Fascism, to be published in 1979.

Neville Kirk is Lecturer in Social and Economic History at Liverpool Polytechnic. He is currently revising his Ph.D. thesis on the decline of Chartism in Lancashire with a view to publication. He is editor of the Bulletin of the North-West Labour History Group.

Alan Lee is Lecturer in History at Hull University. His publications include The Origins of the Popular Press, 1855-1914 (1976) and contributions to the Dictionary of Labour Biography, as well as several journal articles.

Colin Holmes is Senior Lecturer in Economic and Social History, Sheffield University. He is the editor of Immigrants and Minorities in British Society (1978) and author of Anti-Semitism in British Society, 1876-1939 (1979).

Sheridan Gilley is Lecturer in Theology at Durham University. He has contributed to Dyos and Wolff (eds.), The Victorian City (1973) and Holmes (ed.), Immigrants and Minorities in British Society (1978) and has published articles on modern Irish and Roman Catholic history.

Gregory Anderson is Lecturer in the Department of Economics at Salford University. He is the author of Victorian Clerks (1976), and several journal articles, and is a contributor to Crossick (ed.), The Lower Middle Class, 1870-1914 (1977).

Bill Williams is head of the Manchester Studies Unit at Manchester Polytechnic. His volume, The Making of Manchester Jewry, 1740-1875, appeared in 1976 and he is at present working on the history of Jewish immigration and settlement in Manchester in the period 1870-1939.

Joe Buckman is Principal Lecturer in Economics in Further
Education, having been lecturer at the University of
Strathclyde and an Economic Consultant and Mission Member
with the OECD. He has presented papers to learned
societies and is at present engaged on a large-scale study
of the alien economy of Leeds.

Kenneth Lunn is Lecturer in the Department of Historical
and Literary Studies at Portsmouth Polytechnic and a former
Douglas Knoop Research Fellow at Sheffield University.
In addition to several articles on the history of minority
groups in Britain, he is co-editor of British Fascism,
to be published in 1979.

Tom Lane is Lecturer in History in the School of Social
Science at Bradford University. He has contributed to the
Journal of American Studies and is completing a long study of
American labour attitudes towards immigration between 1865
and the 1920s.

Preface

The origins of this collection of essays lie with the papers
presented for a conference of the Society for the Study of
Labour History held in May 1978 at Sheffield University. As
a result of discussions before, during and after the proceedings,
it was felt that, with certain revisions, the papers ought to
be published in one volume, since much of the information and
interpretation seemed of significant interest for a wider
audience.

In the course of preparing this publication, many
organisations and individuals were of assistance. First in
line for acknowledgement must be the Society for the Study of
Labour History, for deciding upon the conference theme, and
particularly the organising committee of the conference, for
their efforts in bringing about the proceedings. Particular
mention should go to Beverley Eaton, Beryl Moore and David
Martin, who were responsible for the typing, collation and
distribution of the original papers.

During the editing of the volume, I received valuable
assistance from my former colleagues at Sheffield University,
particularly Colin Holmes. The index was painstakingly
prepared by Sybil Lunn. The publishers, and especially
Robert Seal, were of constant help during the production.
Finally, I would like to thank the contributors for their
interest and cooperation in bringing such a project to
fruition.

Kenneth Lunn
Portsmouth Polytechnic
November 1979

1
Introduction

Those who are now young in Britain live in a country which
has recently witnessed the settlement of immigrant groups on
a previously unparalleled scale.   But even those who are
older have been reared in a society which has provided a
temporary or permanent home for a variety of immigrant
groups.   Indeed, with varying degrees of intensity,
immigration has been a feature of British society since Roman
times onwards, and some movement almost certainly occurred in
even earlier years.   'The British are clearly among the most
ethnically composite of the Europeans', suggests Geipel,[1]
and it is not only in remote, far-off outposts of the Empire
that the British have entered into contact with a variety of
racial and ethnic groups.[2]

   In the nineteenth century, as in earlier years, the
newcomers who came to Britain included individual political
figures fleeing from persecution in Western and Eastern
Europe, who found a more generous atmosphere for their
beliefs and activities.[3]   As in the past the country also
witnessed the arrival of immigrant groups.   Included in this
category were Jews, fleeing from anti-semitism, eager for a
better life in a new world, moving from east to west, and
providing yet another reminder that migration is an integral
part of Jewish history.[4]   In addition, the country
encountered groups such as the Italians who, as part of a
larger movement away from Italy, came to Britain under the
push and pull of economic influences.[5]   And there were

1

others, too, such as the small communities of Chinese and
Africans in or near the ports where they were recruited and
released by shipping firms.[6]

At the present time Britain still contains communities
of refugees who have been separated from their birthplace on
account of political differences. The Polish emigracja
(exile community) is a case in point.[7] Furthermore, Britain
still has a Jewish minority, which is now more widely dispersed than it was for most of the nineteenth century.[8] It
still draws from Europe a supply of workers, including
Italians, who constitute a reserve army of labour, even if
their real earnings in Britain are greater than in their own
countries.[9] And Britain still retains a small number of
Chinese and African immigrants.[10] But there are significant
changes and differences between nineteenth and twentieth
century developments. From the early Danish invasions of
the country until recent times the immigrant influx has been
composed mainly of urban groups, but a great deal of
immigration of the past few years from the West Indies,
India, Pakistan and Hong Kong, consists of former rural
dwellers. The result, it has been written, is that
'Kingston, Karachi and Kowloon are often less familiar to
them than London, Leeds or Liverpool'.[11] Furthermore, the
contemporary immigration from what is called the New
Commonwealth has provided Britain with a far greater number
of newcomers than any other recorded influx in its history,
and it is the presence of such immigrants - the precise
numbers of whom nevertheless elude us - which has given
recent immigration into Britain its distinctive character.
It is also an influx which has led to the emergence in
Britain of a 'race relations industry' and to the activity of
a considerable number of pressure groups attempting to
advance their own specific interests in the immigration
debate.[12]

2

In former years, some immigration into Britain was of a temporary nature: the immigrants were sojourners rather than settlers.[13] Many Jews in the nineteenth century used the country as a staging post on their way to the 'goldene medina' of Hester Street, New York, and refugees such as the Belgians, fleeing from the German Army in 1914, regrouped in Britain before returning to the Continent to resume the fight against Germany. And this tendency still persists so that some contemporary immigrants, particularly those from the Indian subcontinent, also regard their stay as temporary and are interested essentially in accumulating funds to set them up for retirement in the lands from where they came.[14] There is also - as there always has been - a temporary immigration of the young, intent upon the acquisition of skills before returning home. By contrast, however, some of the movement now, as in the past, bears a permanent stamp. The graves of Jews, Germans, Poles and Africans are all reminders of past permanence and in our own day many West Indians and the majority of political refugees from Europe will never leave Britain. In addition, some immigrant Pakistanis, originally intent upon return, will find that government legislation and the acculturation of their children might restrict their future mobility. In themselves, of course, such contrasting attitudes towards Britain serve to remind us that the term immigrant obscures a diversity of intentions.[15] And opponents of newcomers, who lay a stress upon 'Britain for the British' are capable of extending the concept even further, so that it embraces the second generation of those born and bred in this country. We ought to be aware of such nuances.

Britain, then, is a country of immigration of varying kinds. After illustrating this, we might ask how the host society has reacted to such developments. It should be said at once that immigration has always been a double-edged

3

weapon. Receiving societies are not unified wholes and immigration is hardly likely to be viewed in one-dimensional terms. Britain is no exception. In early times, for example, while foreign businessmen were regarded by the state as a welcome asset, their native rivals in business could perceive them differently.[16] Similarly, while at the time of the great Jewish immigration from the Russian Empire there were those who welcomed the Jewish immigrant and heaped Smilesian virtues on him, a different reaction was apparent among those who believed themselves to be facing competition from such labour.[17] Such historical cries against immigrant competition have come not only from the proletariat. Certain professional circles in the 1930s were equally anxious about their prospects, when they believed that they might face competition from those escaping from Hitler's descending persecution.[18] We need to be generally aware, in fact, of this history of economic hostility towards immigrants, and it is an emphasis which is given an important place in the present volume.

The Jewish immigrants who encountered such responses have been relatively well studied. But it was not they alone who ran into opposition from sections of the receiving society. Chinese seamen, although welcomed by some shipping lines, found themselves targets of hostility over what was regarded as undercutting by cheap labour. Tension deriving from this source could extend into other areas so that in a night of rioting in 1911 all the Chinese restaurants in Cardiff were destroyed.[19] Opposition arising out of a fear of economic competition was also present in the hostility directed towards the German clerks who sought employment in the City of London in the late nineteenth century. Faced with what they considered to be unfair competition at a time of status panic, English clerks were not attracted to the view that such an influx aided in the development of an

4

international service economy in which the City of London
would play a major role.[20]

In addition to discontent stemming from fears of competition for employment, friction has also developed out of
demands for another scarce commodity, housing. It is clear,
for instance, that the agitation over Jewish immigration in
the late nineteenth and early twentieth centuries assumed
different emphases at different times, with the result that
tensions relating to employment were eventually replaced by
those derived from competition in the housing market.[21]
More recently, similar fears have played their part in the
hostility displayed towards contemporary immigrants from the
New Commonwealth. This conflict is particularly apparent
between council tenants in slum properties awaiting demolition
and immigrants in lodging houses.[22]

But, at times, man lives by more than bread alone and
tension has arisen over other than economic issues. In the
East End during the great Jewish immigration there were
frequent complaints about the strange habits which were
introduced into the area as a result of the immigration from
Russia. Whitechapel, it was widely believed, was becoming
the New Jerusalem. 'Their ways are different from ours' was
the theme of opposition and, in the short term, it was a
claim which could not be entirely dismissed.[23] In addition
to Jewish groups, Gypsy newcomers found themselves facing
similar opposition, on account of their allegedly dirty and
dangerous ways.[24] And while the Chinese minority in Britain
could be regarded by the police as respectable citizens -
opium-taking did not worry the authorities at the beginning
of the present century - there were those in Britain who
became seriously concerned about what they perceived as a
significant Chinese involvement in gambling, illicit sexual
activity and drug-taking. Those who raised these issues
regarded such behaviour as running counter to national

standards.[25]   Moving closer to our own day, it is also
possible to find the arguments against New Commonwealth
immigrants assuming a similar form, in the sense that an
emphasis is placed upon behaviour which, it is alleged, is
antipathetic to a variously defined British way of life.
Hence we encounter references to groups encamped in a green
and pleasant land, of which they know little, wish to know
little and who, by contrast, are intent upon pursuing their
own life styles and maintaining close links with the countries
of their birth.[26]   Comment such as this, which in earlier
times was often manifested in religious terms, as in the
opposition to Anabaptists,[27] has been a recurring feature in
the historical strands of opposition to immigration.

Faced with the prospect that immigration has been
capable of producing tensions, explicable for the most part
in essentially social terms, bearing in mind that we must
take account of the attitudes and behaviour of both groups in
the conflict equation, the attitude of the state until
relatively recently has been one of limited interference.
However, in the period of the French Revolution and the
Napoleonic Wars several acts were passed, culminating in the
1793 Aliens Act, which were concerned with excluding aliens
from Britain during time of war.   In the early nineteenth
century, this legislation was repealed and replaced by the
1826 Aliens Act and the 1836 Aliens Registration Act.
These did not aim at restricting entry;   their concern was
simply with the registration of immigrants and even that
was not vigorously pursued by the authorities.[28]   In fact,
it took the relatively large Jewish immigration and the
First World War to bring about a change in the character
of legislation.   It was at such times that the 1905 Aliens
Act, the 1914 Aliens Restriction Act and the Aliens
Restriction (Amendment) Act of 1919 were passed.   Under such
acts the admission and expulsion of aliens were controlled by

powers exercised by Order in Council, and these measures
remained in force until 1971.[29]   Such legislation was not
draconian in character and certainly did not prevent the
admission of alien immigrants on humanitarian grounds, with
the consequence that in the 1930s Jewish refugees were
allowed to come to Britain, even if their entry was not as
smooth as some would have wished, and after the Second World
War Polish immigrants, the European Volunteer Workers, and
later still the small number of Hungarians fleeing from the
repression of the 1956 Revolution, were all allowed to enter
the country.[30]

At first, the New Commonwealth immigrants who entered
Britain were not even touched by any of these restrictions.
As Commonwealth citizens they enjoyed the right to enter the
United Kingdom.   However, the 1960s witnessed the end of
such freedom.   The 1961 Commonwealth Immigrants Act introduced the system of vouchers for entry into the country and,
from that point onwards, a series of measures were forthcoming,
each of which was intended to restrict freedom of entry.   In
1965 the White Paper on 'Immigration from the Commonwealth'
stiffened controls through the voucher system, and the 1968
Commonwealth Immigrants Act brought within the control
provisions those with UK passports who were not born,
naturalised or adopted in the United Kingdom or who did not
have a parent or grandparent who was so born, naturalised or
adopted.   In the following year the Immigration Appeals Act
tightened up the control over the credentials of immigrants,
and then in 1971 through the terms of the Immigration Act -
which came fully into force in January 1973 - the distinction
between New Commonwealth immigrants and aliens was largely
abolished for immigration purposes.   There had clearly been
a decisive transformation in official attitudes towards the
former in the 1960s.[31]

At the same time as it was implementing such legislation

the government also introduced laws designed to promote and
improve race relations and to protect recent immigrants and
their families from the hostility of the receiving society.
And, since governments like individuals have no difficulty in
clothing their behaviour in respectable garb, it was
emphasised that restrictive legislation on entry was quite
compatible with laws designed to promote racial harmony.
Indeed, it was suggested that some control over entry would
enable the taks of improving race relations to be facilitated.
The most urgent need, it was maintained, was for integration,
and it was with this in mind, while control was being extended
over entry that the Race Relations Acts of 1965, 1968 and 1976
were placed on the statute book.[32]   The need for such measures
calls into question, of course, the existence of that fund of
goodwill, supposedly present and manifested in Britain towards
newcomers, as part of an essential sense of tolerance and fair
play residing within the nation.[33]

So much for the responses of the receiving society.
How, we might now ask, have the immigrants themselves
responded to their environment?   In our consideration of
hostility towards newcomers it was suggested that we needed
to take account of the attitudes and behaviour of both sides
involved in the conflict situation, and in examining the
various responses made by immigrants to British society, we
also need to bear in mind that reactions have not depended
upon the newcomers alone.   It should be stressed again that
the receiving society is not a unitary concept: what is
'necessary' or 'desirable' from the point of view of one
class may not be 'necessary' or 'desirable' from that of
another.   This means that a range of reactions with newcomers
may be possible.   We also need to be aware that immigrant
groups are themselves divided into social categories, with
their own special interests, and also that the relationship

of newcomers to the host society operates on more than one
axis.[34]

If we consider what this has meant historically it can
be said that most immigrants have gone through an initial
stage when they have enjoyed only a minimum contact with the
homeland and, at the same time, have established only a
tenuous link with their new environment through their bond of
employment. After some time, following on from this stage,
immigrants have tended to build up a primary community system
with their fellow-immigrants. Concentrations of this kind
have arisen partly out of the endogenous needs of newcomers
in a strange environment but such communities have also owed
something to the practice of discrimination by elements within
the receiving society. Consequently, Britain has witnessed
its own 'ghettos', such as the concentration of Jews in
Stepney at the turn of the century, a phenomenon emphasised
in the 1903 Royal Commission on Alien Immigration, the
emergence of a distinct Chinese community in Limehouse, which
fuelled the fears of Sax Rohmer and invoked the romanticism
of Thomas Burke, and the creation of a new black 'Babylon'
among recent immigrants in Handsworth, Birmingham.[35] It is
in such areas that the major examples of primary immigrant
communities have developed.

The consequent relationship between such structures and
the wider society has been governed historically by a complex
interacting process which, in some cases, has led to the
significant abandonment of the primary immigrant community.
In the nineteenth century this occurred in the case of some
Germans and, nearer our own time, the process has been
repeated by some of the younger Polish immigrants who came
to Britain after the Second World War.[36] But it needs to be
underlined that host-immigrant relations have been and still
are characterised by complex, shifting, interacting forces
and this does not allow us to write about inexorable and

inevitable developments here.[37]

On that note, having indicated that Britain is a country
of immigration and that this has provided the context for the
emergence of a variety of relationships between host and
immigrant, we might now turn to a consideration of the specific
studies contained in the present volume.

Concentrating in the main on the period 1870-1914, the papers
first of all provide an indication of the wide ethnic range of
newcomers who entered Britain at this time. The numerical
superiority of Eastern European Jewish immigrants has caused
us to overlook the full extent of this multi-cultural influx
and has led to generalisations about the newcomers and the
reactions of the host society which ignore the wide range of
differing immigrant experiences. In this respect, three
studies of non-Jewish immigration provide a wider perspective.
Colin Holmes considers the hostile reaction towards a
relatively few German Gypsies who found their way to Britain
in the early years of the twentieth century, only to face
police harassment, political opposition and eventual deportation, and contrasts this experience with that of the
Jews, who faced little overt persecution, either on arrival
or in the years following. In Gregory Anderson's study of
reactions towards the employment of German clerks in the
late nineteenth century, we find a detailed consideration of
what appears at first glance to be 'simple' aversion towards
foreigners who pose (or appear to pose) an economic threat to
certain groups in British society. However, placing this
Germanophobia in its wider economic and social setting,
Anderson indicates the other factors at work on the English
clerk's status and thus suggests that the Germans provide a
classic illustration of the scapegoating process. Since the
causal factors of social change were difficult to identify,
an out-group could be treated as the source of the uncertainty

10

and the changing nature of such employment. In another area
of the labour market, the Scottish coalfields, the native
workforce found itself in competition with 'Polish' or, more
accurately, Lithuanian migrants who came mostly from a rural
background. This situation appeared to duplicate in many
ways the mid-century experience of Irish workers being introduced into the mines, although in the case of the Lithuanians,
the numbers were considerably smaller. In addition, Kenneth
Lunn shows that restrictionist demands by organised labour
were made against the Catholic 'Poles' long after such cries
against the Jewish immigrant had ceased. Have we, as
historians, become so overwhelmed by the unwritten adjective
'Jewish' before 'immigration' that we have often tended to
overlook the fact that although other immigrant newcomers
have frequently encountered similar experiences at particular
times, the recent history of individual groups displays
striking differences. For example, Holmes suggests that the
existence of a Jewish minority before the 'Great Emigration'
had a cushioning effect, whereas the Gypsies had no
satisfactory reference group nor any political influence in
British society. Neither did they exhibit values deemed to
be useful or synonymous with the culture of the majority of
the natives. Contrast this with the case of the Lithuanians,
who had no forerunners and encountered great initial hostility,
yet by dint of hard work and unionisation, perhaps even class
solidarity, rapidly became accepted, in certain circumstances,
by most of their workmates, if not by the hysterical middle
class of Lanarkshire. Clearly, there are a whole series of
comparative situations which require analysis before new
conceptual work on the immigration and settlement processes
is produced.[38]

The question of differing responses to immigrants is
also raised by A.T. Lane's paper, which examines the
experiences of Britain and the USA. He points out that

11

the American labour movement demanded greater restriction of immigration and was generally more hostile towards newcomers than its British counterpart. In his attempt to explain this, he considers not merely the problems associated with the concentration and size of the immigration into the USA at this time but discusses other factors which might have produced such a heightened response. By so doing, Lane contributes a model which historians and other social scientists can use as a basis for further work. His final question - was the American response really any different from that of Britain, given the relative size of each country's immigration? - is one which needs careful and detailed consideration. Too often, social scientists here have been content to shelter behind the simplistic view which contrasts a racist situation in the United States with the relative racial harmony of a liberal Britain, the haven of refugees and immigrants. A re-evaluation is long overdue.

Perhaps, too, some of the generalisations about the British experience are a product of the concentration on the London situation. To some extent, such an approach is justified since, over the centuries, the city attracted the majority of immigrants, as well as internal migrants. However, as both Joseph Buckman and Bill Williams show, generalisations based on evidence from London can produce distorting pictures. In their case, studies of Jewish trades unions in Leeds and Manchester reveal significantly different experiences from that of the capital and raise serious questions about the inherent 'Jewish' nature of such activities that previous writers have described. Williams's work on the early Jewish unions in Manchester gives us the wider context for such a study, describing the strengths of the movement as well as its divisions, and suggests that some of the problems are better explained in general economic and class terms than by attributing them to particular 'Jewish' qualities. Similarly, Buckman's very closely researched work on Leeds unionism indicates the necessity for detailed study of a complex series of relationships in the tailoring trades and how we can move away from the somewhat simplistic con-clusions of earlier work published on London. He states that certain districts of Leeds revealed a greater concen-tration of immigrants than London, and this should be borne in mind when the responses of the native Leeds workforce are considered. Furthermore, if Lane's views on the significance of concentration are to be tested, Leeds would seem to be an appropriate subject for such a study.[39]

Many of the conference papers make clear the political dimension of race and ethnicity in the years since 1850. While John Rex focusses on the post-1945 situation and offers a contemporary analysis of Britain's immigrants, Neville Kirk's work on the responses to the Irish in the mid-nineteenth century indicates that political organisations are no strangers when it comes to playing the 'race card'. In Kirk's analysis of the various factors behind the tension between Irish and English in the cotton towns of the north-west, he also suggests that the successful fostering of working-class Toryism in this period owed a good deal to the exploitation of ethnic tension by the middle-class Conservatives. Taking the Irish question into the twentieth century, Sheridan Gilley provides a well-documented account of the Catholic hierarchy's resistance and hostility towards socialist ideas in Glasgow and the resulting problems for the ideological basis of the labour movement. As with the Jews, it has been common practice to describe the Irish as a weakening influence in the labour and trade union movement, and Gilley provides us with evidence of the institutional barriers which were raised against full participation. It should be said, however, that both he and Kirk (and, to some extent, Lunn) indicate the allegiance and support frequently given by the Irish to trade unionism and

13

radical politics.   Richard Thurlow continues the political
analysis and shows how, after the First World War, negative
images of minority groups were used by politicians, some on
the fringes of the political scene, others in the mainstream.
Emphasising a legacy of ideas, he suggests that the ideology
of these individuals and movements is linked to popular
cultural prejudices which reflect working-class attitudes and
behaviour patterns.   In conjunction with this theoretical
paper, the reader should examine Alan Lee's contribution,
which sees the failure of anti-alienism (essentially anti-
semitism) before 1914 to gain great political credence as
related partly to the fact that there was no fundamentally
hostile image of the Jew in British working-class culture for
politicians to exploit.

The major theme of Lee's work is, in fact, an analysis
of the means by which images of minority groups are formed,
with particular reference to the working-class stereotype of
the Jew before 1914.   He raises questions about the nature
of the opposition towards the immigrant and the origins of
such hostility, as well as studying the transmission of images
in a culture whose sources were frequently oral rather than
literary.   The process of transference of these stereotypes
is of some relevance, since several contributors to this
volume (Kirk, Holmes and Thurlow, for example) refer to the
importance of pre-existing images of various minorities and
the influences these ideas had on responses to such groups.
In this area, as in many others, it is clear that we are only
just beginning to move beyond the basic generalities about
the effects of immigration on British society, and the
material contained in this volume suggests some possible
avenues for more detailed exploration.

It appears to us that we need further research both on
immigrants themselves and on the reactions towards them by

the host society. In the former area, the time seems ripe
for a reassessment of certain generalised ideas about
immigrants, and one of the ways to question such views is
through micro-studies such as those found in this volume.
Clearly, more studies of the areas where immigrants have
become established members of the community would help to
identify settlement patterns, distinguish the significant
factors contributing to the differing experiences of various
groups, and highlight the regional variations in such
experiences. It is almost certain that such studies would
suggest that we cannot accurately talk about the 'British
experience' of, say, Jewish immigrants, except in very broad
terms. For a more historically sound analysis, we must in
fact turn to particular examples, taking cities such as
London, Leeds, Manchester and Glasgow as our case studies.
The 1975 conference of the Jewish Historical Society of
England moved in this direction when it provided evidence of
the wide extent of nineteenth and twentieth century Jewish
settlement,[40] and Bill Williams has more recently produced
the first volume of a major study on Manchester Jewry.[41]
Such investigations have begun to redress the emphasis on
London which has characterised so much previous work.[42]
With perhaps the exceptions of the Irish and New Commonwealth
settlers, very few other immigrant groups have yet received
the detailed attention which is necessary for the revision of
existing interpretations. Similarly, many major towns and
cities in Britain do not have a satisfactory account of their
'immigrant history'.[43] Indeed, we still await a fully
detailed study of the East End, the crucible of modern
British immigration and adaptation.[44]

We also know little about the variety of immigrants who
have come to Britain. Again, the concentration has been in
the Irish, the Jews and the New Commonwealth migrants after
1945. others such as the Italians, Poles, Lithuanians and

Gypsies have received scant attention, although J.L. Watson's Between Two Cultures has recently pointed out the multiplicity of ethnic cultures present in British society. Watson also raised an extremely relevant issue when he commented that many of his collaborators were familiar with the country of origin of the various newcomers. This, he argued, was essential for understanding the causes of movement, of why immigrants were coming to Britain. But, more than this, past experiences and expectations helped to govern the responses of the new-comers to British society. In short, a knowledge of the country of origin was suggested by Watson as a crucial element in any attempt to obtain a rounded perspective of immigrant experience.

But immigrant responses do not depend solely on their own pre-existing experiences. The reactions of the receiving society also exert an influence. In this regard, perhaps the first concept we ought to question is that which refers to a tradition of toleration in Britain towards strangers. Although some of the contributors in this volume have remarked on the cooperation they found between certain sections of the native population and the immigrants, and Alan Lee has raised an interesting point about the popular stereotype of the Jew at the turn of the century, questioning the existence of a consistently hostile image, can we not refer to a tradition of intolerance? Practically every immigrant group has met with initial opposition and hostility, which in some instances have not been moderated with the passage of time; in the case of West Indians and Asians antipathy has in fact increased since the end of the Second World War. We have already noticed that in his contribution to the present volume A.T. Lane has questioned the strength of a British tradition of toleration towards immigration and his conclusions would reinforce our own feelings. Should we not, therefore, in considering host-immigrant relations, take, as the starting

point of study, the heritage of intolerance and then proceed
to examine from both perspectives those factors which have
eased social tensions?

In this respect the transmission of stereotypes assumes
a significance. In the present volume Lee has raised points
about how such cultural images might be passed on, but his
conclusions are still tentative. We need to know more about
the images of foreigners which existed at particular times,
whether they were related specifically to certain groups or
to foreigners in general, and how deep-seated these
categorisations were in British society. In this discussion
we also need to recognise that we cannot justifiably refer to
a single British culture.[45] It should be emphasised that
society is composed of a number of cultures and it is
essential to identify not only those images which were present
in the mainstream tradition but those which existed outside
it. The identification of pre-existing stereotypes and the
contexts in which they were held[46] would significantly help
to explain the nature of the reactions shown towards
immigrant groups and in this, it would seem to us that oral
history has an important and much neglected part to play, as
it has in the whole field of immigration studies.

These are a number of major areas in which future work
is needed. In pursuing research in them we should extend
significantly our knowledge of immigration into Britain.
But, while encouraging this process, we might conclude by
emphasising that all such studies would gain additionally if
developments in Britain were placed within a comparative
context. The importance of this approach is that it would
raise our horizons and aid us to recognise those characteristics
which are central for an understanding of the specifically
British experience.

17

NOTES

1. J. Geipel, The Europeans: An Ethnohistorical Survey
(1969), pp. 163-4.

2. A point made in C. Holmes (ed,), Immigrants and Minorities
in Society (1978), p, 1.

3. See the references by V,G. Kiernan in 'Britons Old and New',
in ibid., pp. 49-50. More specifically, see E.H. Carr, The
Romantic Exiles (1933).

4. L. Gartner, The Jewish Immigrant in England 1870-1914
(1960), J.A. Garrard, The English and Immigration 1880-1910
(1971), B. Gainer, The Alien Invasion (1972).

5. R. Foerster, The Italian Emigration of Our Times
(Cambridge, Mass., 1919).

6. K. Little, Negroes in Britain (1947: reissued 1971),
J. Walvin, Black and White: The Negro in English Society
1555-1945 (1972), J.P. May, 'The British Working Class and the
Chinese' (unpublished MA thesis, University of Warwick, 1973),
cover such minorities.

7. S. Patterson, 'The Poles: An Exile Community in Britain',
in J.L. Watson (ed.), Between Two Cultures: Migrants and
Minorities in Britain (Oxford, 1977), pp. 214-41.

8. S.J. Gould and S. Esh (eds.), Jewish Life in Modern
Britain (1964).

9. See the essays in Watson, Two Cultures pp. 242-331,

10. See ibid., pp. 181-213, for a discussion of the Chinese
and ibid., pp. 151-8, and A. Craven, West Africans in London
(1968), for reference to Africans in Britain.

11. Watson, Two Cultures p. 6,

12. See the First Report from the Select Committee on Race
Relations and Immigration, Session 1977-78, Immigration vol. 1
(1978), p. x, Ibid., p. xv, comments on our statistical
ignorance. The history of immigration into Britain during
these years, and the developments related to it, has yet to
be written. New Commonwealth immigrants embraces all Commonwealth immigrants who do not hail from Canada, Australia and
New Zealand. Until 1972, this definition would include
Pakistanis. In that year, however, Pakistan seceded from
the Commonwealth.

13. For a general discussion see P.C.P. Siu, 'The Sojourner',
American Journal of Sociology, 58 (1952), pp.34-44.
E. Bonacich, 'A Theory of Middleman Minorities', American
Sociological Review, 38 (1973), pp.583-94, is also useful on
such matters.

14. See B. Dahya, 'Pakistanis in Britain: Transients or
Settlers?', Race, 14 (1973), pp.242-77.

15. As noted in the S.C. Race Relations etc., p.ix.

16. Kiernan in Holmes, Immigrants, p.28.

17. The most recent discussion is in C. Holmes, Anti-Semitism
in British Society 1876-1939 (1979), ch.2.

18. Ibid., chapter 13. A.J. Sherman, Island Refuge, Britain
and Refugees from the Third Reich 1933-1939 (1973) also
discusses this influx.

19. May, thesis, is concerned with such outbreaks.

20. See the essay by G.L. Anderson in the present volume.

21. J.J. Bennett, 'East End Newspaper Opinion and Jewish
Immigration, 1885-1905' (unpublished M.Phil. thesis, Sheffield
University, 1979) provides the fullest evidence on this point.

22. J. Rex and R. Moore, Race, Community and Conflict: A Study
of Sparkbrook (1967), is a study of such tensions.

23. Holmes, Anti-Semitism, ch.2.   See also Garrard, Immigration
and Gainer, Invasion.

24. See the essay by C. Holmes in the present volume.   For
more general comment, see D. Martin,'Hard Travelling', in
The Times Literary Supplement, 2 January 1976, p.2.

25. As May, thesis, generally· illustrates.   For a condensed
version see his essay 'The Chinese in Britain 1860-1914' in
Holmes, Immigrants pp.111-24, particularly 113-14, 117.

26. B. Smithies and P. Fiddick, Enoch Powell on Immigration
(1969), p.75, in his Eastbourne speech of 16 November 1968.

27. V.G. Kiernan, 'Immigrants in England', unpublished ms,
p.60.

28. P. Foot, Immigration and Race (Harmondsworth, 1965), p.83.

29. S.C. Race Relations etc., p.xi.

30. Sherman, Island Refuge and J. Tannahill, European Volunteer Workers in Britain (Manchester, 1958), discuss these immigrations.

31. S.C. Race Relations etc. pp.xii-xiii outline these changes. See also the comment in R. Moore and T. Wallace, Slamming the Door: The Administration of Immigration Control (1975), pp.1-28.

32. See A. Sivanandan, Race and Resistance: the I.R.R. Story (1974) pp.8-10, particularly the comment by Roy Hattersley, 'Without integration limitation is inexcusable, without limitation integration is impossible'. It was the 1968 act which established the Community Relations Commission which was charged with encouraging harmonious relations between the different ethnic groups in Britain - a task which, since 1964 had occupied the voluntary body, the National Committee for Commonwealth Immigrants. The 1976 Race Relations Act abolished the Race Relations Board and the Community Relations Commission and set up the Commission for Racial Equality.

33. R.J. Benewick, The Fascist Movement in Britain (1972), ch. 1 could identify this. So could James Callaghan, see Sunday Times, 14 June 1970. For critical comment see Holmes, Anti-Semitism chs. 7 and 12 and his article 'Anti-Semitism and the BUF' in K. Lunn and R.C. Thurlow (eds.), British Fascism (forthcoming).

34. Rex and Moore, Race, Community and Conflict (1974 ed.), pp.13-14.

35. See the Royal Commission on Alien Immigration, Parliamentary Papers ix (1903), vol.1, p.14 and Appendix ix, p.42; Ng Kwee Choo, The Chinese in London (1968), pp.18-19; see the references to West Indian segregation in J. Rex's paper in the present volume.

36. See Patterson in Watson, Two Cultures, for some observations on the Polish experience.

37. Rex and Moore, Race, Community and Conflict (1974 edn), p.14. For a further reference to the complexity of host-immigrant reactions, but from a different ideological viewpoint, see S. Patterson, 'Immigrants and Minority Groups in British society', in S. Abbott (ed.), The Prevention of Racial Discrimination in Britain (1971), pp.27-53.

38. For an account of the importance of such work, see John Higham, 'Anti-Semitism in the Gilded Age', Mississippi Valley Historical Review, 43 (1956-7), p.569.

39. Some work on Leeds has already been done: a basic outline can be found in E. Krausz, Leeds Jewry (Cambridge, 1964) and a more sophisticated study can be found in J. Buckman, 'The Economic and Social History of Alien Immigration to Leeds 1880-1914' (unpublished Ph.D. thesis, University of Strathclyde, 1968). However, as Buckman states in his essay in this volume, more work needs to be done.

40. See Provincial Jewry in Victorian Britain, papers for a conference of the Jewish Historical Society of England (1975).

41. Bill Williams, The Making of Manchester Jewry 1740-1875 (Manchester, 1976).

42. Note, however, the work on Leeds cited above and the pioneer study, Cecil Roth, The Rise of Provincial Jewry (1950).

43. For example, see the recent suggestions in Sydney Checkland, The Upas Tree: Glasgow, 1875-1975 (Glasgow, 1976).

44. Chaim Bermant, Point of Arrival: a study of London's East End (1975) may be used as a guideline for future work.

45. Such a view is to be found in J.H. Robb, Working-Class Anti-Semite (1954), p.3.

46. For a recent work on these lines, see Michael Billig, Fascists: A Social Psychological View of the National Front (1979).

2
Immigrants and British Labour: the Sociological Context
JOHN REX

I have been given the task, qua sociologist, of putting the
particular studies which have been assembled for the purposes
of this symposium into a general theoretical perspective, I
can only express my delight that historians should look to
sociologists for this kind of aid. But I must also show
some humility. Like most sociologists I have been forced
away from general theory to contemporary history and I really
feel capable of speaking only as one historian among others
with the limited perspective which comes from focussing
attention on a particular immigrant minority at a particular
point in history, ie on the West Indian and Asian migration
to Britain since 1945. Indeed it is my work, affected as it
is by the particularism which arises from topicality and
orthodox historical work referring to immigrations and
immigration scares which are now long since passed, which is
capable of putting this present into perspective.

On the other hand, I am a theorist and my attempts to
generalise and systematise have not been confined to ad hoc
theorising about Jamaicans or Pakistanis. They arise from
the following experiences: (1) being a South African Democrat
who had lived with the interrelated politics of race and class
and who was born into an English-immigrant-descended poor
white family, which protected itself against unemployment in
the 1930s by supporting industrial colour bars; (2) par-
ticipating with African politicians in lobbying for African

majority rule in East and Central Africa, where white
minorities were seeking to consolidate the de facto white
supremacy which they had established: (3) joining in the
academic and political debates about pluralism in colonial
societies and the Fanonist debate about the relative
importance of national as against working-class revolutions:
(4) undertaking research on the settlement and particularly
the housing situation of West Indian and Pakistani immigrants
in Britain between 1965 and 1978, and taking part in anti-
racist politics during the period after 1962 when coloured
immigration became a major issue: and (5) being invited to
participate in the UNESCO experts committee which was set up
in 1967 on the nature of race and racism. [1]

My theoretical odyssey really starts from that last
conference.   The conference was one of a series which was
initiated by the U.N. in 1945 to rid the world of the scourge
of racism, by which was meant, primarily, anti-semitism.
But by 1967 two things had happened: (1) the biologists
had made it quite clear that the concept of race as they used
it had no relevance to the political differences amongst men
and that the problem of defining the field was one for
sociologists: and (2) the problem of anti-semitism was no
longer the central focus, having been displaced by a concern
about racist oppression of blacks by whites.

I was one of those who was subsequently called upon to
define for sociological purposes the significant
differentiating features of a race relations situation and I
did try to offer a definition on a level of generality which
would take in both anti-semitism and white/black relations.
I suggested that a race relations problem existed wherever:
(1) there was a situation of severe competition and conflict
or exploitation: (2) this situation occurred between groups,
with little prospect of an individual transferring his
membership from one group to another: and (3) the whole

system was rationalised and explained in terms of some sort of deterministic theory of which genetic theories were only one possible sort.[2]

The application of this general perspective, however, had to take account of two separate elements: (1) colonial situations in which entrepreneurs from the metropolis set up economic structures in which native and imported ethnic minorities were brought together in a plural economy and society,[3] and (2) metropolitan societies which were variously constructed of class and ethnic segments, which at varying stages of their history absorbed ethnic minority elements.

My empirical area of interest has led me under the latter heading to be concerned with the transfer of Indian and West Indian populations from a variety of colonial situations to ambiguous positions within an established British class structure or an ongoing class struggle.[4] A more general theory, however, would have to include (1) a theory of dependency which explained the quasi-colonial relationship of the more economically backward Southern European peripheral countries to the more successful capitalist centres: (2) a special account of societies like the U.S.A. and South Africa where a new 'metropolitan' centre had been established by settlers adjacent to and within the same territory as an existing colonial society: and (3) an account of the incorporation of refugee and pariah groups into metropolitan societies.

Obviously then my general theory will take in a wider variety of situations than those which are being discussed here. Here, I take it, we are considering the structure of British and American society and the incorporation into them at various points in their history of a number of groups of immigrant or non-immigrant minorities. The range includes German clerks in Victorian Britain, Jewish refugee immigrants between 1880 and 1914, Germany gypsies, Glasgow Catholics,

24

Polish miners in Lanarkshire, Jewish trades unionism as types of minority situation, and Tory and far-right radicalism, attitudes of dockers and miners in Britain, and a comparison of British and American labour, as types of responses. To these I would want to add my own concern about coloured immigrants in the post-war period.

The first thing that a general theory has to do in this area, it seems to me, is that which A.T. Lane describes as a consideration 'of the differing circumstances, political, social and economic, under which organised labour in the two countries (Britain and America) was forced to conduct its activities and to establish policies for the protection of its members'. This will involve us at looking at the class and ethnic structure of these two societies, at the moment at which any minority enters it.

So far as Britain is concerned it may be said that its ethnic composition is astoundingly homogeneous, but its class formations are strongly developed. This has certain important implications. In the first place it means that the social bonding of the various segments of the capitalist class is dependent upon traditional class-cultural bonds, rather than on ethnicity. Thus while there have been societies in which control of capital in parts of it was in the hands of an ethnic minority - and, of course, the notion that Jews form such a minority which controls finance capital has lived on in Europe since the middle ages - in Britain the control of the higher reaches of capitalism, especially merchant banking, is in the hands of overwhelmingly mainline British people united in their possession, if not of a distinctive ancestry, at least in the possession of an elite education. For this reason the possibilities of mounting a Jewish conspiracy campaign which locates the Jewish threat in finance capital is limited. At most what can be claimed by the ideologists of the right is that British capital is subordinate

to a more distant and vaguely defined international finance
capital managed by the Jews. In the main, however, Britain
has been a difficult country for anyone wishing to divert
class hostility against capitalism into anti-semitism.

Amongst the working classes, there has, of course, been
continuous immigration since the beginnings of the industrial
revolution, but it has been overwhelmingly the immigration of
an ethnically very similar group, namely the Irish. This
predominance of Irish immigration has only been modified by
refugee settlement by European Jews in the late nineteenth
and early twentieth century, by the settlement of displaced
persons after the war and by the recent arrival of Asians and
West Indians.

The closeness of Irish and British culture has made the
incorporation of the Irish into the working-class relatively
easy. Usually within three generations Irish families were
able to move into core working-class positions and beyond
them. Indeed Irish ethnicity helped if anything to strengthen
the bonds of working-class culture. Something similar is
probably possible with Portuguese and Spanish immigrants in
France, but greater difficulties occur in France, Belgium and
Holland in absorbing North African refugees, while in Germany
the use of the derisory term 'gastarbeider' suggests that
there is no intention of absorbing them. In the case of
Britain's West Indian and Asian immigrants, one has a problem
of entirely new dimensions and I shall consider below what
the relations of these minorities to the class structure are
likely to be. To indicate my line of thought in advance I
propose to question the notion that the West Indian and Asian
experience is in any sense prefigured by the Irish or the
Jewish one.

Before we turn to this question, it is important that we
should say something about American ethnic and class structure,
which is in so many ways different from what we have been
describing.

26

In the first place American society belongs completely neither to the metropolitan nor the colonial role in our classification. On the one hand it includes a colonial plantation society. On the other it contains a society of settlers which has become a new capitalist metropolis. It is as though the British capitalist economy had grown around or alongside of the West Indies.

The metropolitan society in the American case is also very different in class structure from that to be found in Britain. It is anything but ethnically homogeneous, being based upon wave after wave of European immigration. The consequence of this is that individual workers have looked to their ethnic group rather than to trades unions, parties, or the working-class movement to defend them. Each separate group has bought its way into the political system through its bosses and is structured in terms of patron-client relations as well as relationships of common class interest. The one group which did not enter this system as a successful eth-class were the 'native' American Blacks. Lloyd Warner suggested that there was a caste-like barrier between them and the white class system in the thirties, which might tilt but would not be breached.[5] Only in the sixties, for a variety of reasons including their own 'revolution' and the impossibility of a viable American foreign and imperial policy being sustained abroad if there was the possibility of a hundred Vietnams at home - only then did the boss system begin to operate on behalf of the blacks.

Now we must return to the crucial difference between the American and the British political class systems. This is that no one buys his way into the system through a political boss. Social rights, trade union protection and welfare have been won through the labour movement based upon the trades unions, and there is no way through for an incoming group, other than through the labour movement.

27

One way of analysing complex industrial societies which has some usefulness is that which derives from Max Weber's revision of Marx. For Weber a class situation exists wherever there is a market situation, and there is a market situation wherever there is any resource which is controlled as property.[6] I was therefore able to suggest in 1967 that one could look at Birmingham, England,[7] not simply in terms of industrial classes and an industrial class struggle, but in terms of housing classes and a housing class struggle. Moreover it does not seem to me to be far fetched to speak of educational classes or medical classes referring to groups differentially placed in relation to the control of educational or medical resources.

But the problem which this poses is why there are not, alongside the Labour Party which speaks about trade union rights of workers, tenants' parties, students' parties, patients' parties and so on. Here the fact of the matter is that the Labour Party has pre-empted the formation of such parties by operating in all areas. Thus, whatever lobbies there may be at local council level representing local interests in the various markets or allocative sectors, it is the Labour Party which the underprivileged have to lobby.

I believe that one understands something of the immigrant worker's situation if one recognises: (1) that he may be in a specially weak position in any of these allocative sectors: and that (2) he is not necessarily represented by the Labour Party. Indeed, what the Labour Party can be thought of as doing is to win a privileged position for its own native-born members in employment and the various welfare sectors and to concern itself with protecting those privileges against competition. The question is how quickly, if at all, immigrants or minorities can break into control of the Labour Party and share in these privileges.

Undoubtedly many of the Irish, Jewish and European immigrants of an earlier generation, were once in the position

of being outsiders to Labour's welfare deal and then either
came to participate in it or went beyond it to middle-class
property-based status, or bypassed it by entering middle-class
commercial occupations straightaway. So far, however, there
has not been a parallel development amongst West Indian and
Asian minorities. I will now turn to the position of these
minorities before returning to the general theme of the
symposium.

What one sees is something like the following: whereas
among whites in inner-city Birmingham one-third are in white-
collar jobs and one-quarter are in semi-skilled and unskilled
jobs, among West Indians and Asians only about 8 per cent are
in white-collar work and nearly 50 per cent in unskilled work.
The coloured immigrants, moreover, are heavily concentrated
in heavy, dirty industries, do more shift work and work
longer hours for less money. In times of unemployment their
unemployment rises disproportionately.

Since many of the immigrants who came to settle in the
late fifties or early sixties have been in stable employment
for the past five years, however, we should not think of an
unemployed, unemployable, ghettoised underclass. Rather we
should think of a replacement labour force. The really
important question is whether they will only be tolerated
industrially so long as they accept their role as mere
replacement labour. This is the question which was sharply
posed in disputes such as those at the Mansfield Hosiery Works
and Imperial Typewriters. The immigrant workers, under-
protected and neglected by their union in the unskilled jobs,
came out on strike and forced the union into making the strike
official. They also developed demands for entry into the
better-paid jobs. They were met with open hostility by white
workers who were opposed to their aims, and, though arbitration
of the disputes went in their favour and the Transport and
General Workers' Union officially accepted the need to have

more Asian shop stewards, the victory was a pyrrhic one in which the firms concerned closed down their plants.

One cannot really be certain at the present time that some kind of permanent dual labour market situation and a situation of a dual working class might not develop in Britain based upon a partial colour bar. It is true that immigrant workers are overwhelmingly trade union members and express satisfaction with them. It is also true that they support the Labour Party (particularly the Indians who do so over-whelmingly). There is evidence of defection to far left and immigrant groups in politics, however, and there are even signs of immigrant groups developing within if not outside and opposed to British unions.

Even more striking than the separation of the coloured immigrant worker industrially is his residential segregation. Nothing could be more striking evidence of the extent to which he is at present excluded from the working-class and labour movement's Welfare State deal than his under-representation in the public housing sector. Despite the availability of a planning instrument which could be used to correct the disadvantages which the free market imposes on coloured buyers and renters of publicly provided rented housing without social stigma, that instrument has been used systematically against coloured immigrants. The result of this is that many immigrants of the 1950s and 1960s were forced into buying old houses with the aid of council mortgages, into houses converted into multiple occupation by immigrant landlords, or into flats produced out of old houses by housing associations. The result of this has been the concentration of immigrants in the worst remaining property in the city.

That there has not been a fundamental alteration of the immigrant's situation when he did eventually qualify for a council house can be seen from more recent housing history.

On the one hand the earliest immigrants to be rehoused were
concentrated in central city tower blocks. On the other a
few were dispersed, that is, offered a council house on a
suburban estate, with the proviso that no other coloured
immigrant should be housed in the six houses on either side.
Thus the immigrant was offered a choice between being cut
off from his natural community entirely or being segregated
in squalor.

The effect of residential segregation through housing
policy then is this: insofar as there is any kind of
developing solidarity between native and immigrant workers
at work, it is not reinforced and strengthened by the
creation of a residential community of a multi-racial kind.
At night, white and black workers separate at the factory
gates and the black worker is assigned to what amounts to
stigmatised housing.

A different set of considerations arise in relation to
schooling. There can, of course, be no denial of the right
to schooling on a queueing basis as there can to housing in
the public sector. But residential segregation inevitably
produces educational segregation, and indeed segregation is
inevitably multiplied in the school system since immigrants
are in the more fertile age groups and have more children
than their white neighbours. Thus, although there was no
ward in Birmingham with more than forty-nine per cent of its
population with both parents born in the New Commonwealth,
all secondary schools in this ward had more than sixty per
cent immigrant population and some primary schools had more
than ninety per cent.[8] The vast majority of the immigrant
population therefore, attend immigrant majority schools and,
given teacher autonomy, there can be no guarantee that the
education in these schools is not inferior. The reply that
although these schools are separate, they are nonetheless
equal, is ironic. It means that in 1978 in Britain the

31

situation has reverted to that accepted in the Plessey vs.
Ferguson judgment in the USA in 1396.

Within the school system, moreover, there is one known
area of failure. West Indian children are doing systematically
less well in almost any test than their English or Asian peers.
It is very likely that as this becomes increasingly apparent,
biological arguments will be adduced to explain the failure.
It is, however, interesting to notice that Professor Eysenck
has now discovered that English children do less well than
Chinese children in Singapore. We may soon see a situation
in which Asian children start doing better than English
children in school. The question will then have to be faced
as to what the cultural problems are which produce under-
achievement.

West Indians, like American Blacks in fact, face a
cultural situation unlike any other immigrant minority group
in British history, a situation which is best described as
cultural castration. Other groups of immigrants have had to
learn English and to live within English culture, but they
have at least kept the memory and knowledge of their own
culture. In fact, in the case of Asians this culture is
strongly retained so that young children live within two
cultures using each instrumentally to operate more successfully in the other. The West Indian by contrast knows no
culture of his own[9] and has to live within an English culture
which represents him, not merely in school text-books, but
through a thousand cultural clues, as inferior. Thus, while
all immigrant children suffer disadvantage in being in
immigrant majority schools, West Indian children suffer a
double disadvantage of not being equipped to perform
adequately even in those schools.

I now want to sum up what I have said about the life-
chances and the class situation of immigrants in the three
major 'markets' - that for jobs, that for housing, and that

for educational opportunity. Obviously it is true that a
minority do as well as the indigenous working class in all
these areas and a smaller minority still actually get into
middle-class jobs and neighbourhoods and get their children
into the most desirable schools. But the striking fact
about the present situation is that the majority of
immigrants live within the underparts of a dual labour
market as replacement labour, are concentrated in poor owner-
occupied inner-city property and in the worst council housing,
and send their children to ill-provided, largely segregated
schools. How then do they react to this situation and what
is the relationship between their organisations and that of
the native working class? The reaction for the two
communities is, I think, different. I will first discuss
the position of West Indians.

West Indian workers are trades unionists and vote Labour
more consistently than their English neighbours. But it is
also true to say that if one asks what the focal point of
West Indian identity is, it is not within the labour movement.
A West Indian who is active in the Labour Party or even in
white organisations further to the left as his main activity
is likely to be thought of as an Uncle Tom. The real centre
of West Indian life is to be found among the brothers-on-the-
block, i.e. in community-based organisations, the main focus
of activity is in helping one's neighbours and particularly
in helping the young men who get into trouble with the police
on the streets.

There is one surprising word at the centre of most West
Indian ideology today. It is 'Babylon'. The main theme
of the Ras Tafarian religion is not the absurd notion that
Haille Sellassi was divine, but the historically correct
notion that Jamaicans are an African people who have spent
four hundred years in captivity. My belief is that about
half of the Jamaican population aged between fifteen and

twenty-five see themselves in this way.   They may express
their beliefs by listening to reggae music, smoking marijuana
and reading the Bible, all quite common activities among
Jamaican youth, and a few may study the writings of Black
writers like Garvey, Fanon, Huey Newton and Stokeley
Carmichael and take an interest in the liberation of Southern
Africa.   They may see socialism of a kind (their own kind)
as an answer to their problems, but generally they look with
approval on any black man who succeeds, including black
capitalists.

   There has been a very rapid growth in West Indian
political consciousness of this kind.   It has been somewhat
arrested by the fact that probably several hundred potential
local and national leaders have found their way into the
paternalistic apparatus of the Commission for Racial Equality
as salaried servants of the state.   But this cannot arrest
the process of politicisation for long.

   It could be, of course, that militant black politics will
be primarily expressive, or that they will simply have a
psychologically stabilising effect, which through restoring a
sense of black identity, adjusts men and women to living in
Britain.   And it could be that the black leadership will
eventually realise its political potential, and by selling
its vote dear to the Labour Party, buy an institutionalised
place within the British political system.

   So far as the Asians are concerned, their position is
very different.   Most of them have been conscious of, even
if they have not lived within, the Asian diaspora for several
generations.   Asian traders, Sikh soldiers, matriculated white-
collar workers, as well as coolies and lascars, have participated
in the functioning of the British Empire for many generations.
Moreover with their strong ethnic identity and lineage-based
organisations they are well equipped to succeed at most of
the things they turn their hand to.   To understand the

various Asian communities one should think of tightly knit
lineages of men and women used to a low material standard of
life engaged in the business of accumulating a family estate.
An original immigrant works long hours of overtime in a
foundry and buys up a few slum houses and a shop to provide a
basis for other members of the lineage to settle.   The
capital of the lineage will then be put to further use in
buying education for their young men and women as well as for
investment in small businessses.

The strong economic orientation of these communities
means that some of them may come to dissociate themselves
from the working class, industrially and politically, and it
should be noted that many Asian workers think of their
British counterparts as lazy and unenterprising.   Some,
moreover, might respond to Tory and Liberal wooing and try to
buy into, not the working class, but the bourgeoisie.   But
we would be wrong, as would men like William Whitelaw, if we
thought this would happen easily, for the exploitation of
India by British Conservatives and its attainment of
independence under Labour is not easily forgotten.   Moreover Indian liberation politics had a Marxist dimension which
survives in bodies like the Indian Workers Association and
leads to an orientation of these bodies to the labour
movement.

Those who have studied Jewish immigration will recognise
that what I am saying was true also of the Jews.   Some of
them were to succeed in business and see their sons and
daughters enter the professions, and some few actually
became Conservatives.   But as with the Indians, the Jews
were seen as not merely responding to British socialist
teaching but of spreading international socialist doctrine.

Will it be the case, then, that the West Indians will
buy into the system collectively and the Indians attain an
English Jewish future?   We cannot answer this question

superficially.   There is no natural cycle of immigration and
race relations such as Robert Park in America and Ernest Krauz
in England have suggested.[10]   Everything depends upon how
British people and particularly working-class people react to
the presence, not simply of another group of immigrants, but
immigrants from the most inferior roles and statuses in the
Empire.   What we have seen during the past twenty-five years
is a collapse of the anti-racist element in British Conservative, Liberal and Socialist ideology and the widespread
acceptance of the view that immigration (meaning coloured
immigration) is the greatest evil from which Britain suffers
at present.   There seems to be no end to the auctioning of
principles in order to win the anti-immigrant vote, and with
each new abandonment of a principle demands grow on the
right for more.   Mr Enoch Powell is no longer content with
voluntary repatriation.   He wants inducements.   The
National Front bids to become a more effective political
force than the Liberal Party, and a city councillor from
Blackburn is offered good wishes by a judge when he responds
to the murder of an Indian boy with the remark 'one down, a
million to go'.   It is hardly surprising that some West
Indians and Asians believe that they may be headed for 'the
final solution'.

It is hardly surprising either if in the face of these
threats immigrant organisations become more militant.   The
choice of strategy is not theirs to make.   They have the
right to defend themselves and will do so.   We will deceive
ourselves if our liberal or socialist analyses lead us to the
complacent belief that all will work out peacefully in the
long run without the deployment of power by all the groups
concerned.   Possibly in the long run the British people will
assimilate three million Asian and West Indian descended
citizens into its professional, business and working-class
communities, and a new cultural strain will be absorbed into

a multi-racial Britain.   But this adjustment to the legacy
of Empire is unlikely to be an easy one to make.   One finds
it particularly hard to envisage while doing research in the
city of Joseph Chamberlain.

NOTES

1. The statement prepared by this conference and its pre-
decessors is published with a commentary in A. Montague,
Statement on Race (1972).

2. See J. Rex, Race Relations in Sociological Theory (1970)
and Race, Colonialism and the City (1973).

3. See J. Rex, 'New Nations and Ethnic Minorities', in Race
and Class in Post-Colonial Society (UNESCO, 1977).

4. Reported in J. Rex and R. Moore, Race, Community and
Conflict (1967) and J. Rex and S. Tomlinson, Colonial
Immigrants in a British City: A Class Analysis (1979).

5. W. Lloyd Warner, 'American Class and Caste', American
Journal of Sociology, XLll (1936), pp.234-7.

6. Max Weber, Economy and Society, vol.2, ch.9.   Note that
this is a different analysis of social class and an
analytically clearer one than that which appears in vol.1, ch.
4 of the same book and which was actually written later.
See Economy and Society (Bedminster Press, New York, 1968).

7. See Rex and Moore, Race, Community and Conflict: J. Rex
'The Concept of Housing, Class and the Sociology of Race
Relations', Race, Xll (1971), pp.293-301.   For a discussion
of the concept of class extended to the other spheres, see
Rex and Tomlinson, Colonial Immigrants.

8. Rex and Tomlinson, Colonial Immigrants.   For national
data, see D. Smith, Racial Disadvantage in Britain (Harmondsworth, 1977).

9. Of course, these are African survivals in West Indian
culture, and over the centuries English culture has been
varied in the West Indies and has also produced elements of
a culture of resistance.   Nonetheless there is nothing to
parallel, say, the continued existence of a Punjab Sikh
culture in Britain.

10. E. Krausz, <u>Ethnic Minorities in Britain</u> (1972).

11. It would be of some interest to trace the familial connections of the present residents of wards like Sparkbrook and Handsworth in Birmingham and those who supported Joseph Chamberlain's imperialism ninety years ago.

3

Satan and Sambo: the Image of the Immigrant in English Racial Populist Thought since the First World War

RICHARD C. THURLOW

Popular attitudes towards immigration into England during the twentieth century have ranged from benign neglect to the more malevolent obsession with the subject in contemporary political culture. A recent study of the subject has made clear that hostility has been shown to a wide range of immigrant groups in those reception areas where the majority of them have settled.[1] With the partial exception of the Irish, however, public concern has centred on the political campaigns to restrict Jewish immigration up to 1939 and so-called coloured or 'New Commonwealth' immigration since the Second World War.[2] This public concern has usually been expressed in a generalised xenophobia and articulated in a non-systematic manner through 'common sense' racism and ethnocentrism based on cultural prejudice.[3]

For those who were classically prejudiced or who wished to use the issue for political purposes against the established party system, anti-immigration has been used as a dynamic element in a corpus of ideas which has been designed to challenge the assumptions of Britain's liberal political culture. Anti-immigration and repatriation proposals have formed the central plank, or an important part of the ideas, of fringe political movements which may be termed racial populist.[4] These have used the discredited ideas of racism and ethnocentrism as part of what has been termed the 'underground of rejected knowledge'[5] to help form an English volkish ideology.[6] If the sometimes complementary and at other times contradictory notions of racism and ethnocentrism can be seen as the root of the volkish system of thought, then this has been linked to other ideas which deny humanitarian liberal principles, such as social darwinism, the corporate state, mercantilism and a conspiratorial view of history.

Of these other elements social darwinism was used as a causal rationalisation to justify the struggle against so-called inferior class, racial or national groups both inside and outside the defined community, and was used to argue for an imperialist policy. The corporate state was viewed as the means of harmonising social conflict and the precondition for economic theories based on the production function rather than the laws of scarcity to develop. This was to be achieved through mercantilism, where the community could be isolated from the economic fluctuations which prevented stability in liberal regimes. The conspiracy theory was used to explain how either the golden age of past imperial glories and social harmony had been superceded by liberalism, or how modern society prevented the new utopia from being formed. This effect was achieved by the projection of 'heated exaggeration, suspiciousness and conspiratorial fantasy'[7] on to outgroups. The most extreme form of this paranoid style was conspiratorial anti-semitism in which Jews were often ascribed magical powers.

In general terms the volkish ideology can be viewed either as the expression of the inter-section of personal and collective fantasies by ideologists in the tradition,[8] or as a projection of personality disorder or cultural prejudice allied to a developed intellectual system of ideas. A combination of both approaches would seem to be in order since the volkish tradition incorporated a wide range of

personality types ranging from the well-adjusted to the psycho-
pathological and received its intellectual inspiration from
different sources. On the issue of immigration the differences
are less pronounced and can be viewed in psychological terms.
From an examination of the mainly virtuous qualities ascribed
to the national or racial group of the volk and the negative
image of the outgroup it can be argued that the former
represented an ego-based stereotype and the latter its id-
equivalent.[9] The plausibility of such an image would however
depend on social and cultural factors which enabled communities
to see racial and ethnic outgoups as having a well-earned
reputation for social problems, as well as being a convenient
scapegoat.[10]

The volkish tradition developed in various competing
systems of thought between the two world wars in England.
In general terms, apart from the locally influential British
Brothers League in the East End of London, political movements
based on various combinations of racism, ethnocentrism and
conspiracy theory had not emerged before the First World War.
In the inter-war period the main contributors to the
development of an English volkish tradition have been Nesta
Webster of the British Fascisti in the 1920s; Henry Hamilton
Beamish, the founder of the Britons Society and Publishing
Company in 1919; Arnold Leese, the leader of the Imperial
Fascist League (1929-39); and Sir Oswald Mosley, the leader
of the British Union of Fascists (1932-46). Since the
Second World War, Leese developed his thought until his death
in 1956, and Mosley has been active in Union Movements since
1948. Perhaps the most significant synthesis of the inter-
war traditions was that achieved by Arthur Kenneth (A.K.)
Chesterton, the Director of the League of Empire Loyalists
(1953-66) and the first Director of the National Front (1966-
70). Other important contributions to its development have
come from the racial nationalist thought of John Bean of the

National Labour Party (1958-60), the British National Party
(1960-6) and the National Front since 1966, John Tyndall, the
founder of the Greater Britain Movement (1964-7) and the current
chairman of the National Front and Colin Jordan of the National
Socialist Movement (1962-7), and since then of the British
Movement.[11] The rest of this paper will analyse the ideas
of these individuals and the groups they represent with regard
to immigration into Britain and its effects. The two main
groups of immigrants which have provoked concern are the Jews
and the coloured immigrants. The two subjects will be analysed
separately as very different images are involved and the sources
of such thought come from two distinct traditions. The range
of response and the intensity of the obsession is a heightened
form of popular xenophobia.

The image of the Jew in the ideology has as its roots the
fantasies of European anti-semitism, as well as the populist
response to social problems created by mass immigration.
In particular images deriving from the medieval anti-semitism
tradition, the ethnocentric anti-semitism of the enlightenment
and nineteenth-century mystical and scientific racial anti-
semitism can clearly be distinguished. The apocalyptic
vision created by the fusion of such elements represented the
most virulent form of anti-semitic prejudice,[12] and its
intensity, if not its dissemination and impact, was as
pronounced in England as in modern German anti-semitism.[13]
These images have been linked to various forms of personality
projection and cultural prejudice to form the image of the
Jewish immigrant.

The English tradition of anti-semitism in the twentieth
century had as its deepest root the tradition which derived
from the subconscious of the medieval world, which resurfaced

42

as a response to modernisation and social change in late nineteenth and early twentieth-century Europe.[14] Most of the elements of medieval anti-semitism have been used by ideologists in the tradition and have been projected onto immigrant Jews. Thus the role of the devil in using Jews to undermine christian civilisation has been seen as part of an argument to show that sinister forces operated behind the activities of English Jews and international Jewry. Nesta Webster thought that the 'cult of Satan' was 'practised today in our own country',[15] and that the 'powers of darkness', in alliance with Jews, Pan-Germans, Theosophists and Illuminati, were plotting to destroy the British Empire.[16] The Britons believed that what 'the Jews term anti-semitism is "anti-Satanism"'.[17] This view was taken up by Arnold Leese who thought that Freemasonry was merely the latest stage of the plot organised by the 'forces of darkness...since the Jews first conceived the idea of organising world control'.[18] Although Mosley was not tainted with such atavistic obsessions some of his followers used such imagery. Major-General Fuller, an expert on the occult, wrote that 'wherever the Jew has gone, Satan has followed to heel'.[19] Since the Second World War the main exponent of such arguments has been A.K. Chesterton, who believed that 'The Devil is an extremely competent supreme commander'[20] of the 'great Jewish-Capitalist-Communist conspiracy against Christendom'.[21] The image of the Jew as the agent of the devil has also been pursued by Colin Jordan, who believed in the 'Satanic ambition of World Jewry pursued throughout the ages to achieve a millennium of world domination'.[22]

Linked to the medieval idea of the Jew as in league with the Devil has been the image of Jewish apocalyptic political Messianism. This has been linked to the secularised modern version portrayed in the <u>Protocols of the Elders of Zion</u> whose publication was taken over by the Britons. For

43

Beamish, 'the Jews' Messiah is an earthly tyrant who lives on massacres'.[23] Fuller's researches into the Zohar and Talmud led him to believe that Jews believed in the coming of a Messiah which would lead to the 'extermination, moral, intellectual and physical of all peoples outside Israel'.[24] Chesterton believed that with the destruction of the British Empire, the Jews who 'have a collective Messianic mission are on the threshold of complete world domination'[25].

Thus hostility to Jewish immigration depended not only on xenophobic fears but on irrational, atavistic beliefs by those who articulated the ideology of anti-semitism in England. This was compounded by the projection of two other medieval stereotypes onto the Jewish population, the Jew as a sorcerer and the Jew as usurer. For Nesta Webster it was 'under the more modern terms of magicians and loan mongers that we detect their presence behind the scenes of revolution from the seventeenth century onwards'[26]. Webster took her views from the French anti-semite Gougenot des Mousseaux who had mistaken and misunderstood the nature of the Jewish sacred book, the Kabbalah.[28] This atavistic fear of black magic had as its mirror image her own belief in mysticism, particularly her view that she was probably the reincarnation of an eighteenth-century French aristocrat, the Comtesse de Sabran.[29] This ambiguous relationship to the nineteenth-century occult revival[30] was also mirrored in the beliefs of Major-General Fuller. As an ex-follower of the notorious Aleister Crowley and a leading expert on the occult, Fuller was in a better position than most to know the real nature of Jewish mysticism and magic, yet he preferred in his days as a member of the British Union of Fascists to propogate the myth that 'demonology and magic were definitely Jewish cults'[31] which were behind the growth of witchcraft in medieval Europe.

Most of the ideologists in the tradition who used magical anti-semitism were extremely vague about the nature

of the methods adopted by Jewish witches and sorcerers.
However Arnold Leese supplied the argument by which Jewish
magic supposedly perverted the natural social order by
utilising Nesta Webster's fear of black magic and hypnotism.
For him Jewish magicians perfected the art of 'mass hypnotism'
which produced 'physical wrecks' and destroyed'the will power
of resistance'.[32]   Since the Second World War anti-semitism
has only been possible in coded form in volkish circles as a
result of the defeat of Hitler and Colin Jordan's National
Socialist Movement fiasco of the early 1960s.   However the
old atavistic image of Jewish black magic perverting the
natural society still lingers on.   Now, however, John Tyndall
talks of society being 'hypnotised by liberalist attitudes'
which condemn all 'concept of strong authority and worship
the cult of permissiveness'.[33]   Symbolism and coded form is
an important aspect of the anti-semitic mentality, as the
obsession of the Imperial Fascist League with finding hidden
meanings in the Star of David showed.   Each point of the
star symbolised one of six areas where Jewish thought attacked
modern society.[34]

      Other aspects of medieval anti-semitism also became part
of the twentieth-century heritage.   The Britons published a
pamphlet on ritual murder and Leese could write that 'there
is no doubt that Jewish Doctors frequently do deliberate
damage and murder on Gentile patients'[35].   Even as late as
1963 Martin Webster could still write in The National Socialist
that not only did the medieval Jew 'suck Britain dry of gold,
he had to drain away the blood of the nation's children'[36].

      If most of the medieval images of the Jew found their
way into the English version of modern anti-semitism so did
the ethnocentric and conspiratorial emphasis of the
enlightenment's view of the Jew.   In particular the Jews as
the international people who, despite emancipation, would not
assimilate to the cultural norms of the emergent nation states

of Europe was a particular theme. Various political reactionaries linked the changes in society associated with the process of economic, social and political upheaval in the eighteenth century with Jewish influence and blamed that change on the subversion of secret societies such as the Freemasons and the Illuminati. This joint theme of social reaction combined with nationalism could be seen most strongly in Nesta Webster. The Jew became the symbol in her thought of the force which both undermined the English national state and the class structure of society. The effect was heightened by combining stereotypes which made England's national enemy, Germany, as jointly responsible with the Jews for the ills of society: Lenin was merely 'the agent of the great German-Jewish company that hopes to rule the world'.[37] However for Webster not all Jews were guilty of such behaviour and she believed that even the plotters could be reformed. For this view she was roundly criticised by Beamish because 'If it would be "kindness" to a homicidal maniac to permit him the freedom to exercise his mad tendency, then it would be "kindness" to allow a similar freedom to the Jew.'[38]

This difference highlighted an ideological split in the image of the Jew between those such as Nesta Webster and Mosley whose objections to Jews were chiefly on ethnocentric and nationalist grounds and racial nationalists such as Beamish, Leese, and Jordan. The former took the view that only some Jews were guilty of crimes against the state whilst the latter saw all Jews as racial carriers of the virus which undermined society. Others in the tradition oscillated between the two views or altered them for genuine or cynical reasons over time. Thus Leese moved from an enlightenment ethnocentric view to the nineteenth-century racial nationalist standpoint between 1929 and 1931 as a result of Beamish's influence. Chesterton stopped using imagery which

46

failed to differentiate between types of Jewish influence
after the Second World War, and both Tyndall and Webster have
recently restricted their attacks on the Jewish community to
the machinations of international financiers and Zionists.
The National Front however has adopted the racial nationalist
stance on new commonwealth immigration.   The reason for this
is that due to historical circumstance the historically
discredited scapegoat image of the Jew has been replaced by a
more visible threat to believers in the ideology, and this
used prejudices with more roots in the political culture of
the community.

The enlightenment image of the Jew was perhaps most
forcefully revived in English culture by Sir Oswald Mosley.
There is no evidence that Mosley was interested in anti-
semitism before 1931, and although some of the images he
employed derived from his left-wing critique of finance
capital in the 1920s, from a tradition of cultural prejudice
in the East End of London, and from a development of a growing
hostility to so-called Jewish finance from various anti-semites
in his entourage, the main image he portrayed was that which
closely paralleled Oswald Spengler's view, whose <u>Decline of</u>
<u>the West</u> he had read in 1931.[39]   Thus Mosley's obsession
with showing that Jews and Englishmen were of different
cultures and had different loyalties, had its root in the
Spenglerian distinction between the Faustian and Magian
cultures.   This fact of difference led to the 'appalling
hatred'[40] between the two groups in European society, the
one rooted in the soil, and the other the wandering Jew
stereotype.   Both Mosley and Spengler ridiculed the concept
of a pure race.   Mosley also followed Spengler in another
crucial determinant of his anti-semitism: the difference
between 'good' Jews who assimilated to a national culture
and 'bad' Jews who did not.   The 'bad' Jews were those who
not only used international finance to undermine nationalist

47

solutions to the world's problems but also those who attacked Mosley physically by trying to break up his meetings and this was due to members of the Jewish 'razor gang which takes its orders from Moscow in this matter'.[41] Mosley followed Spengler too in linking these two phenomena in arguing there was a common interest between international finance and international socialism. Unlike Spengler however, Mosley sometimes referred to the supposed connection in anti-semitic terms during the 1930s.

The individual who most neatly combined the enlightenment conspiratorial and nationalist images of the Jew proved to be A.K. Chesterton. He was able to combine these elements with both medieval imagery and nineteenth-century racism to develop a mature English volkish idealogy. Chesterton's basic fear was that there was a conscious conspiracy which only 'dunderheads' could not see which had as its aims the projected 'bastardisation of mankind' and the 'ruthless elimination of the British Empire'.[42] This conspiracy was controlled by Jewish financiers such as Baruch, Lilienthal, Morgenthau, Kuhn Loeb and Company and the Rothschilds.[43] For Chesterton only the minority of Jewish international financiers and Zionists represented a threat to British national interests after the Second World War.

Chesterton has also been at the forefront of a successful campaign since the Second World War to keep racist arguments out of the mainstream of English volkish thought, as far as the image of the Jew has been concerned. He strived for over forty years 'to keep Rosenberg's racial rubbish out of British patriotism'[44] and to oppose the 'clotted nonsense of Houston Stewart Chamberlain and Rosenberg'.[45] Ironically, given the vitriolic attack on Rosenberg, Chesterton's conspiracy theory of Jewish bankers financing the Russian Revolution can be traced both to the White Russian and Rosenberg view of Russian anti-semitism.[46]

48

Similarly racial anti-semitism was what Mosley was attacking
when he criticised Colin Jordan's 'racialist twaddle',[47] as
Mosley's attitude to coloured immigrants was much less
virulent than other volkish thinkers. Yet racial anti-
semitism and the myth of Aryan man were of importance
throughout this period and added to the negative image of the
Jew in the corpus of racial populist thought.

The image of the Jew as a contaminating agent which
'biologically speaking is drinking our life's blood',[48] and
leading to racial deterioration of the British people,
became the basis of H.H. Beamish and the Britons' ideology.
Beamish saw the racial and cultural opposites he described
as competitors in a social darwinian battle for survival.
This battle was described in pessimistic terms, with Jewish
influences undermining the racial and cultural defences of
'rugged individualism' of the European races and turning the
products of modern civilisation into 'robots'.[49] This fear
of modernisation necessitated the alliance of 'all the Aryan
races to join forces against the common enemy of our
civilisation and christianity'.[50] In general, Beamish's
thought showed little sign of development, except that the
racist content became more pronounced. The inherent logical
contradiction between the ethnocentric nationalist arguments
and the belief in the unity of the Aryan race was mirrored,
as it was with Leese, in his ambivalence towards Hitler.

If Beamish's racism was mixed with images of an older
christian anti-semitic tradition, it was Arnold Leese who
provided the leap to a racial nationalist viewpoint. For
Leese 'the real colour problem is more subtle...it is the
acceptance of the Jew as a citizen of this country'.[51]
Leese's objection to the Jews was that in his opinion they
were not a pure race, but combined the blood of the weaker
Alpine and Hither Asiatic 'white'races with a 'Mongolian
yellow element'. This mongrel mixture represented a threat

to Britain because Jews were marrying into the best elements
of the British race, the aristocracy, and therefore 'the
poisoning of our Anglo Saxon blood by this yellow negroid
horde is proceeding apace'[52]. Leese believed in two of the
principal myths of the uncritical positivism of mid-nineteenth-
century anthropology. He argued that individual characteristics could be meaningfully applied to groups without
qualification, and he adopted a pessimistic race-class
degeneration critique which ultimately derived from
Gobineau.[53]

Leese's racial anti-semitism has produced some echoes in
volkish thought since the war, although the basic image is
that of the Jew as a power-mad fiend. For Andrew Fountaine,
the chairman of the British National Party, 'almond-eyed
Esters (sic) with the lure of cash were paraded before the
more dim-witted or improvident sons of the nobility'.[54]
Although racial anti-semitism has been considered generally
beyond the pale since the war, the Jew has still been linked
to the threat of racial contamination. He is now seen as
the organiser of a much greater racial threat, that posed by
the commonwealth immigrant. This type of argument originated
with Leese who argued that it was 'of course in Jewish
interests that this policy of subordinating the White Race to
the coloured is made'.[55] For A.K. Chesterton coloured
immigration was a 'Jewish racket'[56], for which anti-toxins
would have to be produced to stop the breeding of 'a multi-
coloured hugger-mugger in twentieth century Britain'[57].
For Colin Jordan the Jews supported coloured immigration
because it led to 'the breakdown of racial identity and
racial pride'.[58]

As well as deep-rooted historical stereotypes the image
of the Jew in racial populist movements has also depended on
cultural prejudice and personality projections. In terms of
cultural prejudice it was the British Union of Fascists who

tried to reactivate the British Brothers League tradition in the East End of London. E.G. ('Mick') Clarke was the most renowned exponent of giving an anti-semitic gloss to the social problems of this area. He criticised the unfair trading, insurance and bankruptcy swindles, cut-price tactics and sweated labour conditions in the East End and complained: 'Today the Englishman in East London is the slave of his Jewish master and his part of the City of London has become "the land of the waving palm".'[59] For Mosley, 'while Britons are unemployed, the aliens who now hold jobs should not be permitted to retain them'[60]. Mosley went further and blamed the Jews for creating the violence which led to social disturbance and the need for the Public Order Act. He instituted 'research' into the Jewish problem which showed, according to Chesterton, that 'the whole of the capitalist racket, the whole of the National Press, the whole of the British cinema, the whole bunch of purely parasitical occupations were found to be Jew ridden'[61]. Basically the aim of the cultural prejudice was to create an image of the Jews having a well-earned reputation of creating hostility. Since the Second World War, criticism of the Jew has been confined to the influence of the international aspirations of Jewry through banking and finance and Zionist political pressures. Even extremists such as Colin Jordan have in the main failed to utilise cultural prejudice in an intellectual and moral climate not conducive to it.

The image of the Jew has also been buttressed by various personality projections and the generalised transference of frustrations and anxieties onto the outgroup. In general, aspects of modernity which the individual or organisation concerned does not like are blamed upon the Jews. Thus, for the Britons, treasonable activity in the war, which passed by the name of the 'Hidden Hand', included signalling German raiders, passing dud shells, sending pilots to fight in

51

obsolete planes and suicidal infantry attacks on the Western
Front, and this was all part of the 'Jew begotten treason',
which was responsible for 'one quarter of the casualties' of
the war.[62]   Beamish believed that he could prove 'up to the
hilt that a large proportion of the vices of white peoples
are the result of the contact with Jews',[63] and Leese that
the majority of his fellow inmates in jail were there because
of the 'Jewish blood' in their make-up.[64]   For A.K. Chesterton
in the British Union of Fascists the Jew was responsible for
'Yahoo domination, and every value in consequence is turned
upside down'.[65]   The Jew as the bringer of modernity is a
potent image in anti-semitic thought since the Second World
War although it is usually presented in a coded form.   For
the National Socialist Movement, 'Progress produces "MODERN
MAN" that synthetic abortion of nature and reversing every
biological instinct that nature bestows.'[66]

Since the Second World War however, racial populist movements
have concentrated more of their attention on the more visible
problem of the effect of coloured immigration on English life.
Like the anti-semitic image, this has combined in-built
atavistic prejudices with cultural and personal fears.
Winthrop Jordan has argued that even before the beginnings of
colonial expansion of European powers in the sixteenth century
there was a negative image of the inhabitants of other con-
tinents in Europe caused by the traditional stereotypes of
white symbolising purity and black evil, the lack of a notion
of cultural relativism and the technological superiority of
European powers.[67]   These negative images have been
reinforced by the historical experience of slavery in the
Americas and colonial rule in the rest of the world which
combined to give an air of assumed superiority in racial and
cultural terms to European hegemony.[68]   This deeply-rooted
prejudice was given a spurious intellectual validity by the

development of scientific theories of race during the nineteenth century,[69] which combined with the non-scientific
theories such as the Sambo stereotype and 'retrogressionist'
justifications for colonialism to form an entrenched view
impervious to rational argument.[70] Of particular significance
was the combination of the intellectual fashion of uncritical
positivism with the development of nineteenth-century racist
ideas.[71] The thought of racial populist movements in
twentieth-century Britain has shown the power of stereotypes
to survive the conditions in which attitudes were formed,
for despite radical alterations in liberal attitudes to race,
the ideas to be examined remain unalterably fixed in nineteenth-
century assumptions, even with the additions of some modern
ideas.

Scientific attitudes towards race have represented a
synthesis of German, English and American influences.
Beamish and the Britons appeared to owe most to the English
zoologist G.P. Mudge and geneticist Karl Pearson who developed
crude measuring techniques based on nineteenth-century
assumptions with regard to physical characteristics and
intelligence tests.[72] Leese produced a more coherent theory
based on the principle of uncritical positivism and the
negation of the liberal belief that individual rather than
group differences were the most significant. For him 'The
Races of Man have virtues just as have the races of animals.'[73]
Leese adopted the monist position of racial nationalism and
saw the nature of man in social darwinian terms.[74] Leese's
argument, based as it was on a fear of racial contamination,
has greatly influenced post-war volkish thought. Even
Mosley has come close to a racist position in his espousal of
apartheid for 'It is absolutely necessary that the racial
bearers of such cultures should be segregated from each
other.'[75] Mosley, or at least his research assistant, had
read widely to see how 'science' justified racial differences

and he has used the work of Darwin, T.H. Huxley, Mendel, Sir
E.B. Tylor, Professor C.D. Darlington, Professor Waddington
and Dr Gayre of Gayre to support his view that 'a man should
be as determined to preserve his own race as to preserve his
own family'[76]. In the 1950s and 1960s scientific racial
nationalism was resurrected by John Bean, who managed to
trace his ideas back to Chamberlain, Wagner and Gobineau.[77]
More recently, 'scientific' racial nationalism has become
more sophisticated, with Richard Verrall, the editor of
Spearhead and one of the leading ideologists of the National
Front, producing arguments which utilised I.Q. tests,
identical twin experiments, phrenology and physical anthropology to prove that 'The intellectual inferiority of the
Negro, then, is a genetically inherited mental trait.'[78]
The ideology and argument has become more sophisticated but
the same assumptions of the degeneration critique, the
failure to differentiate between individuals and the
inductive positivism unite the tradition from Beamish to
Verrall. The obsession to find scientific evidence to
refute liberal and humanitarian ideas of race was used as
the base for the projection of the image of the coloured
immigrant as an inferior being.

The more pretentious scientific racism has also been
buttressed by arguments deriving from popular 'common sense'
attitudes to race. A.K. Chesterton in particular has
developed basic prejudice to portray attitudes identical to
those in scientific theories. For him the British would
'be unfitted to perform any further services to the world if
our stock is to be mixed with negroid stocks'[79]. Similarly
a crude social darwinian equation of the human with the
animal world and the implication that the Negro was of the
same order as a pig or an ape was implied in Chesterton's
critique of heart transplant operations. He argued that
such operations were supposed to provide evidence that

Europeans and Negroes 'should mix it up socially and sexually'
and if this were true why shouldn't the same principle be
applied to 'men and pigs or to men and apes'.[80] For John
Tyndall, too much racial integration meant the loss of
identity and 'the particular genius that has been Britain's
gift to history',[81] namely leadership qualities. As with
scientific theories the image of contamination and degeneracy
represented the fundamental fears behind such arguments.

The racial qualities possessed by the Negro and Indian
races were also considered to be undesirable. Strangely
enough, 'expert' assessments of Indian and Negro attainments
were very similar with regard to violence fantasies. Thus,
before British rule, Leese saw the history of India as
'centuries of tyranny, bloodshed and oppression',[82] whilst
Chesterton saw African history as a saga of 'Mau-Mau
unchecked'.[83] Similarly there appeared to be a widespread
belief among racial populist groups that the Negro produced
no culture or civilisation worth talking about, while the
'babu'[84] intellect of India merely aped European leadership
or fomented rebellion.

The image of the coloured immigrant therefore contained
these deep cultural and personal prejudices and like that of
the Jew bore little relation to the real human predicament.
For Leese, in the inter-war period, the colour problem,
particularly in the seaports, was created by 'Arabs, Negroes,
Somalis and Chinamen contaminating the white blood of our
race with the assistance of the lowest of the low of white
women',[85] and was of minor importance compared to the Jewish
'problem'. However it set the tone of the basic fear and
image portrayed when coloured immigrants replaced the Jew as
the main scapegoat in the demonology of such groups. The
image of the coloured immigrant was a particularly malign
one. Sex, violence, crime, health, employment, education
and welfare fantasies were projected indiscriminately onto

coloured immigrants. This created much greater problems in
those areas than their numbers in the community could justify
and few benefits. Little or no distinction was made between
different immigrant cultures, although West Indians had more
parties, Pakistanis had numerous fiances and Indian Sikhs
wore turbans. The threat to the English race and culture in
immigrant reception areas was continuously emphasised and an
exaggerated stress was put on the numbers of immigrants
entering the country. Perhaps the best summary of racial
populist attitudes towards immigration was expressed in a
headline in Union, Mosley's post-war newspaper: 'Life blood
flows out, sewage flows in.'[86]

Probably the most extreme views were those of John
Tyndall and Martin Webster, the Chairman and Activities
Organiser of the National Front. For Tyndall, in his Nazi
days before his thought changed, the coloured immigrant was
bringing 'the rule of the jungle on Britain and America'.
As he saw it, the coloured immigrant brought more of his 'sub-
human brothers' into Britain each year, thus polluting Britain
with the 'crime, disease and filth by which their society is
shaped in Africa.'[87] Webster developed the Sambo image of
the coloured immigrant. He argued that 'coloured people
individually - and more particularly in groups - have the
mentality of children'.[88] The most sustained and single-
minded campaign against coloured immigration was that staged
by John Bean of the British National Party in the 1960s. He
was fired to enthusiasm by such thoughts as the fact that
English families usually have between two and four children,
while 'Afro-Asian families frequently have twelve or more'.[89]
The threat of immigrants bringing in leprosy was another
phobia. A.K. Chesterton probably most succinctly summed up
the fears of the tradition. For him the aim of stopping
coloured immigration was to stop the breeding of 'a multi-
coloured hugger-mugger in twentieth century Britain', an

56

image which combined race, sex and violence fantasies.

The image of the immigrant in twentieth-century racial populist thought has been far more dependent on deep-rooted atavistic prejudices than on the newcomers' own behaviour patterns.   The very different images of the Jew and coloured immigrant had their origins in separate fantasies.   The image of the Jew was a contradictory one as a result of combining a conspiracy theory with various volkish mixtures of racism and ethnocentrism within the tradition.   On the one hand the Jew was a member either of an inferior race or culture to the member of the Aryan or the English volk; on the other he was considered intelligent enough to be on the verge of world domination.[90]   The coloured immigrant however provided no ambiguous complications for racial populists. Coloured immigration provided a threat to the racial or cultural homogeneity of the English volk and contamination would lead to the destruction of the English nation.   Crude xenophobia was rationalised by nineteenth-century racist theories which portrayed the darker-skinned coloured immigrant as closer to the apes than to the white Europeans in personality traits.   The images of the Jew and coloured immigrant in racial populist thought were constructed of different layers of prejudice superimposed on each other. They contained Jungian archetypal elements as well as reflecting cultural prejudice and personality projections.

The relevance of this unsavoury subject to labour history is that the ideology of racial populist movements presents in an extreme form popular cultural prejudices which reflect attitudes and behaviour patterns of some sections of the working class.   This is particularly true of the image of the coloured immigrant, and the growth of the National Front can be related to its policy of scapegoating the coloured immigrant for social problems in inner-city areas.   This

is potentially more dangerous than the campaign of the British
Union of Fascists against Jews in the 1930s because a larger
proportion of the populace feel threatened by the more visible
impact of coloured immigration in several geographical areas
than the basically localised impact of the Fascists in the
East End of London.   However, as Hitler proved, anti-semitism
and racism as ideologies were more important in supplying the
dynamism behind his personality than they were in convincing
others to vote for him.[91]   Fortunately none of the racial
populist leaders show anything like Hitler's skill in
manipulating political situations to their advantage.

The significance of such groups and their ideologies is
regrettably to provide a bee-sting effect on the major
political parties.[92]   If issues such as immigration strike
a chord in popular consciousness, then sooner or later one
or both of the major political parties will adopt part of
the platform of the emergent group, in an attempt to destroy
the threat posed to the establishment.   This is what has
occurred with the response to coloured immigration, as both
Labour and Conservative parties have outbid each other to
close the loopholes in immigration law.   Fortunately there
appears little chance of attempting to outbid the National
Front in their plans for repatriation of immigrants.   This
represents the modern variant of the British Fascists' plan
for sending British Jews to Madagascar in the inter-war
period.   Hopefully it will share the same fate as that idea.

NOTES

1. See C. Holmes (ed.), Immigrants and Minorities in
British Society 1870-1914 (1978) for range of examples.

2. See B. Gainer, The Alien Invasion (1972); J. Garrard,
The English and Immigration 1880-1910 (1973); P. Foot,
Immigration and Race in British Politics (1965) for details.

3. J. Rex, Race Relations in Sociological Theory (1970), ch. 6 and R. Thurlow, 'Ideology of Obsession', Patterns of Prejudice, vol.8, no.6 (Nov.-Dec. 1974), pp.23-5.

4. R. Thurlow, 'Racial Populism in England', Patterns of Prejudice, vol.10, no.4 (July-Aug.1976), pp.27-33.

5. J. Webb, The Occult Establishment (La Salle, 1977), p.10.

6. See K.D. Bracher, The German Dictatorship (1973), p.23n for a definition of volkish as an ideology which includes racial, ethnocentric and national elements.

7. R. Hofstadter, The Paranoid Style in American Politics and Other Essays (New York, 1967), p.3.

8. See D.B. Davis, The Fear of Conspiracy (Ithaca, 1975), p.xii for a discussion of this syndrome with regard to American history.

9. E.R. Hilgard, R.C. Atkinson and R.L. Atkinson, Psychology, 5th ed. (New York, 1971), p.408. For previous application to historical material, see G. Mitchell and C. Holmes, 'In His Image', Patterns of Prejudice, vol. 9, no.1 (Jan.-Feb. 1975), p.20.

10. B. Zawadski, 'Limitations of the Scapegoat Theory of Prejudice', Journal of Abnormal and Social Psychology, XLIII (1948), pp.127-41.

11. The major contributions to published work in the field are C. Cross, The Fascists in Britain (1961); W.F. Mandle, Anti-Semitism and the British Union of Fascists (1968); R. Benewick, Political Violence and Public Order (1969); R. Skidelsky, Oswald Mosley (1975); M. Walker, The National Front (1977); N. Nugent and R. King (eds.), The British Right (1978); R. Miles and A. Phizacklea (eds.), Racism and Political Action in Britain (1979); G.C. Lebzelter, Political Anti-Semitism in England 1918-39 (1979); C. Holmes, Anti-Semitism in British Society 1876-1939 (1979) and M. Billig, Fascists (1979).

12. N. Cohn, Warrant for Genocide (1967), p.203.

13. For a description of the nature of modern German anti-semitism, see G.L. Mosse, Germans and Jews (1970), pp.18-19.

14. J. Trachtenberg, The Devil and the Jews (New Haven, 1943), pp.4-5.

15. N. Webster, World Revolution (1921), p.325.

16. N. Webster, Secret Societies and Subversive Movements,
4th ed. (1928), p.405.

17. The Hidden Hand, Sept. 1923.

18. A. Leese, Freemasonry (1935), p.5.

19. J.F.C. Fuller, 'The Cancer of Europe', Fascist Quarterly,
vol.1, no.1 (Jan. 1935), p.77.

20. Candour, Dec. 1965.   This is Chesterton's own private
newspaper published since 1953.

21. Candour, 21 May 1954.

22. C. Jordan, Britain Reborn (n.d.).

23. The Hidden Hand, December 1920.   The Britons produced a
monthly newspaper between 1920 and 1925 which periodically
changed its title.   The main changes were from Jewry Uber
Alles (Feb. 1920 - Aug. 1920) to The Hidden Hand (Sept. 1920
- Apr. 1924) and the British Guardian (May 1924 - 1925).

24. Fuller, Fascist Quarterly vol.1, no.1, p.70.

25. Candour, 12 Apr. 1957.

26. Webster, Secret Societies p.178.

27. Webster, World Revolution p.viii.

28. Webster, Secret Societies p.11; Cohn, Warrant for
Genocide, pp.46-50; Trachtenberg, The Devil ch.5.

29. N. Webster, Spacious Days (1949), p.173.

30. See Webb, Occult Establishment for details.

31. Fuller, Fascist Quarterly vol.1, no.1, p.78.

32. Leese, Freemasonry pp.5-6.

33. J. Tyndall, Six Principles of British Nationalism (1967),
p.25.

34. Anon., The Great Jewish Masque (n.d.)

35. The Fascist, Jan. 1934.   This was a monthly newsletter
published by The Imperial Fascist League between 1929 and
1939.

36. The National Socialist, Aug. 1963. This was an occasional newspaper published by the National Socialist Movement between 1962 and 1965.

37. Webster, World Revolution p. 11.

38. British Guardian, Sept. 1924.

39. Skidelsky, Oswald Mosley p. 465.

40. O. Spengler, Decline of the West, vol. II (1928), p. 321.

41. Blackshirt, 30 Sept. - 6 Oct. 1933. This was one of The British Union of Fascists' newspapers.

42. Candour, 5 Oct. 1956.

43. Candour, 12 Apr. 1957.

44. Candour, Apr. 1971.

45. A.K. Chesterton, 'The "Myth" of Race', Truth, 4 Aug. 1950.

46. W. Laqueur, Russia and Germany (1965), p. 90.

47. Notes on speech made by Sir O. Mosley in S. Africa, 22.1.64, Wiener Library Files.

48. Refugees before Britons (n.d.), p. 4.

49. Letter from Beamish to R. Edmondson, 22 Dec. 1936, Wiener Library Files.

50. The Hidden Hand, Feb. 1923.

51. The Fascist, June 1932.

52. Ibid.

53. M.D. Biddiss, 'Myths of the Blood', Patterns of Prejudice, vol. 9, no. 5 (sept.-Oct. 1975), p. 13; Biddiss, Father of Racist Ideology (1970), p. 124.

54. Combat, May-June 1963. This was the newspaper of the British National Party between 1960 and 1966.

55. The Fascist, Feb. 1931.

56. Candour, 24 Nov. 1961.

57. *Candour*, Sept. 1969.

58. *National Socialist*, no.6 (n.d.).

59. E.G. Clarke, *The British Union and the Jews* (1937), p.2.

60. *Blackshirt*, 30 Sept.- 6 Oct. 1933.

61. *Action*, 7 Nov. 1936.

62. *The Hidden Hand*, Oct. 1920.

63. *The Hidden Hand*, Feb. 1923.

64. *The Fascist*, Jan. 1938.

65. *Action*, 27 Mar. 1937.

66. *The National Socialist*, Aug. 1963.

67. W. Jordan, *White Over Black* (Chapel Hill, 1968), ch.1.

68. V. Kiernan, *The Lords of Human Kind* (1972), particularly pp. 325ff.

69. C. Bolt, *Victorian Attitudes to Race* (1971), pp.1-28.

70. See S. Elkins, *Slavery* (New York, 1963), pp. 81ff.; G.L. Frederickson, *The Black Image in the White Mind* (New York, 1971), pp.244-82, and H. Gutman, *The Black Family in Slavery and Freedom* (Oxford, 1976), pp. 531ff.

71. Biddiss, *Patterns of Prejudice* vol.9, no.5, p.13.

72. *The Hidden Hand*, Nov. 1921.

73. *The Fascist*, Oct. 1937.

74. D. Gasman, *The Scientific Origins of National Socialism* (1971), pp. 31ff.

75. *Union*, 22 Jan. 1949.

76. O. Mosley, *Mosley Right or Wrong* (1967), pp.18-19.

77. *Combat*, Aug.-Oct. 1961.

78. *Spearhead*, Apr. 1976.

79. *Candour*, 4 Sept. 1959.

80. Candour, Jan. 1968.

81. Tyndall, Six Principles p.15.

82. The Fascist, Mar. 1934.

83. Candour, 19 Feb. 1954.

84. The Fascist, Mar. 1934: A.K. Chesterton, Stand By the Empire (Croydon, 1954), p.13.

85. The Fascist, June 1932.

86. Union, 11 Dec. 1948.

87. Spearhead, Aug.-Sept. 1964.

88. Spearhead, Feb. 1965.

89. Combat, Apr.-June 1964.

90. Billig, Fascists, was published some time after the presentation of this paper. Although there is some agreement on interpretation, the author thinks the ideology of the National Front represents more of a synthesis of various traditions rather than ascribing primary importance to a concealed Nazism.

91. Cohn, Warrant for Genocide p.220; W.S. Allen, The Nazi Seizure of Power (Chicago, 1965), pp.77-8 and 209-12; H.A. Winkler,'German Society, Hitler and the Illusion of Restoration', Journal of Contemporary History, XI (Oct. 1976), p.12.

92. R. Hofstadter, The Age of Reform (1962), p.97.

4
Ethnicity, Class and Popular Toryism, 1850–1870
NEVILLE KIRK

Labour historians have long been aware of significant changes
in the development of the labour movement and class relations
in Britain between the second and third quarters of the
nineteenth century. For, despite the Webbs' proneness to
exaggeration and A.E. Musson's insistence upon the basically
unchanged nature of the trade union movement between the 1830s
and the 1870s,[1] there is little doubt that major discontinuities
were in evidence. Hobsbawm, Harrison and others[2] have pointed
to the ebbing of class conflict after Chartism, the increasingly
'reformist' nature of the labour movement, the decline of mass
independent working-class politics, and the sharpening of
divisions and the growth of 'corporate' consciousness within
the working class. In short, the Chartist attempt to create
a new social order was shelved: the labour movement and large
sections of the working class, while prepared to fight hard
on specific issues, increasingly came to accept capitalism as
given and worked for improvements within the system.

The onset of 'reformism' and the lowering of social
tensions after Chartism have been largely explained in terms
of changes within the economy and class structure. Of crucial
importance here were a number of interrelated developments:[3]
the re-stabilisation and expansion of the economy on the basis

of railway development and the growth of capital goods
industries: the modest but nevertheless significant improvements in the standard of living and regularity of employment
of large numbers of workers:[4] the absence (with the exception
of the Cotton Famine) of major, protracted depressions: the
decline and virtual disappearance of certain occupational
groups, such as handloom weavers, which had provided much of
the radical and even revolutionary impetus behind Chartism:
the re-establishment of the labour process on the basis of
modern industry:[5] the rise to dominance within the labour
movement of a politically moderate and relatively privileged
'labour aristocracy' which detached itself from the mass of
workers: the very real advances made by sections of the
labour movement, which involved sections of the working class
far more deeply in the status quo than previously: and the
increased toleration and even formal recognition of trade
unions by major employers. All these factors contributed
(with varying degrees of importance, and despite the existence
of powerful countervailing influences, such as the persistence
of industrial conflict) to the weakening of class combativity.

This chapter sets out to incorporate the dimension of ethnic
conflict into our explanatory framework. It should, however,
be noted from the outset that 'ethnicity' is not afforded
explanatory primacy. I fully endorse Stedman-Jones's view
that the ebbing of class conflict after Chartism must be
attributed primarily to overall changes in the nature of
British capitalism (in particular, railway development and
the growth of capital goods industries lessened imbalances
within the economy, provided a broad, secure foundation for
economic and social advancement, and conferred upon the
economy a degree of stability hitherto lacking) and not
simply or mainly to 'special' features, such as the rise of
a 'labour aristocracy'. Given the centrality of structural

65

changes at the economic level and their profound implications
for social relationships, I contend that within one geographical area - the cotton towns of south-east Lancashire
and north-east Cheshire[6] - 'ethnicity' operated at a secondary
level to weaken working-class solidarity and the appeal of
independent labour politics.   In the cotton districts, as at
the national level, the stabilisation and expansion of the
economy, the various economic, social and institutional
advances made by labour, and the sharpening of cultural and
social divisions within the working class constitute the wider
context in which ethnic allegiances must be situated.[7]

With the massive increase in Irish Roman Catholic
immigration into the cotton towns at the end of the 1840s
came an exacerbation of tensions and an escalation in conflicts
between sections of the immigrant and host communities.   Such
conflicts revealed themselves most dramatically in the
extremely riotous years of 1852 and 1868, but persisted, with
varying degrees of intensity, throughout the 'golden years'.
Ethnic antagonisms exercised a debilitating influence upon
that impressive labour solidarity which had manifested
itself in the manufacturing districts during the Chartist
years.[8]   And a working class fragmented along ethnic (and
wider cultural) lines greatly facilitated the (re-)assertion
of bourgeois controls upon the working class, and helped to
attach workers more firmly to the framework of bourgeois
politics.   Just as the majority of labour activists were
drawn, for a number of reasons, to the 'progressive' Liberal
camp,[9] so ethnic frictions pushed sections of the English
workforce into the receptive arms of anti-Catholic Conservatives and Orangemen: strengthened the authority of the
priesthood in Irish Catholic communities: and were
instrumental in persuading large numbers of immigrants to
support their Liberal defenders.

Before examining these trends in more detail it is first

necessary to define the terms 'ethnicity' and 'class'. 'Ethnicity'[10] is used to refer to collectivities of people who share a common origin, ancestry, and cultural heritage, and who express their common interests in ideas, value systems and institutions. Ethnicity is used, therefore, both as a structural category (the behaviour of people in specified social situations, within structural constraints and determinations) and as a cultural phenomenon (consciousness). Ethnicity further implies: the existence of 'boundaries', which ensure internal group cohesion and create an external category of non-members: and can also carry with it connotations of varying degrees of conflict both within and between ethnic groups. It should also be emphasised that ethnicity is viewed as a dynamic social phenomenon. Ethnic feeling is not automatically given in a static or unhistorical manner: rather ethnic allegiance can diminish or increase over time depending upon specific historical determinations and the ways in which objective determinations are experienced by people.

As with ethnicity, 'class'[11] is interpreted not as a static thing but as a historical relationship, as something which happens over time. Class is also rooted both within objective determinations (mainly the productive relations into which people enter involuntarily) and in consciousness (in the ways in which people, 'live their productive relations, and as they experience their determinate situations, within "the ensemble of social relations", with their inherited culture and expectations, and as they handle these experiences in cultural ways')[12]. Class, as E.P. Thompson has insisted, owes as much to agency as conditioning. And while class experience is largely determined, class consciousness is far less so. Again, consciousness is not given in a simple, mechanistic way by objective determinations, but is rather the result of lived experience within certain specific

67

structural constraints.

How, then, does class stand in relationship to ethnicity? Our preceding sketch suggests that while any analysis of class which ignores or underplays cultural traditions and the ensemble of social relations is inherently unsatisfactory, nevertheless particular importance should be attached to social relations of production. By way of contrast, our definition of ethnicity, while cognisant of material factors, takes as its point of departure cultural traditions, origin and ancestry. This is not to imply, however, that classes and ethnic groups must always stand in mutual opposition and separation: the relationship is often more complex, fluid and dynamic than this. For example, while we could not deny the importance of ethnicity in moulding social structure and attitudes in the United States, we would take issue with any suggestion that workers in America have always been motivated by ethnic as opposed to class interests. Ethnic groups, as with classes, are not usually undifferentiated and monolithic wholes: a sense of cultural distinctiveness can be combined with a very real sense of class.[13]

RESPONSES TO IRISH IMMIGRATION, 1830-1870

We can now return to the situation in Lancashire and Cheshire at the middle of the nineteenth century. We propose, first, to outline reactions to Irish immigration between 1830 and 1870: secondly, to examine the material roots of assimilation and conflict: and thirdly to trace the socio-political effects of escalating tensions in the post-1850 period.

Contemporary attitudes towards Irish immigration have been well documented. Our purpose here is not to rehearse these attitudes in detail, but to focus upon the major points of emphasis.[14] As is well known, contemporary reactions were, for the most part, unfavourable. Irish immigration was widely believed to constitute an example of 'a less civilized

68

population spreading themselves, as a kind of substratum, beneath a more civilized community'. Schooled in a poverty-stricken agrarian society, the Irish were reputedly separated from the 'host' society by economic situation, politics, religion and culture. Concentrated on the bottom and lower rungs of the occupational ladder and huddled into their cramped quarters in the major urban areas, the Irish constituted, according to Faucher, 'the most abject part of the population', prepared to tolerate a lower standard of life than all but the very poorest of the English workforce. The Catholic Church's antipathy towards Chartism and trade unionism, the popularity among sections of the immigrants of the anti-Chartist O'Connell, and the use of the Irish as strike-breakers served to reinforce beliefs that Irish involvement in the labour movement was of little significance, and that the Irish were a direct threat to the English workers' standard of living. The Irish reputation for 'rough, intemperate and improvident' behaviour, their supposed lack of 'industrious and regular habits' and their attachment to an 'alien' religion completed the picture of an ethnic minority at odds with the host population.

An emphasis upon strains and divisions has also figured prominently in some of the more recent research. Werly, for example, has seen the emergence of Irish quarters in Manchester in the 1830s and 1840s as symptomatic of a lack of immigrant integration into the life of the city.[15] And Treble maintains that Irish involvement in Chartism was not particularly strong.[16]

And yet, while problems of assimilation undoubtedly existed, we must be careful not to present an unbalanced picture for the two decades before 1850. Relations between English and Irish workers were more complex and fluid than many contemporaries realised. The researches of Thompson and Foster,[17] and to a lesser extent Treble, suggest that although the mass of immigrants constituted an 'uneasy element' within the emerging working class, nevertheless patterns of integration and the capacity for united class action were by no means absent.

A growing sense of class solidarity was most evident in relation to the labour movement.   Irish participation in Chartism, for example, has sometimes been understated.[18] Several Irishmen held leadership positions in north-west Chartism and the movement at Oldham did attract significant immigrant support. At a national level Chartist leaders, with their belief in international proletarian solidarity, made strenuous efforts to attract Irish immigrants to the cause.   Such efforts met with a mixed response and limited success.   We are dealing here with a chequered history, a story of fits and starts, of rebuttals and renewed attempts at unity.   In south Lancashire, for example, the cordial relationship between the Chartists and members of the Repeal Association was, for a time at least, badly damaged by the events of 1841 when Chartists and Irish supporters of O'Connell clashed on the streets of Manchester, Stockport, Hyde and Stalybridge.[19]   After 1841 repeated efforts were made to wrest control of the Repeal Associations away from O'Connellite influence but without any notable success.   However, even in the immediate post-1841 years Chartist influence over sections of the immigrant community was not negligible: Irish operatives took part in the general strike of 1842 and O'Connor enjoyed some popularity amongst immigrant workers.   Furthermore, institutional links between Chartists and Repealers were resurrected in 1848 when the increased emphasis placed upon socio-economic demands by Mitchell and his followers and their disillusionment with the results of 'moral force' agitation facilitated the creation of an alliance with the Chartists, which lasted throughout the spring and summer months.

Exaggerations and oversimplifications were also present in contemporary claims that English workers automatically reacted with hostility to Irish competition in the labour market.   For those workers influenced by Chartism, this was

70

not necessarily the case. Indeed the <u>Northern Star</u> claimed
in 1841 that many workers had 'taken the very competition by
the hand, and treated them (the Irish) not as aliens but as
brethren'.[20]   According to Richard Sheridan, a handloom
weaver, responsibility for the ills of his craft lay less
with the poor, unsuspecting Irish than with the employers'
cheap labour policies:

> ...the capitalists have sent over false
> reports that they wanted hands, in order
> to induce the Irish to come over that
> they might lower wages. I am at a loss
> to know whether the Irish gentleman or
> the English capitalist has done more for
> the destruction of the working classes,
> both of England and Ireland.   21

The solution, for Chartists, lay in the creation of an
alliance of English and Irish workers against the divisive
acts of capitalists.

Neither were the Irish totally devoid of trade union
experience.[22]   To be sure, trade union traditions among the
mass of immigrants from rural Ireland were weak, but some of
the craft and skilled workers from urban areas had been
schooled in trade unionism. As members of the shoemaking
and tailoring unions in Manchester the Irish played a part in
virtually every trial of strength with employers in the 1830s
and 1840s. Irishmen were amongst those who attempted to
form a national weavers' organisation in 1841, and in
Manchester Irish building trades labourers were solidly
organised. Noted by many employers for their 'rebellious
and insubordinate' character, the Irish, in cotton at least,
were as likely to be strikers as strike-breakers.[23]

It is also easy to overestimate the extent of
ghettoisation and the level and incidence of ethnic conflict
during the Chartist period. Irish quarters did come into

71

existence in some towns, but these rarely constituted large
formal ghettoes from which non-Irish families were totally
excluded.   And in other towns, for example Oldham, it
appears that Irish and English operatives were quite happy to
live as neighbours.[24]   Indeed, after living in England for
some time the Irish became, according to some contemporaries,
more acceptable workmates, social companions and marriage
partners for the English.[25]   And, despite frequent battles
between English and Irish railway navvies and the O'Connellite
disturbances in 1841, instances of overt anti-Irish direct
actions were rare in south Lancashire in the 1840s: Irish
'rows' often amounted to internal faction fights among the
Irish, and were not usually directed against host communities.[26]

We must take care, therefore, not to exaggerate the
extent of tensions and separations for the Chartist period.
While not fully accepting Thompson's conclusion that 'it is
not the friction but the relative ease with which the Irish
were absorbed into working-class communities which is
remarkable',[27] we can suggest that a limited process of
assimilation was at work and that at times class solidarity
reduced the potential for ethnic conflict.

With the increase in immigration in the late 1840s this
scenario changed somewhat. While the capacity for toleration
and even joint action did not totally disappear, the
increasingly fragile nature of class unity and the mounting
undercurrent of anti-Irish sentiment were demonstrated by a
widespread upsurge in violent ethnic confrontations. In
1849 and 1850, for example, newspaper reports of skirmishes
between English and Irish operatives multiplied.   At
Stockport hundreds of Irishmen regularly congregated in the
streets 'speaking in the most hostile terms of the English
and daring any John Bull man to come out and fight'.   At
Ashton and elsewhere the Irish were accused of 'taking the
bread out of the mouths of Lancashire workingmen'.[28]

As tensions mounted, Chartist pleas for toleration and understanding of the plight of the poverty-stricken Irish increasingly fell on deaf ears. After 1848 Chartism in Lancashire, while by no means defunct, became a pale shadow of its former self: a force capable of challenging religious and cultural prejudices within the working class no longer enjoyed a mass base. With the increase in immigration and the demise of Chartism the various small and largely middle-class Protestant organisations redoubled their efforts to generate anti-Catholic sentiments among workers:[29] scurrilous anti-Papist tracts were distributed, a sustained drive for working-class recruits was undertaken and a series of well-attended and sensationalist lectures exposing the Pope's desire for 'universal domination', his antipathy to 'English liberties', and the manifold 'horrors and superstitions' of Roman Catholicism were delivered at Manchester, Stockport and Ashton. The Irish were portrayed as Papal puppets, intent upon lowering wages and 'transforming England into a great workhouse'.[30]

Extreme Protestants did not succeed, at this stage, in creating a strong working-class following, but their prophecies of imminent Papal domination in England were strengthened by the Pope's restoration of the Catholic hierarchy in England and Wales in September 1850. This action triggered off a loud and aggressive Protestant back-lash, which while mainly middle-class in character, served to legitimise and render respectable anti-Irish Catholic feelings of workers and to highlight Irish attachment to an 'alien' religion. Serious anti-Popery disturbances broke out in London, Cheltenham and Birkenhead, and in south Lancashire irate Church of England Protestants held crowded and agitated protest meetings.[31] Hugh Stowell, a leading figure in Manchester and Salford Protestantism, warned that the Catholic Church intended 'to get England under her

power...to persecute and prosecute every Protestant...to set
up the inquisition in our land...and to make Queen Victoria
a Papist'.[32]   No major outbreaks of rioting resulted from
the Protestant backlash in the area, but the signs were
ominous.   In December 1850 there was a street brawl in
Manchester's 'Little Ireland' between English and Irish
operatives: at Stockport Irish Catholics attempted to
disrupt Protestant meetings and Church of England services,[33]
and at Ashton and Stalybridge local Orangemen combined
virulent attacks on Roman Catholicism with support for the
economic grievances of English workers.[34]

Mounting unrest reached a climax in 1852 when anti-Irish
disturbances occurred in a number of towns.   The most serious
riot took place at Stockport in July when the authorities'
decision to permit the Catholics to hold their annual scholars'
procession on the last Saturday in June sparked off several
days of violence.[35]   Irate Conservatives and Orangemen
maintained that the holding of the procession contravened a
royal proclamation of June, which forbade the exercise of the
rites and ceremonies of the Catholic religion in other than
their usual place of worship, and swore to have their revenge.
On the Sunday the borough was relatively peaceful, but on the
Monday evening a crowd of some one hundred English factory
lads carried an effigy of Canon Frith, the Catholic priest,
through the streets of an Irish neighbourhood, tore it apart,
and then did battle with the outraged Irish inhabitants.
The events of Monday formed a prelude to the more serious
rioting of Tuesday evening when, following further street
battles in Hillgate and the stoning of a Church of England
school, a crowd of several hundred English workers, shouting
'Pull the Papist bastards out', attacked and ransacked Irish
houses in Rock Row.   The crowd, which increased to some two
thousand people, then proceeded to carry out extensive damage
at the Catholic chapel at Edgeley, and was only prevented

from ransacking the Catholic chapel of Saint Michael's by
the arrival of troops and special constables. On Wednesday,
Stockport was still in an agitated state. Some English
operatives, to the cry of 'Five pounds for an Irishman's
head', carried out further attacks against Irish houses, but
encountered stubborn Irish and police resistance. The
remaining months of the year witnessed numerous street
battles, and on their return to Stockport in August the
Englishmen found not guilty at Chester assizes were received
by 'one of the most enthusiastic gatherings that ever occurred
in Stockport'.

The riots at Stockport, in which one man was killed and
some one hundred seriously injured, represented a settling
of old scores, a battle for mastery of the borough. A
favourite stamping-ground for 'pulpit-drum' ecclesiastics
during the 'Papal Aggression Crisis',the town, according to
the superintendent of police, had experienced 'for some years'
increasing religious tensions. Pot-house brawls between
English and Irish inhabitants were 'as common as daylight',
and since the late 1840s cotton manufacturers had allegedly
practised discriminatory employment policies in favour of
Irish operatives. By June 1852 the conduct of some Irish
mill workers had become so overbearing that many English
operatives were refusing to work alongside them.[36] The Irish
were disliked because they were 'bloody Papists, bloody
rednecks'. Irish homes in Rock Row were daubed by the
invading English workers with the slogan of 'England for Ever',
and English rioters marched to the tune of 'Rule Britannia',
a pattern to be repeated in the course of every major
disturbance during the following twenty years. Perhaps the
most important clue to the outbreaks of rioting was provided
by an English factory operative. 'There never will be any
good done with them', he declared, 'it is the Irish who keep
wages down.'[37]

The inflamed atmosphere at Stockport was highly infectious.
In July the Irish districts in Manchester were in an 'excited
state': Hulme experienced fights between English and Irish
labourers and factory operatives, and at New Cross (an area
of some Chartist influence) Protestant candidates who stood
at the parliamentary elections received some enthusiastic
working-class support.[38]   Election day at Wigan witnessed a
running battle between some five hundred English and Irish
people.[39]

The remaining years of the decade were often tense and
sometimes riotous. At Stockport weekend battles and
skirmishes continued to plague the lives of 'respectable
citizens', and the Protestant Association registered a sharp
increase in its popularity among the cotton workforce. At
Stalybridge and Ashton, where contemporaries noted a marked
decline of Chartism and a widespread growth of anti-Irish
feeling, repeated clashes took place. In September 1854,
for example, a full-scale riot erupted at Ashton[40] when
between two and three hundred men and youths retaliated
against Irish attacks on the homes of English operatives by
invading the Irish quarter of Flag Alley. In the ensuing
years the Ashton Protestant Association built up a considerable following among the town's cotton workforce. At the
1857 parliamentary election Booth Mason, a prominent local
Orangeman, stood at Ashton on a platform of 'No Popery' and
support for manhood suffrage. Mason received the show of
hands at the hustings but was defeated at the poll.[41]   At
Oldham ethnic polarisation was one aspect of the decline of
working-class solidarity in the 1850s. Here, as at Preston,
Blackburn and Wigan, Protestant street preaching and Orange
parades often resulted in violence.[42]

Despite the upsurge in conflict in the 1850s some towns,
and most significantly Stockport, did experience a lowering
of ethnic tensions towards the end of the decade and in the

early 1860s.   During the Relief Riots at Stalybridge in 1863
English and Irish operatives acted in concert.   When the
police attempted to transport the Irishmen arrested during
the disturbance from the police station to the railway station
a crowd of 'not less than fifteen thousand' English and Irish
operatives made an abortive attempt to rescue the prisoners.[43]
Stockport remained untroubled by major conflicts in the 1860s,
and in 1864 relations between host and immigrant communities
at Ashton and Stalybridge were said to be relatively tranquil.
When Booth Mason stood as parliamentary candidate for Ashton
in 1865 his anti-Irish Catholic tirades failed to spark off a
riot.[44]

Conflict ebbed in part because of the increased alacrity
with which the authorities in the urban areas swore in special
constables and enlisted military aid at the first hint of
trouble.   Furthermore, local Nonconformist Liberals saw the
Irish as potential political allies against Church of England
Conservatives, and accordingly set out to cultivate the
friendship of leading figures within the Irish communities.
Liberals spoke at major Irish Catholic social functions and
praised immigrant attempts at assimilation.   Local Liberal
organisations thus constituted an important countervailing
force against the anti-Catholic fulminations of Orangemen and
Tories.[45]   The Catholic Church (particularly the priesthood),
while prepared to defend and propogate the faith on all
occasions, made strenuous efforts to render the Irish more
culturally acceptable to the 'respectable' sections of the
host society by promoting habits of industry, thrift and
sobriety within the flock.   Temperance drives (often short-
lived) were undertaken, branches of the Catholic Young Man's
Society established (to spread habits of 'regularity, discipline,
and manly Christian piety'), and the adoption of 'innocent
amusements' and 'respectable behaviour' encouraged within the
rapidly expanding Catholic schools and mutual improvement

societies.   In this way the Catholic Church tried to transform the 'pre-industrial' attitudes and behaviour of the Irish:
'respectability' became the keynote.[46]

Countervailing influences met, however, with limited
successes.   Ethnic frictions varied in intensity but rarely
subsided completely.   Ashton, Stalybridge and Oldham
experienced some tensions in the generally more placid years
between 1860 and 1865.   In June 1861 a Catholic chapel at
Ashton was stoned, and during wakes week some two hundred
colliers and Irishmen were involved in disturbances at Hurst
Brook.   At Oldham the early summer months of 1861 saw
frequent skirmishes and a full-scale attack against a Catholic
chapel.[47]   At Stockport, despite the 'improving' endeavours
of the priesthood, the mass of Irish retained their reputation
for unruly behaviour, and in all probability the borough was
spared serious rioting in 1868 only because Murphy did not
visit the town.   For by the end of 1868 thousands of Lancashire operatives had rallied to the Conservatives' election
battle-cry of 'No Popery', and major riots had occurred in
several towns.

Three factors provided the backdrop to the dramatic
developments of 1868:   the growth of Fenianism, severe economic
distress in the winter of 1867 and the success with which
extreme Protestants exploited anti-Catholic feelings.   The
upsurge in Fenian activity in 1866 and 1867 (the planned
seizure of arms from Chester Castle, and the Clerkenwell and
Manchester 'outrages'[48]) served, despite the opposition of the
Catholic Church towards Fenianism,[49] to strengthen the view of
the Irish as subversive aliens.   By the end of 1867 the
manufacturing districts were rife with rumours of imminent
insurrection.   At Stockport there were fears of a repetition
of the events of 1852, and at Manchester Fenian threats to
fire workhouses and other buildings created considerable alarm:
operatives were armed and special constables sworn in for duty.[50]

The belief of the priesthood that Fenian activities could only serve to deepen the rift between hosts and immigrants was, for the most part, justified. Fenianism did enjoy significant support and sympathy among the Irish in Lancashire. Despite the favourable responses of the International Workingmens' Association and left-wing elements in the Reform League, the mass of the host population reacted with anger towards revolutionary nationalist aspirations. In London and Birmingham Liberal demonstrations of sympathy towards the plight of convicted Fenians paled before the aggressive outbursts of English crowds. At Manchester the trial of the 'martyrs' took place within an atmosphere of mounting anti-Irish hostility.[51]

Anti-Fenian sentiments and high unemployment in the latter part of 1867 combined to produce the prospect of an 'ugly winter'. According to the Spectator, only 'occasion' was needed to transform the 'inextinguishable feud' between immigrant and native workers into 'a fatal war of races and creeds'.[52] In south-east Lancashire and north-east Cheshire 'occasion' arrived in the form of a group of Protestant demogogues headed by William Murphy of the Protestant Electoral Union.[53] In December 1867 Murphy and his colleagues, aided by Booth Mason and other local Orangemen, commenced a series of scurrilous anti-Catholic lectures at Ashton and Stalybridge which continued throughout 1868. The lectures consisted of sensationalist exposes and violent denunciations of Roman Catholicism (the association of Popery with mumbo-jumbo, political despotism and Fenianism, and the alleged gargantuan sexual appetites of the priests were favourite themes) and attacks upon the immigrant Irish Catholics as puppets of the Pope, sympathisers with Fenianism, and as a profitable source of cheap labour for Liberal employers. Murphy, surrounded by his personal bodyguards, the 'Stalybridge lads', swaggered into lecture halls holding aloft a revolver and proceeded to

work through his repertoire of horror stories. Many of those
present carried an assortment of weapons to the meetings, and
invariably greeted Murphy's entrance with loud renderings of
'Rule Britannia'. Toleration had no place in such an atmosphere. For the greater part of 1868 Ashton and Stalybridge
endured chronic disturbances.

The full history of these turbulent episodes cannot be
recounted here.[54] What we can do is to sketch in certain
incidents. Between January and April large English and Irish
crowds, increasingly decked out in Orange and Green, repeatedly
clashed on the streets. Frequent sorties were made against
heavily-defended Catholic chapels and Irish neighbourhoods,
and Liberal pro-disestablishment meetings reduced to chaos by
Murphyite intruders. In April a full-scale riot occurred at
Stalybridge when a crowd of several hundred men and youths,
shouting 'We'll pull the bloody cross and the bloody Virgin
down', stoned a Catholic chapel. In May riots, 'unprecedented
for brutality and destruction of property', occurred in Ashton.
Several uproarious Irish Church meetings were followed on 9
May by a 'Great Protestant Demonstration' in Ashton Town Hall.
Approximately one thousand sat down to tea, and were afterwards
addressed by Booth Mason and the Reverends Heffill and Touchstone on the theme of Papal aggression. The audience, many of
whom had travelled from Stalybridge and Dukinfield, was a sea
of orange. No immediate disturbances resulted from the
meeting, but on the Sunday afternoon young factory lads and
lasses, 'displaying party colours', began to taunt Irish
Catholics in the streets of the borough. A group of Irishmen
responded by assaulting English inhabitants. A crowd of some
one thousand outraged operatives had their revenge by attacking
'Little Ireland': homes were ransacked and furniture thrown
into the streets. The crowd, which had increased to over two
thousand people, then wreaked havoc at Saint Ann's Catholic
chapel: windows were smashed, the confessional curtains torn

down, the altar damaged and images of the Virgin Mary and the crucifix smashed to pieces. The Riot Act was read and the crowd dispersed, only to regroup later to launch an assault against Saint Mary's. On that occasion the police broke up the crowd before entry to the chapel had been gained. Ashton remained in a 'most excited state' throughout Monday. Despite the attempt of the authorities to quell the disturbances - five hundred special constables were sworn in and the aid of two companies of the 70th Regiment enlisted - rioting flared up again. Only by the Wednesday had order been restored. A total of thirty-four people were arrested during the distur- bances and hundreds injured.

Rioting of this magnitude did not spread to Stalybridge in May, but the borough had acquired a notorious reputation for ethnic strife. The Ashton Reporter noted that over the previous six months Stalybridge had been, 'in a chronic state of excitement...There have either been street rows on a large scale, or riots on a small scale, to be chronicled every week ...'[55] The remaining months of the year, while less turbulent, witnessed a multitude of battles at Ashton and Stalybridge.[56]

As in 1852, anti-Catholic disturbances were widespread in 1868. Rochdale, Oldham, Preston and Blackburn all experienced major outbreaks of rioting, and in September a Murphyite meeting in Manchester resulted in a brawl involving three hundred people.[57] As late as 1871 the Ashton Reporter could observe that the 'disreputable spirit of Murphy' was 'by no means extinct'.[58]

The preceding narrative points to the magnitude, and the pervasive and tenacious nature of ethnic conflict. We simply cannot accept the viewpoint of one writer that 'the amount of overt anti-Catholic opinion in Lancashire was never terribly great during the whole of 1846-1871'.[59] Despite variations in the scale and intensity of conflict, relations between English and Roman Catholic Irish workers from 1850 onwards were

tense and discordant rather than relaxed and harmonious.
Rioting embraced hundreds and at times thousands of operatives.
Far from being of incidental importance, ethnic animosities
constituted, therefore, a staple feature of working-class life
and the popular politics of the period.

One further point needs to be emphasised. Contrary to
the view expressed at the time by many Liberals, the riots
cannot be dismissed as the work of the 'rags and tatters' or
as a manifestation of youthful rebellion. For while conflicts
were often triggered off by the provocative actions of teenage
factory lads and lasses, there is no doubt that working-class
adults, many of them respectable factory operatives, were
heavily involved in all the major disturbances of the period.[60]

THE MATERIAL EFFECTS OF IRISH IMMIGRATION

An explanation of reactions towards the Irish, and more
particularly of escalating conflict after 1850, requires
further examination of the material effects of Irish immigration, of the roots of conflict and assimilation. We have
thus investigated a number of important areas: patterns of
immigration; Irish influences in the labour market (did, for
example, the English and Irish compete for the same jobs?
Did the Irish receive lower wages?); patterns of residence
(to what extent did ghettoisation take place?) and cultural,
religious and political relations between immigrants and hosts.

Irish immigration into Britain, while by no means
negligible in the pre-Chartist period, observed its most
dramatic increase in the late 1840s. Outside of London, the
manufacturing centres of Lancashire and Cheshire were areas
of heavy concentration. Of the 400,000 Irish-born inhabitants
of Great Britain in 1841, 105,916 resided in Lancashire and
11,577 in Cheshire. By 1851 these figures had almost doubled
to 191,506 in Lancashire and 22,812 in Cheshire. By 1851
Irish-born amounted to 10 per cent of the population of

82

Lancashire and 5 per cent in Cheshire.   Between 1841 and 1851
Irish born, as a proportion of the population of the borough
of Stockport, increased from approximately 7 to 10 per cent;
in the borough of Liverpool from 17 to 22 per cent; and in
the district of Manchester from 12 to 17 per cent.   By 1851
Irish-born constituted almost 7 per cent of the district of
Ashton-under-Lyne and 8.3 per cent of the district of Salford.
Apart from decreases in the boroughs of Manchester and Liverpool, these percentages remained roughly constant or increased
between 1851 and 1861.   By 1871 6.66 per cent of the population
of Lancashire were Irish-born; the total percentage of Irish,
including those born outside Ireland, was of course considerably
higher.[61]

We are dealing at mid-century, therefore, with a vast
increase in the numbers of (overwhelmingly) Irish Roman
Catholics from rural backgrounds entering the Lancashire mill
towns.   Yet increased numbers, in themselves, do not constitute
a satisfactory explanation of worsening relations.   Manchester,
for example, with a higher percentage of Irish-born than Ashton
or Stalybridge, was less troubled by serious rioting.   We must
turn, therefore, to the economic, social and cultural characteristics of the Irish to understand host reactions.

As contemporaries realised, the immigrants were generally
of low socio-economic standing.   Evidence presented in the
1836 Report and other sources demonstrates that the Irish found
little employment at the skilled level; rather, the vast
majority worked at low-status jobs.[62]   Of importance at a
general level were three areas of employment: labouring (in
the building trades, the docks and on the railways); a variety
of crafts and depressed occupations such as handloom weaving,
tailoring, shoemaking, hawking and dressmaking; and factory
work - in cotton the Irish were concentrated in the low-paid
jobs in the carding, blowing, tenting, and the weaving
sections of the industry.

The general pattern of employment is well known: what
is often less clear is the local employment situation. We
have accordingly consulted the census enumerators' books for
occupational data relating to Stockport, Ashton and Stalybridge for the years 1841, 1851, and 1861. The major finding
to emerge from this source is a greatly accelerated trend
towards employment of the Irish (particularly girls and
unmarried women) in cotton, and a relative decline in the
numbers employed in the casual and poorer artisan trades.
And although many male family heads still worked as labourers
at mid-century, a growing number of younger men and male
teenagers joined Irish females in cotton factories. In short,
by the early 1850s the majority of the employed Irish in south
Lancashire and north-east Cheshire were cotton operatives.
At Stockport in 1851, for example (see Table I in the Appendices)
57 per cent of 2,281 Irish living in the centre of the town
were to be found in cotton. Employment in cotton factories
was not a totally new phenomenon: we find a number of Irish-
born tenters, throstle spinners and weavers listed for
Stockport in 1841. What must be stressed, however, is the
mass influx into cotton at the end of the 1840s. At Stockport
women and girls were heavily concentrated in throstle spinning,
in weaving and tenting. Boys and girls worked as bobbiners
and doffers, and young men were either piecers or involved in
a variety of occupations in the card and blowing rooms. Few
attained positions of high remuneration (there were, in the
1851 sample, only two self-actor minders, three male spinners
and two overlookers). Shoemaking and tailoring accounted for
5 per cent of the total employed and labourers made up 17 per
cent. Representation at the skilled manual and non-manual
levels was negligible.

A strikingly similar pattern emerged at Ashton and
Stalybridge (see Tables 2 and 3 in the Appendices). Of
1,392 Irish occupations sampled in Stalybridge in 1851 960

(69%) were in cotton, with dense clustering in the card room, in tenting and in piecing. While there were 25 male spinners, immigrant representation at the craft and skilled levels was of little importance (4% in tailoring and shoemaking). Labourers made up 14 per cent of the total employed. Ten years later, the overall situation at Stalybridge had changed little, except for a heavier involvement in tenting and weaving (mainly female occupations), an increase in the number of Irish spinners and self-actor minders (106 out of a total sample of 2,133), and a slight decrease in labouring (from 14% to 12%). By 1861 the Irish at Ashton were concentrated, in large numbers, in tenting, weaving, piecing and to a lesser extent in labouring.

The fact that the Irish entered cotton in great numbers is of extreme significance in that direct competition in the labour market between English and Irish cotton operatives became more acute, and was more keenly resented by sections of the English than in previous decades.[63] For while we have seen that complaints concerning Irish competition were not new, they did take on a new urgency after 1850 and were widely voiced during the riots of the period.

There is, however, less reason to support the popular view that the Irish presence in cotton resulted in a general lowering of wages in the industry, at least in the twenty-five years after 1850. Cotton, after all, benefited greatly from the mid-Victorian boom:[64] markets expanded, prices stabilised, the crisis of profitability was largely overcome and, with the notable exception of the Cotton Famine, the industry did not experience a slump of the magnitude of 1837-42. Stabilisation and expansion made for more regular employment and an improvement in real wages. For although the latter did not advance considerably in the 1850s (due to price increases), they did so by about 40 per cent between 1864 and 1874.[65]

Despite this increase in wages, the view that the Irish

presence had a deleterious effect upon living standards persisted with some considerable force between 1850 and 1870, and
obviously requires some explanation. It is important to
remember in this context that popular attitudes and ideologies
are not reducible to the economic level: inherited traditions
and values do not change simply at the whim of the economy.[66]
This general point is significant in that by 1850 the view
that Irish competition lowered wages was of some importance,
and could not be expected to dissipate quickly.[67] Furthermore, such attitudes were not without a material base.
Fears of downgrading were reinforced by increased immigration
and by the accusations made by operatives in a number of towns
that employers sometimes discriminated unfairly in favour of
the Irish. Finally (and without suggesting a cause-effect
relationship), those sections of cotton in which the Irish
congregated were generally poorly paid, and did not experience
wage increases comparable to some other sectors of the industry.[6]
Such factors served, along with the propaganda peddled by
Orangemen and others, to keep alive unfavourable impressions.

 Irish involvement in the periodic attempts to form and
consolidate trade unions in cotton in the post-1850 period is
difficult to chart with any degree of precision. Many
sectors of cotton remained without permanent trade union
organisation until the upsurges of the 1870s.[69] Irish
operatives were probably involved in the growth of weaving
and carding trade unionism in the late 1850s and 1860s.
Examples of the Irish acting as strike-breakers were certainly
rare. In the famous Preston dispute of 1853 attempts were
made by employers to recruit blackleg labour, but, significantly,
the majority of immigrant cotton workers seem to have adopted
an anti-employer stance, and employers were forced to look
across the Irish Sea for labour. On arriving in England some
of the potential blacklegs were persuaded to return home by
local English and Irish workers.[70] This brings us to a more

general point. In periods of rising industrial militancy
(in 1853-4, 1859-61, 1866-7 and 1869) Irish and English
cotton operatives generally acted together against the forces
of capital.

Unity during periods of heightened class tensions was
not accompanied by any significant movement towards integration
in terms of patterns of residence. An examination of the
census enumerators' books for Stockport between 1841 and 1871
and Ashton and Stalybridge for 1851 and 1861 reveals the
physical separations between the two communities. For
although the mass of immigrants were not segregated into
large, formal ghettoes, the period did witness the
accelerated development of distinct Irish neighbourhoods.[71]
At Stockport in 1841 Irish quarters were beginning to emerge
in the centre of the town around Rock Row, Adlington Square
and Jacksons Alley. By 1851 few non-Irish families were to
be found in these streets. The streets leading off Middle
Hillgate (Crowther Street, Covent Gardens and Cross Street)
constituted, by 1851, a further area of heavy Irish concentration. Again, few non-Irish families inhabited this
densely-packed neighbourhood. Twenty years later a similar
pattern of residence was in evidence.

By 1861 the streets around 'Flag Alley' in Ashton were
known locally as 'Little Ireland'. Adelphi Court,
Worthington Square, Back Charles Street, Back Portland and
Back Cavendish Streets were all areas of dense Irish settle-
ment, and the scene of repeated conflicts in the 1860s. At
Stalybridge the Irish settled in four major areas: around
the Castle Street mills, particularly on Back Melbourne
Street, Back Castle Street and Bennett Street: around the
King Street mill in Beardsley's Yard, King Street and Chapel
Street: in Leech Street, Cross Leech Street and Back
Grosvenor Street: and around Spring Street, Back Cross Street
and Pearson's Yard. In all these areas a marked pattern of

ethnic clustering was in evidence between 1851 and 1861, with the vicinity around Back Castle Street the site of heaviest concentration and the scene of frequent disorders in the 1860s.

As we noted earlier, the development of Irish quarters was not, however, synonomous with complete ghettoisation. A small minority of the Irish (mainly older folk) were to be found living amidst non-Irish families, and even in the Irish neighbourhoods non-Irish were sometimes not totally excluded. More significantly perhaps, there were a large number of streets in all three towns which were occupied by both the Irish and non-Irish. This, in fact, was the dominant pattern at mid-century. Nevertheless we would be wrong to interpret it as symptomatic of a high degree of integration. For even on these mixed streets there existed an extremely strong tendency towards ethnic clustering, and on many occasions the Irish steadily encroached upon streets which had formerly been predominantly English in character. A few examples will serve to illustrate these two trends. At Stalybridge in 1851, Castle Street, while mixed, was characterised by distinct Irish and non-Irish 'ends': the houses from 39 to 19 were for the most part Irish, while the houses below number 19 were English. Bennett Street, while containing some non-Irish families in 1851, had become mainly Irish by 1861. Both these streets experienced considerable tensions at mid-century. On Caroline Street at Stalybridge the Irish, occupying mainly the odd numbers between 15 and 71, were in 1851 effectively sandwiched between the non-Irish who lived at the lower and top ends of the street: by 1861 the Irish had begun to move into the even-numbered houses once occupied by non-Irish families. The tendency towards ethnic clustering operated with equal force at Stockport and Ashton.

As we have seen, ethnic separations in terms of housing patterns were accompanied by a marked lack of political, religious and cultural integration. The major force in

emphasising the separate religious identity of the Irish was
of course the Catholic Church. For, despite the severe
problem of declining church attendance, the urban catholic
parish remained 'the pivot of emigrant community life', and
the priest was the central figure in Irish neighbourhoods.
Parents sent their children to local Catholic schools whenever
possible, and organised their social lives around the clubs
and societies set up by the church.[72] As detailed earlier,
in its associations with the 'tyrannical machinations of an
alien power' and spiritual intolerance and 'mumbo jumbo',
Catholicism constituted a major source of friction between
hosts and immigrants. Frequent protestations of loyalty to
the monarchy on the part of the priesthood failed to bridge
the religious divide.

Furthermore, for the 'respectable' among the host
population, the majority of the Irish remained culturally
unacceptable. Throughout the 1850s and 1860s, and despite
the 'improving' efforts of the church, and the influence of
the steady rhythms of factory work, large sections of the
immigrants retained their reputation for 'wild and unruly'
behaviour. Fights with the police were common, and weekends
were often given over to drinking sprees. English families,
apart from those living in close proximity to the immigrants,
rarely took in Irish lodgers. A brief survey of census
material for Stalybridge in 1861 suggests that intermarriage
was of minor importance, particularly for those families
living at the heart of Irish neighbourhoods. Irish and non-
Irish, at least in the more mixed areas of Stalybridge and
Stockport, sometimes drank at the same pubs, although weekend
fights were by no means uncommon. While support for the
Liberal Party in particular served to acquaint immigrants
with mainstream political life, the growth of Fenianism acted,
once again, to resurrect fears of the subversive leanings of
the Irish.

In summary, the roots of mounting tensions after 1850
must be sought within the material effects of Irish immigration.
For although popular beliefs that the Irish lowered wages, acted
as strike-breakers and resisted assimilation must be either
qualified or corrected, nevertheless, with the vast increase
in immigration in the immediate post-Famine period the
potential for conflict rose.   Direct competition in the
labour market and fears of economic downgrading weighed heavily
on the minds of English operatives.   The Irish did congregate
in their own neighbourhoods and cluster together on the mixed
streets.   They did remain, for the most part, culturally
distinct: and in their Catholicism and nationalism were
viewed as subversive aliens.   Such sources of friction were
exploited to the full by demagogues like Murphy.

We wish to make three further points in relation to
causation.   First, tensions and outbreaks of rioting cannot
simply be reduced to that overworked and limited concept of
'distress'.   From the mid-1840s onwards there appeared to be
little correlation between immediate 'distress' and instances
of rioting.   Apart from the incidents at Oldham, Ashton and
Stalybridge in the early 1860s, relations between the two
groups appear to have been more harmonious during the
depressions of 1847 and 1861-5 than in the relatively
prosperous years of 1851 and 1868.

Secondly, an aversion to narrow economic reductionism
must not, however, be interpreted as a dismissal of the
importance of the economic 'level'.   We have repeatedly seen
that economic fears (competition in the labour market etc.)
were widespread.   Such fears, which were real to their
holders, constituted the material roots of conflict and were
of crucial significance in informing the consciousness of the
rioters.

The material roots of conflict must, therefore, be
stressed.   But, thirdly, we wish, while offering a

materialist interpretation of strains and disturbances, to
eschew a mechanistic 'base-superstructure' model, in which
the political and ideological 'levels' are seen simply as
passive reflections of the 'base'.   We maintain throughout
this chapter that consciousness is not totally determined at
the economic or any other 'level' and that the 'relative
autonomy' of the political and ideological 'levels' must be
recognised.   These theoretical concerns are of immediate
relevance in that outbreaks of rioting and ethnic frictions
cannot be seen as resulting solely from economic factors.
Religious and political fears were real and significant and
cannot be dismissed as masks for the 'real' underlying
economic causes. Hence English workers saw the Irish
Catholics as a threat not only to their standard of living
but also to their settled way of life, their whole pattern of
existence.   The 'alien' nature of Catholicism (its alleged
machinations against 'the traditional liberties of Freeborn
Englishmen' etc.) and cultural and political divisions -
these were factors of extreme importance in inducing a
belligerent attitude towards the Irish.   The 'battle tune'
adopted by the English rioters, 'Rule Britannia', and the
extremely popular cry of 'Murphy, Garibaldi and the Queen',
reflected fears of alien domination.

POLITICAL RESULTS

We argued at the beginning of the chapter that the decline of
class combativity after Chartism must be attributed primarily
to the restabilisation of the economy and changes in class
structure.   Ethnic conflict operated, against the background
of the apparent inevitability of capitalism, to restrict
further the potential for class solidarity in Lancashire and
Cheshire, and to provide sections of the bourgeoisie with the
opportunity to assert their authority, in a fairly direct way,
upon workers.   For while we must be careful to see the riots

91

not simply as the result of one-sided manipulation from above -
ethnic tensions arose out of the real experiences of workers,
and many middle-class Liberals and some Conservatives openly
condemned mob violence and the excesses of Murphy[73] - nevertheless, sections of the middle class did make conscious
efforts to exploit ethnic animosities and to attach workers
to middle-class political and cultural leadership. The most
dramatic example of this process was the way in which
Conservatives and militant Protestants attempted, with
increasing success, to build a mass movement around the issue
of 'No Popery'.

We can, in this final section, briefly examine these
developments. In the course of the 1860s the Conservative
Party's political fortunes underwent a remarkable trans-
formation in south Lancashire and north Cheshire. Condemned
for so long to second-class political citizenship, the party
finally came into its own in the elections of 1868 when the
Liberal ascendancy in Lancashire was overturned.[74] At
Ashton, newly-enfranchised Stalybridge, Salford and Bolton,
the Conservatives made a clean sweep. Stockport (like
Ashton), for so long a Liberal stronghold, returned one
Liberal and one Conservative, and Manchester elected one
Conservative and two Liberals. The shift towards the
Conservatives continued in 1874 when twenty-six Conservatives
and seven Liberals were elected to parliament from Lancashire.[75]

The 1868 elections were of significance in that they
revealed, often to the surprise of both Liberals and Conservatives, the depth of working-class support for
Conservatism. Leading figures in both parties were
convinced that the working-class vote had proved decisive in
the Conservative triumphs. At Stalybridge, for example,
Sidebottom, the successful candidate, had been 'brought out'
by some 2,000 working people.[76] The elections at Ashton and
Stalybridge represented the climax of months of intensive

worker activity on behalf of the Conservatives.

Gains made among cotton operatives by the Conservative
Party have traditionally been attributed to four major
factors: the sympathy with which workers responded to the
anti-Manchester School views of Tory Radicals such as Stephens
at Stalybridge and Callender at Manchester: the success with
which Conservatives seized upon John Bright's opposition to
the Ten Hours Bill during the 1868 election: the belief that
Conservatives were less dismissive of robust popular culture
than the Liberals: and the fact that responsibility for the
1867 Reform Act lay with the Conservative Party.[77]

Time and space do not permit an examination of such
views here.[78] We suggest, however, than any explanation of
popular Toryism which fails to take into account ethnicity
and religion is incomplete. The 1868 elections, for instance,
revolved primarily not around John Bright's attitudes towards
factory legislation and trade unionism, but around the
questions of continued Protestant supremacy in Ireland and
the more general theme of Protestantism versus Catholicism.
Alarmed by Gladstone's proposed disestablishment of the Church
in Ireland, Conservative candidates throughout the cotton
districts took up 'No Popery'as their election cry. One of
Sidebottom's placards at Stalybridge reflected the tone of
contests in the area. 'THE QUEEN OR THE POPE', the placard
began,

> which will you have to reign over you -
> will you suffer Mr Gladstone to destroy
> the supremacy of your sovereign and
> substitute the supremacy of the POPE?
> SIDEBOTTOM CALLS to English freemen to
> assert their rights.   79

Sidebottom saw the Irish Church as 'the question of the hour',
and constantly reassured his supporters that he was 'opposed
to Popery in all its details'.[80] Fears of creeping
Catholicism dominated the elections elsewhere. Tipping, one
of the two Conservative candidates at Stockport, warned his

audiences that the Catholic Church was, 'a dense, compact
body, acting as one man all over the globe'. 'To destroy
the Irish Church', he continued, 'would be to drop the flag
and lower one's colours as a Protestant power before that
aggressive Church in Ireland, and would be perfectly
suicidal.'[81]

Working closely with Orangemen[82], Conservative candidates
successfully appealed to the anti-Catholic sentiments of those
workers courted by Murphy and his colleagues.[83] The Murphyite
crowds at Ashton and Stalybridge, for example, provided support
for Mellow and Sidebottom. Murphyites continually disrupted
Liberal meetings and held demonstrations outside the homes of
prominent Liberals. While Sidebottom and Mellow were
portrayed as 'true Protestant heroes', the Liberal candidates
were branded as crypto-Papists who wished 'to scatter the
Established Church of England to the four winds of heaven.'[84]

All shades of political opinion agreed that religion was
both the dominant and decisive issue in the elections.
Gladstone, in the opinion of the Manchester Guardian, had been
'kicked out of Lancashire for not being a Protestant'.[85]
Working-class antipathy towards the Irish Catholics had
provided Conservatives with the essential ingredient for
victory.

This chapter has pointed to escalating ethnic tensions in
Lancashire and Cheshire after 1850 and the effects of such
tensions upon behaviour and attitudes. In conclusion we
wish to outline some of the wider implications and assumptions
of our study. First, we do not suggest that ethnicity
operated to the total exclusion of class feeling. The
industrial history of Lancashire and Cheshire in this period
reveals a number of occasions, particularly the disputes of
1853-4 and 1861, when class conflict was acute. Similarly
the notion of 'independence' in working-class behaviour was

94

not completely eclipsed. Rather we have claimed that,
unlike the 1830s and 1840s, class issues were not paramount
in politics. Secondly, we have assumed the existence of a
high degree of working-class solidarity in the Chartist
period which some scholars would dispute or reject. Thirdly,
we have not set ethnic relations in the cotton towns within
a wider national context. The question as to why relations
were more strained in Lancashire than in other parts of the
country must constitute the object of further study.
Finally, we wish to emphasise that changes in class relations
and behaviour after Chartism are not to be explained primarily
at the level of ethnicity. Ethnic feeling was one aspect of
a wider process of fragmentation which must be set against
the changed nature of English capitalism in the 'golden
years'.

APPENDICES

Table 1:   Occupations of a section of the Irish in Stockport, 1851

Bakers	3	Managers	1
Blacksmiths	5	Messengers	2
Blowing room	14	Milliners	4
Bobbiners	54	Nurses	6
Bookbinders	2	Overlookers - cotton	2
Bricklayers	1	Painters	3
Brushmakers	1	Pedlars	12
Cabinet makers	1	Picture-frame makers	1
Capmakers	16	Piecers	25
Card room	27	Printers	5
Charwomen	4	Reedmakers	2
Clerks	1	Reelers	6
Confectioners	1	Rope makers	11
Coopers	3	Saddlers	1
Cotton mixers	8	Sawyers	1
Dealers	6	Schoolmasters	1
Doffers	63	Self-actor minders	2
Domestics	53	Shoemakers	54
Dressmakers	18	Spinners (male)	3
Errand boys	3	Staymakers	25
Factory hands - cotton		Stonemasons	5
	568		
Fruiterers	2	Strippers and grinders	17
Gardeners	1	Tailors	77
Glaziers	6	Tenters	87
Greengrocers	1	Throstle spinners	329
Hatters	1	Tradesmen	1
Hawkers	69	Warehousemen	3
Housekeepers	50	Warpers	1
Joiners	7	Washerwomen	32
Knitters	2	Weavers - powerloom	98
Labourers	400	Weavers - handloom	2
Lap carriers	11	Whitesmiths	1
Lodging house keepers	7	Winders	52

Total = 2281

Notes:

1.   The table relates to the occupation of the Irish in the central area of Stockport, mainly in St Mary's Ward and Middle Ward, both areas of heavy Irish settlement.   It is not a survey of the total Irish employment situation.

2.   The table covers Irish-born.   The sons and daughters of Irish-born are included.

Table 2: Occupations of a section of the Irish in Stalybridge, 1851

Basketmakers	1	Minders	5
Beaters	1	Mixers	1
Blacksmiths	2	Nailmakers	3
Bobbiners	4	Nurses	5
Bricklayers	4	Painters	1
Chairbottomers	1	Pedlars	2
Charwomen	8	Piecers	217
Coalminers	4	Plasterers·	2
Doffers	1	Printers	1
Domestic servants	33	Reelers	6
Card room hands	201	Roller carriers	5
Coopers	1	Sawyers	1
Doublers	2	Shoemakers	34
Dressers	6	Spinners (male)	25
Dressmakers	5	Staymakers	7
Foremen	1	Stokers	1
Glaziers	1	Stonemasons	14
Hawkers	5	Strippers	36
Iron turners	2	Tailors	24
Factory - cotton	203	Tenters	148
Grinders	22	Throstle spinners	12
Iron foundry	1	Tin plate workers	2
Labourers	197	Washerwomen	63
Lap tenters	2	Weavers	57
Lodging house keepers	4	Winders	8

Total = 1392

Table 3: Occupations of a section of the Irish in Stalybridge, 1861

Basket dealers	1	Nailmakers	7
Blacksmiths	1	Nurses	4
Blowing room	25	Overlookers	4
Bobbiners	1	Painters	1
Booksellers	1	Piecers	214
Bricklayers	3	Print workers	1
Card room	181	Provision dealers	1
Carters	6	Reelers	13
Chair bottomers	2	Rope makers	1
Charwomen	14	Shirt makers	1
Coalminers	4	Shoemakers	23
Coopers	1	Silk weavers	2
Cotton factory	364	Spinners + self-actor minders (male)	106
Doffers	3	Spinners (female)	12
Domestic servants	22	Staymakers	1
Doublers	7	Stokers	5
Dressmakers	9	Stonemasons	9
Firemen	1	Strippers	59
Gardeners	1	Tailors	15
Gasmakers	4	Tenters	417
Greengrocers	2	Toy dealers	1
Grinders	72	Travellers	2
Hawkers	2	Umbrella makers	1
Iron moulders	1	Warehouse	1
Joiners	3	Washerwomen	39
Labourers	259	Watchmakers	2
Lap carriers	1	Weavers	137
Machinemen	2	Winders	55
Musicians	1		

Total = 2133

NOTES

1. For A.E. Musson's opposition to the Webbs' notion of a 'watershed' see his British Trade Unions, 1800-1875 (1972), esp. ch.6; Trade Union and Social History (1974), esp. ch.2; 'Class Struggle and the Labour Aristocracy', Social History, 1 (1976), pp.335-56.

2. R. Harrison, Before the Socialists: Studies in Labour and Politics 1861-1881 (1965), esp. I: E.J. Hobsbawm, Industry and Empire (Harmondsworth, 1969), chs. 6 and 7; G.S. Jones, 'Class Struggle and the Industrial Revolution', New Left Review, 90 (1975); J. Foster, Class Struggle and the Industrial Revolution: Early Industrial Capitalism in Three English Towns (1974), esp. ch.7; P. Anderson, 'Origins of the Present Crisis', New Left Review, 23 (1964).

3. See Harrison, Before the Socialists, esp. I: Hobsbawm, Ind. and Emp. chs. 6 and 7: E.J. Hobsbawm, 'The Labour Aristocracy in Nineteenth Century Britain', in his Labouring Men: Studies in the History of Labour (1968), pp.272-315; Jones, N.L.R. 90, pp.66ff.

4. There still exists disagreement among historians as to the extent to which living standards for the mass of workers improved, if at all, after Chartism. Certainly any suggestion that Chartism's demise was the 'natural' result of economic improvement is an oversimplification. See A. Briggs, 'National Bearings', in his Chartist Studies (New York, 1967), p.291; Foster, Class Struggle pp.205-6; G. Barnsby, The Standard of Living in the Black Country during the Nineteenth Century', Economic History Review, 2nd series XXIV (1971), pp.220-39.

5. See, in particular, Jones, N.L.R. 90.

6. We will pay particular attention to developments at Stockport, Ashton-under-Lyne and Stalybridge. The cotton industry dominated all three towns and was characterised, for the most part, by large units of production and a high concentration of ownership. At Stockport, for example, 56 cotton mills employed approximately 17,000 operatives in the 1850s. See Stockport Advertiser, 21 April 1854. See also Manchester Guardian, 6 March 1863 and 7 May 1864 for the industrial structures of Ashton and Stalybridge. As at Oldham, a small elite of highly-visible, tightly-knit, and extremely wealthy cotton families exerted considerable influence upon the affairs of these towns. See Foster, Class Struggle, ch.6; P. Joyce, 'The Factory Politics of Lancashire in the Later Nineteenth Century', Historical Journal, XVIII (1975), pp.525-53.

7. For these developments, see N. Kirk, 'Class and Fragmentation: Some Aspects of Working-Class Life in south-east Lancashire and north-east Cheshire, 1850-1870' (unpub. Ph.D. thesis, Pittsburgh Univ. 1974).

8. For the influence of Chartism in the cotton towns see Foster, Class Struggle, esp. ch.5: D. Read, 'Chartism in Manchester', in Briggs (ed.), Chartist Studies; C.A.N. Reid, 'The Chartist Movement in Stockport' (unpub. M.A. thesis, Hull Univ. 1974); D. Thompson, The Early Chartists (1971), intro.

9. For working-class Liberalism, see B. Harrison and P. Hollis, 'Chartism, Liberalism and the Life of Robert Lowery', English Historical Review, LXXXII (1967); J. Vincent, The Formation of the British Liberal Party 1857-68 (Harmondsworth, 1972); Kirk, thesis, III.

10. For interpretations of ethnicity see A. Cohen (ed.), Urban Ethnicity (1974), esp. intro. and ch.I; R. Ballard, 'Ethnicity: theory and experience', New Community, V (1976), pp.196-202.

11. We subscribe to E.P. Thompson's view of class. See E.P. Thompson, The Making of the English Working Class (Harmondsworth, 1968), esp. the preface; E.P. Thompson, 'Eighteenth-Century English Society: Class Struggle without Class?', Social History, 3 (1978), pp.146-50.

12. Thompson, Soc. Hist. p.150.

13. For useful studies of the effects of ethnicity upon the working class in America see D. Montgomery, 'The Shuttle and the Cross: Weavers and Artisans in the Kensington Riots of 1844', in P. Stearns and D.J. Walkowitz (eds.), Workers in the Industrial Revolution (New Brunswick, 1974); D. Brody, Steelworkers in America: The Nonunion Era (New York, 1969), esp. V.

14. For the views of contemporaries see L.H. Lees, 'Patterns of Lower Class Life: Irish Slum Communities in Nineteenth Century London', in S. Thernstrom and R. Sennett (eds.), Nineteenth Century Cities (1969), pp.359ff.; K. Marx - F. Engels, On Britain (Moscow, 1953), pp.123-7, 506: J.A. Jackson, The Irish in Britain (1963); J.H. Treble, 'The Place of the Irish Catholics in the Social Life of the North of England 1800-1851' (unpub. Ph.D. thesis, Leeds Univ.1969).

15. J.H.Werly, 'The Irish in Manchester 1832-1849', Irish Historical Studies, 71 (1973). Werly probably overestimates the extent of ghettoisation among the Irish in Manchester, particularly in the area around Olham Road.

16. Treble, thesis, pp.245-51, 268ff.

17. Thompson, The Making pp.469-85; Foster, Class Struggle, chs. 5 and 7.

18. See R. O'Higgins, 'The Irish Influence in the Chartist Movement', Past and Present 20 (1961).

19. For these disturbances see Northern Star, 15, 22, 29 May, 5, 12, 26 June 1841; Manchester Guardian, 5, 8, 26 June 1841; T. Middleton, Annals of Hyde and District (Hyde, 1899), pp. 103-4; N. McCord, The Anti-Corn Law League 1838-1846 (1958), pp.102-3.

20. Northern Star, 12 June 1841.

21. 1836 Poor Enquiry (Ireland). Appendix G. Report on the State of the Irish Poor in Great Britain, pp.69-70. (Hereafter referred to as 1836 Irish Poor.)

22. 1836 Irish Poor, pp. vii, xxi, 68; Marx-Engels, On Brit. p.127; Jackson, The Irish in Brit. pp.116-17; Treble, thesis, p.60.

23. Treble, thesis, pp.245-50; 1836 Irish Poor, pp.64-7; Marx-Engels, On Brit. p.157; H.A. Turner, Trade Union Growth, Structure and Policy (Manchester, 1962), p.48.

24. Foster, Class Struggle pp.8, 244.

25. 1836 Irish Poor, pp.61, 82-4.

26. Thompson, The Making p.476.

27. Thompson, The Making p.480.

28. Stockport Advertiser, 5 Sept. 1850; W.M. Bowman, England in Ashton-under-Lyne: The History of the Ancient Manor and Parish (Altrincham, 1960), p.411.

29. The most active Protestant organisations were the Orange lodges, the Protestant Reformation Society, and the Operative Protestant Associations. Prominent figures in the Manchester area were Richardson, Bardsley, Consterdine, Doble, Heffill, Touchstone, Stowell and Mason. The leading spokesman in Manchester and Salford was Hugh Stowell at Christ Church. Stowell was a staunch defender of 'Protestant liberties', a committed enemy of socialism, and president of the Operative Protestant Association. See Manchester Courier, 10 Nov., 15 Dec. 1849, 11 Jan. 1851 for the various organisations. For Stowell see J.B. Marsden, Memoirs of the Rev. Hugh Stowell

(1868); R.L. Greenall, 'Popular Conservatism in Salford, 1868-1886', Northern History, IX (1974), p.133. In the Ashton area Booth Mason (brother of the Liberal Hugh Mason) was the leading Orangeman. For an account of Mason's life see the obituary in Manchester Guardian, 11 Sept. 1888.

30. For Protestant activities see Manchester Courier, 9 Feb. 1850; Manchester Illuminator and General Catholic Record (Manchester, 1850); Theological Tracts (Manchester Central Reference Library).

31. J. Denvir, The Irish in Britain (1892), pp.163-6, book X.

32. Manchester Guardian, 6, 16 Nov., 7 Dec. 1850.

33. Stockport Advertiser, 28 Nov. 1850, 20 Feb., 25 Dec. 1851.

34. Manchester Guardian, 7 Dec. 1850.

35. For the Stockport riots and their aftermath see Stockport Advertiser, 2, 9 July 1852; Manchester Courier, 3, 10 July 1852: Manchester Guardian, 3, 7, 14, 17, 21, 24, 28 July 1852; Northern Star, 10 July 1852. For a more detailed treatment see Kirk, thesis, IV.

36. Manchester Courier, 3, 10 July 1852; Stockport Advertiser, 2 July 1852.

37. Manchester Guardian, 7 July 1852.

38. Stockport Advertiser, 6 May 1852; Manchester Guardian 14 July 1852.

39. Manchester Guardian, 14 July 1852.

40. Manchester Courier, 16 Sept., 4 Nov. 1854.

41. Manchester Courier, 12, 19 Dec. 1857.

42. Foster, Class Struggle pp.219-20, 243-6; Manchester Guardian, 8, 14 July 1856, 16, 23 May 1857. The Lancashire Public Records Office at Preston holds material relating to disturbances at Wigan. See C.P.R.8.

43. For the decline in tensions at Stockport see Stockport Advertiser, 26 March 1858, 18 Oct. 1861; Stockport News, 23 March 1861, 28 June 1862. For the relief riots see Manchester Guardian, 23 March 1863.

44. Ashton Reporter, 15 July 1865.

45. For the growing ties between Irish Catholics and Liberals at Stockport see Robinson, Catholicism in Edgeley (Stockport Public Library), p.62. Vincent notes that Liberal attempts to win the Irish Catholic vote were not a complete success. Catholic politics revolved around 'confession, class and nationality', and only in 1868 did all three issues fully coincide with support for the Liberals. In 1859 and 1865 Garibaldi and the Irish question brought Irish Catholic support to the Tories. As workers, however, Irish Catholic immigrants were generally supporters of Liberalism. Vincent, Formtn of Brit. Lib. Pty p.298.

46. W.J. Lowe, 'The Irish in Lancashire' (unpub. Ph.D. thesis, Trinity College, Dublin 1974), pp. 344-54: Robinson, Catholicism in Edgeley.

47. Ashton Standard, 15 June 1961: Foster, Class Struggle pp. 243ff., Ashton Reporter, 15 June 1861.

48. For Fenian activity see Denvir, The Irish in Brit. book x.

49. The Catholic Church opposed Fenianism for three major reasons. First, the brotherhood was seen as a threat to the dominant position enjoyed by the church within Irish communities. Secondly, the church was hostile to the physical-force methods advocated by the Fenians. And thirdly, for some of the Catholic hierarchy, Fenianism was akin to socialism. The Fenian leadership, while not explicitly anti-Catholic, nevertheless wished to exclude the church from political involvement on the grounds that clergymen had often proved to be incompetent as politicians, and that the Catholic Church had been known to act against the interests of Ireland. For a while it seemed that Irish nationalism would ally itself with anti-clericalism. See D.M. McCartney, 'The Church and Fenianism', in M. Harmon (ed.), Fenians and Fenianism (Dublin, 1968).

50. Manchester City News, 29 Nov. 1867: Manchester Courier, 25 Nov., 2 Dec. 1867.

51. For reactions to Fenianism see P. Rose, The Manchester Martyrs (1970), pp. 68ff.: Harrison, Before the Socialists pp. 91, 141, 220: N. McCord, 'The Fenians and Public Opinion in Great Britain', in Harmon (ed.) Fenians: Greenall, North. Hist. IX: J. McGill and T. Redmond, The Story of the Manchester Martyrs (Manchester, 1963).

52. Spectator, 5 Oct. 1867, p. 1108.

53. For an account of Murphy's career see W.L. Arnstein, 'The Murphy Riots: A Victorian Dilemma', Victorian Studies, XIX (1975), pp. 51-71.

103

54. The best sources are local newspapers. See, for example,
Ashton Reporter, 11, 15 Jan,, 1-29 Feb., 7-28 March, 4, 11
April, 16 May 1868; Manchester Guardian, 12, 13 May 1868;
E. Taylor, An Account of Orangeism: A Key to the Late
Religious Riots and to the Frantic Opposition to Irish Church
Disestablishment (1868); file CPRI in Prest. Pub. Recds.
Office. Full treatment of the events of 1868 in Kirk, thesis,
IV.

55. Ashton Reporter, 16 May 1868.

56. See, for example, Ashton Reporter, 4 July 1868,

57. For the Rochdale riot see Manchester Guardian, 4, 5, 6,
20 March 1868; file CPR5 in Prest, Pub. Recds. Office,
For Oldham, Manchester Guardian, 26 May 1868. For Preston
and Blackburn, Manchester Guardian, 3, 7 Nov. 1868: Ashton
Reporter, 18 July 1868. For Manchester see Manchester
Guardian, 11, 19 May, 1, 2, 5, 7, 8, 14, 16 Sept. 1868.

58. Ashton Reporter, 21 Jan. 1871,

59. Lowe, thesis, p. 468.

60. For the involvement of working-class adults see
Manchester Guardian, 3 July, 14 Aug. 1852; Ashton Reporter,
21 March, 16 May, 15 Aug, 1868; Manchester Courier, 14 Aug.
1852.

61. The population of the municipal borough of Ashton was
30,676 in 1851; Stockport 53,835 in 1851; Stalybridge
35,114 in 1871. Figures and percentages relating to Irish
immigration calculated from the Population Census. See
Population Census 1841 Ireland: Report of the Committee
Appointed to take the Census of Ireland, esp. appendix to
the report: Tables England and Wales 1851 2, tables 2,2,
pp. 659-664; Population Census England and Wales 1861 2,
pp. 655-63; Population Census England and Wales 1871 3, pp.
438-40.

62. 1836 Irish Poor, pp. v, viii, ix,

63. In 1851 there were 17,554 cotton operatives in Stockport
(32% of the total population); at Stalybridge in 1861
10,404 (41%); and at Ashton in 1861 10,856 (31%).

64. Hobsbawm, Ind. and Emp. chs. 6 and 7; T. Ellison,
The Cotton Trade of Great Britain (1886).

65. G.H. Wood, History of Wages in the Cotton Trade
(Manchester, 1910); D. Chadwick, 'On the Rate of Wages in

Manchester and Salford and the Manufacturing Districts of Lancashire and Cheshire 1838-59', Journal of the Royal Statistical Society XXIII (1859).

66. G. McLennan, Ideology and Consciousness: Some Problems in Marxist Historiography, Centre for Contemporary Cultural Studies Occasional Papers (Birmingham, 1976), esp. the intro.

67. 1836 Irish Poor, pp. xxxiii, 49, 61, 67, 70.

68. Wood, Hist. of Wages p. 131,

69. Turner, Trade Union Struct. pp. 114, 124, 141-4, 160-2: Kirk, thesis, I.

70. Manchester Guardian, 19 Oct. 1853; H. Ashworth, The Preston Strike (Manchester, 1854).

71. Foster, Class Struggle p. 244; Stockport Advertiser, 9 July 1852 ('The advent of one low Irish family into any locality is generally the signal for the flight of all the English from the neighbourhood').

72. W.J. Lowe, 'The Lancashire Irish and the Catholic Church, 1846-71; The Social Dimension', Irish Historical Studies, XX (1976), pp. 129-55.

73. Foster, Class Struggle pp. 243-6.

74. Vincent, Formtn. of Brit. Lib. Pty. p. 27; H.J. Hanham, Elections and Party Management: Politics in the Time of Disraeli and Gladstone (1959), p. 313.

75. Vincent, Formtn. of Brit. Lib. Pty. p. 27.

76. Ashton Reporter, 24 Oct., 21 Nov. 1868.

77. For working-class Conservatism see P.F. Clarke, Lancashire and the New Liberalism (Cambridge, 1971), pp. 25-82; Vincent, Formtn. of Brit. Lib. Pty. p. 148; Joyce, Hist. Jnl. XVIII; W.H. Mills, Sir Charles Macara Bart - A Study of Modern Lancashire (Manchester, 1917), pp. 65-7; Hanham, Elects. and Pty. Mangmt. pp. 313ff.; Ashton Reporter, 15 Sept., 24 Nov. 1860, 14, 21 Feb. 1863, 10 Feb., 22 Dec. 1866, 23 March, 1 June, 14 Sept. 1867, 1 March 1868, 2 April 1870 for the continued political importance of Stephens.

78. Some brief qualifications are, however, in order. By no means all Conservatives were sympathetic to the causes of factory legislation and trade unionism and Stephen's social

radicalism met with limited approval. The dominant concerns
of many Conservatives, both before and after 1867, were the
preservation of political and social inequalities. Furthermore, Liberalism had mellowed somewhat; by the 1860s many
Liberals had come to accept and even welcome factory legislation,
and some had come to terms with trade unionism. See Ashton
Reporter, 27 Jan. 1866, 1 June, 14 Spet. 1867, 24 Oct. 1868;
Ashton Standard, 10 Feb., 27 April 1866; Kirk, thesis, II
and III.

79. Ashton Reporter, 5 Sept. 1868.

80. Ashton Reporter, 22 Aug., 17 Oct. 1868.

81. Stockport Advertiser, 2 Oct. 1868.

82. Relations between Orangemen and Conservatives were
particularly close. In south-east Lancashire the Order was
almost a branch of the Tory Party; the men who ran the
Order were often the same men who ran the clubs and local
Conservative Party Associations. In 1868 many Conservative
candidates were either self-proclaimed Orangemen or close
sympathisers with the Order.

83. By the late 1860s Orangemen and other extreme Protestants
had built up a large working-class following. See Foster,
Class Struggle pp. 219-20: Ashton Reporter, 21 Nov. 1863;
Ashton Standard, 21 July 1866, 26 Jan. 1867, 17 July 1869,
5 Feb., 12 Dec. 1870. Extreme Protestants frequently set
themselves up as champions of the working-class interest
against the machinations of Manchester School manufacturers.
See Manchester Courier, 6 April, 4 May 1850, 12 June 1852;
Ashton Reporter, 4 April 1863, 12, 28 Dec. 1867, 25 Jan.,
5 Sept., 24 Oct. 1868.

84. Ashton Reporter, 7 March, 11, 18 April, 7 May, 20 June
1868.

85. Manchester Guardian, 16 Feb. 1869.

5
Aspects of the Working-Class Response to the Jews in Britain, 1880–1914
ALAN LEE

The reception accorded the Jews in Britain in the latter half of the nineteenth century was overwhelmingly conditioned by the immigration of the 1880s, which made the issue one of response less to tiny minorities and token politicians than to a relatively large number of newcomers who quickly became conspicuous in the limited areas of their settlement. Such a response, in itself highly complex, was mixed with another, namely to the Jew as the supporter, underwriter and perhaps parasite of and on the financial and industrial system. Even those whose interest it was to encourage such support tended in Britain as elsewhere to adopt a double standard of treatment. A Jew's money was as good as the next man's, but a Jew in 'Society' almost certainly was not. From those of a class who had less to gain from this system and from those who felt unfairly dealt with by it, it was easy to associate its apparently most obvious providers, the Jews, with its shortcomings.[1] The debates in socialist circles and among trade unionists in the 1890s were often confused by transferring this more traditional image of the Jew onto the new poor 'jewish' immigrants from the East, who far from being the financial props of an unjust system were, as was widely recognised, too often its most abject victims. The two

107

sides of this composite image were derived, I suggest, from
two rather different sources. On the one hand there was the
direct experience of everyday life: on the other there were
the shared and learnt ideas of the Jew which had little to do
with ordinary working-class life, or with experience of the
Jewish immigrant, even in areas of heavy Jewish settlement.
Moreover, and simplifying the process, the direct experience
was by and large that of the poor immigrant, while the ideas
were of 'Shylock' or 'the Wandering Jew' or the general type
that these referred to, of whom the workers can have had
little if any direct experience. Obviously there were bad
Jewish landlords, Jewish sweatshop masters and Jewish money-
lenders, but the idea that rack-renters, sweaters and userers
were quintessentially Jewish was derived from other than
direct experience or knowledge.

Stereotypes are often created not out of reality but
instead of it, to meet the need of being able to identify a
particular individual or group. The modern stereotype of
the Jew, as Dr Shachar has argued, arose with the decline of
medieval restrictions on and stipulations of dress, during
the seventeenth century.[2] At first the eyes and the
distinctive beards and side-locks came to be used as points
of reference, but with their gradual disappearance other
facial features were resorted to, the cheekbones, the
complexion and, of course, the nose. The poor East European
or Russian immigrant of the late nineteenth century, coming
for the most part from more traditional Jewish communities,
may have reinforced the older stereotype, but they did not
erase the newer one, and besides brought with them to those
among whom they settled a newer experience of living with
relatively large groups of strangers. How then did their
new hosts respond?

Reactions to the immigration before the First World War
have been the subject of intensive and valuable research.[3]

We are now familiar with the evidence presented by the aggrieved to the enquiries into sweating and immigration, and with 'anti-alienism' in general. We know something, although still perhaps rather little, about specifically anti-alien organisations, like the British Brothers League. We know in some detail about the politics of the Aliens Act, although, as Gainer points out, the private papers of the politicians most involved seem remarkably reticent on this matter, contrary to what the protagonists of 'high politics' would have us expect.[4]

We still lack, however, a closer examination of the social and cultural contexts within which such responses were made. We need to know how the anti-alien and party-political responses related to the ideas and responses of the rest of society, and whether such connections were ones of typicality or affinity, were reflections or refractions, and this remains an area of darkness.[5] Conceptually the problem is not simple. In some areas responses cut across class and other social divisions, while in others they are clearly conditioned by them. It would make little sense, then, to claim there were specifically 'working-class attitudes' to be studied in isolation from others. While this essay tries to look at the working-class response, this was not totally different or isolated from other class responses, however much the working class may have been becoming culturally introverted during this period.[6] In so far as there was a dominant class ideology, then working-class responses to and images of the Jewish immigration were mediated through that ideology, or more rarely were formulated in opposition to it.[7] Ideas and attitudes originating and identified with other classes filtered down the social scale, and, indeed, in the perception of racial and perhaps of religious differences there seems to have been a greater degree of ideological consensus between classes than on most other issues.

109

If working-class responses were neither sui generis nor
adopted in isolation, neither should a false homogeneity be
attributed to them. Workers in a trade threatened as they
perceived it by technological change and by immigrant labour,
like the boot and shoe operatives, the tailors and the
furniture-makers, were vociferous in their anti-alienism,
however ill-founded such perceptions might have been.[8]
Others, like the dockers, while not directly threatened with
the competition of immigrant labour, could still see themselves as possible victims of a knock-on effect from its use
elsewhere.[9] There were also those on the fringes of the
working class, the small trader and shop-keeper, who were apt
to blame immigrants for the general decline of trade in their
area.[10] Most workers, however, would not have had such
experiences or such perceptions, and it is important to stress
that whereas a study of responses must necessarily focus upon
the areas of contact, the majority of the working population
would have had to go on hearsay and reportage.[11]

There are other serious methodological difficulties.[12]
Images generated through experience or learnt in other ways
are variously mediated, so that we cannot really hope for a
definitive image, or response, and the historian, unable to
poll the dead, cannot manufacture evidence of imagery and
attitude as the sociologist does.[13] What material he has,
indeed, is more likely to be hostile and antagonistic, for
that is more likely to survive, and even more likely to be
generated than evidence of tolerance and fraternity. But if
good news is no news this should not mislead one into seeing
hostility as the major or only response during this period.
It has often been noted that apparently contradictory beliefs
and values may be held by the same person at the same time,
provided that he can compartmentalise them sufficiently to
prevent the incongruity becoming apparent to him. This can
be done most easily, of course, the less systematic is the

belief-system involved, and the greater the area of ignorance
of contradicting evidence and ideas.[14] The ways in which
people may be expected to have made sense of their experience
of the Jews, therefore, were dependent not only upon that
direct experience, but upon the ways in which they made sense
of other aspects of their everyday lives. The task is to see
how such intrusive factors were fitted into the general ideological orientations of the working class, and the purpose of
this essay is to examine a few of the possible ways in which
this might have been done.

What the immediate experience of the presence of 'alien
immigrants' was, is well-known. Environmentally it put most
obvious strain upon local housing, both quantitatively and
qualitatively, and left its most obvious mark upon the
appearance of the areas of settlement. Poor immigrants
could afford only the roughest of accommodation. Knowing
little English, and probably less of the law, and fearing the
consequences of resistance, they could be exploited by
unscrupulous landlords and shopkeepers. To scrape together
enough rent they often took in lodgers, and thus increased
the problem of overcrowding. As soon as they were able the
'native' residents sought to move to more salubrious neighbourhoods, and, initially at least, leave the immigrants
behind them. Immigration was, thus, inextricably linked to
the problems of urban decay. The worst parts of the cities
which attracted immigrants, London, Leeds and Manchester
mainly, but also Birmingham and Hull and other smaller towns,
assumed the appearance of foreign enclaves, which, indeed,
they had often become. In 1896 the Clarion spoke of being
'in a foreign country' in Whitechapel, and George Sims described
a similar visit to Wentworth Street and the Commercial Road
in 1904 as 'off the beaten track'.[15] The Leylands, the
analogous area of Leeds, was separated by a low wall from the
eastern side of the city, and was described in the Leeds Times

in 1888, with surely Biblical inspiration, as 'more Jewish than any part of Palestine'.[16] It is fair to assume that such would also have been the impressions of the average working-man confronted with these areas.

The impression of strangeness was enhanced by the appearance of the people themselves, their clothes being for long those they had brought with them from the East, and their speech seeming to the insular English a babel of tongues.[17] Their behaviour, too, attracted attention. In Leeds it was claimed that they stood around in the streets more than the English workers, and although it was admitted that it was a habit they shared with the Lancashire men, it was claimed that it did set them apart from their English neighbours.[18] The aliens' liking for the old English rural practice of hiring-markets was, naturally enough, frowned upon in Whitechapel.[19] On Sundays they were particularly visible, as Poilishe Yidl pointed out in 1884:

> Go any Sabbath afternoon to Whitechapel and
> stand for a few moments in a doorway near
> where some English workers lounge with their
> pipes in their mouths, and you will hear,
> every time a Jew passes by, the loving call
> 'Bloody Jew'.   20

The implication here that Jews were easy to recognise is here accepted by the Jewish observer.

While the effect of large-scale immigration upon the everyday life of a community could be dramatic, some reactions were palpable rationalisations of grievances having their root in more general urban decline. The much-repeated complaint that immigrants deprived local traders of custom, for example, came significantly from the older residents. The population of the East End was a young one, with high birth, death and migration rates.[21] The complaints, however, came from shop-keepers who spent between a quarter and a half a century in Stepney, and were now blaming its decay upon the most recent and conspicuous element of change.[22] A printer deplored the

loss of respectable residents, churchgoers who provided him
with a living printing church literature, and claimed that he
had been left with a mixture of aliens and 'the lower class
of British'.[23]   It must often have been the case, but the
admission was perhaps much rarer.   In some cases it was
evident that the immigrants had actually improved the slum
districts they had come to, but they were not thanked for it.
A Leylands woman claimed that she liked the area better before
the Jews had come, because the now defunct brothels had
attracted 'the gentry'.[24]

        Some reactions were more obviously to do with the
immigrants as strangers.   The English were not known as great
lovers of foreigners, perhaps especially in this the heyday of
imperialism, and the working class were themselves rather
parochial.   The big cities, however, were centres of migration,
from the countryside and from Ireland, as well as from abroad.
It would be interesting to know more of the reception accorded
the native Hodge-come-to-town, in order to compare it with that
accorded the East European peasant, albeit a semi-urban
peasant.[25]   That newcomers were the rule rather than the
exception, might be thought to have worked in the Jews' favour,
but unfortunately they were, next to the Irish and the
presumably less visible Hodge, the most numerous groups of
immigrants, and had come well after the major Irish inflow of
the mid-nineteenth century.   So there was a hierarchy of
groups with the Jews very near the bottom.   The odd foreigner,
a Frenchman or a Dane perhaps, provoked little if any protest.
The Irish were still set apart, but by the 1890s, with the
exception of the religious conflicts in Lancashire and
Scotland, they were easily tolerated.[26]   Germans were the
focus of some hostility in the 1880s and 1890s, not because
they were Jews, but because they were thought to be taking
clerical jobs away from the English, and could be pointed to
as a possible security risk.   Their numbers, however, were

too small to arouse much general response.[27]   The Italians,
still seen in terms of organ-grinders and ice-cream vendors,
probably came off worse than the Germans, but again their
paucity lent them a degree of camouflage.[28]   Generally, the
only group to be more disliked than the Jews, as a group,
however, were the Chinese, and this tended to be a highly
abstracted form of hostility, there being so little contact
between the observers and the objects of their criticism.[29]

The relative novelty and quantity of Jews in the cities,
made it likely that they would be the butt of what xenophobia
there was, although this may not necessarily have been aimed
at their Jewishness.   They were made even more vulnerable by
their religious clannishness, which engendered the expected
out-group antagonism.[30]   Sometimes, however, it conflicted
with the purposes of the anti-alienists who wished to
demonstrate how many of the immigrants were living off the
English (as opposed to the Jewish) Poor Law Guardians.   That
they were identifiably foreign also meant that the anti-alien
campaign could find support from the Fair Trade League and
the Primrose League, and from general expressions of patriotism.[31]
The immigration had come at the very time when Britain was under
pressure both as an imperial and an economic power.   The
attitude towards 'the foreigner' was, thus, hardening precisely
when there was a need to show more tolerance.

Many of the antipathetic responses rested on charges that
may be characterised broadly as 'un-English' behaviour, these
resting upon a set of prior self-images on the part of the
English observer.   One of the commonest charges was that the
Jews were 'dirty', 'content to live like pigs', as one non-
manual working-class Stepney man put it, with no doubt
unconscious solecism.[32]   Much of this tended to be blamed
on the slovenliness of their wives.   The point here is not
that the Jews were not dirty, as the poor could hardly help
this, nor that many of the natives were as bad, for the same

114

reason, but that cleanliness was a necessary attribute of respectability, and, therefore, of Englishness.   Small things mattered.   A mid-wife, Mrs Ayres, complained that the Jews would not offer her 'a nice fresh cup of tea or coffee', only brandy.   More central to the issue, she found the habit of Jewish husbands remaining near their wives during their confinement 'utterly indecent'.[33]   Some sensitive souls were disturbed to see them sleeping in their yards in summer, and at their being seen going to bed through the windows of their homes.[34]   On such things it was easy to build a more coherent picture.   Remembrance of things past prompted Mrs Ayres to draw the following comparison:

> (Samuel Street) used to be a street occupied
> by poor English and Irish people.   In the
> afternoon you would see the steps inside
> cleaned, and the women with their clean white
> aprons sit in the summertime inside the doors,
> perhaps at needlework with their little
> children about.   Now it is a seething mass
> of refuse and filth...   35

The contrast and causal connection must often have been too tempting to resist.

If the Irish were accused of being roughs and drunkards, the Jews tended to be charged with more sinister transgressions. They were supposed to be inveterate liars, and were often accused of petty crime, and less often of vice.   Evidence to the effect that they seemed far less guilty of such things than the native population generally, made little difference, of course, to the image that was created from these ideas. It was, however, an image which owed something to experience. Many of the objections applied more perhaps to the peasant than to the Jewish, or even foreign origin of the attitudes and behaviour in question.   Much of the criminal reputation was associated with the Jews' supposed 'cleverness' and 'smartness'.   For the academic the image might evince a degree of admiration, as in this passage from Alfred Marshall:

> Nearly every branch of the Semitic race has
> had some great genius for dealing with
> abstractions, and several of them have had
> a bias towards the abstract calculations
> connected with the trade of money dealing,
> and its modern developments.   36

Less sophisticated observers, closer to the ground, saw

matters rather differently.   'They beat you down', commented

an old Stepney haberdasher.[37]   While there was widespread

recognition of the Jews' apparent intellectual prowess, and

schoolteachers found their Jewish pupils generally as bright,

and often brighter than their Gentile peers, critics could

blithely ignore such evidence, and accuse the Jews both of

general illiteracy and of flooding the Board Schools, without

conscious inconsistency.[38]   Intellectual ability was often

accompanied by the desire for upward social mobility, which

in its turn induced hostile feelings among the workers whose

level the ambitious wanted to leave.[39]   A Bethnal Green woman

recalled many years later that 'we were Jewish immigrants, and

so we had no class really.   It was different for us.   The

English working class had a fear of being thought snobs,' and

so attached a low priority to their own children's education.[40]

Closely associated with such attitudes were those images of

the Jews as inclined to 'intellectual' or non-manual jobs, more

often than not, it was felt, concerned with 'making money'.

They were thus seen as affronting the dignity of labour, and

setting themselves apart from the horny-handed sons of toil.

Belfort Bax, in an attack on the 'blackguard' character of the

Englishman noted that:

> Symptoms are not wanting of a danger that
> the world of the future may be absorbed
> by two racial types, all others being
> extinguished - to wit the Jew and the
> Anglo-Saxon.   They doubtless both had
> their places in the natural evolution
> of the species: but a humanity composed
> solely of pushing Jew and swashbuckling
> Briton - of which twain the latter is
> the worse - is to me an appalling thought.   41

Reynolds News was more to the point in 1882, and did not bother with sideswipes at the English. Commenting on a plan to extend charity to the refugees from Russia it asked

> What is the use of going whining about the world over the sufferings and persecutions of Jews and Turks, while not a thought is given nor a sigh drawn for afflicted and down-trodden Englishmen and Irishmen?
> We would also like to ask the question whether the Jews have ever carried hods to the top of a ten-storey building, or descended a two hundred fathom shaft to dig coal? Nobody ever heard such a thing. 42

This was a familiar stick with which to beat the allegedly 'sickly' Jew, who was unfit for and thus sought to avoid proper, heavy work, and who consequently was 'not called upon to expend and make up so much animal tissue as an Englishman'.[43]

Different occupations, however, lent different perspectives. Labourers might claim that the Jews avoided proper work, but handcraftsmen, or even machine workers claimed quite the reverse, that the Jews were able to work harder, longer and on less food than the English.[44] The image of the Jew as 'economic man' was, of course, made respectable by social reformers like J.A. Hobson and Beatrice Webb.[45]

Similar attacks were made on the Jew as consumer. The immigrants' habit of actually inspecting their wares before purchase, and worse still, of haggling over the price, only seemed to strengthen the 'grasping', 'calculating' stereotype. A Stepney greengrocer, whose business had suffered from a general decline in trade, claimed, disappointedly, that 'you cannot get a thing out of them'.[46] In its extreme form this amounted to prejudice akin to anti-semitism,[47] as, for example, in the case of George Acorn, an East End carpenter, who recalled a childhood picture thus: 'The Jew came to buy a fowl for dinner, provided it is cheap, poking and pulling the bird about until every atom of flesh has been calculated and no feather left unturned.'[48]

These views were closely allied to those which were taken
of the Jews as competitors in the labour market. The protests
of the boot and shoe operatives, the tailoring workers and the
furniture-makers are well-known. They claimed that the
immigrants worked longer for less, produced shoddy goods, and
kept out properly trained men, reducing the level of skill in
the trade. Simplified, in Keir Hardie's words to the Select
Committee of 1889, 'every foreigner throws one British workman
out of employment', it was a point easy enough to grasp.[49]

It is perhaps useful to look at such responses partly as
a matter of fairness. Admittedly such rationalisations are
common in the rhetoric of the prejudiced, but it is not wise
to assume that it was always just rationalisation, and even
if it were, it was still an important if not a crucial part
of the response we are examining. The secretary of the
Leeds Boot Manufacturers Association told the Royal Commission
on Labour that 'we hardly think it fair that these people
should come invading us and taking work out of the hands of
our own people'.[50] An erstwhile political agent and self-
styled carpenter argued that 'our people are not philosophers,
and we see these people taking our place, and one by one we
are driven out'.[51] It was a view, of course, to be found in
the repertory of the anti-semitic deputy chairman of the
British Brothers League, Robert Parkes: 'to my mind all the
authorities in the parish seem to favour the aliens in
preference to favouring those who have been here for years,
that is my opinion'.[52] Here was a strong element of populist
alienation from government and authority, a feeling that
protection ought to be given against forces over which they
had no control.[53]

Much of this evidence of the felt experience of the
immigration is well-known, but it must form an essential
part of the explanation of the response to that immigration,
and a few general points arise from it. First, in almost

118

every case the criticism made of the immigrants assumed that
they were Jews, as they usually were, and that objections to
the one were also legitimate objections to the other. From
one point of view this could easily serve as a cover for true
anti-semitism, but I suggest that it was often evidence that
such a cover was necessary, and that the association was a
consequence rather of sloppy and unsystematic thinking.
Such a surmise is, perhaps, incapable of direct proof, but it
seems to make contextual sense. Most anti-alienists took
great pains to dissociate themselves from such unworthy views
as racialism or anti-semitism, in itself evidence that the
accepted norms of tolerance would not brook such appeals.
Arnold White himself, whose avowed purpose was, by subsidising
alien immigrants, 'to bring matters to a head', and who
preferred the possibility of a Judenhetze to a continuation
of the existing situation, was obsessively insistent upon
avoiding the word 'Jew' in his evidence to the 1888 Select
Committee.[54]   Robert Sherard, an outspoken anti-semitic
observer of 'social problems', also vehemently denied being
anti-semitic.   Such disavowals were all but universal, and
remain so.[55]   Even the ordinary working-man felt the moral
pressure, it seems.   George Acorn, after several passages of
anti-semitic diatribe, wrote:

> I desire not to be mistaken.   That there
> are good and bad in every nation in almost
> equal proportions I firmly believe.   I
> only regret that my own life has brought
> me into close contact with more of the
> repellent new type of Jew I have indicated
> than with any other.   56

'Jewish immigrant' was at this time a tautologous label, but
the emphasis was overwhelmingly upon the latter rather than
upon the former term.

A second general point is that the criticisms made,
whether refuted or not, were points that could have been and
were made against sections of the English working class.

119

Environmental deterioration was as much associated with
Gentile as with Jewish poverty and pauperism. The introverted nature of the immigrant communities was mirrored,
religious culture aside, in the equally introverted and
parochial lives of the English working class.[57] The
'respectable' English workers were as disapproving of their
own 'roughs' as of the poor Jews, themselves more rarely,
perhaps, 'rough'.[58] Those workers who were actually active
anti-alienists or even anti-semitic seem to have been drawn
from the skilled working class or the lower-middle class, a
social composition repeated in today's racialist organisations.[59]
The anti-alienists were at pains to identify the issue of
immigration as a working-class one, and to a degree this was
correct.[60] The immigrants lived with the workers, were of
the workers. But the responses bore a close resemblance to
responses to other groups. / In fact there seems to have been
remarkably little active and distinctive response to the
immigrants. Riots were rare. Dr Alderman has suggested
that those in South Wales in the late summer of 1911 were
fomented during a time of unusual economic hardship, in an
area of recent and rapid migration and industrialisation, and
with the possible addition of middle-class incitement.[61]
There had been at least one other anti-immigrant disturbance
in the area around that time, at Dowlais in 1903, and the
Welsh, like the English, had not drawn the line at violent
attacks on the immigrant Irish in the mid-nineteenth century.[62]
But if one looks at the areas of major settlement, the East
End, the Leylands or Cheetham, no major incidents seem to have
occurred, loudly though the anti-alienists prophesied that
they would. The rule in Britain, it bears repeating, was
not, as it was in Europe, one of persecution.

There was, of course, a measure of violence involved in
communal relations, but street fighting was after all not an
uncommon accompaniment of Victorian life. The gangs would

have it out whether or not there were ethnic or religious differences to exploit, and where there were such differences they were not necessarily central to the violence. Willy Goldman recalled that gang fighting was part of everyday life in the East End, but that the violence was directed at the Jews only when the Gentiles were drunk (the relative sobriety of the Jews did not endear them to some of their fellow residents!).[63] The threat remained, however, and the Whitechapel Jew did not venture into Gentile Wapping.[64] In Leeds there were 'periodical weekend raids by bands of hooligans who would cross the "frontier" armed with cudgels and weapons of all descriptions', attacking any Jew they could find.[65] Much of this activity was probably a part of normal adolescent culture. As a Whitechapel police super-intendent observed, the Jews were molested mostly 'by the lower order of British rough', and a Radical Anglo-Jew told the Royal Commission of 1903 that the Jews were hit by 'the ignorant people' in St George's.[66] Their youth was perhaps attested by the Stepney butcher who remarked that 'frequently, late of a Saturday night, you see some of the "boys" as they call them, pummelling into the aliens'.[67] The bullying of Jewish children by their schoolfellows was similarly not an unusual activity among schoolchildren, and the tormenting of Jewish residents by children's practical jokes, even in the admittedly morbid form of hanging dead chickens on doors, was an established tradition of childish behaviour.[68] Occasionally there was more direct action against the immigrants, as when Jews were forcibly prevented from moving into Cornwall Street in St George's, but this seems to have been exceptional.[69] As this was a transitional area of settlement, with from 5 to 24 per cent of Jewish population, it also demonstrates how the so-called ghetto areas helped to keep actual friction to a minimum. The reluctance of either the Jewish or the English working class to venture out of their territories was further

strengthened by the fact that they were also separated at
work, the Jews usually working for Jewish employers in all-
Jewish workshops, something that would account for the
apparent lack of cases of men refusing to work with Jews, as
they did on occasion with blacks.[70]

The discussion so far has been of the working class's
experience of the Jewish immigrants, an experience more
likely to result in physical hostility than was so among
other classes, for whom punch-ups were a less common part of
life. As Theodore Herzl chillingly put it, 'prejudice may
be a smile in Society, and a coup de poing in Stepney'.[71]
But experience and linked behaviour is only a part of the
question of working-class response. We must now turn to the
ideas used to make sense of that experience.

Whether or not the Victorians were unusually prone to
categorise people according to nationality and race, it is
obvious that such categories were important parts of the
common discourse of all classes, and of laymen as well as of
ethnologists.[72] The characterisation was usually in terms
of moneylending, shady finance, and sharp business practice.
The more generalised distrust and dislike of the plutocracy
in the late Victorian and Edwardian England may have added to
the difficulties of the Jews, who were associated with it.
On the other hand, the growing respectability of trade,
commerce and finance would no doubt have helped their acceptance. Both acceptance and rejection, however, tended to be
in terms of the stereotype. The colloquial meaning of the
term 'to jew' was 'to cheat', and 'a Jew' was standard English
for a hard-bargainer.[73] In London especially, the noun and
its derivatives normally referred to the world of petty crime.
An exception, 'jewing', was used mainly in the navy to refer
to 'mending', and was an obvious reference to the common
trade of the late-nineteenth-century immigrant. There was
similar usage in the countryside, although it is worth noting

that in dialect English the words often referred to the Jews'
old mining activity in the south-west of England before the
expulsion, and generally there was a greater residue of the
myth and the exotic attaching to the Jew in the country than
in the towns.[74] Not all references were derogatory, however,
as, for example, 'sheeney', and it was not the Jew alone who
was credited with meanness and a propensity to cheat.[75] The
Scots, the Welsh, the Irish and Yorkshiremen, to name only
the major groups, were all fair game. Presumably, although
I do not know any specific source of evidence, the Jew also
joined the above groups as a convenient and much-used butt
for ethnic and related jokes. It is difficult to assess
such influences, but it would certainly be unwise to under-
estimate the cumulative effect of such usages upon the actual
responses to the Jews.

The tradition of the Oriental moneylending Jew was
firmly established in literature, of course, but how much of
it filtered down to the elementarily literate working class
is difficult to say. More perhaps would have found its way
through to the skilled autodidactic artisan, devoted to
Carlyle, to Scott, or perhaps even to Shakespeare. For an
earlier period Louis James tells us that the Jews were
generally portrayed favourably in lower-class fiction, partly,
he suggests, on account of their exotic appeal, and partly
because it was written for the Jews themselves. It may even,
he adds, have indicated 'an acceptance of Jewish elements into
the working-class communities who read these novels'.[76]
Unfortunately there is no similar study of the lower grade of
literature for our period. P.J. Keating's work is really
about a genre aimed at the middle, or perhaps lower-middle
classes, by writers of the middle class. How popular the
social realists were among the subjects of their social
realism is far from clear, and it is not easy to see how one
can assess the impact of Dickens, Scott, Trollope and Du

Maurier.[77]   Rather than embark upon such a task here, I want
to look a little closer at the pictorial image of the Jew
presented to the working-man.

In this, the age of physiognomy, when Madame Tussaud
wanted at first to call her Chamber of Horrors 'the Chamber of
Physiognomy', there was, of course, a physical stereotype of
the Jew.   While not, perhaps, as interested in the Semite as
the Celt, the ethnologists offered detailed accounts of the
dark hair, strange eyes, dark complexion, thick lips and noses
that could be drawn by writing a six with a long tail.[78]   The
stereotype transcended class for most purposes, rich and poor
being painted with the same brush, and it was a stereotype
which was most evident in pictorial form, which as Dr Shachar
has shown, 'preceded verbal stereotyping by three quarters of
a century'.[79]   Many claimed that it was a faithful characterisation.   A contributor to the Eugenics Review in 1911 noted
that 'the street arab who calls out "Jew" as some child
hurries on to school is unconsciously giving the best and most
disinterested proof that there is a reality in the Jewish
expression'.[80]   Some eyes seemed keener than others.
Llewellyn Smith, for example, found it easy to distinguish
between 'the high cheek-bones and thickened lips of the Russian
or Polish Jew, (and) the darker complexion and unmistakeable
nose of his Austrian co-religionist'.[81]   As Robert Sherard
put it more pithily, 'faces that were not with us at Agincourt
peer at you from every doorway'.[82]

Did the working class share such images?   They almost
certainly lacked the pseudo-scientific theory and jargon, but
to the extent that they were exposed to pictorial representations
of this type, they may well have done.   To know whether they
were so exposed we need a more systematic study than is yet
available.   Cruickshank's illustrations for Oliver Twist were
certainly well-known, as probably were Tenniel's portraits of
Disraeli.[83]   We find Walter Crane using the type of the rich

moneylending Jew, with characteristic nose, in his 'The Strong
Man'.[84]   The art of caricature required such stereotypes, but
they originally 'emerged in satirical context', and there is
little indication that in Britain the cartoonist succeeded in
mythologising the world of politics to the extent that he did
elsewhere.[85]   Outside the world of caricature, in fact, the
use of the stereotype seems to have been very restrained.
The Illustrated London News, for example, was as sparing in
its use of types when dealing with the Jewish immigrants as it
had been when dealing with the Irish.[86]   We need to know more,
however, of how he was portrayed in the working-class press of
the period.

Other possible sources of the pictorial image include the
music hall and the schoolbook, but existing studies provide
little evidence on the subject.   Religious schoolbooks in
particular might well repay further investigation.   Attitudes
towards the Jews in Britain after the mid-century were rarely
associated with religious problems, but it is significant that
someone recalling Hull in the late 1880s remembered a
particular Jew who used to help the migrants, and 'whose pale
(sic) complexion emphasised the Jesus likeness as we knew it
from the lessons in our elementary school'.[87]   Most Bibles
were illustrated, and as will be recalled from Hardy's Jude
the Obscure religious teaching at that level was often done
with pictures, so it would have been surprising if children
so brought up had avoided seeing the Jews in such a context
thereafter.   Finally, there is also some evidence of the
image as above even in the early cinema, although it is
difficult to know how typical it was, or how faithfully
catalogue descriptions were reproduced on film.[88]

All this is relatively fragmentary and sparse evidence,
but it can be seen as an indication of the sort and source of
ideas about the Jews in general, as opposed to actual
experience of them, that the working class in all probability

shared. Attention, of course, has here been confined mainly
to the poor immigrant, but as noted at the start, for many the
image of the rich, scheming Jewish financier was at least as
strong. It was possible to conflate such an image with the
more general one of the 'capitalist', but it seems that it
was often transferred from the rich to the poor Jewish
immigrant. The association of capitalism and Jewry was, in
any case, not an easy one to make. Certainly George Acorn,
anti-semite though he undoubtedly was, had quite other,
although compatible explanations of the way in which the
industrial system ground the worker down. In fact the failure
of anti-semitism, and even of anti-alienism as a political
movement in Britain, at this seemingly most opportune of times,
suggests that such appeals, so effective in other countries,
fell on deaf or uncomprehending ears. The reasons for this
must be sought in a wider examination of working-class ideology
than is possible here. That there was little correspondence
between popular racialism and theoretic racism may have played
its part, but it must be remembered that this disparity did
not prevent a politicised movement elsewhere.[89] In Britain
it seems that antipathy to Jews or even aliens was hardly an
available response for the governing class to tap. There
was no real 'nativist' ideology or movement in Britain, in the
sense of 'an intense opposition to an internal minority on the
ground of its foreign...connections'.[90] Such attitudes may
have been directed, in the case of this major imperialist
power, to people outside the heart of empire, but they found
little purchase in the case of Jews.

The Jews in particular were at this time, with Zionism
only in its cradle, fortunate in being politically neutral.
The occasional association of the Jews with 'anarchism' never
amounted to much.[91] There was no Home Rule problem as there
was with the Irish, and governments, while discouraging
incitement to assassinate foreign monarchs, behaved in the

126

main tolerantly.[92]   The immigration itself was a local
focussed and a temporary problem.   Economically the trades
which had most felt the impact of immigrant competition were
themselves either declining or being transformed, a trend
reflected in the movement of the Jewish trade unionists into
the English trade unions.   Although there was little intermarriage, or even social mixing, the gradual assimilation of
the immigrants into Anglo-Jewish communities of longer-standing,
and even into the wider working-class communities, came to make
Jewishness a less outstanding or important characteristic than
it had appeared previously.   The very development of class
polarisation in society and politics in the later nineteenth
century served to reduce the significance of ethnic groupings
and images generally, until the more visible presence of
increasing numbers of coloured imperial subjects after the
First World War.   Many of the images of the Jews held before
1914 were, as we have seen, based upon the experience of their
poverty and economic competition, and the decline of those
conditions weakened many of the responses which were tied to
them.   It was class, and not race or religion, which became
the fundamental line of cleavage in Britain, but it would be
unwise to ignore the admittedly less fundamental fractures,
of the kind discussed here, in any general estimate of class
attitudes.

NOTES

1.   There is a need to investigate further British working-
class conceptions of 'capitalism', including the part which
'gold' and 'money' played in them.   For the USA see John
Higham, Strangers in the Land (New Jersey, 1955), pp. 93ff.

2.   I. Shachar, 'Studies in the Emergence and Dissemination
of the Modern Jewish Stereotype in Western Europe' (unpub.
Ph.D. thesis, University of London, 1967), pp. 315ff.

3.   L.P. Gartner, The Jewish Immigrant in England, 1870-1914
(1960; 2nd ed. with new foreword, 1973), on the immigrants
themselves, but also valuable for reactions; J.A. Garrard,

The English and Immigration (1971), on the organised opinion of the political parties and trade unions; B. Gainer, The Alien Invasion (1972), on anti-alienism in general.

4.   Gainer, Alien Invasion p.287.

5.   Cf.M. Biddis, 'Racial Ideas and the Politics of Prejudice, 1850-1914', Historical Journal, xv (1972), pp. 581-2.

6.   For 'introversion' see G. Stedman Jones, 'Working-class culture and working-class politics in London, 1870-1900', Journal of Social History, vii (1974), pp. 460-508, and S. Meacham, A Life Apart (1977).

7.   K. Mannheim, Essays on the Sociology of Culture (1956), p. 100.

8.   Gainer, Alien Invasion pp. 57-99; M. Landa, 'The Economic Aspect of Alien Labour', Economic Review, xvi (1906), pp. 43ff.

9.   Garrard, Immigration pp. 163-4.

10. Gainer, Alien Invasion pp. 31-5.

11. Cf. Higham, Strangers p. 213.

12. M. Bulmer, 'Some Problems of Research into Class Imagery', in M. Bulmer (ed.), Working-Class Images of Society (1975), pp. 163-79.

13. Ibid., pp. 170-1.

14. Cf.R.E. Lane, Political Ideology (New York, 1962), p. 377.

15. Clarion, quoted in Garrard, Immigration p. 50; G.R. Sims, 'Off the Beaten Track in London', Strand Magazine, xxvii (1904), pp. 416-23.

16. J. Connell, 'The Gilded Ghetto: Jewish suburbanisation in Leeds', Bloomsbury Geographer, iii (1970), p. 51; Leeds Times quoted in J. Buckman, 'The Economic and Social History of Alien Immigration to Leeds, 1880-1914' (unpub. Ph.D. thesis, University of Strathclyde, 1968), p. 409. For Birmingham see M.D. Blanch, 'Nation, Empire and the Birmingham Working Class, 1899-1914' (unpub. Ph.D. thesis, University of Birmingham, 1975), especially ch. 9. For Hull see F. Rands, 'When Hull was used by Jews as a gateway to their freedom', Hull Times, 29 Dec. 1972.

17. Gainer, Alien Invasion p. 45; Sims, Strand xxvii, pp. 416-17.

18. Select Committee on Emigration and Immigration (Foreigners), Parliamentary Papers, 1889, x, Q.1061: W. Evans-Gordon, 'Aliens in England: the Immigrant Problem', Illustrated London News, 30 Apr. 1904, p. 657.

19. Royal Commission on Alien Immigration, Cd.1742 (1903), Q.9402.

20. Quoted in W.J. Fishman, East End Jewish Radicals, 1875-1914 (1975), pp. 90-1, my emphasis.

21. Gartner, Jewish Immigrant p. 172.

22. RC on Alien Immigration, QQ.8651ff. (42 years residence), 8812ff. (45 years), 9213ff. (30 years), 9545ff. (39 years), 9645ff. (46 years) and 9251ff. (20 years).

23. Ibid., QQ.9251ff.

24. Buckman, thesis, p. 417.

25. Arnold White had begun his political career by assisting the emigration of English agricultural labourers, SC on Emigration, P.P., 1888, xi, QQ.1316ff. See also the same context used by H. Llewellyn Smith, 'The Influx of Population', in C. Booth, Life and Labour of the People in London (1902 ed.), 1st series, vol. 3, pp. 58-9.

26. SC on Emigration, P.P., 1888, xi, QQ.2639ff., and Royal Commission on Labour, P.P., 1892, C.6795-III, xxxvi, Q.20096, P.P., 1892, C.6795-II, xxxvi, Q.9505.

27. G. Anderson, Victorian Clerks (Manchester, 1976), pp. 64f., 132-3. On numbers see H. Kellenbenz, 'German Immigrants in England', in C. Holmes (ed.), Immigrants and Minorities in British Society (1978), pp. 75-6.

28. RC on Alien Immigration, QQ.1736ff.: Buckman, thesis, pp. 181ff.: SC on Emigration, P.P., 1889, x, Q.1045.

29. In general see J.P. May, 'The Chinese in Britain, 1860-1914', in Holmes (ed.), Immigrants pp. 111-24. Also L. Barrow, 'The Socialism of Robert Blatchford and the Clarion' (unpub. Ph.D. thesis, University of London, 1975), p. 432, and E. Silberner, 'British Socialism and the Jews', Historica Judaica, xiv (1952), p. 40, n. 68.

30. On sectionalism see Connell, Bloomsbury Geographer iii, p. 51, on the Leylands as 'a collection of urban villages'. On vulnerability to xenophobic attack see M. Simon, 'Anti-Semitism in England', The Jewish Review, ii (1911-12), pp. 301-2. Willy Goldman recalled that the Jews felt that they

were always treated as foreigners, East End My Cradle (1940),
p. 19.

31. Gainer, Alien Invasion pp. 64, 132ff.; Garrard,
Immigration pp. 56, 72; Blanch, thesis, p. 170.

32. R.C. on Alien Immigration, Q.2461.

33. Ibid., QQ.9425, 9428.

34. Ibid., QQ.9457, 9311.

35. Ibid., Q.9418.

36. A. Marshall, Principles of Economics (1890; 8th ed. 1920),
p. 761, n.1.

37. R.C. on Alien Immigration, Q.8831.

38. Gartner, Jewish Immigrant pp. 229-30; Buckman, thesis,
pp. 434ff.; J. Smith, 'The Jewish Immigrant', Contemporary
Review, lxxvi (1899), pp. 426, 434; Evans-Gordon, 'Aliens in
England', p. 657.

39. B. Webb, 'The Jewish Community', in Booth, Life and Labour
pp. 186ff.; M. Loane, The Next Street But One (1907), p. 32.

40. M. Young and P. Willmott, Family and Kinship in East
London (1957), p. 177.

41. Letter in Reynolds News, 7 Jan. 1900, p. 4.

42. Leader, ibid., 22 Jan. 1882, p. 4.

43. R.C. on Alien Immigration, Q.8558 (British Brothers'
League evidence).

44. Select Committee on the Housing of the Working Classes,
P.P., 1884-85, C.4402-I, xxx, Q.5232; R.C. on Labour,
C.6795-III, xxxvi, Q.15103; R.C. on Alien Immigration, QQ.
287, 1594, 9569.

45. For a discussion of Hobson see C. Holmes, 'J.A. Hobson
and the Jews', in Holmes (ed.), Immigrants pp. 125-7. For
Beatrice Webb see, for example, My Apprenticeship (Harmondsworth,
1938), p. 488, n.2.

46. R.C. on Alien Immigration, Q.9022.

47. 'Anti-semitism' here meaning 'an attitude of hostility
towards the Jews as such', J.H. Robb, Working-Class Anti-Semite
(1954), p. 11.

48. G. Acorn, One of the Multitude (1911), p. 71.

49. S.C. on Emigration, P.P., 1889, x, Q.1469.

50. R.C. on Labour, C.6795-III, xxxvi, Q.14097.

51. R.C. on Alien Immigration, Q.9097.   On this witness see ibid., Q.19934.

52. Ibid., Q.8720.

53. Cf. Lane, Political Ideology pp. 161ff.

54. S.C. on Emigration, P.P., 1888, xi, QQ.1826 (pp. 1857ff.), 1909, 1953f.

55. J. Rex, Race Relations in Sociological Theory (1970), p. 145.

56. Acorn, One of p. 71.

57. H. Macleod, Class and Religion in the Late Victorian City (1974), pp. 42ff.

58. R. Roberts, The Classic Slum (Manchester, 1971), passim.

59. G. Alderman, 'The Anti-Jewish Riots of August 1911 in South Wales', Welsh History Review, vi (1972), pp. 196-7; Simon, The Jewish Review ii, pp. 294ff.   The chairman of the British Brothers' League in Birmingham was a labourer, however, see Blanch, thesis, p. 170.   For today see D. Scott, 'The National Front in Local Politics: Some Interpretations', in I. Crewe (ed.), British Political Sociology Yearbook, vol. 2 (1975), p. 223.

60. R.C. on Alien Immigration. Q.8558 (p. 288); Garrard, Immigration pp. 54, 66.

61. Alderman, Welsh History Review vi, passim.

62. Evans-Gordon, 'Aliens in England', p. 657, who also cites Limerick.   On Wales see J. Hickey, Urban Catholic (1967), pp. 127ff.   Sam Shaw noted that Welsh miners used the term 'shylock' for 'mean', Guttersnipe (1946), pp. 137, 139.

63. Goldman, East End pp. 16ff.

64. Ibid., p. 16.

65. E. Krausz, Leeds Jewry (Cambridge, 1964), p. 22.

66. S.C. on Emigration, P.P., 1888, xi, Q.909; R.C. on Alien Immigration, Q.9320.

67. R.C. on Alien Immigration, Q.9389.

68. Krausz, Leeds Jewry p. 22; Acorn, One of pp. 48-9.

69. R.C. on Alien Immigration, QQ.2253, 2612ff.

70. R. May and R. Cohen, 'The Interaction Between Race and Colonialism: A Case Study of the Liverpool Race Riots of 1919', Race and Class, xvi (1974), p. 118.

71. R.C. on Alien Immigration, Q.6306.

72. Cf. P.N. Stearns, 'National Character and European Labour History', Journal of Social History, iv (1971), pp. 95-124.

73. E. Partridge, A Dictionary of Slang and Unconventional English (1961).

74. J. Wright (ed.), English Dialect Dictionary (1905).

75. On 'sheeney' see J. Hotten, The Slang Dictionary (1881 ed.).

76. L. James, Fiction for the Working Man (1974 ed.), p. 104; but cf. J. Wiener, The War of the Unstamped (1969), p. 227.

77. E. Rosenberg, From Shylock to Svengali: Jewish Stereotypes in English Fiction (1961).

78. Shachar, thesis, pp. 315ff.

79. Ibid.

80. R.N. Salaman, 'Heredity and the Jew', Eugenics Review, ii (1910-11), p. 190. For eugenist views of Jewish immigration see G.R. Searle, Eugenics and Politics in Britain, 1900-1914 (Leyden, 1976), pp. 39-40.

81. Llewellyn Smith, 'Influx', p. 100; also Webb, Apprenticeship p. 182.

82. R. Sherard, The Child Slaves of Britain (1905), p. 65.

83. C. Dickens, Oliver Twist (Oxford, 1960 ed.); F. Sarzano, Sir John Tenniel (1948), pp. 77-8.

84. W. Crane, Cartoons for the Cause (1896; 1976 ed.).

85. Shachar, thesis, p. 359; E.H. Gombrich, _Meditations on a Hobby Horse_ (1963), p. 139.

86. 'The Jewish Law in the East End', illustrated by P. Frenzeny, _Illustrated London News,_ 8 Aug. 1902, p. 212; 'The Alien Invasion and the British Exodus', illustrated by Max Cowper, ibid., 22 Aug. 1903, pp. 278-9; 'Aliens in England: The Immigrant Problem', illustrated by H.H. Flere, ibid., 30 Apr. 1904, pp. 653-6. For the ILN on Ireland see L.P. Curtis Jnr., _Apes and Angels_ (Newton Abbot, 1971), pp. 83ff.

87. Rands, 'When Hull...', p. 4; also Sims, _Strand_ xxvii, p. 417.

88. R. Low, _The History of the British Film, 1896-1910_ (1948), pp. 56ff.

89. Cf. Higham, _Strangers_ p. 165,

90. Ibid., p. 4.

91. Fishman, _Jewish Radicals_ pp. 73, 287ff; C. Holmes, 'In Search of Sydney Street', _Bulletin of the Society for the Study of Labour History,_ 29 (1974), pp. 70-7.

92. A. Kimball, 'The Harassment of Russian Revolutionaries Abroad', _Oxford Slavonic Papers,_ vi (1973), pp. 48-65.

6

The German Gypsy Question in Britain, 1904–1906

COLIN HOLMES

Racial and ethnic conflict situations assume a variety of forms. For instance, differences can be emphasised between members of one nation, as when Gobineau drew a distinction between the French aristocracy and a Gallo-Roman rabble. This was an incompatibility which, he believed, had a fundamental significance for French society.[1] Alternatively, hostility can be directed towards an external object, on the basis of national or transnational interests. This provided a dynamic not only for West European imperialism in the late nineteenth century, when beliefs about the 'white man's burden' acted as a rationalisation of imperialist activity, but also for the gathering contemporary forces of Pan-Germanism or Pan-Slavism.[2] Or again, hostility can develop towards an alien minority, when conflict arises between sections of the host community and alien newcomers, when the latter are perceived as posing a threat to economic or cultural interests - or in some cases to both.[3] In this respect, German, Italian, French, Spanish, Greek, Turkish and East European workers - to refer to a sample drawn from the European experience alone - have all encountered hostility as minorities within receiving societies. Such antipathy has often been of a transient nature, arising out of a particular constellation of social circumstances, and disappearing as conditions changed. But there are groups, such as Jews and Gypsies, without a settled permanent home of their own, against whom a tenacious receiving hostility has been displayed.

Before turning to a consideration of the Gypsies, and in particular the hostility which was displayed towards the German Gypsies in Britain between 1904 and 1906, it is necessary to set that conflict against the perceptions of Gypsies which had already developed in British society.

Although they originated in northern India, over the course of time the Gypsies had been involved in their own diaspora which had taken them into most European states and the first of their number entered Britain in the fifteenth century. They came from the Balkans, which was then undergoing Turkish occupation, in the course of which Gypsies were uprooted from their settled communities and sedentary occupations and pushed towards Western Europe, where they formed a part, although a special part, of the multitude of beggars and displaced persons who were considered a burden on European society. On the basis of their own statements they were known as natives of Egypt, and as Christians on pilgrimage. West European man would have been amazed to learn that they had in fact originated in the fabulous land of India which he was trying desperately to reach. But at this stage he was unaware of this and a prolonged debate was to take place about the origins of the Gypsies before the mass of tradition, rumour and deliberate falsehood were penetrated and the geographical origins of this 'singular people' were finally established.[4]

Almost from the beginning Gypsies encountered a strong strain of European hostility. In the sixteenth century, for instance, while they could find themselves as entertainers in receipt of royal and aristocratic favour in Scotland, the same years also witnessed legal attempts being made to expel them

135

from the kingdom.[5] A similar severity towards Gypsies was apparent in the English law of the sixteenth century and was in fact reflected in most European countries.[6] And this hostile strain continued to be displayed in society's responses to the Gypsy presence. In economic terms the Gypsies lived an interstitial life, darting in and out on the margins of the economy.[7] They were entertainers, often acrobats, hawkers, pruners, fortune tellers, rag collectors, horse traders, living a life of movement, responding to changing economic opportunities and the political compulsions of the authorities. Although little of this economic life brought them into face to face competition with non-Gypsies, it has been commented that the 'intermittent stranger' is likely to be perceived through 'dark negatives and reinforced spirals' and this is even more likely if, as happened, there was a culture-clash involved. We have been told that the societies which received and repelled the Gypsies 'classified their bodies and their ways as dirty and dangerous' and, in turn, the Gypsies reciprocated such sentiments. Tensions could also occur through the rejection by the Gypsies of 'bureaucratic organisation' and any political unity beyond 'the web of family and kin'.[8] It was on this account that Sir Roger de Coverley could refer to them as an 'idle, profligate people, who infest all the countries of Europe and live in the midst of governments in a kind of commonwealth by themselves'.[9] Much later, Goldwin Smith could write in the same tradition and lump together Jews, Armenians, Parsees, Greeks and Gypsies as 'cases of parasitism', living off society, drawing from it, but not generously contributing to it.[10]

But attacks upon the Gypsy minority through the instrument of the law, and the persistence of hostile attitudes towards them, do not reveal the full range of society's responses. Both in Britain and elsewhere other images developed of an

effusive romantic nature which carried different emphases.
The defiance of ordered society by the Gypsies exercised an
appeal in some circles who could cover such values with a
haze of romanticism.[11]   To the romantics the Gypsy was 'a
faultless child of nature',[12] a sentiment which finds its
later expression in the claim that he stands for 'freedom' in
'an increasingly conformist world'.[13]   Painters such as
George Morland[14] and, much later, Augustus John, found their
life-style appealing[15] and it was in the same vein that
George Borrow could present his enormously influential scenes
of Gypsy life in Lavengro and Matthew Arnold could refer to
the Scholar Gypsy. The gypsy lover image developed out of
the same romantic tradition and it was to some extent pressure
from those who had a romantic conception of Gypsies that led
to the founding of the Gypsy Lore Society in 1888.[16]

But these kind of influences, which became apparent in
the eighteenth and nineteenth centuries, which applauded the
spirit of Gypsy life and welcomed it as a source of social
richness, had to contend with that other tradition which led
to the perception of the Gypsy as a nuisance who should either
be excluded from society or 'tamed' and brought into line with
social convention. In line with this more dominant viewpoint
George Smith of Coalville could campaign for legislation to
register Gypsy vans, segregate the sleeping quarters of the
sexes, maintain minimum hygiene standards and ensure some
education of Gypsy children. His biographer commented that
Smith cared little for the origins of the Gypsies:

> ...his great concern was that there were
> tens of thousands of vagabonds living lives
> that he considered a disgrace to civilisation
> and Christianity and making money by thieving
> and chicanery, whilst honest men were starving
> and...tens of thousands of little children
> were being brought into the world and trained
> to walk in the devious footsteps of their
> fathers.   17

Hence his campaign aimed to influence Gypsy life through the
provision of education and legislation such as the Moveable
Dwellings Bill.[18]   Smith's references to Christianity also
serve as a reminder that the Gypsies had to contend with a
religious opposition to their presence. The Evangelical
imagination could stereotype the Gypsy as 'a deprived and
miserable outcast' who should be filled with the knowledge of
the one 'true' religion. Consequently, the Gypsy was
encouraged to leave his spirits behind him and to enter into
the comforting folds of Christianity and it was to this end
that much missionary work was devoted. The Quaker mission
was founded in 1815,[19] and the London City Mission started
work in the 1850s. It was in the course of such zeal that
some activity degenerated into an attempt to destroy the
whole range of Gypsy culture while supposedly gathering
converts for Christ.[20]

There were, in short, a stock of favourable and
unfavourable images of Gypsies which were in circulation in
British society by the end of the nineteenth century and it
is against this background that we might consider the German
Gypsy question.

The issue was first brought to the attention of the
Home Office in a letter which was written on behalf of the
Port of London Sanitary Committee by the town clerk at the
Guildhall. On 20 November 1904 information was received by
the committee that a party of fifty foreign Gypsies, including
seventeen children, who had been expelled from Holland, were
expected to arrive at Queenboro' from Flushing. However,
the Zeeland Steam Ship Company declined to convey them and
consequently the group moved to Hamburg. At this stage it
was believed that the Gypsies would not therefore come to
Britain but to the surprise of the London port authorities,
they arrived by another route and at the time the town clerk
was writing his letter they were encamped just outside the

City boundary. The letter continued:

> It is clear from the facts that the Dutch
> Government, although expelling these gipsies
> from their own country as 'undesirables' had
> apparently no objection to transporting them
> on their own steamers to this country: and,
> in the present state of the law, nothing
> could have been done to prevent their landing
> and proceeding to London, or distributing
> themselves throughout the country.
> The committee deplore the possibility of
> such a state of affairs as is disclosed and
> urge upon the Government the necessity for
> immediate steps being taken by legislation or
> otherwise to render such incidents impossible
> in the future.

A minute by a Home Office official suggested that the Gypsies
were brought from Rotterdam to London by the S.S. Batavia on
1 December 1904.[21]

For the next two years the immigration of German Gypsies
was a problem to which the Home Office had to direct its
attention. Shortly after the receipt of information from
the Port of London authorities another letter was directed to
the Home Office, this time by Percy Webb of Walton-on-Thames
Urban District Council, in which an objection was raised to
police action in driving Gypsies across county boundaries
between Middlesex and Surrey. The Gypsies, it was claimed,
were being constantly harried and wished to return home but
did not have sufficient funds for this purpose. Webb's
letter continued:

> I very respectfully submit that the method
> which, as above mentioned, is being employed
> in dealing with this matter is little short
> of a scandal. These people have been allowed
> to land here and so far as they confine
> themselves to the lawful business of showmen
> they would appear to be within their rights
> in travelling through the country. If
> however they break the law they will I presume
> be punished by some other means than that of
> battledore and shuttlecock between the counties.

139

His letter went on:

> It is perhaps not for me to suggest any
> alternative course but it does seem to me
> that it would be more in accordance with
> the dignity of this country if they could
> be sent back even at the public expense,
> to their own country.   22

Consequent upon such developments discussions were soon
taking place between the Home Office and the police.   Home
Office opinion clearly showed that a number of delicate
issues were involved.   If it were true, as Webb suggested,
that the Gypsies wanted to leave Britain, enquiries had to
be started to ascertain to which country they should be sent
and whether that country would receive them.   Whatever was
done, the implications of any decisions had to be kept in
mind since the attitude of the British government towards the
dumping of unwanted nationals of other countries was involved.
These issues which were now exercising the police and the
government arose through the presence of a minority which had
not broken any immigration regulations by entering the country,
and one which had to be treated carefully from the angle of
precedent.[23]

It was soon ascertained that the Dutch authorities would
not re-admit the Gypsies: the police in Rotterdam had
provided the Gypsies with passage money to allow them to
enter Britain and they were in no mood to take back their
human exports.[24]   But it was then discovered that the
Gypsies were in fact German and that they had very few funds
of their own.[25]   At this point, therefore, attention turned
in the direction of the German consul.   Enquiries started to
be made about possible help from this quarter and a degree of
urgency was injected into the situation by the arrest of
Adolph Ficker, the leader of the Gypsies, on a warrant of
cruelty, which had been issued at the insistence of the
Society for the Prevention of Cruelty to Animals.   It was

transmitted to the Home Office that if the Gypsies were to
leave the country no evidence would be offered against him.[25]

But the problem remained complicated. Although the
Gypsies could be identified as German, it was pointed out
that there was an agreement between the British and German
authorities - which had been invoked more than once - that
each would care for destitute nationals of the other within
its borders and it could be argued that there was consequently
no lever which could be used against the German authorities in
order to secure the deportation of the Gypsies. On the other
hand, it was believed by one Home Office official that the
British government appeared to have some cause for complaint
against the Dutch, if the actions of the Netherlands government had been properly reported. Gypsies with German
passports had been allowed to pass through Holland and take
passage to England but permission was being refused to return
the same way. Elsewhere in the Home Office it was believed
that the Foreign Office ought to be drawn into the problem in
order to deal with the Dutch and German governments and the
same official doubted, while recommending this action, that
the British government had any grounds to support a protest
either to the Dutch or German authorities.[27]

A Foreign Office opinion, expressed on 16 January 1905,
was that the Dutch and German governments had not been
provided with all the evidence which they needed if they were
going to co-operate.[28] But the Home Office managed to achieve
very little when it did spell out the problems to the German
and Dutch representatives.[29] It was not until February 1905
that significant developments began to take place. The
Hertfordshire Constabulary had suggested that a voluntary
organisation, the Society of Friends of Foreigners in Distress
(SFFD) might undertake the arrangements for the transport of
the Gypsies to Germany. In a letter of 1 February, which
was forwarded by the Commissioner of Police to the Home Office,

the SFFD indicated that, together with the German Benevolent
Society, it had decided to make arrangements for the return
of the Gypsies to Germany.[30] The Society had arranged to
despatch the party almost straightaway from London to
Cologne via Hull and Hamburg and had also provided for the
reconveyance to Britain of any persons whom the German
authorities might reject. The Home Office understood that
the German Consul had not been very sympathetic in the matter
and had suggested possible difficulties about readmission
into Germany.[31] Nevertheless, it was reported shortly
afterwards that on 8 February the Gypsies had left Great
Central Station for Grimsby en route for Hamburg with
Cologne as their ultimate destination. 'So far so good', a
Home Office minute commented and, at the same time, said that
the police should be complimented on a discreet and well-
planned action.[32] The problem of the Gypsies seemed to have
been solved without the need for governmental involvement.

With the Gypsies safely back in Germany, the first stage
of the German Gypsy question and the authorities' response to
it might be regarded as over. But the problem did not go
away. Soon the Scottish Office sent to the Home Office a
report from the Procurator Fiscal of Perthshire giving details
of eighty German Gypsies in that county. The report of 14
April 1906 spelt out that the Gypsies could hardly be proceeded
against by the 1905 Aliens Act which had been passed after the
first stage of the German Gypsy problem had been settled.
None of the band had been convicted of any crime warranting
imprisonment; none of them had received parochial relief;
it could not be said that they were without means of subsistence.
Furthermore, the provisions of the third section of the 1905
act, which allowed for the deportation of undesirable immigrants,
scarcely seemed applicable to a band of people in which there
may have been forty adults and as many children.[33] The hopes
which the Home Office had entertained that the 1905 act would

142

easily take care of the Gypsy problem were proving ill-founded.[34]   Indeed, in addition to the problems raised by the Procurator Fiscal, the Home Office realised that none of the ships which landed the Gypsies in Britain constituted an immigrant ship within the meaning of the 1905 act and, to make matters worse, the Home Office had reason to believe that the trade in Gypsies was being carefully organised in Hamburg.[35]

This second wave of German Gypsies attracted more attention than the earlier influx.   In fact, in 1906 the newspapers were constantly reporting the progress of the Gypsy bands,[36] in the course of which it was indicated on a number of occasions that Gypsy groups found themselves in conflict with various local populations.   In April 1906, for instance, a party 'camped on Bannockburn Green'[37] and such an action stirred certain Scottish hearts.   'When I tell your lordships', Lord Balfour of Burleigh told the House of Lords, 'that they even encamped upon the historic plains of Bannock-burn the House will understand how much feeling in the locality was stirred.'[38]   But it was not only in Scotland, the major landing place for the immigrants, that hostility could manifest itself.   On 8 August 1906 it was reported that the German Gypsies had camped at Thornton, midway between Fleetwood and Blackpool in Lancashire, following which a number of police with 200 workmen from the Alkali Works pulled down the canvas screens and dragged the vans into the road.   The police and the men then drove the 'gang' out of the field, and when the women in the Gypsy party lay down they were carried from the site.   Finally, after this assault, the police attempted to pacify the leader of the Gypsies by refunding the amount he had paid for the rent of the field.   Soon afterwards when the Gypsies turned up at Preston they were hustled across the Ribble Bridge into Penwortham, and there was apparently another clash with the

police at Warrington which forced the band to proceed to
Manchester.[39]   There was similar evidence of police
hostility in the Midlands and even tension between different
forces over police action.   The Warwickshire police, for
example, took great exception to the activity of the
Leicestershire force in driving the Gypsies across county
boundaries.[40]   Still in the Midlands, the Chief Constable
of Northampton made no attempt to disguise his assessment of
the problem when he wrote to the Home Office on 30 November
1906.   To him the Gypsies were an intolerable nuisance.
They were, he commented, 'a most objectionable band to have
roaming about the Country - they are apparently in possession
of some means but to a great extent they live by masterful
begging and thieving when they can.'   In short, he regarded
them as 'a standing menace to law and order'.[41]

However, not everyone perceived a problem along these
lines.   The Gypsy Lore Society took a keen interest in
monitoring the journeyings of the Gypsies, and John Sampson,
a well-known student of Gypsy life, used their presence to
extend his knowledge of Gypsy culture.[42]   But opposition was
more the order of the day and Sampson commented that even the
English Gypsies approved of police action against the German
newcomers, presumably fearing that their presence might
activate hostility towards the local Gypsy population.   More
significant was the opposition which manifested itself in
Parliament.   Lord Balfour of Burleigh, whose concern over the
encampment at Bannockburn we have already noticed, complained
that the Gypsies found the country 'such a land of promise
that they circulated reports of their prosperity' and thereby
encouraged others to come to the country.[44]   And this opinion
was soon being reflected by Mr Mitchell-Thomson, the MP for
Lanarkshire North West, as well as Claude Hay, the Tory member
for Shoreditch Hoxton, who had played a part in earlier issues
relating to alien immigration.[45]   Very soon these opposing

voices were joined by Anthony Fell, the Tory MP for Yarmouth
and Sir Howard Vincent, the member for Sheffield Central, both
of whom, like Hay, had interested themselves in the earlier
battles over alien immigration.[46]   'How are we to get rid of
these wretched people?', Vincent asked in the House.[47]   What
arrangements could be made 'for their deportation to the lands
whence they came?'[48]   Such clamant forces were also joined
by Major Evans-Gordon, the member for Stepney, who had
organised the parliamentary opposition to Jewish immigration.[49]

It was in this kind of atmosphere that government policy
evolved towards the Gypsy problem.   One of the earliest
measures involved action against James Currie and Company of
Leith in Scotland.   In a letter from the Home Office on 5
May 1906 the firm was told that in the event of further
passengers of the class of German Gypsies being brought into
Britain in their ships, the Secretary of State would be
obliged to consider the question of reducing, in the case of
Currie's ships, the number of alien steerage passengers who
determined the status of an immigrant ship under the 1905
Aliens Act.   In its reply on 8 May the company asked for
guidance in the matter, arguing that only 'a strong and precise
expression of the Government's desire could justify the refusal
of a passage to persons prepared to pay the ordinary fare'.[50]
In the event the government went ahead and, in the case of
Currie's ships, reduced the number of steerage passengers
required for classification as an immigrant ship from twenty
to two.   Currie's expressed surprise at the action which it
described as unnecessary and oppressive.[51]   But taking action
to prevent British ships engaging in the traffic of Gypsies
from Germany did not solve the problem.   Following this, in
response to pressure from various sources, the government
began to move towards action which would remove the Gypsies
from Britain.

In order to achieve this the government turned to the

police. In a letter of 14 November 1906 to all chief constables in areas through which the Gypsies were likely to
pass, Herbert Gladstone, the Home Secretary, stated that the
only direct power which the government possessed for the
departure of these aliens was contained in Section 3 of the
1905 Aliens Act, which allowed for the deportation of
undesirable aliens.[52] Up to the despatch of the letter only
one case had fallen into this category and it was recognised
that this procedure was likely to operate only very slowly.
The letter continued: 'and observing that it has been stated
that the Gipsies are now anxious to leave the United Kingdom
he thinks that it would be well to give them all possible
assistance and inducement to carry out their desire'. In
view of the harassment to which they were subjected it is
hardly surprising that the Gypsies wanted to leave the
country, but this still left unanswered the question how this
was to be achieved. In this respect, encouragement was
given to the suggestion that the police should strive to
congregate the Gypsies in Hull or Grimsby as a prelude to
their deportation. Gladstone's letter also made it clear
that the chief constables of Hull and Grimsby should assist
in every way the Gypsies who arrived within their jurisdiction
for the purpose of leaving the country, to the extent of
supplying any money they needed for their passage. The
Home Office made it clear that any sums would be reimbursed.[53]

After police action of this kind the actual transference
of the Gypsies to Germany once again fell to the SFFD.[54] A
small party was admitted in early November and the organised
exodus took place at the end of the month.[55] The total cost
of the action was estimated by W.J. Cable of the Society at
£500-£600, and by the end of the year the government was able
to compliment itself upon an action which had led to the
German Gypsies being returned into the heart of Germany. An
unofficial letter of thanks went to the chief constables of

Dumfries, Hull and Grimsby as well as to the SFFD, which
also received a cheque to cover the cost of its expenses.[56]
Once more the government had been able to engage in a
discreet handling of its Gypsy problem.

So much for the details of events between 1904 and 1906.
In considering the episode it soon becomes apparent that the
German Gypsy question cannot be discussed as an isolated
case study: it needs to be placed within the context of the
wider discussion over alien immigration which was taking
place in British society.   In effect, this public debate
was mainly concerned with Jewish immigrants, but those whose
voices were prominently raised in this connection were also
vociferous in the debate over the Gypsy question.   Claude
Hay, Anthony Fell, Sir Howard Vincent and Major Evans-Gordon
were among the leaders of the anti-Jewish immigration lobby
and they, we have noticed, turned their attention towards
the German Gypsies.[57]   In the second 'invasion' they
envisaged an opportunity to test the 1905 Aliens Act and
secure a tightening in its provisions.   The original act
had specified that an immigrant ship was one which was
carrying twenty steerage passengers, but this definition
could be varied at the discretion of the minister concerned,
and Ackers Douglas, the Conservative Home Secretary, had
fixed the number at twelve.[58]   As we noticed, in the case of
James Currie of Leith, the Liberal Home Secretary, Herbert
Gladstone, who succeeded Douglas at the Home Office after the
Conservative defeat in the 1906 election, was prepared to
reduce the number down to two, and this was quickly seized
upon by the anti-immigration lobby, so that on announcing
his decision in the House Gladstone was asked by Claude Hay
whether he would reduce to two the number for vessels
entering the Port of London.   Predictably, Gladstone replied,
'No Sir: but if I am told there is any necessity I will look

147

into the question.' Here we can detect an attempt to drive the wedge of an argument towards the centre.[59] A similar strategy was also apparent at a later stage when Howard Vincent, after noting that the German Gypsies had been deported, asked Gladstone whether he would introduce legislation to prevent any renewed entry into the country and whether he would instruct the Immigration Board not to admit them again. Gladstone did not have to be the most astute Home Secretary to realise what lay behind this question and his reply, 'My hon. friend knows that I have no power to do that', is hardly surprising.[60] Responses to the Gypsies could be used as precedents in the major campaign against Jewish immigration. In short, the debate over the Gypsy question witnessed the concerted action of anti-alien forces, at a time when alien immigration issues were in the air, to exploit the Gypsy 'invasion' in order to secure a tighter measure of control over the entry of immigrants into Britain. However, although anti-alien agitation continued after 1906, it did not direct itself significantly towards Gypsies, even though small transient bands came and went.[61] In 1907, for instance, Servian groups, about whom reports were made at frequent intervals, appeared in Britain.[62] And sightings of these bands, with their bears, donkeys, monkeys and scantily clad children passing through England and Scotland, sometimes under the influence of police harassment, were still being made in the following year.[63] In 1909, by contrast, it was reported that the British Isles had been 'very little troubled by the presence of foreign Gypsies' but Britain did find itself attracting the Gypsy coppersmiths who wandered through Western Europe between 1911 and 1913 and whose culture was a source of delight to the Gypsy Lore Society.[64] None of these groups seems to have been large and none received the attention which attached itself to the German Gypsies between 1904 and 1906 in the face of an organised export

148

trade in Gypsies and in the midst of the debate surrounding
the Aliens Act of 1905.   It was in such circumstances that
a small-scale issue - the German Gypsies in Britain between
1904 and 1906 hardly numbered 200 - could assume a transient
significance.   It was the context of the immigration debate
which guaranteed that attention was directed towards the
Gypsy newcomers rather than towards the local Gypsy population.

Although the responses to the German Gypsies need to be
considered within the context of the 1904-6 debate over alien
immigration which, it might be emphasised again, was chiefly
related to Jews, the experience of the Gypsies differed
markedly from that of the Jewish immigrants.   Nobody attempted
to shunt Jews across county boundaries as they did the Gypsies.[65]
Nobody arranged for the deportation of the Jewish immigrants,
even if exclusion was advocated in some circles.[66]   The
'greeners' from Russian Poland found a Jewish community which,
with whatever hesitancy, provided help and a base from which
they could adjust to British society.   Nothing comparable
awaited the Gypsies on their arrival in Britain.   Indeed,
where could the Gypsies have found their advocates?   Certainly
not in Parliament where cries were raised for their deportation
and an active defence was conspicuous by its absence: there
was in fact a striking contrast between parliamentary reactions
to Jewish immigration and the responses displayed towards the
Gypsy influx.[67]   The sentiments present among the intellectuals
who constituted the Gypsy Lore Society, who viewed the Gypsy
as a primitive who should not be chained by civilisation, were
hardly likely to advance the German Gypsy case with the
authorities.[68]

In fact, once under way the German Gypsy issue revealed
the limits of toleration in British society.   There is a
powerful strand of opinion which would claim that Britain
possesses a measured, civilised, tolerant system of social
behaviour which is reflected in the treatment of minorities.

It is of course perfectly true that in comparison with their experiences in a number of other states minorities in Britain have been relatively well treated. But one must be careful in relating this to a British tradition as if Britons are all heirs to some kind of special conditioning process. A continuity of the political system in the absence of strains which have been apparent in some other societies, such as Czarist Russia and Nazi Germany, has guaranteed protection for some minorities, but this should not encourage us to place on one side in casual or convenient fashion the long tradition of hostility towards a wide range of newcomers which has also been present in British society. The treatment of the Gypsies reveals the other side of the coin to that of the state as the guardian of tolerance. The state is in fact likely to encourage the settlement of minorities and to protect those groups whose interests are perceived as coinciding with those of the state. If they diverge, and particularly if the minority is weak and powerless, liberal tolerance can be forgotten. The treatment of the Gypsies which resulted in their being hounded until they were ready to return to Europe and the careful preparations of the state to arrange this, provide a stark contrast with the reactions displayed towards other minorities such as the German clerks and the Jewish immigrants from Russian Poland.[69] Further, the relations between the police and the German Gypsies, in particular the driving of the Gypsies over county boundaries and the forcible break-up of Gypsy encampments, throws into sharp relief the relations between the police and the Jewish immigrants who were simultaneously arriving in England.[70]

Such developments, to which reference has just been made, occurred at a time of a major Gypsy movement in Europe, which has been likened to that which manifested itself centuries before when Gypsies thrust themselves into the European consciousness.[71] At this later time Gypsies were often

moving as a response to persecution and the attempts to achieve
a tighter control over their lives, which were in evidence in
Europe in the decade before the Great War. Sympathisers with
the Gypsies could refer to 'this present international movement for the repression of the Gypsy race' and draw attention
to earlier repressive measures which had failed to solve 'the
Gypsy problem'.[72] It was not merely Germany which was
attempting to tighten its hold over its Gypsy population at
this time.[73] Similar measures were being debated in France
where suggestions were being made for their expulsion from the
country and where in 1912 Gypsies were obliged to carry special
identification papers.[74] Around the same time there were
also proposals in Britain to subject the local Gypsy population,
unofficially estimated at 12,000, to an increasing degree of
social control as evidenced in the Moveable Dwellings Bill,
which would have provided for the registration and regulation
of moveable dwellings and the enforcement of the school
attendance of children living in such accommodation. Suggested
doubtless from the best of motives, it was opposed in the Gypsy
Lore Society, where the proposal was described as one which
required 'careful watching on the part of those who, in
upholding the liberty of the subject, do not exclude the Gypsies
from the social community'. The danger, it was asserted, lay
'in every attempt, overt or secretly astute, to force the
Romany people to change their whole system of living, to cage
these freedom-loving children and to deteriorate the race
through the foisting of modes of existence unnatural to them'.[75]
Such pressures were believed by the Gypsies and Gypsy sympathisers
to be on the increase in the years immediately preceding the
First World War and it is also against this wider context, as
well as within the narrower ambience of the national debate
over immigration that the German Gypsy question in Britain
should be considered.

In brief, the German Gypsy question in Britain, although

a minor episode in itself, raises a number of important issues
which have a relevance to the debate over immigration into
Britain in the late nineteenth and early twentieth centuries.[76]
It also needs to be placed within the context of the wider
attempt to control Gypsy life which was apparent in Europe
just before the Great War. Through the combined agencies
of immigration legislation, the help of voluntary organisations
and, doubtless, through the testimony of the German Gypsies
themselves, who would be in a position to disabuse their
fellow Gypsies of the belief that Britain was a land of promise,
the problem was short-lived. But the episode almost certainly
had longer-term consequences. Forty years later the whole
nature and dimension of the Gypsy question had changed. By
then half a million Gypsies had been systematically exterminated,
and we might end in sombre mood by reminding ourselves that
some of those who were harassed through Edwardian Britain,
together with their children, would no doubt eventually
encounter a more savage and final response at the hands of
the persecuting Gaujo.[77]

NOTES

1. Michael D. Biddiss, Father of Racist Ideology: The Social
and Political Thought of Count Gobineau (1970), pp. 103-11.

2. Stanley Lieberson, 'A Societal Theory of Race and Ethnic
Relations', American Sociological Review (henceforth Am. Soc.
Rev.), 26 (1961), pp. 902-10, contains some useful discussion
on racial and ethnic conflict situations.

3. The economic arguments tend to have greater emphasis placed
upon them. See Marios Nikolinakos, 'Notes on an Economic
Theory of Racism', Race, 14 (1973), pp. 365-81: Edna Bonacich,
'A Theory of Ethnic Antagonism: The Split Labor Market', Am.
Soc. Rev. 37 (1972), pp. 547-59 and idem, 'A Theory of
Middleman Minorities', Am. Soc. Rev. 38 (1973), pp. 583-94.
Lieberson in Am. Soc. Rev. 26 takes a wider view.

4. The quotation is from Parallel Miracles or the Jews and
the Gypsies (1830) by Samuel Roberts. For Roberts see my

152

condensed essay in Sidney Pollard and Colin Holmes (eds.),
Essays in the Economic and Social History of South Yorkshire
(Barnsley, 1977), pp. 233-46. The early history of the
Gypsies in Europe is discussed in J.P. Clébert, The Gypsies
(1963), pp. 29ff. and Donald Kenrick and Gratton Puxon, The
Destiny of Europe's Gypsies (1972), pp. 13-56. Brian Vesey-
Fitzgerald, Gypsies of Britain: An Introduction to their
History (1944 and 1973), provides useful background reading.
In the late nineteenth century Sir Richard Burton claimed that
it was he rather than the French scholar, Bataillard, who
first discovered the Indian origins of the Gypsies. See the
essay in his posthumous work, The Jew, the Gypsy and El Islam
(1898).

5. C.H. Firth (ed.), Scotland and the Commonwealth: Letters
and Papers relating to the Military Government of Scotland
(Edinburgh, 1895), pp. 28-9.

6. Kenrick and Puxon, Europe's Gypsies, ch. 2 passim. See
also C.J.R. Turner, A History of Vagrants and Vagrancy (1887),
pp. 483-505.

7. See W.M. Adams, 'The Wandering Tribes of Great Britain',
Cassell's Family Magazine (1883), p. 730 and the discussion
by Judith Okely in Farnham Rehfisch, Gypsies, Tinkers and
Other Travellers (1975), pp. 66-8.

8. David Martin, 'Hard Travelling', The Times Literary
Supplement, 2 January 1976, p. 2. Comments made in the course
of a review article on a number of new books on Gypsies
including Rehfisch, Gypsies: Barbara Adams, Judith Okely,
David Morgan and David Smith, Gypsies and Government Policy in
England (1976) and E.B. Trigg, Gypsy Demons and Divinities
(1976).

9. The Spectator (vol. 2, 1827), p. 319. See also W. Ellis,
'The Nuisance and Prejudice of the Gypsy Vagrant', quoted by
Okely in Rehfisch, Gypsies p. 57 for a similar eighteenth
century view and Clarion, 19 August 1910, for a later summary
of such a position.

10. Goldwin Smith, 'The Jewish Question', in his Questions of
the Day (1893), p. 252.

11. Kenrick and Puxon, Europe's Gypsies p. 41.

12. E.B. Trigg, 'Magic and Religion among the Gipsies of
Britain' (unpub. D.Phil. thesis, University of Oxford, 1967),
p. 414. See his Gypsy Demons and Divinities for a more
accessible statement of his views.

13. C. Duff, in his introduction to Clébert, Gypsies, p.v.

14. Sir Walter Gilbey and E.D. Cuming, George Morland, His Life and Works (1907), pp. 102, 124, 130, 224.

15. John Rothenstein, Augustus John (n.d.), pp. 11-12 and plates 68 and 78. See also 'Russian Gypsies at Marseilles and Milan' by Augustus John in Journal of the Gypsy Lore Society (henceforth Jo. Gy. Lore Society), 4, pp. 48-9 and and 356-9. John was for a time president of the Gypsy Lore Society.

16. If one can withstand the hagiography, Dr Dora Yates: An Appreciation (Liverpool, n.d.), by Eleanor Bradburn, provides some information on those involved in the early days of the Society. See also Dora E. Yates, My Gypsy Days (1953). Clébert, Gypsies pp. 91-5 discusses the romantic conception of Gypsies and 'Our Gypsy Visitors', by C. Stein in Baily's Magazine of Sports and Pastimes, 70 (1898), pp. 17-23, offers a nostalgic account of Gypsy life around the time that the Gypsy Lore Society was founded. It needs to be said that it was not unusual to find a romantic attraction towards Gypsies co-existing with a rejection of what were perceived as essential aspects of Gypsy life and the Gypsy personality. See C.G. Leland, The Gypsies (1874), p. 116, where at the side of the picturesque account of Gypsy life, the same could be described as 'one greasy lie'. See also Louis James, Fiction for the Working Man 1830-1850 (1963), p. 105, for the mixture of allure and fear in the Gypsy stereotype. Much later the same is apparent in D.H. Lawrence's The Virgin and the Gipsy. For some discussion of mixed stereotypes see Colin Holmes (ed.), Immigrants and Minorities in British Society (1978), pp. 142-3.

17. Edwin Hodder, George Smith (of Coalville) (1896), pp. 140-1.

18. Hodder, Smith, is useful on Smith's work. See also Gypsy Life (1880), I've Been a Gipsying (1883), Our Canal, Gipsy Van and other Travelling Children etc. (1888) and Gypsy Children (1889). See Thomas Acton, 'The Development of the Gaujo Conscience 1816-1936', in his Gypsy Politics and Social Change (1974), pp. 103-28, for the context of late-nineteenth and early twentieth-century reform developments.

19. J. Hoyland, A Historical Survey of the Customs, Habits and Present State of the Gypsies (York, 1816), p. 191. The autobiography of a famous convert to Christianity is Gipsy Smith, His Life and Work by Himself (n.d.).

20. Trigg, thesis, p. 417.

21. Public Record Office, Home Office, H.O. 45/10313/124855/1.

22. H.O. 45/10313/124855/3. See The Spectator 18 December 1897, pp. 894-5, for evidence of earlier hostility in Surrey towards English gypsies. The Surrey authorities clearly regarded the 'wandering tribes' as a social irritant.

23. H.O. 45/10313/124855/4.

24. H.O. 45/10313/124855/6.

25. H.O. 45/10313/124855/8.

26. H.O. 45/10313/124855/8. A few years before, allegations in Staffordshire involving a member of a racial minority and cruelty towards animals had resulted in the Edalji case. See the convenient summary in Douglas Johnson, France and the Dreyfus Affair (1966), pp. 5-7.

27. H.O. 45/10313/124855/9.

28. H.O. 45/10313/124855/14.

29. H.O. 45/10313/124855/14 for the Home Office note of exasperation.

30. H.O. 45/10313/124855/19 and /18.

31. Minute on file H.O. 45/10313/124855/18.

32. H.O. 45/10313/124855/19. Public Record Office, Metropolitan Police, MEPOL, 2/705, Report from Albany Street Police Station, gives a good account of the departure.

33. H.O. 45/10313/124855/25. Lord Tweedmouth, speaking in the Lords on behalf of the Government said 'It is true that they have, after the fashion of the gipsies been guilty of petty larcenies, but the offences have not been of a serious character.' He also noted that they could earn £3 to £5 per day by giving acrobatic performances. Hansard, 4th series, 1906, 156, p. 207.

34. H.O. 45/10313/124855/23.

35. H.O. 45/10313/124855/25.

36. Henry James Crofton, 'Affairs of Egypt 1892-1906'. Jo. Gy. Lore Society, 1 (April 1908), pp. 373-84, discusses these matters.

37. Ibid., p. 373.

38. <u>Hansard</u>, 4th series, 1906, 156, p. 206.

39. Crofton, <u>Jo. Gy. Lore Society</u> 1, pp. 380-1.

40. H.O. 45/10313/124855/77 and /79.

41. H.O. 45/10313/124855/83. See comment on the Northampton situation in Crofton, <u>Jo. Gy. Lore Society</u> 1, p. 383.

42. See John Sampson, 'The "German Gypsies" at Blackpool', <u>Jo. Gy. Lore Society</u>, 1 (October 1907), pp. 111-21. Sampson was University Librarian at Liverpool and a celebrated Gypsyologist. See Yates, <u>Gypsy Days</u>, for some reminiscences of Sampson.

43. Sampson, <u>Jo. Gy. Lore Society</u> 1, p. 120.

44. <u>Hansard</u>, 4th series, 1906, 156, p. 126.

45. Ibid., pp. 1482-3.

46. Ibid., 1906, 160, p. 1060 and ibid., 1906, 162, p. 1356.

47. Ibid., 1906, 162, p. 1357.

48. Ibid., 1906, 163, p. 1414.

49. Ibid., p. 1107.

50. H.O. 45/10313/124855/34.

51. H.O. 45/10313/124855/38. In H.O. 45/10313/124855/44 in a letter to the Home Office on 26 May 1906 Currie and Company said they had instructed agents in Hamburg not to accept alien Gypsies and to exercise extreme care in selecting other alien steerage passengers. In view of this they requested that the exceptional order be withdrawn. Gladstone ordered this on 8 June 1906.

52. As emphasised by Lord Tweedmouth in the first parliamentary debate on the matter see <u>Hansard</u>, 4th series, 1906, 156, p. 207.

53. H.O. 45/10313/124855/83. The question of payment for the passage had been regarded by the Home Office as crucial from an early date. See <u>Hansard</u>, 4th series, 1906, 160, p. 1061 and ibid., 1906, 162, p. 1357.

54. H.O. 45/10313/124855/104. W.J. Cable of the S.F.F.D. wrote to the Home Office on 27 November 1906, 'I have had to inform the postmaster in confidence the source from which the

expenses will be paid in order to dispel any doubts which he had'. The Home Office Papers make it clear that Gladstone did not tell the whole story to the House when he said that the S.F.F.D. 'by willing and effective action, which I think should be generally appreciated, arranged last week for the repatriation of the two large bands of Gypsies which have been wandering about the country for some time past'. The Times, 28 November 1908, did not know or did not tell the full story when it said that the fares to Germany were paid by the S.F.F.D.

55. The Times, 28 November 1906. H.O. 45/10313/124855/104 contains a letter from H.M. Customs at Newcastle to the Home Office, dated 13 November 1906, which indicated that a small party had sailed for Hamburg on 3 November.

56. H.O. 45/10313/124855/104.

57. See above for the anti-alien lobby. Willy Guy in Rehfisch, Gypsies p. 203, warns against discussing Gypsies in isolation from specific social contexts.

58. J.A. Garrard, The English and Immigration 1880-1910 (1971), p. 104, discusses the administration of the 1905 act by the Liberals.

59. Hansard, 4th series, 1906, 156, pp. 1482-3.

60. Ibid., 1906, 166, p. 749.

61. Garrard, Immigration, pp. 103-33; Bernard Gainer, The Alien Invasion (1972), pp. 199-215 and Colin Holmes, 'In Search of Sidney Street', Society for the Study of Labour History Bulletin, 29 (Autumn 1974), pp. 70-7, all refer to tensions after 1905.

62. Henry Thomas Crofton, 'Affairs of Egypt 1907', Jo. Gy. Lore Society, 2 (October 1908), pp. 132-3, although on p. 133 he noted a public escort for German Gypsies.

63. Henry Thomas Crofton, 'Affairs of Egypt 1908', in Jo. Gy. Lore Society, 3 (April 1910), pp. 287-8. See also The Times, 6 and 12 June 1908.

64. Thomas William Thompson, 'Affairs of Egypt 1909', Jo. Gy. Lore Society, 5 (October 1911) p. 128 refers to the falling off in the Gypsy influx. But see The Times, 20 February and 22 May 1909, as well as 13 May 1910, for continuing sensitivity. E.O. Winstedt, 'The Gypsy Coppersmiths' Invasion of 1911-13', Jo. Gy. Lore Society, 6 (1911-12), pp. 244-303, discusses later immigration. See also Gypsy Coppersmiths in Birkenhead and

<u>Liverpool</u> by Andreas (Mui Shuko), i.e. R. Scott Macfie
(Liverpool, 1913), a reference I owe to David Mayall.

65. See above, p. 143.

66. See Colin Holmes, <u>Anti-Semitism in British Society 1876-1939</u> (1979), ch. 7, for reference to exclusionist sentiment
before 1914.

67. Compare the account being presented here with the
parliamentary and other official responses to Jewish
immigration referred to in Garrard, <u>Immigration</u> and Gainer,
<u>Alien Invasion</u>.

68. Acton, <u>Gypsy Politics</u> pp. 121-2.

69. On the German clerks see G.L. Anderson, 'German Competition
in the Clerical Labour Market in Late-Victorian Britain', paper
given at the Society for the Study of Labour History Conference
in Sheffield, May 1978 and his revised paper in this volume.

70. J.J. Tobias, 'Police-Immigrant Relations in England 1880-1918', <u>New Community</u>, 3 (Summer 1974), p. 211-14, discusses in
outline fashion police relations with Jewish immigrants. The
image of Britain as a tolerant country is present in both major
parties in the current British debate over immigration. The
concept has also been used in the attempt to account for the
failure of fascist anti-semitism in the inter-war years. See
R.J. Benewick, <u>The Fascist Movement in Britain</u> (1972), ch. 1.
For a totally jaundiced, opposing view on our national tolerance
see M. Harrison, 'Gypsies', <u>Sunday Magazine</u>, 74 (1885), pp.
495-6.

71. Crofton in <u>Jo. Gy. Lore Society</u>, 1, p. 373. See also the
piece by Donald Macritchie in the <u>Scottish Review</u>, 26 April
1906 on 'A Gypsy Band in 1604', which was prompted by 'the
present interruption of German Gypsies in Scotland'. See also
<u>The Outlook</u>, 1 June 1907, pp. 721-2.

72. Walter M. Gallichan, 'The State Versus the Gypsy', <u>Jo. Gy.
Lore Society</u>, 1 (April 1908), p. 350 and the first article by
Dora Yates, 'Measures which failed', in ibid., pp. 393-7.

73. See <u>Encyclopaedia Britannica</u>, 11th ed. (1910-11), 12,
p. 40; Arthur Thesleff, 'Report on the Gypsy Problem', <u>Jo. Gy.
Lore Society</u>, 5 (1911-12), p. 91 and R. Breithaupt, <u>Die Zigeuner
und der deutsche Staat</u> (Würzburg, 1907), pp. 70-87, with its
references to the 'gypsy plague', and H. Mode and S. Wolffling,
<u>Zigeuner. Der Weg eines Volkes in Deutschland</u> (Leipzig, n.d.),
p. 168, for comment on the German situation.

74. Gallichan, Jo. Gy. Lore Society 1, pp. 353-6.   See also
Kenrick and Puxon, Europe's Gypsies pp. 49 and 55.

75. Gallichan in Jo. Gy. Lore Society 1, p. 357.   See Acton,
Gypsy Politics ch. 10 passim, for an account which is sympathetic to George Smith who was the leading proponent of
legislation to change Gypsy life through the agency of state
action.   Some reference to Gypsy movement in Britain, free
from state restrictions, is in Raphael Samuel, 'Comers and
Goers', in H.J. Dyos and Michael Wolff (eds.), The Victorian
City (2 vols., 1973), 1, pp. 123-60.   Encyclopaedia Britannica
11th ed. p. 37, gives an estimate of 12,000 for the Gypsy
population of Britain.

76. It is interesting to contrast the experiences of the
Gypsies not only with those of the Jewish immigrants (see
above n. 70) but also with other Germans in Britain.   On
this see Colin Holmes, 'Germans in Britain 1870-1914', in
J. Schneider, et al. (eds.) Wirtschaftskräfte und Wirtschaftswege.
Festschrift für Hermann Kellenbenz (5 vols., Nuremberg, 1978),
3, pp. 581-93.

77. Kenrick and Puxon, Europe's Gypsies takes the Holocaust
experience as the focal point of its discussion of Gypsy life
in Europe.

I should like to thank the Knoop Fund, University of Sheffield,
for financing the research on which this article is based.

7
Catholics and Socialists in Glasgow, 1906–1912

SHERIDAN GILLEY

Since 1789, for both social and intellectual reasons, the
Roman Catholic Church has been a conservative institution.
The ecclesiastical hierarchy was part of the old social order,
the faith was strongest among conservative peasants, and both
the European upper classes and the new romantic apologists
for Rome looked to reactionary religion to save them from
revolution. Yet circumstances also made Catholics rebels:
in Belgium, Poland, Ireland and Italy, a long line of turbulent
priests from Ventura and Lamennais to Patrick Lavelle embraced
the new ideas of the nineteenth century, and saw religion as
the cause of the people. By 1900 the emergence of political
parties representing organised labour posed the problem of
popular politics in a new form for the Church throughout the
Irish diaspora, in the industrial cities of Britain, North America
and Australasia. This challenge had, therefore, an international character, and a comparative study of the Cardinals
Gibbons, Manning and Moran of Baltimore, Westminster and
Sydney would show something of the nature and extent of the
Church's accommodation to the new movements of the urban
working class.[1] There was also an international aspect to
the difficulty which arose wherever these movements claimed
to be 'socialist', and to those controversies over the
meaning of 'socialism' which decided whether Catholics

160

could vote socialist or join socialist parties.

But just as 'socialism' changed its meaning from one
country to another, so there was a complex interaction in
Catholicism between international and local history. In the
nineteenth century, the Roman Church was centralised to a
hitherto unknown degree, and in the modern period has mirrored
the outlook of the reigning pope, from the Marian pietism of
Pius IX to the indecision of Paul VI. Ecclesiastical interest
in modern social questions began in the pontificate of Leo XIII,
an aristocratic liberal; the Church's social attitudes in the
years which concern us, 1906-1912, were dominated by the peasant
conservatism of St Pius X. Thus Catholic social reformers and
conservatives alike looked back to the Encyclicals of Leo for
guidance on issues ignored by Pio; above all to the Leonine
Encyclical Rerum Novarum of 1891, which condemned 'socialism'
while recommending social reform. By 'socialism', Leo meant
those revolutionary movements which sought to abolish private
property, and which on the continent were anti-religious; and
the revolutionary and anti-religious associations of 'socialism'
prejudiced loyal Catholics everywhere against it. It was
however unclear how far the Pope had condemned those forms of
British socialism which were gradualist, non-violent and not
irreligious. The matter was complex, for on religion, British
socialists were divided into three main schools which spent
much time disagreeing with one another: Christian Socialists,
who thought that Christianity implied socialism; secularist
socialists, for whom socialism meant the world's deliverance
from religion; and those neutral socialists who wanted to
keep religion and socialism apart.[2] So Catholics might argue
that a neutral or Christian Socialism was an extension of the
Leonine ideal of social reform, which welcomed trade unions
and state regulation of factory hours and wages, though
rejecting strikes and class warfare. Nor was it clear how
far the Encyclicals represented a massive claim by the Church

to political authority as guardian of the one true political philosophy. Thus in the local setting, the Church had freedom of manoeuvre, and every kind of parochial political and personal consideration might determine both the content of 'socialism', and whether the Church should oppose it.

The Church in Britain already offered Catholics some guidance on social questions. Romantic conservatives from the 1830s were devout believers in a largely imaginary vision of social harmony and cooperative effort which had flourished, they claimed, in the later middle ages. They regarded trade unions as medieval guilds, professed collectivist principles and rejected laissez-faire capitalism as the offspring of Protestant individualism and of the greed of the sixteenth-century reformers. These ideals influenced socialists from William Morris to R.H. Tawney; they formed the ideological substratum to all Catholic theorising about social questions, and underlay Catholic charity. More distinctly radical was the social activism of Cardinal Manning, Archbishop of Westminster from 1865. Manning supported trade unions and state regulation of factory conditions, defended the right of the starving to steal, and in his most famous gesture to the labour movement, resolved the Dock Strike of 1889. He did not profess any political philosophy, though he was called a Catholic Socialist. A narrower system of social ideas was propagated by the Catholic Truth Society, founded in 1884 by a convert London layman to publish Catholic propaganda. The Society's impact was enhanced by Jesuit support, and through the writings of C.S. Devas, called for trade unions, state protection of labour, the abolition of sweatshops and other factory legislation. This radicalism however had well-defined limits. Devas defined his ideal of Christian Democracy as any form of government which ruled in the interests of the people; but it might do so without manhood suffrage. Nor need Christian Democracy oppose inequality:

162

rather it attacked the abuse of inequality.[3]   In a pamphlet
of 1906, Devas sharpened the distinction between socialism
and social reform to show why Catholics could support many
socialist measures, but not on socialist principles.   He
also identified the anti-religious socialism condemned by the
Church: the German socialism of Marx and Bebel, the socialism
of Juares in France, of Vandervelde in Belgium and Ferri in
Italy; the British socialism of the aggressively anti-Christian
Robert Blatchford and his newspaper the Clarion, of the Social
Democratic Federation and of the Socialist Party of Great
Britain.[4]   The English organisations and personalities in
this list were in the secularist tradition; together they
made up a mighty obstacle to Catholics becoming socialists,
and seemed bound to blight the development of Catholic
socialism in Britain.

   Irish Catholicism abroad presented socialism with an even
more intractable problem, for the social attitudes of the
Irish diaspora were complicated as much by nationalism as by
religion.   Every Irish community had a double loyalty, to
Faith and Fatherland, which set Irishmen off from their non-
Catholic and non-Irish fellow countrymen in a pugnaciously
defensive posture equally reflected in polemic on behalf of
Catholic Truth, and gun-running for the Fenians.   The
enthusiasms lavished by Catholic newspapers in refuting No
Popery lectures and convent scandals were quite as much tribal
as religious, and these loves of Faith and Fatherland were
real enough: yet St Patrick's Day rhetoric barely concealed
the divisions within each Irish community.   If Irishmen
enjoyed their scraps with the Saxon, they were never happier
than when fighting other Irishmen.   The ideals of Faith and
Fatherland were ambiguous in themselves, and the resulting
conflicts made communal unity unreal.   The Irish in Glasgow
were typical in this: that in Glasgow as elsewhere, bishops
fought priests, laymen the clergy, the Church strove for and

against the varieties of nationalism, which in turn punched up one another. Thus the Irish in Glasgow in 1906 were already fragmented into sects. This fissiparous tendency in Irish Catholicism, its internal disintegration into sectarian parties, was a fact of life in the Glaswegian Catholic community.[5] To survive in this atmosphere, socialism had to become a sect, an excuse for Irish Catholics to be fighting one another.

Yet socialism had also to penetrate the impressive political and religious establishments of the city, the institutional achievement of half a century of effort by emigrants since the Great Famine. By 1908 the church claimed a Catholic population of 380,000 in Glasgow and the neighbouring industrial towns of Lanarkshire.[6] Some 60,000 Glaswegians were Irish-born; the great mass of them were very poor. Perhaps a fifth of Irish emigrants were Orangemen, who reinforced the anti-Catholic activities of the Scottish Calvinist churches. The confrontation of Orange and Green and seventy years of Protestant revival in the city had enhanced the Irish Catholics' separate sense of self-identity, and kept most of them Catholic. Yet even their Church had at first seemed alien to them, under the rule of Scottish bishops and priests who had aroused violent Irish immigrant opposition into the 1860s. The pope resolved the problem in 1869 by appointing as bishop the scion of an old English landed family, Charles Eyre. Eyre was raised to the rank of Archbishop of Glasgow in the Scottish hierarchy reconstituted in 1878, and during an episcopate of thirty-three years, spent his private fortune on his seminary, churches and charities, and still left £200,000 to his family. More remarkably, he kept the peace with his people by a strict self-rule of non-involvement in politics; and his circumspection passed to John McGuire, his coadjutor from 1894, and his successor from 1902. In background, McGuire was Glaswegian, the son of poor immigrants

164

from Ireland; he was a warm and brilliant orator and excellent
administrator who played it cool. From 1912 he was intermittently insane: but by then he had set his stamp on the
Church's public attitude to labour in the city, as one of
careful temporisation between rival points of view.

McGuire presided over the self-enclosed social world in
which the Church had duplicated every movement of Protestant
and secular social service and charity. There were ninety-
one parishes in the archdiocese, 271 priests, and more than
50,000 school children on the rolls of its poor schools,
which employed over 1,200 teachers.[7] High schools for the
small Catholic middle class were conducted by Jesuits,
Marists and the secular clergy, and by a number of orders of
nuns, who also ran the teachers' training college, a refuge
for destitute children, industrial schools, orphanages,
reformatories, hospitals, old peoples homes, a deaf-and-dumb
institution, hostels for working girls and friendless women,
a home for training domestics and two more for rescuing
prostitutes. There were two industrial schools and a
reformatory for boys, and a centre from which trained nurses
went out to nurse the sick poor in their own homes, which
like the other charities had its own social context: busy
auxiliary committees of patrons, lay helpers, and an annual
bazaar.[8]

This was ambulance work to the human wreckage thrown up
by the Industrial Revolution; the Church's other favoured
social method was that of self-help by mutual aid in community.
Nearly every parish had its own working men's conference of
the Society of St Vincent de Paul, which raised 6,000 pounds
a year for local poor relief.[9] Most parishes had either a
Catholic Benefit Society or branch of the Irish National
Foresters, which claimed over 22,000 members in western
Scotland in 1907.[10] There were the temperance associations
of the League of the Cross, Catholic Young Men's societies,

dramatic societies and billiards and football clubs, the
latter usually affiliated to the famous Celtic club, founded
by a brother of the Society of Mary in 1887 to raise money
for the free breakfasts provided by the St Vincent de Paul
for poor school children.[11]   These institutions overlapped
with one another: the football clubs tended to be temperance
associations, and their members might also belong to one of
the many guilds and brotherhoods dedicated to Our Lady or the
Blessed Sacrament. Each had its little local hierarchy of
officials, and a following who doubtless found in their
special devotions, small sphere of authority and distinctive
uniform, ribbon, or scapular a reinforcement of their sense
of self-identity and worth in a bleak and hungry world.

Presiding over all was the parish priest, invariably
declared in the Catholic press to be 'popular' with his
people. But whether in choir dress or in the papal court
robes of a protonotary or monsignor, or in frock coat and
top hat or cassock and biretta, he was also a figure of
authority, and there are paradoxical elements of fear and
love in this authoritarian power. Nonetheless his setting
was the popular one of the understaffed overcrowded parochial
school, the billiards club and benefit society, while the
faith he represented was popular at the deeper level of
those hundreds of tiny sums acknowledged week by week in the
Catholic press, of donations for St Anthony's bread to
convents which kept lamps burning before the statues of the
saints, for donors whose prayers encompassed all the hopes
and fears of the humble. This was a state of mind which
socialist doctrine could only enter with difficulty.
Catholics thought of themselves as Catholics first, not as
members of a wider working class, and their sense of need
for local community was fulfilled by the parish church.

But the community had other heroes, the politicians who

served the Fatherland. Glasgow Irish politics was nationalist, and by far the largest nationalist body was the United Irish League, which, reinvigorated by recruitment after 1898, directed the Irish vote at the behest of the Irish party in the Commons. Because of poverty only a tenth of the Irish community even managed to vote; but in at least four of the parliamentary constituencies in the Glasgow area, they formed more than 10 per cent of the electorate, and their support was worth seeking.[12] The largest component of the United Irish League in the city was the Home Rule branch, which was at loggerheads with the principal Scottish Catholic newspaper, the Glasgow Observer, one of a chain of twenty-two Irish Catholic newspapers published by the Scottish Catholic Printing House, founded in 1887 by Charles Diamond, a Newcastle Catholic journalist. Diamond and the Observer's editor, D.J. Mitchel Quin were teetotal and puritan where the Home Rule branch was dominated by publicans; both however preached loyalty to the diktat of the Irish MPs, and were opposed to Sinn Fein, which, with half a dozen branches around Glasgow from 1906, offered Irishmen a nationalist alternative to the parliamentary tradition.[13]

Just as delicate was the relationship between the nationalists and the clergy, who suspected Sinn Fein of anti-clericalism, and in 1899 had actually banned another nationalist organisation and insurance club, the Ancient Order of Hibernians, which was allegedly less concerned with insurance than with secret political intrigue. In 1905, the Order expelled its extreme political components, and became a more exclusively benefit society. The Glasgow Observer and even priests attacked the ban still upon it. One clergyman claimed that his best parishioners belonged to the order, few denied them communion and in 1909 the prohibition was abolished.[14] Still this phase of the history of the A.O.H. has left some evidence of conflict between priest and people and of popular dislike

of the clergy.[15]   There were also tensions between the
Church and the United Irish League. The Irish Party generally
told the Irish in Britain to vote Liberal, because the Liberals
supported Home Rule. But Irishmen voted in School Board
elections as Catholics, under the direction of the 'Catholic
Union', to maintain their separate schools; and the divided
loyalty to Fatherland and Faith was sorely tried after 1906
when the Liberal government promoted legislation hostile to
Catholic education. The upshot was that after 1906, at by-
elections in Manchester and Dumfries, the Church divided the
Irish electorate by urging its flock to vote Tory. The Irish
party raised howls of rage; their argument, as Diamond and
Quin hammered it home in the Observer, was that the Irish
parliamentary party was the sole guardian of Catholic
educational interests, and that the Church had no choice but
to trust the Irish party to uphold them, whatever Liberal
measures might be. As John Dillon said in an address to
Diamond's jubilee dinner in 1909, after the election at
Dumfries, the Church could state the principles of Catholic
political action, but it was for the laity to apply them:
had not the priesthood's efforts as politicians destroyed
Catholic education and charity in France?[16]   Here then, was
another reason for McGuire's desire to keep the Church out of
politics, and for restraining the clergy from denouncing
socialist parties as distinct from socialist principles. To
do so would move the Church beyond the spiritual sphere to
which Irish politicians wished to confine it, by reserving
politics for laymen.

        As Glasgow Irish politics was dominated by religion and
nationalism, labour organisations could only win political
support with the active good will of the United Irish League
and of the Glasgow Observer, and the acquiescence of the
Church. There was one such opening in 1906, when the League,
the Irish MPs and Observer supported the candidature of G.N.

Barnes of the Independent Labour Party in the Blackfriars
(Gorbals) constituency. Barnes was a distinctly moderate
politician; he cultivated warm relations with the Irish in
the area, and held the seat until his retirement from
parliament in 1922.[17] His was an isolated achievement.
Despite the many Labour successes in England in 1906, Barnes
and Wilkie in Dundee were the only Labour candidates elected
to parliament from Scotland, and the Irish party continued
until the First World War to direct the Irish vote in
Scotland to the Liberals. The other socialist bodies in
the city were tiny: the Social Democratic Federation and the
Socialist Labour Party consisted mostly of skilled working men,
of whom few were Irish, and despite James Connolly, they
attracted few Irishmen.[18] The Glasgow Observer was in
sympathy with more moderate manifestations of Labour politics,
but the general Irish movement to the Labour Party in Glasgow
only came after the collapse of the pre-war structure of Irish
politics in Britain, through the Liberal government's suppression
of the Easter Rising and the subsequent disgrace of the Irish
MPs. Thus Labour politics in Glasgow before 1914 was of
secondary interest to the Irish in the city; and Catholic
Labour politicians had to struggle for a hearing for as long
as Faith and Fatherland came first.

Yet that movement began in the first decade of the
twentieth century in the conversion to socialism of Irish
Catholics who had been reared as Nationalists and Liberals.
The chief of these was John Wheatley, a miner's son from the
village of Ballieston near Glasgow.[19] Born in 1869, he
became president in 1898 of the Shettleston branch of the
United Irish League. He was a socialist by conviction in
1906, when though not a member of any socialist party, he
acted as polling agent for a Labour candidate in North West
Lanarkshire. Wheatley joined the Independent Labour Party
in 1907, entered parliament as member for Shettleston in 1922,

and as a Labour minister in 1924 was author of the Wheatley
Act for rehousing poor families. His subsequent drift into
the ranks of the left-wing critics of the Labour Party
destroyed his parliamentary career, and he died aged sixty-
one in 1930. Despite his success as a self-made businessman
and petty-bourgeois appearance, with a roly poly tum and
thick round spectacles, he was one of the makers of the legend
of the Red Clydesiders, while as a devout Roman Catholic, his
life epitomised the stresses between socialism and the Church.[20]

Wheatley's Catholicism was of the bedrock kind fostered
by the first generation of missionary clergy who were unused
to luxury. Wheatley's boyhood mentor was the Dutch parish
priest of Ballieston, Father Terkin, who in 1879, took lodgings
in a worker's house, said Mass in a converted stable, lived
for thirty-five years in the parish, and tramped for hours
every day round the nine mining villages which formed his
mission. Patrick Dollan, who was to dominate the Labour
Party in Glasgow between the wars, was Terkin's acolyte and
unpaid secretary during twelve years of childhood and
adolescence, and declared that more than any other man in the
district, the priest made it progressive and prosperous.[21]
Terkin's missionary preaching was famous, his branch of the
League of the Cross was 'the first social centre for men in
the village', which he ruled through a cabinet of colliers.
In other ways Terkin was a conventional priest. He built a
church and presbytery which were the most impressive buildings
of the area; both subscribers and defaulters to church funds
were announced from the altar steps, and though 'a small man,
not more than 5ft. 2ins. high', in his frock-coat, tall hat,
and with black ebony stick, silver-mounted, in hand, he would
'clear the streets on Friday and Saturday evenings, the
carousel time for miners...' He enjoyed sailing into crowds
of unruly men and dispersing them in a homeward direction.[22]
Terkin singled out Wheatley as a lad of promise when as a

grocer's apprentice he met the priest after mass to discuss
the Sunday sermon, and the Dutchman's ministry was calculated
to make his pauper congregation socially mobile.   Dollan
recalled his many proteges who afterwards got on; not least
in the labour movement.   Under Terkin's influence, Wheatley's
wife had become a daily communicant, and the strength of
Ballieston Catholicism as Terkin had remade it kept Wheatley
a Catholic in spite of the church's suspicion of socialism.

Wheatley declared his socialism in February 1906, after
a lecture given by C.S. Devas in the Athenaeum Hall in Glasgow,
under the auspices of the Catholic Truth Society, in the wake
of the Labour victories in the 1906 elections.   Devas
distinguished the 'harmless Socialism' which was not really
socialistic of the newly elected Labour MPs from the anti-
Christian socialism of Blatchford and the Clarion.   In so
far as his lecture had a bearing on practical politics, it
reads as an olive-branch to the Labour Party, and an assurance
that Catholics could support it.   Signing himself 'Catholic
Socialist', Wheatley answered Devas in the first of his dozens
of letters to the Observer.[23]   By doing so he lifted the
debate to the plane of abstract political theory.   He was
not yet a member of any socialist party, and his motives were
both political and intellectual.

The burden of Wheatley's argument was that Catholics
should be socialists because they were Catholics.   Declaring
that Catholics like Devas were trying to influence the Church
against the socialist movement, Wheatley argued that 'such a
course would be contrary to the traditional teaching of the
Church...   The Catholic Church has always leaned more to
Socialism or Collectivism and equality than to individualism
and inequality,' he wrote.   'It has always been the Church of
the poor, and all the historical attacks on it have emanated
from the rich.   Its Divine Founder on every occasion condemned
the accumulation of wealth.'   Wheatley invoked the parable of

Lazarus and Dives, quoted St Paul, St Ambrose and Jerome,
and declared that the medieval Church had held its wealth in
trust for the poor, and loyally cared for them: 'the
Reformation...was due principally to the desire of the
Individualists to capture the property which the Church held
as common...in those days there were neither paupers nor
workhouses...' Wheatley freely admitted that it was the
duty of Catholics to oppose 'the revolutionary, confiscatory,
anti-religious methods of the early, modern Continental
Socialists.' This criticism, however, did not apply to the
methods and aims of the legal evolutionary socialism of Great
Britain, which he identified with Irish land reform and a
further extension of the ownership of public utilities, gas,
water and electricity already exercised by the Glasgow
corporation. Indeed the spread of such a socialism would be
invaluable to Catholicism, by raising Catholics from their
poverty. Wheatley concluded that the economic organisation
of a capitalist society had made the practice of Christianity
impossible:

> The Greed for Private Gain Causes the
> Publican to Encourage Intemperance, the
> landlord to charge extortionate rent,
> the employer to "sweat" labour, the house-
> owner to keep slum property, the shopkeeper
> to sell adulterated goods, the business man
> to tell lies, the weak man to gamble, the
> weak woman to do worse... How can religion
> prosper in such an atmosphere? Is it
> surprising that Indifferentism flourishes
> here?

The nonconformist churches were individualist in their
underlying principles and philosophy; but the natural place
of a collectivist church was on the collectivist side.

The quotations from the Scriptures and patristic
writers, the romantic view of the middle ages, and the
conception of Catholicism as collectivist, point to a Catholic

source for Wheatley's Socialism: and Dollan confirms[24] what
is in any way apparent, that Wheatley had read the book
Catholic Socialism, by a Neapolitan Professor of Economics,
Francesco Nitti, published in 1891 and translated into
English in 1895. Nitti surveyed the social teachings of the
Bible, and synthesised the consensus of the Fathers of the
Church that private property was a result of original sin,
and that Christians should hold their goods in common.
Much of the book was devoted to nineteenth-century Catholic
social reforming movements on the continent, which Nitti
bluntly called 'Catholic Socialism'. In the more conservative pontificate of Pius X however, the phrase 'Catholic
Socialist' was suspect, and not the least of Wheatley's sins
was to write under the pseudonym 'Catholic Socialist' which
was not in good odour with the clergy. Not that Nitti's
book was enough to make Wheatley a socialist by itself;
rather it harmonised with his wider reading of Emerson, Hardy,
Meredith and Tolstoy, which belonged to the idealist and anti-
rationalist frame of mind of the Independent Labour Party,
puritan, teetotal and religious. The ILP's heroes were 'Jesus,
Shelley, Mazzini, Whitman, Ruskin, Carlyle and Morris'.[25]
Its knowledge of economics was slight, and its crusade against
Mammon was in the radical nonconformist tradition. As the
Communist William Gallacher said of Wheatley himself, 'An
honest, earnest socialist was John, but without any understanding of Marxism'. He was a 'staunch Catholic, and that
kept him from any real understanding of dialectical materialism
or of the materialist conception of history'.[26] Wheatley's
socialism was in the pattern of Keir Hardie's, and of that
pre-war Methodist socialist society in county Durham recently
most sensitively described by Robert Moore.[27] Like Hardie
and the Durham Methodists, Wheatley appealed to a Christianity
wider than his own confession, while remaining within it, just
as Dollan had learned his socialism from an Episcopalian

clergyman. Coming from religious or anti-religious backgrounds, the early socialists did not ignore the churches:
they fought them, or sought a compromise. In Wheatley and
Dollan and Hardie the puritan and idealist working-class
culture fostered by the Protestant and Catholic churches was
seeking a common socialist expression, and so Wheatley's
Catholic socialist followers were to invoke the spirit of
Cardinal Manning, and of 'the greatest Christian Socialist
the world has ever seen, "Our Divine Savour"';[28] appealing
both to a Roman Catholic leader and to the general Christian
tradition.

Wheatley had a tougher task than Hardie's: the confessional tradition which he was trying to transcend was
rigid and exclusive, exposed to international pressures and
acutely sensitive to outside criticism. Yet Wheatley had
no difficulty in publicising his opinions through the most
comprehensive institution the community possessed, its
newspaper. The Glasgow Observer took a consistent attitude
to Wheatley throughout, denying that 'Catholic Socialists
were really Socialists, just because they were loyal Catholics.'
The Observer opposed socialism, but in its own eyes at least
was not thereby opposing Wheatley. Indeed it encouraged his
controversial contributions to its columns, presumably out of
a newspaper's first loyalty, to a vested interest in selling
newspapers, and for three years from 1906, it gave Wheatley,
his fellow Catholic socialists and their critics a platform
to develop their ideas.

Wheatley's first concern was with the standing of the
Catholic Truth Society, as a recognised authority on Catholic
dogma: Catholics would too easily conclude that in condemning
socialism, it spoke for the Church. He fastened on a fact to
which he clung throughout, that the Church had banned no
socialist society in Britain, and that Catholics were therefore
free to join them. This was to shift from his original

174

argument that socialism was implied by Catholicism; indeed
it went with an opposing stress that Catholics could be
socialists, because socialism was simply an economic programme
for the nationalisation of the means of production, distribution and exchange quite independent of religion. This
strategy was equally a consequence of the arguments developed
by anti-socialist correspondents to the Observer. Invoking
the aggressive secularist views of some British and continental
socialists, they argued a logical connection between socialism
and atheism: 'there can be no question', it was said, 'as to
the proclivity of Socialist movements in general. They are
always anti-religious.'[29] Worse, they were opposed to
Christian morals, would dissolve 'patriotism,...paternal
affection, kith, kin, and relations'[30] while, as to the family,
the 'whole mass would herd together like rabbits in a warren.'[31]
This,as Wheatley pointed out, libelled his own family life, a
model of Christian fidelity, and 'Another Catholic Socialist'
compared the socialist future with the model family in which
the working members gave their wages to the wife and mother.[32]
This resort to maternal metaphor was utterly Irish and Catholic.
Wheatley found it more convenient to secularise his socialist
ideal, by declaring it to be without religious base; and like
James Connolly in his attack on the Dublin Jesuit Fr Kane,[33]
sought to show that all workers should be socialists, regardless of their morals or religion.

But by defining socialism in a secular sense, Wheatley
did not achieve his aim of withdrawing it from the Church's
jurisdiction. 'Rerum novarum' itself declared the social
question to be a religious and moral one, through the Church's
guardianship of the natural law which was common to all mankind,
and not just to Roman Catholics. One of Wheatley's disciples
risked his arm in rejecting this, declaring that the papal
encyclical was only 'the individual opinion of the Pope and
not an "ex cathedra" pronouncement, binding on the consciences

of Catholics'; indeed on a level with Pope Adrian's gift
of Ireland to England.[34]   This argument was dangerously two-
edged; it played straight into the hands of conservative
Catholics, by pronouncing the Church to be as reactionary as
they, and by threatening to provoke the hostile reaction
from the clergy which Wheatley was anxious to avoid. I
have found no evidence, in spite of modern statements to the
contrary, that in 1906, socialism was denounced in the parish
churches; and there is a problem of relating public anti-
socialist pronouncements to practical politics. In late
September in 1906, the Observer attacked Keir Hardie's
insistence that the ILP was a socialist party;[35] in November,
the newspaper supported a number of Labour candidates in the
Glasgow municipal elections, including Hardie's brother.[36] In
December, Hardie was again denounced for declaring that the
Church on the continent was to blame for socialist hostility
towards her.[37] The same ambiguity appears in the first
clerical denunciation of socialism, by one Father Galton, in
an address to the Caledonian Catholic Association.[38] Galton
was not a parish priest, but a Jesuit; and his diatribe on
the socialist subversion of private property mentions no
socialist bodies by name. His remarks belong to the realm
of theory in which Catholic champions vanquished all the
heresies, and had little relevance to practical politics.
More significant was an address by Archbishop McGuire to a
'monster demonstration' of the working-class League of the Cross.
McGuire warmly welcomed the emergence of the working classes
as an independent political force; by grace of the election
of so many Labour MPs, 'at last there seemed to be a chance
of what Abraham Lincoln called "the government of the people
for the people by the people" in Britain.'[39] The same
goodwill to Labour was expressed by a Glaswegian Franciscan,
Father David, to a parochial gathering in October. David
distinguished a 'speculative' socialism of abstract principles

from an 'economic Socialism' which the Church could commend.
He applauded the election of Labour candidates to parliament,
and hoped that their numbers might increase; and he also
told one questioner - possibly Wheatley - that Catholics
could join the Independent Labour Party, because the church
had not condemned it.[40]

These soothing noises may have encouraged Wheatley to
found a Catholic Socialist Society.[41] In its first two
meetings in early November, fifty members were enrolled,
under Wheatley as chairman. Its aim was to propagate
socialism among Catholics; its membership was confined to
Catholic communicants, though it was addressed by the
propagandists of other socialist societies, and its meetings
were open to anyone. Wheatley had earlier expressed
reservations about a separate Catholic socialist organisation,
which looked like a concession to the very sectarian spirit
which he wanted to overcome. The restrictions on membership
combined with the openness of meetings and the ideological
variety of lectures were intended to attract Catholics to a
Catholic institution, while showing them their proper role
within the wider working class. Wheatley compared his
society's work among Catholics to Fabian Socialist propaganda
to the middle class: on the other hand he defined a second
aim, of making socialism less hostile to religion, and of
permeating the socialist movement with a Catholic spirit,
and showing the relevance of Catholicism to socialism. Thus
the Society's early lecturers included the Ballieston miners'
leader, Jimmy Donaldson, on 'The Church and the Poor in Pre-
Reformation Days',[42] while later speakers extolled the
'Golden Age of British Labour' before the sixteenth century.[43]
Wheatley sought to show that by embracing socialism, the
Church would greatly benefit religion, and destroy the anti-
religious socialists about whom the clergy were complaining.
In fact, he was to be driven to ask for mere tolerance, not

active support. No leading Catholic laymen, no Catholic
priest even joined the Society, and as was to become apparent,
some priests and laymen were out to destroy it.

Yet the Society was to last for over a decade, though
its membership never rose above a hundred in Glasgow, and
apart from a branch at Motherwell with a regular attendance
of fifty, attempts to open branches elsewhere in Scotland
came to grief through apathy or violence. It is unlikely
however that its membership figures are a true gauge of its
influence. It was increasingly part of a wider socialist
world through Wheatley's membership of the ILP and his links
with the socialist journal Forward, which publicised his
activities with those of other Christian socialists. The
Society's gatherings each Sunday afternoon in the Albion Halls
to hear and debate a paper were doubtless of limited appeal.
A speaker who preached up state nurseries for children got
the dusty response that mothercare was best.[44] Nationalism
also put off likely sympathisers, who thought that Irish
independence should come first.[45] When in 1908 James Larkin
addressed the Society just before his trial in Dublin, he
'criticized...the Nationalist and Sinn Fein movements, and
contended that nothing short of Socialism would bring peace
and plenty to Ireland. A number of Sinn Fein advocates...
warmly defended their position', though 'At the close of the
meeting, several new members joined,' including Larkin.[46]
They were often addressed by William Gallacher, who later won
fame as a Communist MP for West Fife, and rather rosily
recalled the hall 'packed' every Sunday:[47] one of the few
accounts alleging an enthusiasm well-concealed in the dull
reports in the newspapers. The Society's pamphlets advertised
Cochrane's tea, and there is also a distinctly decorous quality
to the country rambles which superseded the Sunday debates in
summer, and to the Society's tea parties at which members might
enjoy a humorous sketch by Miss Ida Hamilton and Mr D Stevens,

and an impersonation by Mr Joe Rogan of Henry Irvine in the
'Bells'... The Bohemian Pierrots were represented by Messrs
Donnelli and Bert Lytton... Miss Hamilton and Mr Stevens
sang finely in solos, and the pleasing voice of Miss Lena
Keatings was heard to advantage in 'Flight of Ages'.[48] This
was hardly revolutionary stuff: on the other hand, as a small
propagandist body, the Society fits the pattern defined by
Walter Kendall of those Marxist socialists who

> saw themselves as educators rather than
> as leaders, and...maintained a quite
> artificial separation between industrial
> and political action. The socialists,
> possessed of an inner vision, saw them-
> selves in Connolly's expressive phrase...
> as the "John the Baptists of the New
> Redemption".   49

The failure to grow in numbers may have forced this rather
inactive role of talkshop on the CSS but it suited Wheatley's
discovery of his gifts as a propagandist of socialist ideas,
and the legacy of these years of his life is tens of thousands
of words.

His first clash with a priest, in March 1907, was with
another Jesuit, Father Ashton, whose newspaper articles from
the preceding December were directed not at Wheatley but at
the usual bevy of bogy-men secularist socialists - Marx, Shaw,
Hyndman, Quelch, Belfort Bax, Blatchford and the Clarion.
In short, Ashton objected not so much to Wheatley's economics
but to the socialist connection with advanced progressive
thought, especially in morals. Thus on practical points he
thought that Socialist Sunday schools and hymns represented a
separate irreligious culture, which must alienate Catholics
from the Church, and that by supporting socialist candidates,
Irish Catholics would weaken the effect of their vote, whose
strength lay in union. Indeed Wheatley's attack on Catholic
representatives who did nothing for the working man threatened

179

to divide the community along the lines of class, disrupting
the harmonies of Fatherland and Faith. Yet despite the
large principles involved, Ashton's exchange with Wheatley
was polite. The Jesuit declared he would have never written
were all socialists like Wheatley, who professed to be willing
to surrender his socialism if it weakened his faith.[50] These
mutual compliments contrast favourably with Wheatley's next
major argy-bargy in the Observer, with Father Leo Puissant,
from July. Puissant was the parish priest of St Thomas,
Muirkirk, and not, as has been said, a 'retired Jesuit'.[51]
He was a youngish man, entirely lacking in Jesuitical suavity,
and for two years of busy letter-writing in the Observer,
Wheatley turned to clever polemical use Puissant's unpriestly
violence of manner and rough tongue.

Wheatley and Puissant were in other ways well-matched,
for Puissant was also a visionary. He was a Belgian from a
solidly clerical family: three uncles and an elder brother
were priests, and he was ordained by his cousin the bishop
of Ghent. He had been caught up in the crusade of prayer
for the conversion of England, and at Muirkirk had built his
own church and schools.[52] He now wanted to form a Catholic
Democratic party similar to the confessional parties of
Germany and Belgium, and with his unusual knowledge of
continental sociology, his own social programme was radical
enough:

> the establishment and development of trades
> unions, mixed syndicates, patronages, schools
> of social and domestic economy, technical
> schools, savings banks, friendly and insurance
> societies, old age pensions, housing of the
> working man, work for the unemployed, temperance
> legislation, a minimum labour day and a maximum
> wage, war against speculation on Exchange, and
> the law of divorce.   53

He called tenement houses 'a disgrace to civilisation';

while as a remedy for unemployment he urged 'national and county public works all the year round.' Despite his ferocious anti-socialism, he was not, therefore, the bleak reactionary of socialist legend. Indeed his commitment to Christian Social Reform on the Belgian model left him without a clear answer to Wheatley's demand to know what item in the socialist programme the Church condemned, while he confused matters by using the phrase 'Christian Socialist' in both an approving and hostile sense.[54] In fact as far as immediate economic policies were concerned, the differences between Wheatley and Puissant were slight. Wheatley denied that he wanted entirely to abolish private property, and promised compensation to factory owners for nationalisation, while Puissant had no objections to nationalisation in principle. The difference between them was more fundamental. In the heat of controversy, Puissant privately urged Wheatley to surrender his socialism and instead assume the leadership of a Catholic Democratic Party, which, Puissant declared, Wheatley alone was capable of creating. To Puissant, Wheatley's cardinal sin was to have taken up with a non-Catholic ideology. It was the very sharpness of Puissant's vision of a populist radical Catholicism which so violently estranged him from any social programme not completely controlled by the Church, and from the prospect of Catholic participation in politics beyond the ghettoes of Fatherland and Faith. It was almost a secondary consideration that this emergence from the separate Catholic social context was designed to give them a new loyalty to the working class.

To this Puissant brought a nightmare vision of the morality which a godless socialism would create: 'a new world...whose loftiest ideal would be the production of material wealth; a materialistic world with a materialistic gospel; fodder and lust', people

who sit to eat and drink, and rise to play;
a world with human stud-farms and nursery-

181

pens: a world of vice and filth, without
religion and without grace; a world of
human automata worked like cast iron pulleys
or cogs, without personal freedom or dignity;
a world of powerless slaves and...scheming,
combining, artful, and heartless official
tyrants; a world where the slave...would
have to look grateful and graceful when his
wife and his daughters...would be the sport
of luscious, abominable officals

with the power to reduce the wronged husband and father to
'the municipal scavenger and street-sweep'.[55] To Wheatley
this described capitalism as it was already, in spite of
anything which church authority could do to prevent it:
socialism would prevent it and thereby create a Christian
social order for the Church.

Indeed Puissant's anti-socialist polemic could only bring
church authority into contempt: the authority of encyclical,
of pope and parish priest. His violent language was calculated
to rouse non-Catholic socialists in Glasgow to anti-Catholicism,
provoke Wheatley and his followers into anti-clericalism, and
possibly drive them from the Church. Wheatley was driven to
deny the Church's political power, in the words of O'Connell:
'Our religion we take from Rome: our politics from ourselves'.
The tension latent within the Irish community between priest
and politician came to the surface as Wheatley denied that
'Rerum novarum' was ex cathedra, and ignored Puissant's valid
enough insistence that this made it no less binding on
Catholics.[56] The Glasgow socialist Forward lent fuel to
flames with a series which ran from 1908 to 1912 'Outside the
Chapel Door' by 'Mark Tyme', the pseudonym of an embittered
gravedigger at a Roman Catholic cemetery.[57] Equally
inflammatory was the anti-Christian propaganda of Bruce
Glasier, a member of the Glasgow ILP. Indeed Puissant was
making Wheatley notorious, and drawing Catholics to his side,
as the community gathered protectively around him. In August
1908, the Catholic Socialist Society fell under the lash of

the president of the Catholic Young Men's Society,[58]   In
November it was condemned by a Benedictine,[59] in December by
the Jesuit Father Power,[60] and by the Catholic Bishop of
Salford, whom Wheatley had quoted in his own defence, and who
now pronounced a Catholic Socialist Society as illogical as a
Catholic Wesleyan Society.[61]   The climax came on 20 June 1909,
when a branch of the Society was banned in Leeds by the Bishop,
in a pastoral letter heavy with episcopal thunder read in every
Church in the city: 'It is the Bishop's duty to teach and rule
and guide his flock': he declared '...For this God has made
him a Pastor and given him authority, and for this does God
require the flock to obey and follow him...All Socialistic
societies he utterly condemned as abhorrent to the teaching
of God's Church...'[62] Well might Puissant rejoice; here
was the Church wielding the political power to which he claimed
it had the right.[63]

Yet in Glasgow, the Archbishop was silent, and only one
circumstance lent political importance to Puissant's
thunderings, the Labour Party's commitment to secular
education. It was here that the Church's relations with
both the Liberals and the Irish party were also most difficult
to maintain; but Labour's educational policy gave a sharp
edge to anti-socialist polemic by suggesting that the party
was as anticlerical as its counterparts on the continent.
Side by side with denunciations of the Labour attitude to
Catholic schools, the Catholic press published burning accounts
of socialist attempts to destroy religious teaching in Italy
and France; the _Observer_'s Roman correspondent was an
especially prolific source of atrocity stories of the
crucifix smashed from the class-room wall, which reawakened
older Catholic memories of Protestant educational proselytism
in Ireland. As the _Observer_ declared, 'The overwhelming
bulk of the Catholic vote in Great Britain is a Labour vote',
and would go to Labour just as soon as Labour assisted

Catholic education.[64]   In fact, the Labour representatives
in the Glasgow School board usually voted with the Catholics:[65]
while the TUC's campaign for secular education spurred the
formation in August 1908 of a Conference of Catholic Trade
Unionists,[66] which year by year protested at the annual
conferences of the TUC against the secular principle.   Later
in the year, a Glasgow gathering of Catholic trade unionists
was called to make a similar protest, the Catholic socialists
turned out to parade their Catholicism, and there was
subsequent controversy about their union membership which
Wheatley's followers exploited to the full.   Only in educational
matters did Puissant's anti-socialist tirades touch upon
practical politics, for it was only there that secularist
socialism assailed Catholic interest, and only there that
Catholics were organised as he wished them to be, just as
Catholics united by Catholicism.

These ambiguities reflected a practical difficulty: both
the Church and the Irish Nationalists wanted cooperation with
the Labour Party, and welcomed most of its programme as
promising amelioration of the plight of the poor.   At the
Catholic Truth Society's annual meeting at the end of 1907,
the Society's anti-socialist propaganda was criticised for
threatening the wholly desirable objectives of Labour.   There
was a deafening chorus of clerics on public platforms denouncing
'Godless slum lords, jerry builders, food adulterers, and
grinders of the poor', while Archbishop McGuire reiterated his
enthusiasm for organised labour in his public speeches, most
notably in an address to a meeting in the Albert Hall of
8,000 men, at the Eucharistic Congress in 1908.

> Power is passing, he declared, day by day
> more into the hands of the working-classes.
> It looks as if...the working men will rule
> the world...men who observed the signs of
> the times said the great factor of the
> last General Election was the birth of the
> Labour Party...God knows working-men have

grievances enough...there has been class
legislation,...partial laws...the rewards
of capital have been greater than those of
labour. What did capital risk? Money.
But labour risked its life...when you have
an inefficient General, you give him a
pension; an inefficient working man retires
to the workhouse!

McGuire warned that Labour's victory had great dangers, that
every group who had ever held power had abused it, and that
if workmen were not more generous than their oppressors,
'then nothing but horror can lie before the world.' He
looked forward instead to a better time, 'when man to man,
the world o'er, shall brithers be, for a' that'.[67] His
speech was reproduced in the volume issued by the Eucharistic
Congress, which was bought by every Catholic library in Great
Britain, and it marks the Church's acceptance of Labour men,
as distinct from socialist principles.

An earlier version of this speech had prompted Wheatley
to ask if the Archbishop was a socialist, and even to insist
that McGuire would not dare condemn the Catholic Socialist
Society. The Archbishop's phrase 'The working men will rule
the world', gave Wheatley a motto for his pamphlet The Catholic
Working Man which he published in 1909. This tract for the
times took further captions from Manning, the Catholic Truth
Society, and the Nationalist MP, T.P. O'Connor, while at the
base of each page was the Sunday school exhortation,
'SOCIALISM MEANS - THE GOLDEN RULE AGAINST THE RULE OF GOLD'.
Half the pamphlet was a sorting-out of the nationalist
insistence that Home Rule should prevail over any other
political measure; the other half was an answer to the
Catholic objections to socialism. Here Wheatley displayed
a remarkable skill in the manipulation of quotations. He
cited the Observer to prove that the Catholic Socialist
Society was safely Catholic, and reproduced the arguments of
the Dominican Fr Vincent McNabb, that because British

socialists did not wish to abolish all private property,
'Rerum Novarum' could not be used to condemn them. McNabb
was the intellectual enfant terrible of the Catholic Church
in England. His bombshell bursting in the Tablet had caused
bitter conflict in Glasgow and London. Indeed Wheatley had
any amount of material to show ecclesiastical support for
socialist programmes if not for socialism. He concluded on
the religious note that 'Capitalism was destroying Christianity',
but that socialism would help Catholicism by embodying in the
very social fabric the commandment to 'Love thy neighbour as
thyself.'

This same line of argument appears in another Catholic
Socialist publication, 'Socialism and The Catholic Faith', by
the Fabian Socialist Hubert Bland, a London Catholic journalist
and columnist, with a large working-class readership as 'Hubert'
of the Sunday Chronicle.[68] Wheatley also printed and
circulated a tract, 'Economic Discontent', by Fr T.J. Hagerty,
an American priest allegedly suspended by his bishop for
supporting striking miners.[69] Wheatley himself wrote two more
tracts, on the mining industry, 'How the miners were robbed'
and 'Miners, Mining and Misery', under the Catholic Socialist
Society's imprimatur. His arguments were chiefly economic,
but even here there was a strong underlying moral and religious
stress, that the judgement of God was on the capitalist for
exploiting his fellow men.

The Archbishop of Glasgow had himself said as much, and
his more radical pronouncements were worrying conservative
Catholics. McGuire however was equally out of sympathy with
Wheatley and his priestly opponents. In a letter to Puissant
in 1908,[70] the Archbishop showed no enthusiasm for a Catholic
Democratic party, or for Puissant's first measure towards
creating it, a central Catholic club at which working men
would be taught the principles of Catholic political economy.
This last scheme was rejected outright by the 'Diocesan

Committee on Socialism' which McGuire convened in November.
Only one of the reports of its meetings has survived,[71] but
it indicates the depth of hostility to Wheatley behind the
Archbishop's public silence, and sets forth the clergy's
assessment of the problem which he posed for them.

The committee agreed that the socialist influence among
Catholics was slight:

> an inappreciable number of our people have
> become out-and-out Socialists.,.A good many
> of the Catholic unemployed are drawn to
> hear the harangues at Socialist meetings,
> dazzled by the fair promises of work. It
> has been ascertained on good authority that
> the interests of labour are the bait, and
> remain the only connecting link between
> the workingman and socialism... A few
> individuals here and there, who have been
> practical Catholics, have given up the Faith
> and extend the lists of the Socialist party.
> They are democratic Socialists.

These dangers here were inconsiderable enough: the real
problem in fact was Wheatley.

> A small number of men, and a few women have
> joined the so-called Catholic Socialist
> party, which is under the aegis of a
> mal-content Catholic... The people, who
> attend the so-called Catholic Socialist
> meetings are in a most dangerous position:
> as they associate with speakers brought to
> their meetings, who are agnostics and
> materialists. They are known to have
> received addresses from men of the Blatchford
> Camp and also members of the Fabian Society.
> The Faith and Priesthood have been decried
> and denounced by them at meetings attended
> by the so-called Catholic Socialist party.
> All are agreed that there is great danger
> to the faith of our people, who attend
> Socialist meetings, but especially the
> meetings of "the Catholic Socialist party".
> The qualification Catholic is a snare.

It was, then, as a 'malcontent Catholic' that Wheatley
threatened Catholicism. In a manner more easily felt than
stated, he was that most dangerous foe, a heretic, an enemy
within the citadel of faith from which the Church defied the
world.

The committee therefore urged caution in dealing with
him, concluding that 'Catholic interests would not be best
safe-guarded by direct opposition to Socialism'. Instead
they merely recommended a further intensification of lectures
on 'Rerum Novarum' by informed and approved clergy and laymen,
and remitted to their next meeting the questions of the
'Relationship of our people to the Independent Labour party',
and of Puissant's projected Catholic Labour party, to be
'formed on the lines of the German Catholic Labour party'.
The committee also sent the Archbishop proposals for a
Catholic Working Men's union or association, 'to counteract
the danger of our people being drawn into Socialist Societies',
and suggested that the whole question 'De Socialismo' be sent
for discussion to the deanery conferences of the parochial
clergy.[72] It is not clear whether this was done. The
matter may have been dropped, and it is not until the
following year that there is evidence of Wheatley's estrange-
ment from his own parish priest.

From 1906 to 1912 Wheatley lived in the parish of St
Mark's Carntyne, and in 1911 he complained to the archbishop
that the priest, Robert Paterson, had refused to accept his
church dues or to read his name at services among the other
subscribers. In reply to the archbishop,[73] Paterson insisted
that for years he had gone out of his way to 'show John
Wheatley every mark of kindness with the object of converting
him' to right political opinions. This kindness had cost
Paterson 'the good will and friendship of Dr Ryan and Fr
O'Brien', the priests in the neighbouring parishes. Moreover,
'three of the best families in this parish left the parish as

they thought my kindness to Wheatley was a slur on the other
priests in the district.' Two years before, in 1909,
Wheatley had begun

> to lead astray some of the young men and
> women of the parish; getting them to go
> with him straight from the chapel on
> Sunday to open air Socialist meetings held
> quite near the chapel. The people com-
> plained to me about this and I spoke to
> him about the matter. At this time I
> visited his house just the same as the
> other houses in the parish.

Matters however had worsened in 1910 when Wheatley 'along
with some of the young men he had led astray' started

> going...from house to house selling a
> Socialist paper called the "Forward",
> which week after week contained blasphemous
> attacks on the catholic priesthood...
> This...became a regular scandal in the
> parish and I was forced much against my
> will to warn the people about the danger
> to their faith in buying this paper.
> The week after giving the people this
> warning Wheatley had me Billed all over
> the town.   I paid no attention to this,
> never so much as mentioned the fact in
> church.

Paterson concluded by declaring that Wheatley

> does not care a straw for any Bishop or
> Priest in the Country. The man has lost
> his faith, if he ever had any, and is now
> by selling papers attacking the church
> an enemy of the church. He wishes however
> for the sake of his followers, who have as
> yet some catholic faith about them, to be
> looked upon as a Catholic.

Paterson insisted that

> personally I have no ill will towards John
> Wheatley. I speak to him every time I

189

meet him just as I do to the other people
of the parish, but until he mends his
ways I can do nothing more, least of all
accept his money.

This was a highly indirect way of showing disapproval,
the more so in that Paterson had resolved never to speak of
Wheatley again even in private: the disagreeable business of
being 'Billed' all over Glasgow had silenced him. In 1912,
however, Carntyne was reunited with the neighbouring parish
of Shettleston, in which the parish priest was Andrew O'Brien,
whom Wheatley had already denounced to the Archbishop in 1911
in a letter which does not survive. O'Brien's reply to
McGuire disclaimed any interest in Wheatley, noting that his
address of 'George St is not in this district, and the
individual who complains has been out of my mission for the
past five years.'[74] Wheatley's grievance on this occasion
is unknown, but it is unlikely that right was wholly on his
side, as he made his complaint in the course of a dog-fight
between the priest and Wheatley's friend Daniel McAleer, a
disputatious character with a special grudge against O'Brien.

With McAleer one plumbs the petty jealousies of the
Catholic parish pump. McAleer was a local worthy: district
correspondent of the Glasgow Observer, secretary of the
Shettleston United Irish League, and of the Society of St
Vincent de Paul, President of the St Paul's Dramatic Club and
leader of a faction opposed to O'Brien's predecessor, Fr
Gaule, who in 1902, after an angry confrontation with McAleer
from the pulpit, over the building of a hall for the league
instead of schools, had forced him to resign from the St
Vincent de Paul. On coming to the parish in 1904, O'Brien
had quashed McAleer's anti-Gaulist faction, and later, after
the teachers in the parish school had complained of the tenor
of McAleer's reports to the Observer, had taken the task of
reporting from him, and had made him retire from the Drama

190

Club.   In 1908, McAleer wrote to the archbishop demanding an
apology for the injury done him by Fr Gaule, who had long
since left the archdiocese, while with extraordinary simplicity
McAleer cited O'Brien as a character witness in his favour.[75]
In the following year, McAleer fanned the flames of a dispute
between the United Irish League and a curate at St Paul's,
while he had also become 'an ally of the Socialists of the
neighbourhood, and gave great offence to the Catholic Community
by his public approval of a misleading reference to the Catholic
Clergy, made from a public platform.'[76]   It was in 1910 that
McAleer told the archbishop of a sermon in which O'Brien had
called McAleer 'hardly fit company for a Brothel Keeper' and
his wife 'a secret drunkard' who 'keeps a woman in the house
to tempt her husband'.[77]   O'Brien denied that he had ever
attacked the McAleers, who had not been in church to hear the
alleged offending sermon; in fact the priest seems to have
been berating the favourite sins of no particular one of his
parishioners.   McAleer's further complaint to the archbishop
that O'Brien urged the congregation 'to pray for a catholic
socialist sympathiser and his wife'[78] may have had more
substance, but Wheatley could hardly have chosen to support a
less convincing friend.

Yet O'Brien was an authoritarian, with a violent temper
and conservative opinions from his years in a Spanish seminary.
In 1909, he displeased the archbishop by trying to impose on
the Shettleston Hibernians the ecclesiastical ban which the
church rescinded in December.[79]   O'Brien was however a
formidable foe; independently wealthy from a Glasgow pawn-
broking family, he was a scholar and gentleman, and a devoted
parish priest.   He feared nothing from either socialist or
archbishop.   As a local newspaper put it, he wielded his 'Big
Stick' in a manner 'which says a good deal for his courage if
not so much for his discretion',[80] and it was the depth of his
congregation's loyalty to him which caused violence when

Wheatley criticised him.

The conflict was O'Brien's battle with the Hibernians all
over again; he was fighting it alone. The Church had
abandoned the idea of an anti-socialist campaign, when in the
early summer of 1912, O'Brien denounced the socialists in the
parish from the pulpit, as Wheatley sat in the congregation.
On 29 June, Wheatley defended himself in a measured vein in
Forward, but his article gave great offence to Shettleston
Catholics. Catholic girls in Shettleston went round tearing
up Forward posters, and on Sunday 30 June, an indignant
meeting of parishioners agreed to present O'Brien with a
testimonial and address, and appointed six men to wait on the
archbishop with a protest on O'Brien's behalf,[81] while a
delegation of twelve men and twelve women were nominated to
speak out against Wheatley at an ILP meeting on Monday evening.
A crowd of seven to eight hundred people escorted the delegates
down Shettleston Main Street, and found that though the ILP
gathering had been cancelled, a small meeting was being held.
This they dispersed with violence and advanced to Wheatley's
house, where Wheatley's two children were at home with the
McAleers, who had rushed there to give Wheatley warning.
Wheatley and his wife came back from a walk, and for over an
hour Wheatley and McAleer watched as the actively hostile part
of the crowd, a band of girls, no doubt from the Children of
Mary, burned Wheatley's effigy to the strains of 'Faith of our
Fathers'.[82] In a subsequent encounter, one socialist supporter
had his clothes nearly torn from his back, and another got a
broken nose.[83] The incident was doubtless frightening, showing
the depth of Irish feeling which an outside ideology could arouse;
but it was a storm in a teacup just the same. The following
Sunday, Wheatley and his family were back at mass at St Paul's,
and O'Brien was as stymied as Paterson. Far from supporting
the priest, the archbishop's secretary politely fobbed off the
deputation from the parish,[84] while the Observer treated the

'Anti-"Socialist" Shindy in Shettleston'[85] as a minor joke,
with bad puns: 'A burning topic' and 'form of en<u>light</u>enment'.[86]
In the September 1912 municipal elections, the paper endorsed
a Catholic opponent of Wheatley's whom it reprimanded for anti-
clericalism;[87] but this was part of a general reversal of its
past support for the Labour Party, which was in their eyes
insufficiently pro-Irish rather than just anti-religious.[88]
The whole significance of the Shettleston shindy was its
symbolic force of socialists, to whom it showed up the Church's
hatred for socialism. In fact O'Brien does not fully deserve
this dislike; he devoted his ministry to the working classes,
and in 1922, he was forced to resign his parish when he annoyed
McGuire's successor as archbishop, Mackintosh, a man as cold
as a fish on a slab, by spending the church building fund as
well as much of his own wealth on feeding unemployed miners
and their families. It should be noted that he did this
regardless of creed; and his memory was revered for at least
as long in Shettleston as the socialists reviled it.

Thus the Roman Church in Glasgow was not simply a
'reactionary' institution opposed to socialism, but one with
a variety of responses, which tended to neutralise one another.
The continental influence was especially complex: Puissant's
Belgian Social Catholicism, O'Brien's Spanish training, the
Dutchman Terkin's long years of devotion to pastoral duty, the
anticlerical socialism of Italy and France, and 'Rerum novarum'
itself: all oddly blending and mingling with a nationalism
and religion from Ireland. Thus the outcome was a truce not
often disturbed by public controversy. The founder of the
Catholic Social Guild, Father Charles Plater SJ, visited
Glasgow in August 1912, to lecture on 'Rerum novarum'; and he
was much impressed by the Catholic Socialists, and by some
socialist ex-Catholics.[89] In 1913, Father Vincent McNabb had
the cheek to ask McGuire for his <u>imprimatur</u> on a pamphlet on
the housing problem, to be published by the Catholic Socialist

Society,[90] and in 1914, McNabb caused uproar by arguing that
the worst moral consequences predicted of socialism existed
under capitalism already,[91] while the Archbishop of Liverpool,
described by a Liberal minister for education as the mildest
man who ever slit a throat, predicted that the Church and the
socialists would work together.[92] Clerical conservatism
reasserted itself to dissolve the Catholic Trade Unionist
Federation, when in 1918 the Labour Party adopted a socialist
platform; and the same conservatism showed its strength
during the General Strike. Echoes of Wheatley's controversy
continued to resound: as late as 1948, Gallacher paraded Nitti's
patristic quotations to persuade Catholics to vote for the
Communist Party,[93] and devoted two pages of invective to 'Rerum
novarum' in his autobiography. Nor did he ever forget or
forgive O'Brien.

Yet O'Brien's reaction, if extreme, was not wholly
uncharacteristic of his Church. The girls singing 'Faith of
our Fathers', Puissant at his most apoplectic, the diocesan
committee which found Wheatley's claim to be 'Catholic' a
'snare', all shared the defensive outlook of a faith which
was inbred with fear of the outsider, and which having
suffered exclusion and persecution thought tolerance a difficult
virtue. Thus the Church feared socialism not so much in itself,
but because it might endanger religion. This was the stance
of the whole Catholic Church under Pius X, as he trampled his
modernist critics, but he struck an answering chord in Irish
community life, which appeared in its reaction to socialism.
By their very existence, the Irish church and community were
sworn foemen to the Protestant churches and government of
Britain, but in being rebels, they could not endure rebellion
against themselves, and their own establishments of the sword
and spirit found the rebel within their walls as abhorrent as
the enemy outside. It could be argued that this intolerance
was reflected in the Irish Socialist extreme and among those

Sinn Feiners whose will to be a political establishment was as strong as anyone's. This Irish tendency to factionalism strengthened the authority which tried to put it down, and which was not too squeamish about the means. A more subtle politician like McGuire tried to rise above the tumult of his warring flock, and to ignore what could not be put down. But Wheatley was difficult to ignore: he threatened to divide Catholic from Catholic on lines of class, and to put the workers' interests before Ireland. In that sense, the opposition to his socialism was not just the priests and politicians, who were no more in this than the authentic representatives of the Irishman's hope for this world and the next, as his fathers had taught him. Socialism was opposed by the whole separate and sectarian texture and fabric of Irish Catholic life, and its desperate grip on a hard-won achievement of stable families, political parties, sporting clubs, temperance and self-help societies and schools and mission chapels. These gave meaning to the poor Irishman's existence: is it any wonder if in spite of his poverty, he was cautious when Wheatley offered him more? His was a harder task than Connolly's, because his faith was more fervent; and one can only marvel at the temerity of the man in his effort to harmonise the 'Red Flag' with 'Faith of Our Fathers', and 'God Save Ireland'.

NOTES

1. On Gibbons, see Allen S. Will, <u>Life of Cardinal Gibbons, Archbishop of Baltimore</u> (New York, 1922); on Manning, see V.A. McClelland, <u>Cardinal Manning: His Public Life and Influence</u> (1962); on Moran, see Patrick Ford, <u>Cardinal Moran and the ALP: A Study in the Encounter between Moran and Socialism, 1890-1907</u> (Melbourne, 1966).

2. See for example, the frequent and lively exchanges in the Scottish socialist <u>Forward</u>, on which see below.

3. C.S. Devas, <u>The Meaning and Aim of Christian Democracy</u> (1899)

4. C.S. Devas, Plain Words on Socialism (1906).

5. James E. Handley, The Irish in Modern Scotland (Cork, 1947).

6. John Ritchie, 'Glasgow, Archdiocese of,' The Catholic Encyclopedia (1909), vol. 6, p. 578.

7. Ibid.: see also Sister Martha Skinnider, 'Catholic Elementary Education in Glasgow, 1818-1918', in T.R. Bone (ed.), Studies in the History of Scottish Education: 1872-1939 (1967), pp. 13-70.

8. Catholic Directory 1906, pp. 127, 155-6, 278, 281-3.

9. Glasgow Observer henceforth cited as GO, 25 April 1908.

10. GO 15 June 1907.

11. James E. Handley, The Celtic Story. A History of the Celtic Football Club (1960), esp. pp. 14-15.

12. John McCaffrey, 'The Irish Vote in Glasgow in the Later Nineteenth Century: A Preliminary Survey', Innes Review, 21 (Spring 1970), pp. 30-6.

13. Handley, The Irish pp. 261-301.

14. Ibid., p. 283; GO 5 Jan. 1907.

15. James Morrison, St Mary's, Pollockshaws, to Canon Ritchie, 6 January 1910: the Pollockshaws AOH 'was one of the most violent against the Clergy and especially against myself, as the whole parish knows'. Glasgow Archdiocesan Archives, henceforth cited GAA.

16. GO 31 July 1909.

17. Handley, The Irish p. 290; 'George Barnes' in DNB.

18. Walter Kendall, The Revolutionary Movement in Britain, 1900-21 (1969).

19. The best work on Wheatley is Samuel Cooper's admirable unpublished thesis, 'John Wheatley: a Study in Labour History' (unpub. Ph.D. thesis, Glasgow Univ. 1973). Also 'John Wheatley' in DNB.

20. R.K. Middlemas, The Clydesiders: A Left Wing Struggle for Parliamentary Power (1965).

21. Patrick Dollan, 'Memories of Fifty Years Ago', The Mercat Cross, vol. 6 (1953), p. 39.

22. Ibid.

23. GO 24 Feb. 1906.

24. Dollan, The Mercat Cross, vol. 6 (1953), p. 169.

25. David Lowe, Souvenirs of Scottish Labour; cited Middlemas, Clydesiders p. 31.

26. William Gallacher, Last Memoirs (1966), p. 200.

27. Pitmen, Preachers and Politics (Cambridge, 1974), pp. 170-82.

28. GO 18 Aug. 1906.

29. GO 21 July 1906.

30. GO 25 Aug. 1906.

31. GO 20 Oct. 1906.

32. GO 13 Oct. 1906.

33. Samuel Levenson, James Connolly: A Biography (1973), pp. 180-2; C. Desmond Greaves, The Life and Times of James Connolly (1961), pp. 191-2.

34. J.H., in the GO 4 Aug. 1906.

35. GO 22 Sept. 1906.

36. GO 3 Nov. 1906.

37. GO 8 Dec. 1906.

38. GO 29 Sept. 1906.

39. GO 15 Sept. 1906.

40. GO 6 Oct. 1906.

41. He announced his intention to do so, reversing an earlier reluctance, in the GO 13 Oct. 1906.

42. GO 17 Nov. 1906.

43. GO 5 Jan., 2 March 1907.

44. GO 9 March 1907.

45. GO 24 Nov. 1906: 'Mr Kelly, of the Sinn Fein Society,

claimed that before Ireland could have any Socialistic legislation, it must be cut off from Great Britain.'

46. GO 15 Feb. 1908.

47. William Gallacher, Catholics and Communism (Watford,
1948), p. 4.

48. GO 28 Sept. 1907.

49. Kendall, Revolutionary Movement p. 293.

50. Ashton, GO 16 March 1907.

51. Cooper, thesis p. 39.

52. Cf. GO 4 Aug. 1906.

53. GO 1 Feb. 1908.

54. Ibid.

55. GO 19 Oct. 1907.

56. GO 31 Oct. 1908.

57. See Forward, 31 Aug., 14 and 18 Sept. 1912 on the author's
emigration to Australia.

58. T. Colvin, at the CYMS conference at Coventry, GO 15 Aug.
1908: cf. Colvin in GO 5 Sept. 1908.

59. Dom Columba Edmonds, OSB, in GO 21 Nov. 1908.

60. GO 19 Dec. 1908.

61. GO 26 Dec. 1908.

62. GO 3 July 1909.

63. Ibid.

64. GO 1 Feb. 1908.

65. Cf. D.J. Mitchell Quinn to George Barnes, 15 April 1913,
of Martin Haddow, Labour member of the Glasgow School Board:
'the Catholic members of the Board would rather see almost
any one of their own number excluded than see Mr Haddow
defeated'.

66. GO 8 Aug. 1908.

67. Report of the Nineteenth Eucharistic Congress, held at Westminster from 9th to 13th September 1908 (1909), pp. 548-50.

68. CSS 1910.

69. On Hagerty, see J.L. Kornbluh, Rebel Voices, an I.W.W. Anthology (Ann Arbor, 1964), pp. 11-12; Robert E. Doherty, 'Thomas J. Hagerty, the Church and Socialism', Labor History (Winter 1962); cf. Fr Matthew Power, SJ, to Canon John Ritchie, 1 May 1908, GAA.

70. As is apparent from Puissant's reply to McGuire, 7 May 1908.

71. Diocesan Committee on Socialism, 13 Nov. 1908, GAA.

72. George Ritchie to Canon John Ritchie, 20 Jan. 1909, GAA.

73. Robert Paterson to Canon John Ritchie, 14 Feb. 1911, GAA.

74. O'Brien to McGuire, 11 Feb. 1911, GAA.

75. McAleer to McGuire, 22 May 1908, GAA.

76. O'Brien to Canon Mackintosh, 21 Dec. 1910, GAA.

77. McAleer to McGuire, 13 Dec. 1910, GAA.

78. McAleer to McGuire, 10 Jan. 1911, GAA.

79. O'Brien to McGuire, 22 April 1909, GAA: cf. F. McGuire to Archbishop McGuire, 12 and 19 April 1909, GAA.

80. Cutting, 'Local Lucubrations', The Eastern Argus, 13 Aug. 1910, GAA.

81. Daniel Travers to Canon John Ritchie, 1 July 1912, GAA.

82. Cooper, thesis pp. 47-8: based on Forward 6 July 1912.

83. GO 27 July 1912.

84. Canon George Ritchie to Daniel Travers, 2 July 1912, GAA.

85. GO 27 July 1912.

86. 'Plain and Coloured', GO 6 July 1912.

87. GO 7 Sept. 1912.

88. <u>GO</u> 2 Nov. 1912: 'Hitherto our counsel to Irish electors has almost invariably been to support candidates of the Labour Party in every constituency. That counsel we are no longer able to extend.'

89. C.C. Martindale, SJ, <u>Charles Dominic Plater, SJ</u> (1922). p. 139.

90. McNabb to McGuire, 21 Sept. 1912, GAA.

91. Ferdinand Valentine, OP, <u>Father Vincent McNabb OP. The Portrait of a Great Dominican</u> (1955), pp. 400-3.

92. Ibid., p. 136.

93. <u>Catholics and Communism</u>, p. 16.

8
German Clerks in England, 1870–1914: Another Aspect of the Great Depression Debate
GREGORY ANDERSON

This essay seeks to explore one small and fairly unknown aspect of the clerical labour market in the late-nineteenth century - the impact of German clerks. This apparently minor theme may have certain linkages with other more important developments. Broadly speaking, perhaps three such linkages can be identified. First, the German clerks' problem was an intrinsic part of the more general and well-known Anglo-German economic and political rivalry which emerged during the Great Depression and continued down to the First World War. Secondly, and arising out of that trade rivalry, the German clerks, given the emphasis placed upon their language and other business skills, are an integral part of the debate at that time concerning the value of investment in education in order to maintain economic leadership. Therefore, the German clerks represent one factor in the widespread demands in Britain for improvements in commercial as well as technical education. Finally, the use of German clerks and the reaction to them must be examined against the background of the wider working of the clerical labour market in which other, and arguably more significant, changes were taking place.

The starting point and chronological background to this problem
is the period of the Great Depression itself. Recently, of
course, the whole notion of the Great Depression has come under
careful scrutiny and some economic historians are now sceptical
about the utility of such a concept. In spite of this
revisionism, however, no one has seriously questioned the major
negative characteristics of the period. These are well-known
and it is unnecessary to repeat them at length here. Suffice
it to say that there was a secular fall in prices and profits,
a decline in the rate of economic growth, an at least marginal
increase in unemployment and a steady underlying increase in
foreign competition, especially in overseas markets. The
extent of foreign penetration, real or imagined, in what were
regarded as previously reserved areas for British commerce had
in turn a profound effect on national confidence. Indeed the
period can realistically be characterised as one of growing
national self-doubt and self-criticism. This mood emerges
most clearly in the contemporary debate over the shortcomings
of British institutions and commercial practices compared with
the best examples elsewhere. Elsewhere usually meant Germany.
This, above all other countries, was seen as providing the
model which could guarantee a return to a higher level of
economic performance. Contemporaries believed it then and a
number of historians, writing since, have largely endorsed
their views. Therefore, Hoffman, Aldcroft, Landes, Searle,
Sanderson, Lewis and Kindleberger have all in their various
ways suggested the greater efficiency of Germany's economy
and society.[1] As Geoffrey Searle put it, describing the
ideology of national efficiency:

> If one were to sum up its meaning in a
> single sentence, one might describe the ·
> habits, beliefs and institutions that
> put the British at a handicap in their
> competition with foreigners and to commend
> instead a social organisation that more
> closely followed the German model. [2]

The response to Germany went deeper than a mere admiration of her economic and social organisation. It was complicated by a deep distrust and even hatred of that country. David Landes got some sense of the character of the period when he suggested that, at that time, Germany 'stuck in John Bull's craw'.[3] Germany, therefore, 'assumed the dual role of model and enemy: a state whose threat to vital British interests could be fended off only through an adoption of her own methods and institutions.'[4] This strange mixture of envy, admiration, fear and hatred combined to give its tone to much of the period starting from the Anglo-German trade rivalry in the 1880s and lasting down to 1914.

Against this background the debate over alleged German superiority took place. In this debate, most attention was initially focused on the excellence of Germany's educational system which, it was widely believed, laid the basis for that country's two-pronged advance on the economic front. From Germany's technical schools and universities (Technische Hochschulen) the links were forged with the new science-based industries. While in commerce, Germany's trade schools and business institutes (Handelshochschulen) produced the merchants and particularly the salesmen who were penetrating foreign markets with their direct and dynamic selling methods. It is with this commercial threat that the German clerks' problem is intrinsically connected, with the extra dimension that German clerks were competing internally in the English labour market and in the domestic economy.

Reference to the threat of competition from foreign, and mainly German, clerks can be traced back to the mid-Victorian years. The Report on Technical Education in 1867 drew attention to the problem. 'The German clerk', wrote Jacob Behrens representing the Chambers of Commerce, 'who has a good knowledge of three or four languages, who has been taught to understand the working of the exchanges...the tariffs of different

countries...will find employment and rise to an important
position or to independence much sooner than the English
clerk.'[5]   By 1880 The London Telegraph was arguing, in less
measured language, that English clerks were 'being pushed from
their stools by competitors from Germany'.[6]   The feeling of
insecurity generated by the German clerks reached a peak in
1887 when the London Chamber of Commerce carried out a joint
enquiry with the Association of Chambers of Commerce into the
number of foreign clerks engaged in London's commercial houses.
According to the enquiry's testimony some 35 per cent
of the firms which replied stated that they employed foreigners
while several firms with a purely English staff admitted they
would, in all probability, employ them in future.[7]   Unfortunately, objective enquiries such as that carried out by
the London Chamber of Commerce were rare.   Many other
commentators preferred to base their opinions on the number
and impact of German clerks on a mixture of wild conjecture
and rumour.   Therefore, in 1888, the Liverpool-based The
Clerks' Journal, inspired by the London Chamber of Commerce's
enquiry, could warn ominously but uncritically of the 'incredible
number of Germans employed in London alone'.[8]   As rumours spread
it became difficult to disentangle myth from reality.   In some
people's minds a full-blooded invasion was occurring.   One MP,
for example, quoted as evidence a statement he had heard at a
public dinner, which stated there were 14,000 German clerks in
Manchester alone and 100,000s in London.[9]

Such figures quoted so confidently were, in fact, wildly
exaggerated.   The census returns tell a different story.   From
1871, possibly in response to the public disquiet over this
issue, the number of foreign-born commercial clerks, merchants
and brokers was enumerated separately.   The number of foreign-
born clerks, as table I indicates, increased from 2,512 in 1871
to 6,946 in 1911.   Germans constituted the largest single
national group with 1,262 in 1871 and 2,748 in 1911.   As can

204

be seen foreign clerks did indeed represent a substantial minority among commercial clerks but they were never present in the numbers implied by some commentators. Moreover, although they were expanding in absolute terms they were not increasing as a percentage of the total clerical labour force. In 1871 foreign and German clerks represented 2.8% and 1.4% respectively of the clerical labour force but by 1911 their shares had fallen to 1.5% and 0.6%. Of course, part of this declining share can be explained by the huge increase in female clerks with whom foreign clerks, who were almost entirely male, did not really compete. If foreign clerks are calculated as a percentage of the total number of male clerks then their decline is less marked. Nevertheless in 1901 and 1911 the ratio of foreign clerks to the total number of male clerks was not expanding but was steady at 1.7%.

TABLE I

Foreign Clerks in England and Wales, 1871-1911

Year	All commercial clerks		Foreign commercial clerks		German commercial clerks	
	Number	%	Number	%	Number	%
1871	91,042	100	2,512	2.8	1,262	1.3
1881	181,457	100	3,327	1.8	1,795	1.0
1891	247,229	100	4,049	1.6	1,966	0.8
1901	363,673	100	5,443	1.5	2,170	0.6
1911	477,535	100	6,949	1.5	2,748	0.6

The entry of German clerks into the English labour market was considerably eased by the network of Mercantile Unions (Kaufmannische Vereine) operating in Germany. These self-help organisations, which fulfilled a kind of trade union function, existed in all the country's major commercial centres. In some respects they were similar to the clerks' associations in Britain, although they were far larger, better organised and more numerous. Among their other functions they were the chief mechanism for filling vacancies in Germany, and through their connections with other countries they placed many German clerks in situations abroad. In London a number of organisations, including the German Mercantile Society and the German Young Men's Association, often working with the German-based Mercantile Unions provided assistance with travel costs, accommodation and job search. As a result German clerks were cushioned from many of the costs incurred upon entry into the English labour market.[10]

Once in England the response to German and other foreign clerks was almost entirely hostile. Much of that hostility was, of course, simply an extension of the Germanophobia mentioned earlier. At the same time German clerks were feared and hated by English clerks because of their particular impact on the labour market. It was widely believed, for example, that Germans worked cheaply or without remuneration. In 1895 the National Union of Clerks denounced those employers who opened 'their office doors to the sons of rich merchants trading in Berlin, Leipzig and other German towns. Such foreigners found their way into English offices and accepted berths at small salaries and in many cases for no salary at all.'[11] At a more personal level one Manchester clerk complaining in the 1880s of fierce job competition, feared that if low-paid situations were refused 'the German to whom salary is no object steps forward and offers his services for next to nothing.'[12]

The objective evidence which is available generally supports these views but further suggests that it is necessary to distinguish between two separate supply curves of German

clerical labour. Material collected from the London Chamber
of Commerce, which through its employment department categorised
those clerks available for employment according to job type,
qualifications, salary required and nationality, shows that the
better-connected and most-skilled foreign clerks were concentrated in a highly-specialised area of the labour market.
They were employed almost exclusively as foreign correspondents,
an area in which their language skills made them particularly
suitable. According to the London Chamber of Commerce very
few applied for jobs as managers, company secretaries, book-
keepers, ledger clerks, shipping and invoice clerks. What is
more, as table II makes clear, foreign correspondence was
apparently monopolised by foreign clerks, especially Germans,
to the exclusion of the English.[13] Incidentally, many of the
other foreign clerks, especially the Swiss, Austrians and
Hungarians were German-speaking. It was these clerks,
operating at the top end of the labour market and seeking
valuable experience abroad in an advanced country, which
Musgrove was prompted to describe as part of the 'migratory
elite'.[14]

TABLE II

Foreign Correspondence Clerks by Nationality, 1900-1914.

Nationality	1900	1910	1914
German	33	79	97
British	3	2	-
Swiss	7	17	42
Others	7	52	63
Total	50	150	202

Source: Supplements to the London Chamber of Commerce.

Not all German clerks were so successful in their job search. A number anyway (how many is unknown) operated at a much lower level in the labour market. Organisations such as the Society for the Relief of Distressed Foreigners were providing board and lodging, employment information and even financial assistance in returning to their home countries for a large number of foreign immigrants. Among these were German clerks and commercial travellers, some of whom were unemployed in England for upwards of a year.[15] German clerks faced with this situation soon became demoralised and were often forced into the 'secondary' labour market where work was casual and intermittent, wages were low and there was little or no chance of advancement. By contrast the German clerks who acquired positions as foreign correspondents may be said to have entered the stable and upwardly mobile 'primary' labour market.[16]

Whether working at the top or at the bottom of the labour market one characteristic all German clerks had in common was a willingness to accept wages lower than the average for British commercial clerks. Even quite highly qualified German clerks, equipped with several foreign languages plus a knowledge of book-keeping and shorthand, were prepared to work for wages as low as those paid to British female shorthand typists or junior clerks at the bottom end of the market. Most German clerks, who advertised their availability as foreign correspondents, were prepared to work for wages of between £60 to £90 and some as little as £40. A small minority even worked as 'volunteers' (i.e. without a salary) although judging from the London Chamber of Commerce's reports these were not so common as was popularly feared. Interestingly, the handful of British clerks applying for jobs as foreign correspondents all sought wages of £100 or more.

Various explanations were offered, at the time, to account for the ability of the German clerk to undercut his British counterpart in this way. For some the policy of conscription

in Germany was a factor. According to this argument 'with
the prospect of military service before them, it is useless
(for German youths) to make any definite business engagement'[17]
so that they were prompted to spend a couple of valuable years
away from home, perfecting their knowledge of foreign languages
and business methods. Therefore, German clerks were often
happy to accept lower wages in the short term because (i) they
did not anticipate permanent settlement in Britain but expected
to return to Germany after a few years, and (ii) they expected
a net addition to their income in Germany as a result of the
British experience.[18]

This pattern of re-migration was regarded as an important
social cost implicit in the use of German labour. The
experience gained by the German clerks represented ultimately
a net addition to the human capital stock of a major competitor.
It became easy for some to see, in a conspiratorial manner,
that 'the essence of the German clerks' invasion was not simply
that they were taking jobs but business also'.[19] As the
Chamber of Commerce suggested:

> There is no doubt much weight in the
> objection which is frequently taken, on
> the ground that foreign clerks are mere
> birds of passage, who come here to obtain
> higher pay and acquire greater experience
> than their own respective countries afford -
> an experience which they intend to utilise
> on their return home in direct competition
> with those under whom they served their
> apprenticeship. 20

Not all German clerks may have wished to re-migrate back to
Germany. Non-return migration is expected to be related to
the higher earnings opportunities existing in the country of
destination compared to the country of origin. Those Germans
who operated at the bottom of the labour market were almost
certainly attracted by the prospect of the higher wage levels

and conditions which obtained in England. Many Germans even
when working cheaply in England were better paid than at home.
These poorer German clerks were probably an example of an
attempt at permanent migration. However as a number of German
clerks were repatriated through the benevolent societies acting
on their behalf their goal of permanent migration was not
always realised.

A number of the better-equipped and well-placed German
clerks also anticipated permanent migration. Because of this
they were regarded as a major threat as they were taking jobs
and becoming businessmen in England, thus removing trade from
British control and usurping British clerks' chances of
advancement at home. Certainly as table III suggests,
foreign-born merchants, of which Germans were once more in a
majority, did form a sizeable though not expanding minority
in Britain.

TABLE III

Foreign Merchants in England and Wales, 1871-1911

Year	All merchants		Foreign merchants		German merchan	
	Number	Percentage	Number	Percentage	Number	Percenta
1871	15,903	100	2,301	14.5	1,084	6.8
1881	10,359	100	-	-	-	-
1891	8,460	100	2,676[1]	-	671	7.9
1901	5,151	100	870	16.9	350	6.8
1911	5,536	100	858	15.5	320	5.8

[1]Up to 1891 includes brokers, agents and factors thus over-
stating the number.

This erosion by German clerks of the opportunities available
to British clerks was a source of much comment. According

to one observer:

> More British clerks remain clerks all their
> lives than do those of any other nation and
> the consequence is that even in Britain
> itself an undue proportion of British trade
> falls into the hands of foreigners... The
> foreign clerk becomes the foreign principal
> in our midst, and a dull sub-consciousness
> of this probability makes him a stumbling-
> block and a rock of offence to our commercial
> youth; he is hated because he is dangerous. 21

Just how dangerous is difficult to say but if the Germans
were experiencing greater career mobility than English clerks
then their monopoly of foreign correspondence was undoubtedly
important. Correspondence clerkships were always highly
coveted because of their closeness to the area of decision-
making within the firm. Unlike other more specialised or
routine positions, foreign correspondence provided clerks with
access to the wider workings of a firm and, more particularly,
introduced them to its foreign customers. From such a
position a man might more easily either enter the firm's
management, exploit the opportunities inherent in travelling
abroad to direct overseas agencies or even set up in business
on his own account. Interestingly D.C.M. Platt has noted
that German clerks previously employed by British merchants
were indeed establishing their own firms in South American
markets at this time.[22] Moreover, the specialised language
and other skills required of foreign correspondents meant
that 'ports of entry' were created for German clerks into
what may otherwise have been fairly closed internal labour
markets with most jobs within the firm filled by clerks who
had been recruited at a general entry level and then been
trained and selected for advancement. In Figure 1 a
simplified model described how such an internal labour market
might operate.[23]

Figure 1

A Simple Internal Labour Market for a Nineteenth Century
Commercial Firm

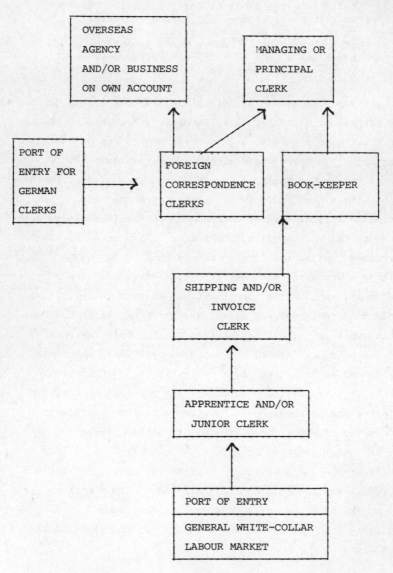

212

Against this background the reasons for the apparent superiority of the German clerk were endlessly debated, the focus shifting almost unconsciously between technical, and therefore possibly measurable explanations on the one hand, and inherent or racial ones, on the other. The latter were never far below the surface. The German, therefore, came to be regarded as somehow steadier, more persevering and reliable. By contrast the English clerk was much less serious 'taking no intellectual interest in his work and seemed to give his mind to sport'.[24] As always the racial response was a peculiar mixture of fear, dislike and grudging admiration. Typically one Liverpool clerk could at once applaud 'the high moral and intellectual capacities of the Teutonic race' and lampoon 'the obsequious German clerk, the dull phlegmatic plodder with neither tact nor judgement'.[25]

Leaving aside these inherent and unhelpful racial characteristics one tangible advantage which the Germans were widely regarded as possessing was access to a superior education. Much of their success was directly related to Germany's commercial schools in which young men were given a sound practical and theoretical background in commerce. What impressed observers in this country was the highly-structured nature of German education in which students having undergone basic training in the elementary and secondary schools could advance into the commercial and/or high schools before either going into business or completing their studies in the Commercial High Schools where they might continue, if necessary, until the age of twenty-five. Apart from these commercial schools, the country's secondary schools, which underpinned the entire system and in which no special commercial subjects were necessarily taught but which provided an excellent liberal training lasting some three years longer than in Britain, were thought to constitute an altogether superior preparation for commercial life.[26]

Britain, by contrast, possessed no comparable system of commercial education. In this country clerks, commercial travellers or employers-in-training left school at the age of fourteen or fifteen and then trained within the firm. Traditionally they served an apprenticeship, usually for three years. In fact with the expansion of routine clerical work the practice of apprenticeship was less common by the end of the nineteenth century, although it still persisted in the best commercial firms and banks. Critics of the British system believed that the traditional early placement of youths in business led in their mid-teens to the loss of the key years of educational opportunity. 'It is possible', write F. Hooper, 'that the earlier provision of a commercial course commencing at fifteen and extending over three or four years might induce parents to keep their sons at school for an additional two or three years at least and would meet the needs of youths who would be likely later on to fill positions below if not up to the employer class.'[27] Interestingly the attack on the old notion of a commercial apprenticeship and the belief in a longer period of formal education corresponds strongly to the thoughts of David Landes and others who have argued that industrial apprenticeship combined with the inadequacies of technical education acted in a similar way as retarding factors on the manufacturing side of the economy.[28]

Those provisions for commercial education which were developed in Britain at this time were linked mainly to the needs of the bottom end of the labour market. This period witnessed an enormous expansion of routine white-collar occupations in which thousands of young clerks, an increasing proportion of whom were female, joined in the hunt to become 'certificated'. Provision for instruction in basic office skills such as elementary book-keeping, shorthand and type-writing blossomed on demand. A hugh increase occurred in continuation (i.e. evening) classes organised both by voluntary

agencies (eg YMCA, Mechanics' Institutes and the Society of
Arts) and local government both under the School Boards and
later under the new provisions of the Education Act of 1902.[29]
While the scale of investment in routine commercial education
in England was undoubtedly high, there was no matching
expansion in the provision for more specialised instruction
in such areas as commercial foreign languages and correspondence. Moreover as the human capital debate, both then
and since, has revolved around the top and not the bottom of
the educational system, it is important to distinguish within
commercial education between higher and lower levels of
training. Primary or lower-level education, given the nature
of late-nineteenth century technological and commercial change,
may only have been important in forming 'a basis for the more
advanced training of white-collar workers and to facilitate
the selection of those most capable of receiving that
training'.[30] While some improvements were gradually occurring
in the technical sphere at the top of the educational system,
Michael Sanderson has shown that, with a few exceptions such
as the Faculty of Commerce at Birmingham, British universities
generally neglected commercial education at this time. The
result of this situation was that although 'it may be argued
that English civic universities were the equivalent of the
German Technische Hochschulen, it would be difficult to point
to any part of the English educational system in the 1890s as
a counterpart of the German trade schools.'[31]

Of course, much of the explanation for this neglect of
commercial human capital formation lies not on the supply but
on the demand side. Given an elastic supply curve of German
clerks any investment in specialised training by English
clerks might be expected to yield little additional income.
After all, German clerks had the advantages of incurring low
or negligible training and migration costs and were prepared
to undercut their English competitors by working for very

moderate wages. English clerks by contrast, in pursuit of
specialised training, incurred both psychic costs (incursion
into leisure time) and entry fees on continuation courses.
English employers were for the most part not prepared to
invest directly in the formal commercial education of their
clerks. This is hardly surprising given the opportunity
cost of such an investment with a cheap supply of highly-
trained German labour available.[32]

Whatever the reasons for the neglect of higher commercial
education in England it appears that Germany was achieving a
high social rate of return on its investment in advanced
education. From the 1880s Germany was successfully launching
its trade drive invading both the British and third markets.
The basis for this success lay in competitive prices, leadership in the new commodities and sales energy. With regards
to the last two causes advanced education may have provided
a large, if somewhat unmeasurable, residual component in
German economic growth. While the connection between
technical education, technological growth and the new
commodities is quite well-known in the German case, the links
between the sales drive and commercial education are less
familiar. However, the impact of German commercial travellers
in third markets, well observed in contemporary British
consular reports, and the penetration of German clerks into
British business, which created such unease in Britain, were
both aspects of the relationship between commercial education
and Germany's tremendous sales effort.[33]

In any assessment of the effect of the German clerks'
influx a distinction must be drawn between their real and
psychic impact. As we have seen they undoubtedly had an
effect in a strategically important but relatively narrow
band of the labour market where British employers exploited
an additional source of cheap but highly-qualified labour.
There is no doubt that they operated further down the labour

market in the area of routine, casual or temporary employment.
There, along with other ill-equipped clerks, they were by no
means so successful but frequently suffered from unemployment
and distress. A number of them, as we saw, had recourse to
benefit societies and were in due course returned home. In
addition they represented only a small and static proportion
of the clerical labour force. Despite these considerations
they were often singled out as the most important threat
facing British clerks. In large part the reaction to them
can only be explained by the changes which were occurring
quite independently in the British clerical labour market.
In the years after 1870 a number of short and long-term
developments coincided to create feelings of uncertainty in
many branches of clerical employment. Evidence from the
clerks' associations and other sources indicates an increase
in unemployment during the Great Depression years as firms
failed or cut their costs in the face of increasing competition
and falling profits.[34] In the longer term the increase in
demand for routine low-status clerks was more than matched by
an increase in the potential supply at the lower end of the
labour market. Female clerks and typists, for example,
became a permanent feature of the occupational scene at this
time. Problems such as unemployment, low wages and job
competition did not seriously affect the better-placed clerks.
The difficulties they faced were different but no less serious.
Traditionally better-placed clerks had sought respectability
by achieving economic independence and setting up in business
on their own. In the last third of the century the failure
of firms in the depression years and the increase in the scale
of business organisation combined to create fewer openings
for clerks, especially in the mercantile sector. In a period
of diminishing opportunities the entry of German clerks,
taking up key positions and possibly setting up in business
on their own account, was a natural source of resentment.

In a sense the German influx was a convenient scapegoat for other and more profound changes which were occurring in Britain's clerical labour market. In reality, the explanations for those changes had little to do with the impact of German clerks.[35]

NOTES

I wish to thank Shirley Woolley for willingly undertaking the task of typing up this essay. I should also like to thank Bob Ward, Research Officer in the Department of Economics, Salford University, for his help in collecting and processing the census material.

1. See, for example, D.H. Aldcroft, 'Investment in and Utilisation of Manpower: Great Britain and her rivals, 1870-1914', in B. Ratcliffe (ed.), Great Britain and Her World (Manchester, 1975); R.J.S. Hoffman, Great Britain and the German Trade Rivalry, 1875-1914 (Philadelphia, 1933); C.P. Kindleberger, Economic Response (Harvard, 1978), ch. 7; D. Landes, The Unbound Prometheus (Cambridge, 1969), ch. 5; W.A. Lewis, Growth and Fluctuations (1978), ch. 5; M. Sanderson, The Universities and British Industry (1972), ch. 7; G. Searle, The Quest for National Efficiency (Oxford, 1971), ch. 3.

2. Searle, Quest p. 54.

3. Landes, Unbound Prometheus p. 327.

4. Searle, Quest p. 57.

5. Parliamentary Papers, Report on Technical Education, letters from chambers of commerce, PP, 1867-1868, LIV, 23.

6. The London Telegraph, 15 Sept. 1880.

7. Details from the Report are available in The Chamber of Commerce Journal, 5 Aug. 1887, pp. 170-2.

8. The Clerks' Journal, June 1888.

9. From a speech heard by Mr W. Field, MP (Dublin) and quoted in the Supplement, The Chamber of Commerce Journal, April 1902.

10. For evidence on the role of the German clerks' associations in the penetration of German clerks into the English

labour market see The Chamber of Commerce Journal, 5 Sept. 1889, for the importance of the Kaufmannishe Vereine, and The Bee-hive, December 1889, for the activities of the Frankfurt-on-Main Clerks' Association.

11. The Clerks' Gazette, 31 Oct. 1895.

12. The Manchester Guardian, 20 Nov. 1886.

13. The figures for foreign correspondence clerks provided in table II should not be taken as representing a national total. They are taken from the lists of clerks who were available for employment published as supplements in the London Chamber of Commerce Journal.

14. F. Musgrove, The Migratory Elite (1963) pp. 4-5.

15. For evidence of German clerks operating at the bottom of the labour market see G. Anderson, Victorian Clerks (Manchester 1976), pp. 63-5.

16. The difference between 'primary' and 'secondary' labour markets is a common enough notion in labour economics. For an explanation see F.R. Marshall, et al., Labour Economics (Illinois, 1976) pp. 275-80.

18. Within the context of this essay migration has been considered as a private investment. The German clerks who migrated to England, whether temporarily or permanently, are assumed to have engaged in a form of rational decision-making that entails costs and engenders increments to lifetime earnings streams. As is mentioned later in the essay there are also obvious community implications of such migration. In the sense that Germany invested in the training of German clerks who later worked in Britain this may be said to represent a net loss for the former community and a net gain for the latter. For the permanent migration this may be true but once re-migration is considered then new difficulties arise in the assessment of costs and gains. Some German clerks were re-migrating, taking new skills and experience back with them to undercut Britain in the trade war. The migration theory utilised here is derived from M.J. Bowman and R.G. Myers, 'Schooling, Experience and Gains and Losses in Human Capital Through Migration', in R. Wykstra (ed.), Human Capital Formation and Manpower Development (New York, 1971) and Julie de Vanzo, 'Differences Between Return and Non-return Migration', International Migration Review X (1976).

19. W.G. Blackie, Commercial Education (1888), p. 12.

20. Quoted in The Chamber of Commerce Journal, 5 Aug. 1887.

21. J. Montgomery, Education and Commerce (1911), p.5.

22. D.C.M. Platt, Latin America and British Trade (1972), p. 136. See also H.S. Ferns, Britain and Argentina in the Nineteenth Century (1960), p. 443, for evidence of German commercial penetration in the 1880s and the superiority of German commercial manpower over British.

23. The concept of the internal labour market is well-known to labour economists. For a detailed theoretical analysis see P. Doeringer and M.J. Poire, Internal Labour Markets and Manpower Analysis (Lexington, 1971). See also Marshall et al., Labour Economics pp. 270-5.

24. Quoted in S.F. Cotgrave, Education and Social Change (1958), p. 51.

25. The Clerks' Journal, Nov. and Dec, 1889.

26. There is a surprisingly extensive body of contemporary material dealing with the contrasts between German and British commercial education. The Parliamentary reports on Technical Education for such years as 1867, 1884 and 1900 are one source. In addition see F. Hooper, Commercial Education at Home and Abroad (1901) and M. Sadler (ed.), Continuation Schools in England and Elsewhere (Manchester, 1907). Much of the debate was carried out in the columns of London's Chamber of Commerce Journal.

27. Hooper, Commercial Education p. 26. The evidence on the retarding effect of the commercial apprenticeship does not all point in one direction. An important and widely-quoted report on 'The Early Training of German Clerks' by the British vice-consul at Mannheim (see The Chamber of Commerce Journal, 5 Sept. 1889) questioned the role of the German educational system in producing excellence and suggested that the persistence of apprenticeship in Germany, in which 'one cannot separate the clerk from the merchant' was the basis of success.

28. See Landes, Unbound Prometheus pp. 340-8.

29. For the expansion of commercial education see Anderson, Victorian Clerks ch. 6. Interestingly much faith was pinned on the power of routine commercial education, and shorthand especially, to raise clerks' status and clear the labour market. In fact the considerable expansion of commercial education was directly related to the demand for routine labour and thereby to the lowering of overall status.

30. See J.D. Gould, Economic Growth in History (1972), p. 312.

31. Sanderson, Universities p. 187.

32. The lack of interest by British employers in the formal training of their clerks was a source of much comment in the late-nineteenth century. Certainly few commercial schools in England matched the emerging 'business schools' to be found in the USA and Western Europe. Likewise many clerks were discouraged from making such an investment by a combination of long working hours, intrusion into leisure and entry fees. In London in the 1880s probably the cheapest available course in German was at the YMCA at five shillings per term but fees could range as high as £1 11s. 6d. at King's College (see The Chamber of Commerce Journal, 5 Aug. 1887). On employers' attitudes to commercial education see Anderson, Victorian Clerks pp. 97-107.

33. The threat from German commercial travellers is more well-known to students of the Great Depression period. See, for example, D.H. Aldcroft and H.W. Richardson, The British Economy 1870-1939 (1969), pp. 155-9.

34. See Anderson, Victorian Clerks ch. 5.

35. For an elaboration of the underlying changes in the clerical labour market see G. Anderson, 'The Social Economy of Late-Victorian Clerks', in G. Crossick (ed.), The Lower Middle Class in Britain, 1870-1914 (1977).

9
Alien Working-Class Response: the Leeds Jewish Tailors, 1880–1914
JOE BUCKMAN

Union organisation by alien immigrants from Eastern Europe
during 1880–1914 has received no more attention than an
occasional glance in general works on immigration, or on
small trade unions. Arguably, further, these have deflected
inquiry from an area of labour history essential to the
exploration of the roots of the Jewish community in Britain,
and from the important response of English labour to the
problems posed by the immigrants. Mrs Lerner's version of
the Jewish tailors as a transplant of Talmudic scholars from
Russia and Poland, for example, hardly produces a picture of
stern unionising material.[1] The Leeds Jewish branch of the
trade, moreover, has enjoyed a cosy presentation, obscuring
its internal economic and class conflicts. Yet, by 1912,
when it was observed that 'the Sweater knows no race or blood
bond', such conflict was an old ghetto commonplace.[2] An
uncritical perpetuation of contemporary propagandist views of
Leeds as a centre of large Jewish workshops, 'orders in
quantity', and 'regular work' - all in idyllic contrast to
the horrendous East End - also invites thoughts of benign
industrial relations based on a sound and static industrial
structure.[3] Above all, the 'communal' approach to alien
settlement either locates the trade unions among proliferous

charity and religious organisations, thereby obliterating
them as the representative institutions of Jewish proletarianism
and as the agents of class struggle; or fails to notice them
or their role in winning alien acceptance, at all.[4]

This is strange, since the most imposing alien union, in
size, influence, and continuity of life, was to be found, not
in the populous and publicised East End, but in the obscure
Leeds slum, 'The Leylands'. Prior to the mass immigration
induced by the assassination of Alexander II in 1881, there
were fewer than thirty Jewish workshops in Leeds, which on the
evidence of their slum locations in domestic premises, could
hardly have employed many aliens.[5] Yet, at this 'prehistoric'
stage of the community, a union of Jewish tailors appeared,
probably as early as 1874.[6] After 1881 immigrant numbers in
Leeds increased rapidly, reaching 25,000 by 1908.[7] Attracted
by the prospect of outwork from a native wholesale clothing
industry expanding from 21 firms in 1881 to 145 by 1911,[8]
tailoring became the chief occupation of the aliens. For the
growth of alien unions, however, there were complex problems.

Significant immigration coincided with the end of peak
Victorian prosperity, with the rise of concern about foreign
competition, and with a period of hectic activity and growth
of English unions. These formed the background to the great
anti-alien movement whose triumph was the Restriction Act of
1905. Apart from objections to their presence on many social
grounds,[9] the aliens were, more dangerously, regarded as highly
undesirable labour competition. This view, and also that their
concentration in particular trades and districts affected English
workers, was endorsed by Parliament as early as 1889.[10] The
objecting voice of English labour came loud and clear through
the Trades Union Congresses of the 1880s and 1890s. 'Pauper
Immigration' was before the Congress of 1888 when it was agreed
that 'it was the duty of the trades to keep the matter under
close consideration'.[11] At the same Congress a resolution of

the Edinburgh Tailors, seconded by Keir Hardie and passed,
deplored the fact that Britain had become 'the refuge of all
the rubbish of the central countries of Europe'.[12] The
worried traditional craft tailors, curiously overlooking the
effect of cheap mass production on their ancient trade since
the 1850s, blamed 'the Jewish system' and the public for
wearing its products 'stained by the sweat of some poor white
slave who has to endure the lash of some Jewish Simon Legree'.[13]
The Jewish bourgeoisie of old settlement were equally
offended. 'The influx of foreign poor' was regarded as a
disturbance which might well affect the even tenor of their
wealthy enclave.[14] Jewish 'society' journals lashed 'the
scum of the Polish ghetto',[15] whilst Jewish MPs campaigned
enthusiastically for the restriction of aliens.

Local opposition, aggravated by the high concentration of
foreigners, was naturally strong. Labour leaders favoured
restriction but worked for the organisation of settled aliens
in the hope that they, too, would welcome protection against
the competition of more aliens.[16] The correspondence columns
of Leeds newspapers testify also to the hostile attitudes of
the wider public.[17] The intensity of opposition to their
presence in the town, plus the dangers of physical confrontation,
contributed to the uniquely strong tailors' impulse to
organisation, and identification with English labour is a
strongly recurrent theme in their history.

Building a union in a hostile society was also attended
by peculiar internal problems. The geographical and
occupational mobility of the alien was high as he readily
moved on or trafficked between occupations. At least before
the 1890s, newcomers learned no more than a single, simple
process by way of 'apprenticeship' with the result that men
were not very specific to their trade. The structure of the
trade also affected membership. Jewish workshops depended
on the large Leeds wholesalers whose excess orders they made

up. Thus, the Jewish branch was merely ancillary and always
liable to lose workers in the frequent trade disturbances to
which the industry was prone.

For a generation after 1881, also, the associated
questions of organisation and discipline created problems.
The alien worker had no organisational antecedents of the
English type and Jewish individualism rejected discipline,
to the exasperation of English leaders. To the Leeds socialist,
Tom Maguire, for example, the Jews were 'an eminently unorgan-
isable people in the absence of a Moses'.[18] The Factory Times,
which generally encouraged the tailors, considered them unstable
and 'very poor at organisation and discipline'.[19] Another
problematic feature was their revolutionary standpoint. Workers'
Friend, the influential Yiddish-language organ, promulgated a
colourful admixture of Marxism and Kropotkinism[20] and the notion
of smashing capitalism entered freely through British ports as
part of the intellectual baggage of many aliens. The newcomer
often viewed the enclosed economy of the ghetto as a microcosmic
image of the macro-system and, if the English unions were not
yet ready for revolution, the alien could certainly set about
the abolition of the most-immediate capitalist class: the
Jewish masters. Thus, a death-threat was injected into Jewish
disputes leading to the polarisation implicit in the formation
of a countervailing Masters' Society, and to a degree of
bitterness in exchanges which often shocked Leeds citizens.[21]

The embryo union of the 1870s appeared in the 1880s in
the form of three separate unions of tailors, machiners, and
pressers,[22] and as union activity increased, the alarmed
masters formed their society.[23] Also apparent and increasing
was the concern of local labour and press at alien conditions
and lack of organisation for protection. The Trades' Council,
through J.H. Sweeney, an official of the National Union of
Boot and Shoe Operatives and a future secretary of the Jewish
tailors, voiced native reactions at its meeting in May, 1884.

225

He thought the tailors had 'little pluck' but that this was
due to their working seventeen hours per day 'in shops not
fit for dogs to be in'.[24]   The Leeds Express was exhortative.
Christian workers, it considered, had 'in a measure thrown
off long hours and poor wages'.   The Jews could do the same
if they were united.[25]   With the unions on both sides in
confrontation, and with English interests in close observation,
the pattern was completed by an idea held by both classes of
the ghetto: that of mutual destruction.   The masters set
about the task on the inception of their Society and, by use
of the blacklist, openly sought to 'crush the societies and
to prevent the leaders of the men from having any employment
in the town'.[26]   The unions announced that all the evils of
the trade were due to the capitalist class and that the
origins of their poverty lay in being robbed of the rightful
fruits of their labour.[27]

In more practical terms, the unions claimed recognition,
but this was firmly rejected by the masters who countered
with a ban of one year on any worker discharged by any one of
their number.   As a strike broke out, Jewish blackleg labour
was imported from Liverpool.[28]   One week later, however,
after press warnings that public opinion would 'certainly not
support either association in simply trying to break down the
other', the masters agreed to recognise the unions.[29]

Characteristically, however, the settlement was far from
permanent.   The men found, as they were to find in the future,
that enforcement was a most difficult task.   As well as the
men, the mobility of masters was high.   The new alien, with
his rapidly acquired skills, could simply disappear from
entrepreneurial ranks as easily as he had entered them.
Small masters were difficult to control and many were ignorant
of the significance of labour agreements as understood by
English unions.   In the following year, the appearance of
Workers' Friend served to focus more sharply the vision of the

Jewish master as typification of the capitalist system.   From
Leeds came the view that, whilst the capitalist did 'not place
so much as a finger in cold water', the Jewish worker ground
away his life and health.   The way to throw off 'the blood-
suckers and robbers' was to open co-operative workshops which,
by working directly for the wholesalers, would eliminate the
masters.[30]

This threat became manifest at a mass meeting of the
three unions in March 1885, which pledged itself to 'rely on
the influence of the Labour Association to procure work from
the warehouses'.[31]   By this date, the unions had as secretary,
J.H. Sweeney, who led the campaign which was now mounted to
abolish the masters.   On 2 May, Isaac Myers, the tailors'
president, made a public appeal to the large Leeds wholesalers,
assuring them that the middlemen were reaping large profits
weekly 'as was shown by their class of residence &c'.[32]   A
co-operative workshop was soon established but failed to
survive the year owing to the low prices received for work.[33]

In the same year, the tailors sent a circular to the
masters demanding a uniform working day for all classes in
the trade: from 8 am to 8 pm.   Prior to the strike provoked
by this document, the Jewish clothing worker's day, with the
single exception of that of the record-breaking Jewish slipper
worker, was of outstanding length in the industry of Leeds.
Machiners, the 'artistocrats' of the trade, already worked the
day demanded but tailors and pressers worked from 7 am to 9 pm,
whilst underpressers - the lowest form of tailoring life -
worked 6 am to 9 pm.   The masters' rejection of this demand
caused a two-week strike.   Having rapidly learned the bitterness of Jewish disputes, local writers warned the men that
their vituperative style would cost them public support, and
that they ought to be courteous to the masters and 'use only
quiet persuasion to those of their fellows who might differ
from them'.[34]   The masters, however, the busy season being

upon them, quickly conceded the point.[35]

This action, unimportant in the wider history of the tailors, yields a first fleeting glimpse of their early ability. The strike was well led and Sweeney was a successful negotiator. Its timing, at the height of the busy pre-Whitsun season, caused the masters to come under pressure from the wholesalers for completion of orders, making it difficult for them to hold out. This timing became a regular feature of the tailors' strikes. Jacob Finn, one of the leaders, considered this the first Jewish strike by the first Jewish union in the modern world. The machiners, he stated, with nothing to gain, took the initiative on behalf of the tailors and pressers. It was a well-organised movement. When blacklegs arrived from London, they were met by pickets, given a 'brotherly talk', and put back on the London train with tickets paid for by the Leeds men.[36]

If the men dominated busy seasons, the masters came into their own in the equally regular slack seasons. The blacklist was soon again in wide use and the strike leaders, including Finn, were forced out of Leeds. The depression of 1885-6 did much to negate the limited victory and many tailors, encouraged by the Jewish Guardians, emigrated. At the same time, a fresh wave of aliens caused worsening conditions in Leeds and there was again talk of eighteen-hour days of the pressers.[37]

Despite these adverse conditions, the unions held together. Lewis Frank, a new tailors' leader, announced that recruitment and education were progressing. At least among smaller masters, he claimed, union power was on the increase. Shops could now be entered by officials to settle disputes and, if the master did not agree with the union, he found himself without labour. Many new union members, he stated, were small masters they had turned into ex-masters. He also reported a major step towards acceptance by English labour in

228

the formal recognition of the unions by the Leeds Trades'
Council - a sign, he considered, that the Jewish workers were
'not shut out of the general company of the English working
classes'.[38]

In their next phase, however, the aliens came under the
influence, not of the Liberal Trades Council, but of the Leeds
branch of the Socialist League, whose leaders were agitating
strongly among the unions of aliens by 1888. This probably
represents the influence of socialism in Leeds alien circles
rather than the attractions of the general unionism with which
the League was then much preoccupied. One sign of leftist
influence was that an overall president of the three unions
had been elected in the person of Morris Kemmelhor, a
revolutionary devoted to the abolition of the Jewish master.
The League's agitation to bring the aliens under its influence,
led by T. Maguire, A. Mattison, T. Paylor, and W. Cockayne,
the Gasworkers' leader, also attracted national figures such
as J.L. Mahon. At a huge meeting in the Leylands on 3 January
1888, he lectured the tailors on Marx, informed them that
socialism was 'only a higher stage of trade unionism', and
hoped that the Jewish workers would not stand back from the
struggle. The speech was translated into Yiddish and widely
read. The voice of the Trades' Council also prompted action.
Its support would be forthcoming if the Jews showed that they
refused to 'work like horses and be treated like dogs'. John
Judge, a Council officer involved in the strike of 1885, compared the fifty-six hour week of the English, with the sixty-
five hour week of the aliens. The general strike to which
he urged should, he said, be to reduce hours, to enforce
trade union shops, and to stop the wild-animal methods of the
masters.[39] Views of this kind were put at many Leylands
meetings by English speakers, and, with a strong revival of
demand, a high alien euphoria was induced which led the
tailors to boast of their strength.[40] In London, the Lords

had set up their Committee on Sweating and it was clear that, since its attention might be directed to Leeds, it would be better for the reputation of the alien workman were he to stand revealed as a well-organised fighter.

With memories of their easy, if temporary, victory of 1885, and exploiting their seasonal advantage, the tailors invited the masters to sign a document agreeing to union recognition throughout the trade. The rejection of this proposition brought out almost the whole of the labour force of over 3,000 men. The strike was made a very open movement with numerous public meetings and many letters to the press. The aliens and the alien question were thrust firmly before the public for the first time. Another new feature was the deep hostility involved. The masters, for example, did not hesitate to exploit anti-semitic sentiment by accusing the men of striking, not against their conditions, but to rid the trade of English female labour. Workers' Friend called this 'Inhuman Bestiality of the Leeds Jewish Masters'.[41] The latter also took steps, as one of their number admitted to the Lords, to cut off credit to the men at the ghetto grocery shops, the better to starve the men into submission.[42] It was, in fact, lack of sustenance from an adequate strike fund which caused the collapse of the strike by 25 May.[43] General action had been a bad error and the 1885 precedent a bad one. The masters were far better prepared in 1888, holding together well, resisting pressure for completion of work by having it done in London, and finding ways to import blackleg labour.

The effects of the general strike were profound. The tailors never again attempted general action and, in the future, paid proper regard to financial problems. The attitudes of the masters perpetuated hostility as a local editor perceived when he wrote that, although the strike was over, it would be a mistake to think that 'the matter' was settled.[44] The noisy appearance of the alien on the streets of Leeds had both national and local repercussions. It helped focus the attention of the Lords' Committee onto the provinces as some London newspapers reported the strike as well as the sympathetic demonstrations of London Jewish workers. Official visits of inquiry were made to Leeds by Beatrice Potter and John Burnett, the labour correspondent of the Board of Trade, eliciting a report on the Leeds Jewish tailoring industry.[45] The strike also provoked fierce local discussion of the aliens. 'A procession of Sweaters (sic),' wrote the Leeds Times, 'must needs be full of interest because they so seldom act in a body or come out into the glare of the public street.'[46] The alien impact on the town was analysed and scrutinised. It was found that the English and Irish residents of the Leylands had 'retired before the Jewish invasion like the black before the grey rat'. The Jewish butcher's shop was 'about enough to make a Gentile turn vegetarian', whilst, although there was something 'in the Talmud to stop the Jews drinking', the taps of the Leylands were 'doing a roaring trade'.[47] At the strike's end, The Lancet sent Commissioner Smith to survey Jewish workshops. Smith's findings were condemnatory,[48] the local authority duly embarrassed, and the town as a whole compelled to regard their new community of the Leylands as a permanent and special problem. The normally hostile Yorkshire Post defended Jewish shops, finding them 'miniature factories'[49] but the Town Council knew better. It sacked the Medical Officer of Health and appointed a Special Inspector of Jewish Workshops.[50] Annual reports and a close watch on the shops were instituted and many actions for nuisance undertaken.[51]

The masters, the unions routed, engaged a punitive reaction towards their co-religionists of a brutality which shocked local opinion. Under the boycott, the leaders were forced out of Leeds. Leaving certificates were instituted recording the previous wage so that no increase could be obtained. There was such hunger among boycotted men that the sympathy even of

of craft rivals was aroused.[52]   Maguire wrote of 'the terrible
sufferings of the boycotted workers' and, by the end of June
1888, the boycott was described as 'large scale'.[53]   The
unhearing masters were informed that, in England, such a course
was 'looked upon as odious in the extreme'.[54]

With their organisation in tatters, the tailors spent
two years in strife, often leading to violence.[55]   Another
co-operative workshop, set up to aid boycotted men, came and
went; collapsing due to a struggle between socialists and
Orthodox Jews.   It would be wrong, however, to conclude, along
with the official historians of the Union of Tailors and Garment
Workers, that there was no further activity until 1893.[56]
Regrouping efforts were, in fact, constant; resulting from
the dual pressures of the masters' enmity and the anti-alien
feeling triggered in Leeds by the strike and its attendant
publicity.

In defeat, the usual problems were aggravated, and 'great
suffering' was reported.[57]   The men had to beg for their jobs
and were sunk in pessimism.[58]   Before the Lords, Sweeney
stated that, so great was the fury of the victorious masters,
union membership was reduced to three in 1889.   Men had been
compelled to tear up their cards before the master and wage
cuts had been imposed.[59]   Quarrels within the ranks were also
destructive as political and religious elements vied as to
future policy, and several small splinter unions were formed,
only to die away by the end of 1889.   A Leeds tailor described
the situation at this time:

> Dark and bitter is the lot of the worker
> working for a small master.   One is chased
> like a dog and oppressed to death.   If one
> works for a large master, the prices are so
> low that it is impossible to make a living.   60

Dark as it was for the tailors, the year 1889 was
brilliantly lighted by the success of the Gasworkers

232

whose Leeds branch obtained the eight-hour shift within six weeks of formation. They were led by the members of the Socialist League who had played a prominent part in the disastrous Jewish strike in the previous year. Early in 1890, as the tailors again began to enrol new members under a socialist president, Lewis Frank, they became the target of a campaign to amalgamate them with the Gasworkers. It has generally been held that Jewish workers would not consider an alliance with English unions opposed to immigration.[61] It is clear, however, that with an urgent need for allies, with socialist leadership, and influenced by the success of their friends in the Socialist League, the aliens could overcome their scruples. Maguire, held by the Jews as a good comrade, was an eloquent anti-alienist,[62] and Sweeney, their Christian secretary who feared the flooding of the labour market, also opposed immigration.[63]

Many meetings were addressed by the League stressing the advantages of an alliance with the Gasworkers. On 16 February 1890, Frank informed a mass meeting of tailors that there was 'a great need for alliance with our Christian brethren'.[64] Four days later, as many tailors returned to the fold, the alliance was officially sealed.[65] It was a remarkable event, for, within ten years of their coming, an alien group had crossed religious, ethnic, and social barriers so far as to form a branch of an English general union. The alliance aroused great enthusiasm since it was felt that English trade unionists might now influence the Jewish tailoring trade and help to regulate it. A delighted Factory Times considered the tailors had 'a great future before them'.[66]

There was an immediate outburst of activity as Gasworkers' officials gave notice of their intentions. They addressed many meetings in the Leylands aimed at increasing the membership, and the tailors noisily joined the Eight-Hours Movement, heading its large-scale processions. The Masters' Society took fright, one of their number proposing a petition to 'the Almighty Queen Victoria' for the deportation of 'the dangerous union men'.[67]   Backed by the new strength of the Gasworkers, the tailors felt sufficiently strong to return to old issues such as the uniform working day.   A circular to the masters on 15 August was rejected with an announcement that their society would resist collectively.   Two days later, over forty shops were without labour.   The strike was quickly spread until it was little smaller in scale than that of 1888. This was the sole resemblance, however, since, on this occasion, victory came swiftly.   Within a few days, fifteen masters had conceded a uniform day, and, when they were followed by a further twenty-six during the next week, the strike was effectively at an end.

The presence of the Gasworkers had been decisive.   The masters had no taste for battle with men who had so recently routed police and troops on the streets of Leeds.[68]   Workers' Friend carried a gleeful description of the terror they inspired with their 'long poles'.[69]   There had also been changes on the side of the masters.   Increasing competition had flawed their former unity.   On the very day their society had announced its intention of resistance, fifteen had capitulated.   'This', said the Factory Times, 'exposes Jewish ways.'[70]

The victory restored the sixty-two-hour week ruling before the 1888 strike, but the usual difficulty of enforcement arose. Thus, the tailors began to call for the closed shop.   Meanwhile, the gas stokers went the rounds of reluctant shops to enforce the agreement.   Many were under police guard.   When sixty stokers appeared at one shop to demand the reinstatement of a group of sacked strikers, the police fled and the men's jobs were restored.[71]   The contrast with 1888 was extreme.   It was now the masters who were left in disarray and the unions were able to advance their power, at least over the smaller

234

shops.[72]   Some were blocked for excessive driving causing
the masters, unable to obtain labour, to go out of business.[73]

The period August-October 1890 represents the high-water
mark of the strange labour alliance. By the end of 1891, it
was over, despite the speedy gains and restoration of alien
morale. Action, often violent, persisted to the end.   In
October 1890, non-union shops were attacked.[74]   Strikes
occurred in June 1891 when union men were sacked at a time
when the masters were said to be 'showing more fight'.[75]
The long struggle against piecework - a detested novelty in
Jewish tailoring - was beginning, and unrest was widespread.[76]
Further strikes occurred in August against attempts to restore
the old hours of work,[77] and, in September, three more disputes
were won.[78]   October saw 'the Jews often in and out in the
Leylands'.[79]

The causes of the severance were complex. To the
Gasworkers, the aliens seemed wild and impractical, demanding,
on one occasion, the use of 200 pickets at a single shop for
a number of weeks. Nor had the Englishmen ever dealt with
such employers. The Jewish master would bow low before the
negotiators, yield every point, and then carry on as before.
It was, said the Factory Times, 'very hard to deal with such
people'.[80]

The initiative, however, came from the Jewish side. It
was first associated with a split between anarchists and
socialists in the London Jewish unions. In Leeds the reaction
took the form of an anarchist drive against the Gasworkers'
alliance. Jacob Caplan, its articulate leader, opposed the
strike for small gains and saw unions as merely the instruments
of struggle against capitalism as a whole. He stood against
the very concept of leadership and demanded a weekly election
to the union chair.[81]   Leadership, he proclaimed, had, by its
despotic tendencies, dissipated the admiration felt by the
aliens for the Gasworkers. Branch power had been lost to

235

the latter, creating delay in the hearing of grievances.[82]
Caplan also felt that the full support of the Gasworkers had
not been received. He instanced the case in which the
tailors had decided to close a sweated shop by blocking labour.
Although the Gasworkers had not been asked to intervene, their
officials had negotiated secretly with the master concerned,
clearing the shop for work. The men had refused, picketed
the shop, and some had been arrested for intimidation. The
Gasworkers' Executive, seeing their authority challenged, had
rushed through an amendment to their constitution requiring a
two-thirds majority of all branches for their removal. The
anarchists, Caplan concluded, would henceforth work for an
organisation free of despotism.[83]

With the departure of the anarchists, socialists remained
in the alliance merely on principle but, after a time, they
also became critical. There was wide agreement that duties
were being neglected, especially when an official was found
drunk. The virtual impossibility of removing officials
under the new rules was also found irksome. A crisis was,
therefore, easily induced when a tailor was expelled for
questioning the value of drunken officials.[84] In December
1891, Jewish delegates moved to consider 'proven charges of
drunkenness and neglect of duties in the union's interest'
and, very soon, large numbers of aliens were leaving the
alliance.[85] Mahon, Sweeney, and Cockayne fought to save the
situation. They addressed stormy meetings at which, also,
'Jew after Jew spoke and chairs flew over their heads, forms
were used, fists and boots were brought into play'. Some
came back, only to fall away by early 1892.[86]

The rupture was widely deplored. Without allies, and
with trade again deteriorating, a wage-cut was imposed, and,
in the resultant strike, the tailors were defeated within
the week.[87] They were now 'in a very weak and foolish
position' and 'in a fix'.[88] Opinion in Leeds was bitter and

disillusioned, and, in its report for 1892, the Trades'
Council voiced its regret that, with regard to the aliens,
'no good results' had been obtained.[89]   In the following
year, with heavy unemployment, the Council passed a resolution
against 'the continual influx of Jews', and it seemed that
local hostility had reached a peak, whilst all alien efforts
at identification had been negated.[90]

In October of the same year, however, the tailors quickly
began a new union with 100 members.   Incorporating tailors,
machiners, and pressers under a single banner, this was the
form it was to retain throughout its life as an independent
union to 1915.   The new movement marks a very sudden and
complete break with the past in terms of unity, leadership,
businesslike procedures, and continuity.   These qualities
brought strength and allowed an advance, however painful,
towards parity with English clothing workers.   From the
point of view of the problem of alien acceptance, the most
significant consequence was that, within a few years, the
attitudes of English labour were transformed.   When, in 1903,
the secretary of the Leeds Trades' Council informed the Royal
Commission on Aliens of the passing of its anti-alien
resolution,[91] this was anachronistic, not only in the sense
that it had been passed a full decade before, but in the sense
that the tailors had already elicited wide praise and many
signs of acceptance by 1900.[92]

It would be difficult to ascribe the metamorphosis of
the tailors to any single cause.   In particular, it is
difficult to explain the neutralisation of political and
religious factionalism which troubled previous organisations.
The anarchists and socialists retained their clubs in Leeds
and their opponents, the Orthodox Jews, probably numbered
half of the total labour force.   These groups often clashed,
both in the philosophical and physical senses.   The anarchists
continued to deride meliorist objectives, formal leadership,

237

and businesslike procedures.[93] Religious riots were known,
not least on the Annual Feast and Ball held by the Anarchists
and Freethinkers on the Day of Atonement - the most solemn
Fast Day of the Hebrew calendar.[94] Yet all could agree on
common cause against the Jewish master, and, even after 1893,
the vision of a Jewish co-operative system had not entirely
disappeared. Out of the copious debate of this period there
was formed a clear policy for the future. Discipline and
rules were to be accepted. Attacks on the leaders must end
since all they got for their pains was the boycott in defeat.
Political outlook must be modified since revolutionary calls
had been heeded for years, but revolution had backfired on
the workers, destroying unity and leaving hatred in its
place.[95]

In the same year, the first paid secretary, Sam Freedman,
was appointed. His principal lieutenants were two anarchists,
Louis Ellstein and David Policoff. Freedman's methods were
important in framing the new outlook. In 1905, it was said
of him: 'He is not a demagogue. He does not enter into long
diatribes and orations. He is a calm, business trade union
secretary. When Sam became General Secretary the union became
more stable and less liable to fluctuations.'[96]

The mounting anti-alien campaign was also a strong
inducement to unity. The Trades' Council resolution of 1893
had merely reflected national feeling. The TUC resolutions
of the 1890s cast a definite shadow and alien workers began
to be confused in the public mind with alien criminal refugees
and anarchists of the Assassin School. 'Fear of criminals,
Socialists, and Anarchists', was Salisbury's muddled justification of the abortive Aliens Bill of 1894.[97] In 1902, the
assassination of President McKinley prompted the Cabinet to
consider the immigration question more closely.[98] In 1896,
the Home Secretary announced Salisbury's continued determination
to legislate,[99] and the Queen's Speech contained reference to

238

such an Act.[100]   The fire was amply fuelled by events down to the Great War, notably the Royal Commission of 1903-4 and the 'Siege of Sydney Street' in 1911, which convinced some Leeds newspapers that the anarchist tailors' club in the Leylands was a centre for desperadoes.[101]

The stability of the new union is further highlighted by a consideration of the immense industrial problems it faced. The tailors suffered badly in the severe slumps, especially in 1896-7 and 1903-6, losing batches of skilled members to America and Canada.[102]   Downward price revisions became commonplace, either through the acceptance by the masters of lower wholesale prices in competitive bidding for work,[103] or by the external imposition of lower prices by the wholesalers.[104]

The background to both forms of price reduction was a sinister, long-term reduction of demand on the Jewish branch disliked, at best, by the large native firms for its strike bound nature.[105]   Independence of alien labour became a proud selling point with some Leeds firms.[106]   These movements were associated with a much-changed role for the Jewish tailor. Almost as the new union was forming, demand was shifting from cheap serge readymades to measure orders which, by 1895, already formed an important fraction of total Leeds output.[107] All the large houses were involved by 1902, by which year readymade clothing no longer predominated in the wholesale trade.[108]   Retailers no longer required large stocks of finished garments since a thick pattern-book suited their new trade better, and demand fell accordingly, depressing prices. Furthermore, as capacity increased during the 1900s, the prices of cheap made-to-measure suits fell as low as 10s.0d.[109] These price-depressing forces were naturally felt in the Jewish branch and only the larger masters were able to survive.[110]

The adaptable Jewish tailor did not stand still.   Russian industrialisation had produced refugees with more skills[111]   and

there are many indications that the alien, associated with
the slop trade in the 1880s, was well involved in the better-
class trade a decade later.   In 1894, for example, it was
noted that the aliens had become such adepts that 'high class
work' was being let out to them.[112]   Before 1914, their
skills were much admired, even by rivals.[113]   By 1909, over
25 per cent of Jewish work was said to be for the quality
trade.[114]   As the demand for their services fell, Jewish shops
of the older type fell away and the extinction of the Jewish
master was regarded as merely a matter of time.[115]   Many
turned to a more precarious existence as makers up of measure
orders for small High Street retailers and travellers.   This
drastically altered the structure of the Jewish trade.   Some
masters continued as outworkers for the large wholesalers in
the readymade trade, but they were inevitably fewer in number.
There also appeared an enormous rash of small bedroom masters
engaged in the small-scale, rather casual, bespoke trade.
By 1903, 180 such shops could be counted in Leeds whilst the
traditional English craft tailors had declined from over 550
in 1873 to 250 in the later year.[116]   In 1906, the Jewish
bedroom workshops were described as 'not more than 3¼ yards
by 4 yards' and were said to contain an average of no more
than six workers.[117]   Two years later, the prevalence of the
bedroom master was blamed for the total ineffectiveness of the
Truck Acts in Leeds.[118]   By this year, it was held that most
Leeds Jewish men were tailors and that they worked 'very
largely in their own homes'.[119]

    It is, therefore, clear that the new union was bound to
function against a background of very limited potential.
Nevertheless, it maintained continuity and rapidly entered
the general community of trade unions.   That acceptance
remained important can be seen in the many overt acts of
identification with English unions, for example, regular
contributions to the strike funds of unions in other trades.[120]

In the _fracas_ of 1903 involving the 1893 resolution of the
Trades' Council, the tailors reacted angrily but refused to
leave the Council, preferring 'to show themselves disciplined
trade unionists'.[121]   Sam Freedman attended the Trades Union
Congress annually, being the sole Jewish representative,[122]
and his men were founder-members of the General Federation of
Trade Unions.[123]   Their outlook is well epitomised in
Freedman's angry letter to the _Jewish Chronicle_ on the
occasion, in 1900, when it carried an advertisement for
blackleg labour to replace strikers in Dublin.   'When we
have tried our best to organise ourselves,' he wrote, 'and
succeeded in coming into nearer relationships with the English
workers, you come out with such advertisements trying to make
the Jews into blacklegs.'[124]

External opinion of the tailors was strikingly transformed.   'Mr Freedman and his union,' observed the _Factory
Times_, 'work well with the other trade unions of Leeds.'[125]
In 1903 the same journal described the tailors as 'one of the
strongest, most prosperous, and philanthropic of Leeds
unions'.[126]   The rival Amalgamated Tailors, speaking of the
'grimy aliens' in 1899,[127] acknowledged a few years later that
the aliens were 'leading the way in Tailoring labour
organisation'.[128]   The tailors' reputation influenced opinion
more widely;   for example, during the anti-alien crisis of
1903-4.   The ILP Congress, debating its attitude to the alien
question, rejected a restrictive motion on learning of the
progress of the Leeds tailors.[129]   English workers were
warned against restriction since this would not keep out the
'German-Jewish financier' who would 'drain the workers dry',
but the Jewish trade union tailor was 'a man who was not as
easily sat on as he used to be'.[130]

The new, more stable, Jewish unionism presaged neither
'responsible' attitudes of co-operation with the masters, nor
a new condition of peace.   As the incidence of falling prices

and the stresses of economic change were felt on both sides
of the trade, conflict was, if anything, heightened during
1893-1914. The masters remaining in the wholesale trade,
fewer but individually larger, were still adamantine enemies;
and the increasing bedroom masters clearly posed problems.
The Jewish workman's easy habit of moving from shop to shop
made it difficult to hold members if a new master were anti-
unionist. Waywardness remained to be cured. On one
occasion, a group of union members banded together to undercut their employer at his suppliers and, having obtained his
work, fellow-members of the union found themselves suddenly
unemployed. This necessitated the setting-up of a special
committee to deal with the problem.[131]

A study of the incessant strikes of this period reveals
grossly uneven progress. The questions of piecework,
internal subcontracting, and union recognition recur in
disputes subsequent to settlements of these various grievances.
On the working day, there was no progress whatsoever until
1911. In other respects, however, impressive advances were
made such that, by 1907, the union had imposed a system of
'compulsory labour' under which the master lost his freedom
of dismissal. From 1897, the union turned its back on efforts
to obtain general agreements with the Masters' Society, and
chose to impose its will, shop-by-shop, by a series of well-
planned strikes. Individual masters, thus attacked, often
fought hard and many of the actions involved violence and
police intervention.[132] During their course, Freedman,
Ellstein, and Policoff were all jailed for intimidation.
This campaign, lasting until the turn of the century, also
gave forth yet another short-lived co-operative shop.[133]

The depression of 1903-6 induced the longest era of
peace prior to 1914. In these years, the chief problem was
to hold the union together since the Jewish workman had 'no
local permanence anywhere' and could always 'be seen, staff

in hand, ready to emigrate'.[134]   The anarchists also threatened a schism by reviving the call for a general strike,
deriding the 'palliative struggle' as merely preliminary 'to
the historical struggle to destroy the wage system'.[135]   The
severity of the depression, however, compelled the anarchists
to acknowledge that only a national federation could henceforth
undertake action on this scale.[136]

With the upswing of the trade cycle in 1906, there was
a resurgence of pent-up activity in the union.   This was
urgent since many members had been lost and the trade had
suffered badly.[137]   In the same year, Freedman was replaced
by Moses Sclare, a former Glasgow official of the Engineers'
Society.   This made him welcome in Leeds skilled labour
circles such as the Trades' Council, and brought the tailors
their first leader with experience of English union practice.

In Leeds the conditions for conflict were developing.
As prices fell, the masters reconstituted themselves into a
Master Tailors' Union with 100 members.[138]   Their policy was
to spread piecework as a cost-reducing device but were
increasingly frustrated by the compulsory labour system of
the tailors' union.   Strikes became so numerous that the
tailors were said to look on harmony 'as a monotonous state
of affairs'.[139]   From 1906 to 1909, the issues of piecework,
subcontracting within the workshop, and union recognition,
lay at the centre of these many disputes.   In 1909, however,
Sclare drafted a programme of grievances, which, he announced,
they would venture to remedy.   In the programme, the old
problem of the working day was resurrected.   The drive which
ensued produced so many stoppages that the masters, early in
1911, decided upon a final stand.   A general lockout was
proclaimed and this became a fact on 3 March.[140]   The masters'
demands show well the extent of the advances of the union as
well as their dislike of the union's tactic of striking
individual shops.   They sought the abolition of compulsory

243

labour, private wage-bargaining, and the settlement of disputes at shop level. It was, they stated, 'neither trades unionism nor Socialism to stab one individual in the back or bleed him to death'. Demands, they concluded, should be made on all equally.[141]

By 1911, however, there was little hope of a solid front of the masters. Their hold on the trade was much weakened and one large wholesaler's remark that it was a joke to think that they nowadays relied on the Jews, must have sounded ominous.[142] Pressure was being applied for early completion of holiday orders and some masters early begged the union to release labour to them, from fear that, in future, their work might be retained indoors.[143] The men were in a strong position and responded by treating the matter as a general strike. No 'free labour' appeared and finances were strong. The evidence of the press is that public sympathy lay strongly with the union. Early in the dispute also, some smaller masters had already asked to be allowed to withdraw the lockout notice. This was refused, Sclare informing the masters that they had wanted 'competition labour'. What the union now wanted was nothing less than a shorter working day.[144]

On 7 March, the masters turned, in desperation and for the first time in any Leeds Jewish dispute, to arbitration, and, on the following day, both sides accepted the Board of Trade offer of intervention. The resultant award represents the summit of the tailors' achievements before 1914. It provided for the abolition of compulsory labour but union members were no longer to be victimised. Internal sub-contracting was abolished and piecework was to be subject to an agreed log statement and to yield wages no lower than could be earned under alternative systems of payment in the trade. Hours were to be reduced by stages to nine per day by 1 January 1912, giving a week of fifty hours and, after almost three decades of battle, parity with English clothing workers.[145]

244

Three months before the outbreak of the Great War, the
Jewish Chronicle observed that it was a 'remarkable record
for a Jewish trade union to have a continuous existence of
twenty-one years',[146] but it might well have added that the
union had also exceeded in size and continuity all unions in
the clothing industry, not excluding the great native wholesale branch, before 1914. In the determination of this,
English labour attitudes, passing from curiosity to hostility,
and then to acceptance, played an important role by adding to
the need for organisation against the Jewish master, the
shadow of anti-alienism.

The background alien controversy, which once had vied
for newspaper space with sensations such as the Ripper
murders and the Dreyfus case, disappeared so rapidly that
Belloc, as early as 1922, was moved to complaint of the
general silence on the Jewish Question.[147] The reception
accorded the aliens, however, is now seen as a complex and
large-scale phenomenon,[148] involving such dangerous political
pressures that acceptance by the hosts was an urgent
necessity.[149] The view taken here is that the sudden disappearance of the alien controversy was ultimately due to
two factors exogenous to the controversy proper: the Trade
Boards Act of 1909 and the outbreak of war, which immediately
transferred the connotation of 'alien' from Jew to German.

For the critical 'holding' period to 1914, several
endogenous factors have been propounded as inducements to
toleration on the part of the hosts. In certain quarters
of English society, the potential assimilability of the alien
may have been telling in this regard,[150] but his foreignness
formed a mere fraction of the total hostility evoked by his
presence. The benign influence of the anglicised Jewish
community has also been very much canvassed,[151] yet the
evidence of the priority of class interests within this
powerful group is strong. Anglo-Jews were years ahead of

245

both press and Parliament in public opposition to immigration, whilst prominent Jews were vocal in support of restriction. Jewish financiers unconcernedly raised loans for the Tsar, and, so high was the priority of profits, offers to potential subscribers were insensitively placed in grotesque juxta-position to reports of pogroms.[152] From the pens of provincial Anglo-Jewry also, came pleas for an end to immigration, often with contemptuous comment on the aliens already present.[153] In its most extreme form, a major contribution by this wealthy community to alien acceptance is claimed as the consequence of its intellectual brilliance and social distinction.[154] This presents a section of Anglo-Jewish society as an abstraction and ludicrously overlooks its material roots in a settled capitalist class, whose own existence presupposes a Jewish proletariat and mutually-hostile class attitudes. Thus, the idea of a unitary Jewish 'system' is dispelled and the paradox of the hatred of the Anglo-Jew for the Russian Jew explained.

The struggles of the Leeds Jewish Tailors' Union, on the other hand, suggest that a more significant contribution to the acceptance gained before 1914 came from Jewish working-class battle in an arena which may have been an exclusive Jewish ghetto, but which was closely surrounded by the troubled host labour market in which lay the greatest danger to the aliens.[155] That contribution has not received due assessment owing to the concentration of the literature upon London and to the perpetuation of myths concerning the Leeds tailoring trade.

The revolution in attitudes to the aliens noted above as the fruits of their advancing organisation and industrial struggle, could not fail to be important to general alien acceptance. The tailors were either led by, or were in close alliance with, Leeds labour leaders throughout. They were also closely observed by such journals as the Factory

246

Times which circulated in Lancashire and Yorkshire, where an
important fraction of English labour was concentrated. Mr
Garrard's view that the reputation of Jewish unions rested
on those of London[156] would certainly have been queried in
northern circles by 1900, by which year the tailors had done
much to alter the sweated-slave image of the alien worker.

Whilst the success of the Leeds tailors has sometimes
been acknowledged, the standard presentation of their
industry and conditions grossly minimises the significance of
their role in the acceptance process. Of a particularly
damaging nature is the persistent exoneration of the aliens
from the charge of displacement of English labour, which
makes of the class struggle in the ghetto an exclusively
alien affair, and, by implication, treats the charges made
by Englishmen as irrational. Throughout the period, however,
local hostility was much coloured by conditions, not in the
tailoring, but in the Jewish slipper industry, in which,
incontrovertibly, both extreme sweating and devastating
displacement of English labour occurred. Anti-alienists
rarely paused to distinguish the two trades so that the
tailors made an equal target for their invective. Nor was
the hostility induced by the alien impact on the tailoring
trade _itself_ as irrational as has been implied by those who
have given that trade a clean bill of health on the score of
alien displacement of labour. Mr Garrard, for example,
cites Beatrice Potter's view of 1888 that Jewish and Gentile
tailoring existed in watertight compartments, and he goes on
to extend this to 1914. He thus concludes that the aliens
did not displace the traditional English craft tailors.[157]
This is, however, to overlook entirely the dynamics of the
burgeoning Leeds clothing industry, the shift of aliens into
the bedroom workshop, their growing involvement in the
quality trade, and the effect on the local population of
English tailors, reviewed above.

These changes, with their proliferation of small shops, also point to the doubtful status of the view that the Leeds Jewish tailoring industry contained no sweating and that its successful unionisation was due to the scale of Jewish shops and the stability of the supply of work based on regular large orders received from the great warehouses of the town.[158] This was certainly the staple diet fed to governmental inquiry by Leeds Jewish labour leaders, but the daily reality of these gentlemen's lives blatantly contradicted the picture, which was calculated to do no more than measure the difference between Jewish working-class, and Jewish bourgeois, attitudes to the danger of England's closure to further immigration.

The term 'sweating' eludes definition but some aspects of the Jewish tailoring trade may be examined in order to assess the reasonableness, or otherwise, of hostility on this major industrial score. Central to sweating is a working week of inordinate length and, as the above narrative indicates, the aliens did not obtain parity with other local clothing workers until the late year of 1911. Thus, there are immediate grounds for thinking that hostility reflecting local suspicions and reactions to alien hours of work was well enough founded.

Those beguiled by the scale of the large Leeds wholesale firms and by the 'benefits' accruing to those in economic harness with them, have yet to prove their thesis. There are, in fact, many reasons to suppose that the large firms contributed to conditions akin to those in London, and which may be regarded as contributory to aspects of the trade in Leeds resembling sweating. Despite the huge scale of the Leeds firms, they were unable to provide greater regularity of work than elsewhere. They were highly vulnerable to the peculiar cycles of the trade, and their fortunes were closely linked to those of the basic industries of coal, textiles, and metals. In addition, they were subject to the well-known

seasonal cycles, and the astonishing regularity of the monthly
movements of demand from 'very bad' through 'bad' and 'improved',
to 'busy' and 'very busy', are quite clear from the official
reports for 1893-1907.[159]   Equally clear is the anxiety with
which trade journals watched other factors such as strikes,
the weather, and the state of the basic industries.[160]   The
export trade could not fill the gaps in domestic demand as
it was badly affected by high tariffs throughout the world,
including British Imperial territories,[161] whilst success in
competition with the well-organised German and American
clothiers involved very steep price reductions.[162]   In these
circumstances, Leeds wholesale firms could not provide a full
week's work for their own employees; still less were they
able to comply with the utopian visions of 'regular work'
based on 'large orders' seen by interested contemporaries and
their latter-day followers, as typical of alien tailoring in
Leeds.   In the English branch, the average working week was
officially put at four days in 1893,[163] and, as late as 1907,
'the swing of the pendulum' was so marked that many tailoresses
were idle for half the year.[164]   For the Jewish branch, the
Board of Trade put the average working week at three and a half
days, and, when set against official reports of a similar week
in London, it is clear that little advantage was gained by
alien tailors in Leeds from the scale of their work source.[165]

There were other 'sweating' costs associated with life
midst the large warehouses, whose managers held sway over the
Jewish masters by their power to distribute work to those of
their own choice.[166]   This system gave rise to intensive
competition among the masters and forced down prices.   In
turn, it contributed much to the driving which formed so
marked a feature of life in Jewish shops.   But, in the long
term, the chief cost was the reduction in the part played by
the aliens in the trade by reason of the gradual retention
of more work indoors.

The apologist view that there was no sweating in Leeds because of the scale of Jewish shops, also remains unsubstantiated. The complex problem of the size-distribution of the industry, and the conditions consequent upon such distribution, will not yield to the method of a simple reference to the scale of the Leeds wholesale houses, and a comparison between the latter and the typical merchant-clothier of London, as sources of alien work.[167]

For the last decade or so of the period, it has been demonstrated that alien shops in Leeds came increasingly to resemble those of the East End in the 'Booth-Potter' period of the 1880s. Contemporary official testimony as to the large scale of the Leeds shops is, in fact, chiefly confined to the period 1880-1900 and, whilst it shows the existence of many large shops, flaws in each account tend to obscure the smaller. In his 1888 report on Leeds to the Board of Trade, for example, John Burnett put the average number of machines at twenty to thirty, but he spent only a single day in the town and interviewed a mere eight Jewish masters, who happened to rank amongst the largest employers.[168] The 1894 report on immigration,[169] upon which, as the most comprehensive document of its kind, great reliance has been placed by commentators, produced similarly optimistic findings in comparing Leeds with London and Manchester, but, as the distinguished investigator, Clara Collet, expressly ignored Leeds shops of less than ten workers, and, as she included this category in her calculations for the other cities, her averages do not bear statistical scrutiny. A similar curious procedure was adopted in the Board of Trade survey of 1893.[170] The chief local source is the Town Council survey triggered by the general strike of 1888, and which yields an average shop-size of thirty-one workers.[171] This survey, conducted in some degree of panic, is categorically deficient in coverage, listing a mere fifty-one shops, whilst, only one year later,

250

the Medical Officer of Health reported the presence of 153 Jewish shops.[172]

There is, on the other hand, abundant testimony to the co-existence of numerous small shops alongside the larger in the Leylands. As early as 1885, the Yorkshire Post noted that many Jewish employers had 'only two or three men in their service',[173] whilst the strike of 1888 called forth the same journal's view that thousands of aliens were employed in their own homes beyond the jurisdiction of factory inspector or local authority.[174] Inspector Rickards of Leeds himself put the number of alien home workshops at 1,000, giving as the cause the cheapness of hire of sewing machines.[175] More telling, perhaps, is the expert evidence of The Lancet in its 1888 inspection of the problem, which put the average size of Leeds shops at twenty machines, but did not overlook the small cottage sweaters 'with two machines and four or five people'. Nor did The Lancet overlook, as have subsequent commentators, the courts of the Leylands teeming with Jewish homeworkers, which caused that journal to conclude unequivocally that, from a sanitary point of view, there was sweating in Leeds.[176] From 1888 also, the omniprescence of the small, unregulated shop can be detected in Town Council activities aimed at coming to grips with the problems it posed. Systematic inspection in 1888 produced a list of thirty-one dwellings used as workshops, in which the average number of workers was four. This, presented to the Lords' Committee on Sweating, was regarded by some members as clearly deficient.[177]

From a consideration of the nature of immigration and immigrants, too, blanket claims that Leeds Jewish shops were simply large, appear untenable. The life-cycle of the Jewish master - from arrival to short apprenticeship to setting up for himself with the minuscule capital required - points to the constant augmentation of the numbers of small shops, and, as Mr Fishman has well said: 'Only a ruthless few made it.

Until the 1930s, the tragi-comedy would be repeated _ad nauseam_.'[178]

In its energetic 'cleansing' campaign following the disclosures of The Lancet, the Leeds Sanitary Committee did not, in any case, distinguish between conditions in large and small alien shops. This fact reveals the essential fallacy in the idea that larger shops implied better working conditions and, by implication, a defence against the accusations of the anti-alienists. The inspectors were aware, as the Leeds correspondent of the Factory Times pointed out, that a 'large shop' of forty workers might well be no more than an attic room, so crowded that some had to work on the floor.[179] The committee showed less complacency than some latter-day commentators on this score, appointing a Special Inspector of Nuisances for the Jewish shops, and, in 1899, a Yiddish-speaking inspector. So unlike model miniature factories were the Jewish shops that, in 1888, action was taken by the Council in 197 out of 252 inspections. New closets were ordered in seventy-two cases, and ninety notices were served in respect of dirty conditions.[180] Similar results are on record for later years and, as late as 1910, the pail-closet system was still prevalent, the standard of sanitation low, and the worst air samples taken in Leeds were from Jewish shops.[181] The clue to these conditions even in the larger shops lies in a Leeds report of 1888, which shows that they were rarely purpose-built but were, rather, 'disused old mills and sheds' and, in one case, 'a tumbledown old workhouse'. Many had no ceiling and were open to the roof and closets were 'defective in many instances'.[182] On the cognate matter of average space per worker, analysis of the data of the Council survey of 1888, involving fifty-one shops, failed to distinguish better spatial conditions in the larger than in the smaller shops.[183]

A close appraisal of the position of the Leeds Jewish

tailors not only contradicts optimistic conclusions as to
the benefits of large scale but demonstrates that the paradox
between their harsh battles and their 'favourable' conditions
is illusory. The tailors' struggles, inasmuch as they were
conditioned by external criticism, were based on the reality
that much of that criticism was only too appropriate. Thus,
their achievements were the fruit of a more arduous campaign
than might be supposed necessary, given the conventionally
favourable picture presented of the industry. The response
of the Jewish tailors to the twin problems of their conditions
and host reaction was of major importance to the alien movement as a whole. It was a uniquely successful response by
the largest alien community in Britain, considered in terms
of percentage of local population, to the source of greatest
danger to immigration. As such, it acquires 'representative'
status and the union the primacy normally accorded London
Jewish unions.

NOTES

1. S.W. Lerner, Breakaway Unions and the Small Trade Union
(1961), pp. 66-7.

2. Factory Times, 4 Jan. 1912 (hereafter FT).

3. L.P. Gartner, The Jewish Immigrant in England, 1880-1914
(1960), p. 89.

4. V.D. Lipman, Social History of the Jews in England (1954);
M. Freedman (ed.), A Minority in Britain (1955).

5. Clothing District Directory of Leeds (Leeds, 1875), passim;
Commercial Directory of Leeds (Leeds, 1878), passim.

6. FT, 16 Dec. 1904. The union was registered on 15 Feb,
1876. See Report of the Registrar of Friendly Societies, 1876,
(P)arliamentary (P)apers 1877, LXXVII, 429, appendix C.

7. Jewish Chronicle, 29 May 1908. (hereafter JC).

8. Directory of Leeds (1881), passim; Robinsons Directory

of Leeds (Leeds, 1911), passim.

9. There is a vast literature. See, for example, The Earl
of Dunraven, 'The Invasion of Destitute Aliens', Nineteenth
Century, XXXI (1892), pp. 985-1000.

10. Report of the Select Committee on Emigration and
Immigration, P.P. 1889, X, pt viii.

11. Report of the Trades Union Congress (1888), p. 23.

12. Ibid., p. 41.

13. Report of the Amalgamated Society of Tailors (1887), p. 4.

14. JC, 20 April 1883.

15. Jewish Record, 6 May 1887.

16. T. Maguire, 'The Destitute Alien', Labour Chronicle,
6 May 1893.

17. All the standard complaints, plus restrictionist remedy,
are well aired in a series of letters to Leeds Evening Express,
18-25 Feb. 1893 (Hereafter LEEx).

18. Maguire, 'Destitute Alien'.

19. FT, 22 May 1891.

20. The journal's life extended from 1885 to 1915.

21. See, for example, LEEx, 9-11 May 1888. The masters'
name for the co-operative shops intended to replace them was
'The Angel of Death'.

22. Leeds Express, 5 July 1884; 23 Aug. 1884 (hereafter
LEx).

23. Leeds Weekly Express, 8 Nov. 1884 (hereafter LWEx).

24. Reported in LEEx, 3 May 1884.

25. LEx, 23 Aug. 1884.

26. LWEx, 8 Nov. 1884.

27. Der Polishe Yidel, (The Polish Jew), 10 Oct. 1884.

28. LWEx, 15 Nov. 1884.

29. Ibid., 22 Nov. 1884.

30. Arbeiterfreund (The Workers' Friend), 15 July 1885, (hereafter WF).

31. Leeds Daily News, 9 March 1885.

32. Yorkshire Post, 4 May 1885.

33. WF, 29 June 1888, in a review of the events of 1885.

34. Yorkshire Post, 4 May 1885.

35. Ibid., 14 May 1885.

36. J. Finn to A.R. Rollin, 27 Oct. 1943.

37. Die Tsukunft, (The Future), 5 March 1886; LEEx 1 Feb. 1887.

38. WF, 9 Dec. 1887.

39. Ibid., 11 May 1888.

40. Ibid., 13 Jan. 1888.

41. Ibid., 18 May 1888.

42. House of Lords Select Committee on the Sweating System, Minutes of Evidence, P.P. 1889, XIV, (331), Q.31785.

43. Leeds Times, 25 May 1888. See also, S. Freedman, 'Sketch of the Leeds Jewish Tailors' Union', The Trade Unionist (July, 1899), p. 449 for the view that the sole cause of the collapse of the 1888 strike was that they 'went out without any funds'.

44. LEEx, 25 May 1888.

45. See Report on the Sweating System in Leeds, P.P. 1888, LXXXVI, (C 5513), passim.

46. Leeds Times, 2 June 1888.

47. Ibid., 12 May 1888.

48. The Lancet, I, (June, 1888), pp. 794, 1146-8, 1208-10.

49. Yorkshire Post, 16 June 1888.

50. For the query, 'What are the inspectors doing?' plus the

advice that Jewish workshops should be closely watched, see
LWEx, 9 June 1888.

51. Leeds Civic Hall, Minutes of the Sanitary Committee of
Leeds Town Council, 1888.

52. LEEx, 4 June 1888.

53. WF, 15 June 1888.

54. LWEx, 7 July 1888.

55. For police intervention, see, for example, WF, 29 June
1888.

56. M. Stewart and L. Hunter, The Needle is Threaded (1964),
p. 118.

57. WF, 18 Jan. 1889.

58. Ibid., 11 Dec. 1891, in a review of the events of 1888-9.

59. SC on the Sweating System, P.P. 1889, XIV, (331), QQ.
30189-91.

60. WF, 27 Nov. 1889.

61. See, for example, Lerner, Breakaway Unions p. 90.

62. WF, 18 May 1888.

63. His views are in SC on the Sweating System, P.P. 1889,
XIV, (331), QQ. 30270-72, 30315.

64. WF, 21 Feb. 1890.

65. Ibid., 28 Feb. 1890.

66. FT, 9 May 1890.

67. WF, 2 May 1890.

68. Ibid., 27 June 1890.

69. Ibid., 24 Aug. 1890.

70. FT, 29 Aug. 1890.

71. WF, 3 Sept. 1890.

72. Ibid., 19 Sept. 1890.

73. Ibid., 17 Oct. 1890.

74. FT, 31 Oct. 1890.

75. Ibid., 19 June 1891.

76. Ibid., 26 June 1891.

77. Ibid., 14 Aug. 1891.

78. Ibid., 25 Sept. 1891.

79. Ibid., 30 Oct. 1891.

80. Ibid., 24 Oct. 1890.

81. WF, 11 Dec. 1891.

82. In 1903, in a consideration of these events, the Jewish Chronicle observed that the 'quick-witted Jewish character could not brook the cumbrous and dilatory process of consulting the executive before the branch could take action'. JC, 17 June 1903.

83. WF, 11 Dec. 1891.

84. FT, 25 Sept. 1891.

85. Ibid., 4 Dec. 1891, 1 Jan. 1892.

86. Ibid., 18 Dec. 1891, 8 April 1892.

87. Report on Strikes and Lockouts for 1892, P.P. 1894, LXXXI, (C 7403), p. 216.

88. FT, 1 July 1892.

89. Ibid., 8 July 1892.

90. Ibid., 8 Feb. 1893.

91. Royal Commission on Aliens, P.P. 1903, IX, (Cd 1741), Q. 14998.

92. See, for example, FT, 23 July 1897, 3 Sept. 1897.

93. See, for example, WF, 15 Nov. 1895.

94. Ibid., 4 Oct. 1899.

95. Ibid., 29 Nov. 1895.

96. FT, 29 April 1905.

97. The Times, 18 July 1894.

98. Public Record Office, Cabinet Papers, 37/60 (1902).

99. The Times, 6 Feb. 1896.

100. The Standard, 30 March 1896.

101. Yorkshire Post, 4 Jan. 1911; Yorkshire Evening News, 7 Jan. 1911.

102. Jewish Express, 4 Dec. 1896; JC, 5 March 1897; FT, 4 Dec. 1903, 15 Jan. 1904, 10 Feb. 1905, 10 March 1905, 25 Feb. 1906.

103. LEEx, 24 Feb. 1893; JC, 9 July 1897.

104. Yorkshire Post, 24 June 1892; JC, 8 Feb. 1907, 15 May 1908. For the German threat to the export trade in cheap readymades, see Men's Wear, 15 July 1905, 13 Jan. 1906.

105. The great strike of 1888 set the process in motion. See Report on the Strikes and Lockouts for 1888, P.P. 1889, LXX, (C 5809), appendix i, p. 82. Complaints abound. See, for example, JC, 18 Aug. 1906, 15 May 1908, 12 June 1908, 2 July 1909, 5 Aug. 1910; Men's Wear, 18 Aug. 1906; Report of the Leeds Auxiliary of the Society for the Propagation of the Gospel Amongst the Jews (1909), p. 4.

106. See the advertising in Men's Wear, 19 May 1906, 28 July 1906.

107. Clothing and Outfitting World, 7 Sept. 1895, 16 May 1896.

108. Men's Wear, 8 Nov. 1902.

109. Ibid., 26 May 1906.

110. Bankruptcies were very frequent. See, for example, LWEx, 4 March 1893; Leeds Daily News, 21 March 1900.

111. WF, 2 Oct. 1908.

112. LWEx, 27 Jan. 1894.

113. Journal of the Amalgamated Society of Tailors, Nov. 1910, p. 9.

114. Departmental Committee on the Truck Acts, P.P. 1908, LIX, (Cd 4443), Q. 5888.

115. <u>JC</u>, 5 Aug. 1910.

116. <u>RC on Aliens</u>, P.P. 1903, IX, (Cd 1741), QQ. 14293-4, 14317-20, 15038.

117. <u>Yorkshire Evening News</u>, 23 June 1906.

118. <u>DC on the Truck Acts</u>, P.P. 1908, LIX, (Cd 4443), Q. 5949.

119. <u>JC</u>, 29 June 1908.

120. <u>FT</u>, 9 Oct. 1897, 24 Dec. 1897, 23 June 1899, 29 May 1903.

121. <u>JC</u>, 10 April 1903.

122. Ibid., 12 Sept. 1902.

123. <u>FT</u>, 20 July 1900.

124. Ibid., 25 May 1900.

125. Ibid., 2 Dec. 1899.

126. Ibid., 3 April 1903.

127. <u>Journal of the Amalgamated Society of Tailors</u>, Sept. 1899, p. 119.

128. Ibid., Sept. 1903, p. 67.

129. <u>FT</u>, 17 April 1903.

130. Ibid., 25 March 1904, 29 June 1906, 15 Aug. 1908.

131. <u>Jewish Express</u>, 6 Dec. 1896.

132. <u>FT</u>, 16 April 1897.

133. <u>LEEx</u>, 20 April 1897.

134. <u>JC</u>, 30 Dec. 1904.

135. <u>WF</u>, 31 July 1903.

136. Ibid., 6 Oct. 1905.

137. <u>FT</u>, 6 Oct. 1905.

138. <u>Report of the Registrar of Friendly Societies for 1911</u>, P.P. 1912-3, LXXXI, (123-xv), part C, p. 58.

139. JC, 9 Nov. 1906.

140. WF, 3 March 1911.

141. Yorkshire Evening News, 27 Feb. 1911.

142. Ibid., 8 March 1911.

143. Ibid., 6 March 1911.

144. WF, 10 March 1911.

145. JC, 7 April 1911; WF, 14 April 1911.

146. JC, 1 May 1914.

147. H. Belloc, The Jews (1922), ch. 4, passim.

148. See especially, J.A. Garrard, The English and Immigration, 1880-1910 (1971).

149. But not according to the Jewish Establishment scholar, James Parkes, who makes very light of the matter, narrowing down the bases of hostility merely to the fears of poverty-line English workers. See J. Parkes, 'The History of the Anglo-Jewish Community', in Freedman (ed.), A Minority in Britain pp. 49-50.

150. Garrard, The English and Immigration p. 13.

151. Dr Parkes, in defence of the untenable, gives as his first reason for the fact that 'no outbreak of anti-Semitic feeling or boisterous zenophobia' occured, the presence of an Anglo-Jewry which was 'at this time very well equipped to receive them'. See Parkes, 'Anglo-Jewish Community', in Freedman (ed.), A Minority in Britain p. 45.

152. See, for example, Jewish Standard, 30 Jan. 1891.

153. See JC, 3 Dec. 1886, 15 Aug. 1894; Manchester Courier, 14 April 1887, for the views of Anglo-Jews in Hull, Leeds, and Manchester.

154. F.H. Modder, The Jews in the Literature of England (Philadelphia, 1944), p. 237.

155. Garrard, The English and Immigration p. 20, also emphasises the importance of the English workers as a source of anti-alien hostility.

156. Ibid., p. 168.

157. Ibid., pp. 166-7.

158. Ibid., pp. 159-60; Gartner, Jewish Immigrant p. 79.

159. Labour Gazette, I-CV (1893-1907), passim.

160. See, for example, Men's Wear, 1 Nov. 1902, 17 Jan. 1903, 4 July 1903.

161. Return of Foreign Import Duties, 1893, P.P. 1893, LXXXI, (401), p. 39: Import Duties Levied Upon Principal Articles Imported into the British Colonies, 1909, P.P. 1909, LXXXIII, (Cd 4784), p. 67.

162. FT, 14 April 1910.

163. Labour Gazette, II (June 1893).

164. Report of a Conference of the Women's Industrial Council on the Unemployment of Women (Oct. 1907), p. 13.

165. Labour Gazette, I, (May 1893), I, (June 1893): JC, 18 March 1898.

166. This power was exerted in other costly ways such as the extortion of bribes. See, for example, Yorkshire Post, 10 May 1888: LWEx, 27 Jan. 1894: Leeds Mercury, 21 Jan. 1898. For a Jewish master's testimony to the necessity for bribing the warehouse manager, plus a Leeds jeweller's assertion that he sold many articles put to this purpose, see SC on the Sweating System, P.P. 1889, XIV, (331), part i, QQ. 31654, 31657, 31665, 31714.

167. Garrard, The English and Immigration pp. 159-60.

168. Report on the Sweating System in Leeds, P.P. 1888, LXXXVI, (C5513), pp. 4-5.

169. Reports on the Volume and Effects of Recent Immigration, P.P. 1894, LXVIII, (C 7406), appendix xv.

170. Labour Gazette, I, (May 1893).

171. Leeds Civic Hall, Minutes of the Sanitary Committee of Leeds Town Council, 12-13 June 1888.

172. Leeds Civic Hall, Report of the Medical Officer of Health for 1889.

173. Yorkshire Post, 9 May 1885.

174. Ibid., 25 Aug. 1888.

261

175. <u>SC on the Sweating System</u>, P.P. 1889, XIV, (331), part i, QQ. 30926, 30928, 30934.

176. <u>The Lancet</u>, I, (June 1888), pp. 794, 1146-8, 1209-10.

177. <u>SC on the Sweating System</u>, P.P. 1889, XIV, (331), part ii, appendix F; ibid., part i, Q. 30431.

178. W.J. Fishman, <u>East End Radicals, 1875-1914</u> (1975), p. 50.

179. <u>FT</u>, 29 Nov. 1889.

180. Leeds Civic Hall, Minutes of the Sanitary Committee of Leeds Town Council, 1 April 1889. 119 Jewish shops were involved.

181. <u>Report of the Chief Inspector of Factories for 1910</u>, P.P. 1911, XXII, (Cd 5693), xvii, pp. 52, 116.

182. Leeds Civic Hall, Minutes of the Sanitary Committee of Leeds Town Council, 25 June 1888. This accords with the descriptions in <u>The Lancet</u> in the same year.

183. J. Buckman, 'Problems of the Alien Economy of Leeds, 1880-1914', paper presented to the Urban History Group Meeting of the Economic History Society, Leeds, 1974.

10
The Beginnings of Jewish Trade Unionism in Manchester, 1889–1891

BILL WILLIAMS

The intention of this paper is to use Manchester evidence as
a means of reassessing the origins of Jewish trade unionism
in England.[1] Essentially I shall argue that in the past
the question has not been set in sufficiently wide a context
to identify all the factors involved. In particular,
explanations both of the rise of Jewish trade unions and of
English attitudes towards them have rested too firmly on the
narrow base of ethnicity.

This is the general tenor of Anglo-Jewish history, dating
perhaps from the late nineteenth century, when Anglo-Jewish
leaders felt the need to formulate a coherent defence of the
community against the hysterical onslaughts of anti-alienism.
They responded to anti-semitic caricature with a pattern of
stereotypes which promoted the inner virtues of Jewish communal
life: the respectability, generosity and civic mindedness of
its anglicised leadership; the piety, industry, sobriety and
domesticity of the new immigrants; the solidarity and harmony
of the community as a whole. These were substantially the
views of Harry Lewis in his classic response to anti-alienism
in The Jew in London (1901). Of the small immigrant workshops of the East End, Lewis wrote: 'there is practically no
class distinction between master and men', and elsewhere he

argued that the common bond of religion created working conditions marked by 'kindness and good feeling'.[2]

Extended into explanations of communal change by
historians drawn from the same elite, the effect of such
defensive stereotypes is to lead the history of Jewish
immigrant life into a cul-de-sac. Anglo-Jewish history
becomes separated from the wider social, economic and
political context in which it took place and the assumption
is made that explanations of communal change must be sought
primarily within the community itself - in some element,
religious, social, even psychological, of Jewish society.
Thus, for example, the rise of Jewish charities is put down
to the traditional emphasis on charity of Jewish religious
teaching or to the special place of philanthropy in synagogue
life. Or Jewish commercial success (as well as the failure
of early Jewish trade unionism) is attributed to the special
individualism and 'entrepreneurial tastes' of the Jewish
immigrant. Anglo-Jewish history is interpreted in a vacuum;
pressures from the wider society are, at the very least,
underestimated; unique cultural inheritance takes precedence
over simple economic and class factors. Jewish history
becomes a ghetto.

This trend has had an important effect on the study of
Anglo-Jewish social and labour history. It has meant, for
example, that class division has rarely been taken seriously
as a mechanism of change in Anglo-Jewry.[3] In so far as
historians have seen Anglo-Jewry as divided, the divisions
have been attributed to communal factors: differences of
ritual taste, of theology or of nationality. The assumption
has been that a wider social coherence - occasionally referred
to quite explicitly as 'Jewish solidarity'[4] - overrode these
inner 'family' differences. In other words, social differences
themselves - differences arising from the place of Jews in the
social and economic spectrum of the wider society - were

264

rarely acknowledged, and even more rarely employed as explanations of change. And yet, in reality, it might be argued that the rifts in Jewish society were the main agents even of religious change. The proliferation of synagogues in the Anglo-Jewish communities of late Victorian and Edwardian England owed as much to social as to religious or national distinctions: each social fragment of the community demanded its own synagogal accommodation.[5] If anything, social division had more effect in the minority than in the majority community, since within the minority it was more territorially and institutionally confined, more inescapable, and therefore more abrasive. Harry Lewis's model of the socially coherent workshop breaks down in face of the fierce and consistent claim by Jewish workers that their chief oppressors were the Jewish masters.

In the case of trade union history, the origins, strengths and weaknesses of Jewish trade unionism have all been traced to the special characteristics of Jewish immigrants or to the special nature of the 'immigrant trades'. In a classic statement of the case, Lloyd Gartner links the origins of Jewish trade union activity in England in the late 1880s to the innate individualism and ambition of the Jewish worker rather than to class division and economic exploitation in the workplace: 'that the social order irretrievably fixed him in his lowly estate never occurred to him'.[6] He goes on to argue that in its origins, Jewish trade unionism was inevitably an independent growth, and he finds the reasons for this in 'the social and cultural gulf between Jewish and English workers and the separateness of the Jewish sectors of the main immigrant trades of garment and boot and shoe making'.[7] Gainer extends this thesis in arguing that the Jewish immigrant was precluded from joining English trade unions by 'English hostility, alien uneasiness, and the immigrants' ignorance of the language'.[8]

265

Moreover, Gartner, Gainer and others have asserted that when independent Jewish unions did arise in London, Leeds and Manchester, they were 'notoriously unstable'[9] and on the whole ineffectual. Successful strikes were exceptional: 'the rule was small and ill-planned efforts, leaderless and futile'.[10] Jewish trade union activity was, at best, 'spasmodic'[11]; between strikes Jewish unions 'all but wasted away'.[12] The reasons for this weakness supposedly lay in the nature of the Jewish trades: 'the fluidity of the labour force, the long, demoralising slack seasons, and the transient nature of many workshops'.[13] Small and unstable units of production sapped potential collective strength; so did the 'entrepreneurial tastes' of the Jewish immigrant. In the typical workshop trades to which he was drawn by prior experience in Eastern Europe or the tight social network of the English ghetto - tailoring, cap-making, waterproof-garment making, boot and shoe making, slipper-making and cabinet-making - the Jewish worker was at once too vulnerable and too ambitious to make an effective trade unionist: 'neither psychology nor economics encouraged trade unionism in the principal immigrant trades'.[14] Against such a background, Gartner saw the London Jewish tailors' strike of 1889 as essentially a flash in the pan: 'a brief period of high tide; the ebb set in at once'.[15] The strike was 'little more than a prolonged demonstration', without permanent gains.[16]

Since the Jewish worker in the Jewish trades is assumed to have been innately so unsuited to steady trade unionism, it becomes necessary to find some explanation for such early trade union activity as occurred. The explanation lay in socialism; and in socialism of an extreme European variety, 'not grounded in utilitarianism and Free Trade'.[17] So, the 'most articulate Jewish trade union spokesmen' were socialists;[18] the early leaders of Jewish unionism 'came mainly from the socialists'.[19] And the socialism in question was identified quite clearly as the anarchism which formed the editorial staple of the Yiddish press.

Setting all these arguments together produces a powerful example of special pleading. Jewish trade unionism had specifically Jewish origins, and these origins both separated it from the mainstream of English trade unionism and afflicted it with special and chronic weaknesses. It is this line of argument that I wish to challenge on the basis of developments in Manchester. Nor can I accept that the conflict between Gartner's model and the Manchester evidence lies in the exceptional character of Manchester Jewish immigrants or the Manchester Jewish trades. It seems to me rather that there are two major sources of error in Gartner's analysis.

One is the implicit assumption that Jewish workers of the late 1880s were very recent arrivals from Russia and Poland. This is part of Gartner's general inclination to see Jewish immigration from Eastern Europe as essentially a phenomenon of the 1880s.[20] In fact, it was a continuous process from the 1840s, and a substantial one from the 1860s. Although immigration reached its height after 1881, before 1880 there was already a large proletariat of Jewish workers of Eastern European origin in London and Manchester.[21] More important for the present discussion, by 1889-90 many Jewish workers had considerable experience of British working conditions and had been open to the influence of the English labour movement for up to twenty years. It was from this sector that the leaders of the first Jewish strikes in Manchester were drawn.[22]

More important is Gartner's failure to locate the origins of Jewish trade unionism in English trade union history. There is in his chapter on the subject not a single reference to the rise of the 'new unionism'. Nor is any connection made between the entry of London Jewish workers into trade union activity in the late summer of 1889 and the successful

267

unionisation and strike action of the London gas workers and
dockers only weeks earlier. In looking at the events of
1889-91 in Manchester I want merely to suggest, in a most
tentative way, that the beginnings of Jewish trade unionism
are best understood in the context of such developments in
the wider society. Whatever the precise sequence of causes
in London, subsequent events in Manchester suggest a strong
connection between the unionisation of Jewish workers and
trends of opinion in English trade unionism. There is
evidence of a two-way process. Jewish workers were awakened
by the new enthusiasm in the English labour movement to the
possibility of improving their own position by union action
at a time when the sweated trades were receiving a particularly
adverse press. English trade unionists saw this as their
opportunity to unionise Jewish workers whose weak bargaining
position acted as a brake on their own aspirations. Their
point of convergence was a succession of five strikes, in
four of which Jewish workers were from the beginning members
of English unions.

II

The first was in a relatively minor local industry which was
only fleetingly attractive to Jewish immigrants in Manchester:
cigarette-making. In some ways, the dispute was a rehearsal:
for the Jewish workers a tentative flexing of the muscles;
for the local trade union movement a small opportunity for
gauging the potential bargaining power of Jewish workers. The
occasion, early in 1889, was an attempt by a Manchester firm,
Muratti and Company of Oxford Road, to reduce piece-work rates
by 3d per thousand, from 2/3 to 2/-, as against general prices
of 4/- per thousand in London and 3/- in Manchester. Since
a first-class hand could make up to 2,500 cigarettes in the
customary eleven-hour day, the reduction was equivalent to

7½d a day.   There were more general grievances: the men 'had
to take work home, and sit up a great portion of the night
preparing for the next day's work or else they could not make
a living, so that really they worked about 15 hours a day'.
They paid girl assistants 4/- to 5/- a week to assist them:
'in one way or another something like a third of their earnings
were expended'.[23]   According to <u>The Commonweal</u> the oppression
under which the Jewish workers laboured was 'indescribable'.[24]

The initiative in opposing the reduction was taken by
'the Jewish section of the employees'.[25]   Wishing to form a
union, but 'largely unacquainted with the methods of working
such organisations', a deputation of Jewish workers approached
the Manchester and Salford Trades Council for advice in February
1889.   The result was the Manchester branch of the Cigarette
Workers and Tobacco Cutters Union, with a Jewish secretary,
Ben Kaplan, and a substantially Jewish membership.[26]   A strike
was declared only days later: according to G.D. Kelley,
secretary of the Trades Council, 'the whole of the foreign
labour had left the establishment, but he was very sorry to
say the English workers had stayed on'.[27]   It was a very
minor affair, involving 21 Jewish workers out of a total
workforce of 28.[28]   It was none the less significant.   It
marked the first indication that Jewish workers in the sweated
trades in Manchester were prepared to fight for better conditions.
It provided the first formal link between a Jewish workforce and
the organised trade union movement in Manchester.[29]

It is significant also that the context of the dispute
was the awakening of the Manchester public to the realisation
that 'sweating' was a local as well as a London phenomenon.
Local press comment in November 1887 on Burnett's Board of
Trade report on the 'Sweating System in the East End' was
based on the assumption that sweating was confined essentially
to London.[30]   The leaders of Manchester Jewry shared this
view.   In pressing a typically impractical scheme for the

redistribution of Jewish workers throughout the Lancashire
textile towns, the president of the Manchester Jewish Board
of Guardians commented: 'although circumstances in Manchester
might not warrant any immediate action, yet it was as well to
take time by the forelock by reason of what was happening in
London and the government report recently issued upon the
labour question there.'[31]   That was in December 1887.   In
March 1888 the Manchester City News described the 'Manchester
system' of producing ladies' costumes as 'an immense improvement on the 'sweating' system in vogue in London, the horrors
of which are only too well known.'[32]

Such illusions were shattered by the publication in
April 1888 of the Lancet's report on the sweated industries
of Liverpool and Manchester.[33]   This made it perfectly clear
not only that there was a 'sweating system' in Manchester,
but that it was not limited to tailoring: it existed also
in footwear, cabinet-making, upholstery, shirt-making, hand-
kerchief-making, and in other occupations 'where the supply
of workers is large and many of the labourers are females,
or foreigners.'[34]

Such revelations came as a severe shock.   The Lancet
had 'dragged into light what has been long hidden from the
public.   The story is as serious as it is painful.'[35]   The
Mayor and the City Council, 'jealous for the honour of the
Corporation', passed the buck to the Factory Inspectorate.[36]
Individuals spoke out in favour of legislation to restrict
the immigration of destitute aliens,[37] and a more full-blooded
restrictionism was inhibited only by residual concern to keep
England's door open to refugees: 'What should be done?   This
is a question that nobody seems able to answer in harmony
with English tradition and sentiment.'[38]   The Jewish community
was equally non-plussed.   The president of the Jewish Board
of Guardians found it necessary to explain the absence of any
reference to sweating in the Board's annual report, issued

earlier in the year. The Board (he told subscribers) had
not then believed that the sweating system existed in
Manchester: 'since the report had been printed, however,
various things had appeared which had implicated Manchester
in the system.'[39]

One effect of the spotlight now turned towards sweating
was to highlight the differential in pay and conditions
between unionised English and non-unionised Jewish workers
and so emphasise the vulnerability of English workers to
lower-paid Jewish competition. The facts were already well-
known to local officials of the Amalgamated Society of Tailors
(AST), who had been conducting their own independent inquiry
since Burnett's lurid account of the East End labour market.[40]
Now they became public knowledge. Unionised tailors were
'alarmed': the struggle for them was 'for continued existence'
against the competition of 'non-unionist males and females'.[41]
Other trades were equally affected. A local reporter commented:
'the foreign quarter of the town is growing, and in the hands
of the sweater it is being used to take away from our countrymen
some of their handicrafts. Tailoring is only one of them.'[42]
Loftus Remond, secretary of the East Manchester branch of the
Alliance Association of Cabinet and Chair Makers, attributed
sweating in cabinet-making to the pressure of Jewish immigrants
who supplied Manchester stores with their cheapest furniture at
starvation rates: even the most expert worked a 12-14 hour day
for 25/- a week.[43] Conditions were similar in waterproofing
and footwear.

The only effective solution, according to a Manchester
City News leader, 'The Invasion of England by Foreign Paupers',
was to refuse entry to indigent labourers. Surely it is
carrying the principle of freedom to too great lengths to
allow a system which increases pauperism in our land and untold
sufferings amongst our own people?'[44] This was the voice of
hysteria. There is every indication that sweating was conceived

271

by trade unionists not as an evil to be rooted out by restrictions on immigration so much as a practical problem of hours,
wages and working conditions to be solved by traditional trade
union methods.[45]   Nor was it a problem of Jewish foreigners
alone.   Sweating in the garment trades owed as much to female
as to foreign labour.   In February 1889, James Quinn, president
of the Manchester branch of the AST, spoke from the platform of
a meeting sponsored by the Trades Council 'to promote the
organisation of female labour'.   Of women workers, he commented:

> in some of the main streets of Manchester
> garments were exposed for sale which, if
> the purchasers knew the amount paid to the
> workers for them, few would wear without
> hesitation.   Thousands of pairs of trousers
> were made at 1/- per pair and made under the
> most horrible sanitary conditions.   46

In the cheaper branches of men's tailoring in the 1880s sweated
women workers made the trousers, while sweated Jewish workers
made the coats.[47]   In March 1889 Matthew Arrandale, president
of the Trades Council, told a public audience that no branch of
trade in Manchester more required a union than the tailoresses:
'trade unions did not object to female labour;   what they
objected to was the prices paid to females in the trade.'[48]

The answer to sweating, therefore, did not lie in restricting
Jewish immigrants, any more than its cause lay in their arrival.
The real solution lay in the effective unionisation of women and
Jewish workers.[49]   And the evidence suggests that by the early
months of 1889 this solution was being applied by Manchester
trade unionists, both through their separate organisations and
through the Trades Council.   This does not imply the absence
of latent anti-alien feeling amonst English trade unionists.
The options of restriction and unionisation were after all not
necessarily incompatible;   through unionisation and an improvement in its working conditions, the native Jewish workforce

might itself be won over to the cause of limited restrictionism for its own self-protection.   Nor did English trade unionists necessarily approve of the presence of Jewish workers in Manchester; Quinn told the Select Committee of the House of Lords that he would rather they had stayed at home and held them at least partially responsible for a decline in wage rates in the tailoring industry since 1861.[50]   The attitude of the English trade union establishment was governed by expedience.   The ultimate object was the improvement of the pay and conditions of English skilled workers.   In 1889 it seems that this might be achieved by first unionising Jewish workers and so removing the anchorage of low-paid competition. But if this option failed, the alternative of restrictionism was always to hand.   At all events, in the case of neither women nor foreigners was unionisation expected to be an easy matter: both represented a readily replaceable semi-skilled labour force on the very periphery of a highly competitive sector of the economy.

In the case of Jewish immigrants, a further difficulty lay in the structure of the labour force in the sweated industries.   In those trades in which Jewish involvement was heaviest - particularly in tailoring - there was a very real danger that their sudden acceptance into English unions would have the effect of depressing conditions throughout the industry.   The argument ran thus: 'If the sweater is abolished the unionist tailor will have to compete with the non-unionists, and the foreign element.'   The 'foreign element' might thus be encouraged to work under better conditions and for somewhat higher rates of pay, but the rates would still be well below the rate per piece paid to unionists.   'Swamped' by foreign workers, the unionists would find difficulty in maintaining 'a reasonable rate of wages'.[51]   And what was the solution?   That in tailoring Jewish workers should only be admitted to English unions after their rates of pay and conditions of work had been 'levelled-up'.[52]

Until that time, Jewish tailors should be encouraged to organise separate unions. Seen from this point of view, the independent growth of union activity amongst Jewish tailors was not, as Gartner has suggested, a result of any 'social and cultural gulf' between Jewish and English workers but a deliberate act of practical policy on the part of English tailoring trade unionists.

On the other hand, in the case of trades in which Jewish workers were a minority - in cabinet-making, for example- they might without danger be admitted from the beginning to English unions. So, when in January 1888 Remond set out to the Trades Council the case of the Jewish sweated worker in cabinet-making, the advice offered was the 'thorough organisation of all members of the trade,[53] and over the succeeding months he set out accordingly to draw Jewish cabinet-makers into the East Manchester branch of the Alliance Association, the branch which represented the cheaper end of the trade, centred in and around the rookeries of East Ancoats.[54]

There was a third trade in which the early predominance of male Jewish workers actually pre-empted any policy which English trade unionists might have wished to pursue. This was waterproof garment making, second only to tailoring as the chosen trade of immigrants. A Manchester observer noted in 1888: 'these Jews seem to have made the macintosh trade a speciality'.[55] In July 1889, a Jewish waterproofer explained that while the trade was 'conducted mainly by Jewish employers, and the great majority of the males employed are Jews, the females with the exception of three or four are Christians'.[56] Unlike tailoring, there was no danger that the unionisation of Jewish labour would depress the wages of English skilled workers, nor were the English workers in any event in a position to protect themselves. The result was a general union established by Jewish male workers and with a predominantly Jewish membership. The Waterproof Garment Makers' Union was

certainly in existence by July 1889, and was probably founded
a month or so earlier.[57]   The secretary and leading spokesman
was Isidore Sugar.   Nor was Sugar interested in Jewish workers
alone; from the beginning he campaigned for the organisation
of the Christian female workforce.[58]

In waterproofing, the usual roles were, in fact, reversed:
any improvement in the working conditions of the alien worker
depended on the progress of the native workforce.   As the
union's delegate, Sugar made this point more than once to the
Trades Council: 'up to now the employers had used one class of
workers to combat the other, and in that they had been so far
successful'.[59]   The survival of the union itself was at stake:
'there was great fear (in May 1890) that they would not be able
to exist for another twelve months.   Even if they did exist
for that time there was no doubt they would be able to do little
or nothing unless the females were organised.'[60]   His own and
the Trades Council's efforts, he asserted, were hampered by the
vulnerability of women to intimidation by the employers.[61]

Yet another result of the new and adverse publicity given
to Manchester sweating after the Lancet enquiry was to make it
clear to Jewish workers that the conditions under which they
worked were not only intolerable to themselves but unacceptable
to public opinion and to English trade unionists.   Quite apart
from its effect on working conditions, collective opposition to
sweating would provide an effective answer to the voice of
anti-alienism.

A further catalyst at work in the Jewish immigrant milieu
during 1888-9 was socialist propaganda, issuing both from the
London Jewish anarchists and (probably more powerfully) from
the Manchester branch of William Morris's Socialist League.
Although the cautious and conservative Trades Council had played
the major public role in organising the cigarette workers,
behind the scenes the Socialist League was at work in Manchester,
as it was in London and Leeds, propagating the virtues of union

275

membership. A 'strong effort' in January 1889 to organise
Manchester Jewish workers had led to the formation of an
International Working Men's Club, situated close to the main
areas of immigrant settlement in Strangeways and Red Bank.[62]
Apart from the 'enlightenment and education' of Jewish workers
'on all subjects bearing on the labour question,' the object
of the club was 'to combine the workers employed in different
trades for the purpose of co-operating with the English workers
in their struggle against the sweating system.'[63] It may well
have been the Socialist League which in February 1889 persuaded
the Jewish cigarette workers to approach the Trades Council for
practical advice and support.

Thereafter, the League was active throughout 1889 both
directly in the Jewish workforce and indirectly by providing
a link between the London Jewish anarchists of Berner Street
and Jewish workers in Manchester. In its issue of 23 March
1889, The Commonweal, the League's journal, invited 'all comrades
in and around Manchester wishing to see the cause of Socialism
advanced' to meet William Wess, a member of the Berner Street
Club, at an address in Cheetham Hill. Those who could not
'take the risk of doing active work' were encouraged to assist
in the distribution of leaflets. In August the League was
independently at work within at least one sector of the Jewish
workforce: 'We have been assisting the cap-makers, men, women,
and girls, to form a union, which is very much needed in this
industry, where sweating is the order of the day.'[64] In the
following month, when the League organised a demonstration in
Manchester in support of the Jewish tailors on strike in London,
Nathan Diemschitz, another member of the London International
Working Men's Club, was one of the speakers to an audience of
some 3,000 people.[65] Another was John Marshall who, as an
organiser of the AST, a Socialist Leaguer and a member of the
Trades Council, was in a strong position to provide a bridge
between Jewish workers, English tailors and the Manchester trade

276

union establishment.   It was almost certainly Marshall who
organised a meeting in Strangeways in November to consider
ways in which Jewish tailors might best unite with the AST in
fighting for improved conditions in the tailoring trade.   It
was this meeting, in turn, which gave practical shape to the
agreed strategy for improving conditions in the tailoring
trade: separate unions of Jewish and English tailors working
towards a common end, 'so that when one demands an increase in
wages the other will assist them in that direction.'[66]

III

The immediate result was a meeting at the Free Trade Hall on
3 December 1889 when 400 Jewish workers in the Manchester
tailoring trade organised the Jewish Machinists', Tailors' and
Pressers' Trade Union, Manchester's first, and only, specifically
Jewish union.[67]   Events in Manchester were not simply a reflection of London developments.[68]   It seems far more likely that
similar conditions produced similar results, with the London
strike acting only as the final catalyst.   In particular, the
Manchester trade union movement took advantage of a new sense
of injustice amongst Jewish workers to promote a policy that
had evolved slowly over the previous twelve months.   The
initiative at the Free Trade Hall was taken by English tailoring
unionists and members of the Trades Council.   It was Quinn of
the AST who proposed the resolution for the foundation of the
union;   of Jewish workers he said: 'at last they have awakened
to the belief that their labour should be adequately rewarded'.[69]
Arrandale, president of the Trades Council, commented that if
Jewish workers united they would soon secure for themselves the
same rates of pay as members of the English union;   he and the
Trades Council would 'give them every assistance in their
power'.[70]   Behind the formation of a Jewish union lay not a
cultural gulf but English union strategy;   fear, perhaps, but

277

certainly not hostility.   Within twelve months the JMTPTU had
nearly 800 members.[71]

At the inaugural meeting Quinn had advised Jewish tailors
to work for better conditions by cautious negotiation; a strike
was 'the most remote idea he wished them to have in their minds'.
In the event, however, a strike proved to be the only means by
which conditions were likely to be improved, particularly in
Jewish-owned shops.   Early in April 1890 a deputation of Jewish
tailors laid a series of grievances before the Trades Council,
and 'from the advice given' they determined on a strike which
began on 13 April and involved some 1500 male and female
workers.[73]   Forgetful of the minor action of the cigarette-
makers, the <u>Manchester Guardian</u> believed it to be 'the first
strike of Jews that has taken place in Manchester'.[74]   The
demands were modest enough: a working day from 8 am to 8 pm
with recognised breaks for lunch and tea, an increase in piece-
work rates of 3d a garment for machinists and 2d a garment for
pressers, and an improved log for workers in the bespoke trade.[75]
The significance of the strike lay more in its character than
in its objectives.

One aspect of this was the leadership of the strike by
more anglicised Jewish workers basing their claims not on
socialist ideology but upon the stark contrast between Jewish
and English working conditions.   Barnett Levine, the first
president of the JMTPTU, declared at an early meeting

> that no workmen were treated as were he and
> his Jewish fellows. They had been accustomed
> to hear England spoken of, and to speak of it,
> as a land of freedom, but the Jewish working
> man was under present conditions in a state
> of slavery (cheers).   76

Nathan Cohen, leader of the strike committee, spoke of improved
working conditions as a logical extension of the political
emancipation of Anglo-Jewry, secured earlier in the century.[77]

278

The strikers adopted the traditional tactics of English unionists, partly, no doubt, on Trades Council advice: open-air meetings in such traditional focal points of Entlish strikes as Stevenson Square and New Cross, a parade through the main streets and squares of the city headed by a brass band and a huge red banner bearing (remarkably) the device of a white cross and the words 'Jews' Union'.[78] Cohen told another meeting: 'we wish for nothing more than to be something like you English workers.'[79] Even the Anglo-Jewish elite, which might otherwise have felt threatened by an awakening of the Jewish masses, found solace in the 'true English style' of the strikers.[80]

Another notable feature of the strike was the sustained support of the strikers by English unionists. Kelley attended most of the major meetings and repeatedly pledged the Trades Council's support; after taking the matter up, the Trades Council would not leave Jewish workers 'at the mercy of men who outwardly posed as philanthropists and yet were perhaps members of sweating firms'.[81] Jewish masters were sufficiently irritated to suggest that their workers had been 'misled and badly advised' by the Trades Council.[82] John Marshall, who served for a time as secretary to the Jewish union, told a strike meeting in Stevenson Square that English tailors were agreed that Jewish workers were right to press their claims; they must go on and carry the strike to a successful conclusion. Marshall's final sentiment that the Jewish worker should become as 'his English fellow-man' was 'applauded by many of the Englishmen around the square'.[83]

The applause was not altogether disinterested. More significant still was the formulation of new demands by English tailors of the AST only two days after the commencement of the Jewish strike. The logical connection between the two events was spelt out by a spokesman for the English workers:

> They have worked all this time with a
> knowledge that there had been a gradual

cheapening of articles of wearing apparel,
and that so much of the trade was in Jewish
hands that if they came out it would have
been with a dread that their industry might
have been well-nigh swept away from English
fingers altogether. The Jewish working man
having now, for the first time in their (sic)
history in this country, come to a sense of
'their rights' it would be foolish on the
English workman's part..,to let the opportunity
to secure an advance pass, perhaps for an
irremediable time. 84

Hence the logic of a separate Jewish union and of English
support for a Jewish strike. It had now become possible for
the AST to fight for a modest revision of the 1869 log with
only a minimal risk of the master-tailors replacing English
with Jewish workers, English with Jewish methods. Both
strikes were pressed to a successful conclusion, the Jewish
strike in only a week, the strike of the AST over a rather
longer period. The Jewish strike ended in a compromise
engineered by the Trades Council and mediated by the Lord
Mayor in the less heated atmosphere which followed the
'enforced quiet' of the Jewish Sabbath.[85] The masters gave
way on hours, but the claim for an increase in piece work
rates was reduced by half.[86] In the case of the AST, the
tailors faced concerted and tough opposition from English
masters. Unable to obtain a collective settlement from the
Association of Master Tailors, they dealt with employers
'separately and individually': their new log did not find
general acceptance until the middle of May.[87]

IV

One immediate effect of the Jewish tailors' strike was the
further exposure of sweating in Manchester. The Manchester
Guardian commented: 'Few were aware that amongst the Jewish

community in Manchester such a state of things existed as had
been laid bare...the strike must be the forerunner of a
healthier condition of things.'[88]   The 'public eye' had been
directed to 'conditions of labour among the Jewish nationality...
such as no man in a country like England can be long expected
to fulfil.'[89]   The Anglo-Jewish elite rationalised a revolt
of the Jewish masses as part of their own war on sweating.[90]
Others hoped that the strike would 'have delivered a blow to
the sweater from which he would never recover'.[91]   Such hopes
were wildly over-optimistic.   In the end, sweating did not so
much depend on the worker as on the consumer, not so much on
the Jewish worker as on the whole casual labour force.   More
realistic was Lewis Lyon's appraisal: the House of Lords
Committee, having sat for two years and asked 36,000 questions,
'had now retired for recreation to leave the solution of this
sweating business to the working-classes themselves'.[92]   What
the modest success of the strike achieved was a chain reaction
amongst Jewish workers in other sweated trades.

In cabinet-making, the problem was not altogether dis-
similar from that in tailoring: the need of the 'better class'
of workers was for an initial 'levelling-up' of rates of pay
in the less skilled sector prior to a stabilisation of wages
and conditions and a more general advance on a broad front.
As in tailoring, the Jewish worker was seen as a check on the
ambitions of English workers.   But since the Jews did not
monopolise the unskilled branches to anything like the degree
to which they had captured 'slop tailoring', the levelling-up
was spearheaded by a branch of the general union which
represented the whole of the cheaper end of the trade: Remond's
East Manchester branch of the Alliance Association of Cabinet
and Chair Makers (AACM).   In the twelve months following his
initial appeal to the Trades Council in January 1888 Remond had
succeeded in unionising 380 makers of 'the rough and very cheap
classes of furniture';   of these, 140 were Jews.[93]   So similar

281

were English and Jewish working conditions that in several instances Jewish and English cabinet-makers worked side by side in the same workshops.[94]

Exactly a week after the conclusion of the Jewish tailors' dispute, Remond convened a meeting to publicise the demands of his members. It was, quite explicitly, 'a movement for the levelling-up of prices': the aim was not to achieve an 'all-round advance' but 'to try to compel the low-paying employers to come up to the standards of the better shops.' There was no complaint against the 'very fair rate' paid by 'the manufacturer of sounder and more costly goods'. To achieve its aim, the union would use 'all peaceable means', but if any employer would not give in 'they were determined not to lay down their weapons until the victory was won'.[95] The result, Remond believed, would not only be to achieve higher rates of pay but also to improve standards of craftsmanship by eliminating the 'quack' products of under-skilled, under-paid and overworked cabinet makers: 'there was an amount of quackery in the cabinet trade at the present day which would have to be swept away. There were quack manufacturers of furniture, quack dealers and people who took in the quackery.'[96] The demands embodied in a new log would drive the amateur out of the trade: 'they would be dealing a blow at the "slop" furniture methods'.[97] They would also benefit the 'fair employer' by eliminating his cut-price competitor.[98] But most of all they would check conditions of deteriorating wages under which 'the cabinet makers of Ancoats...were the most hard-worked, cruelly crushed people in the world'.[99]

The object was not to drive Jewish aliens out of the trade. On the contrary, Jewish workers played a major part both in formulating the demands and in agitating for their acceptance. Of the committee of seven workmen who met the masters on 10 May 1890 two, including the vice-chairman, Edward Marcus, were Jews.[100] When the masters subsequently rejected the men's demands, it was

'the Jewish workmen affiliated to the union' who first came
out on strike, often leaving work-in-hand in an unfinished
condition.[101]   It was only after a meeting of the general
committee of the branch that it was resolved 'to advise English
workmen to follow their example'.[102]   By noon on 14 May 'the
whole of the men engaged in the cheaper class of cabinet-making
in Manchester' were on strike.[103]   Jewish workers were amongst
those most aware of the injustice of their position, amongst
the most oppressed, and, from the point of view of the English
worker, most in need of 'levelling-up'.   Again, the key to
events was the coincidental awakening of the Jewish and the
native workforce.

The cabinet-making strike shared other features of the
dispute in tailoring.   One was the support from the beginning
of the Trades Council; Arrandale told the strikers that 'there
were plenty of trade unionists in Manchester who would see that
they did not fail through lack of funds'.[104]   The AACM also
pledged its help; a representative of the union's national
executive found conditions in Manchester 'disgraceful', pressed
the men to 'maintain the struggle until the employers had given
in', and promised a special levy, if needs be, on the membership
in London, Liverpool, Birmingham, Glasgow and Edinburgh.[105]

As in tailoring, the special target of the strike was the
Jewish employer, with his easier access to pliable immigrant
labour.   The Manchester Guardian reported: 'The dispute is
strongest between the Jewish employers and their men';[106]   the
conduct of the Jewish master towards his employees was said to
be 'neither more nor less than sheer oppression'.[107]   Concluding
a report of a mass meeting in Stevenson Square, the Guardian
reporter commented: 'Much enthusiasm prevailed, and at the close
cheers were given by the crowd for the Jewish men who have come
out, as it is still stated that the Jewish masters are those
who are most strongly determined to maintain their own amended
price list.'[108]   Another way of looking at English trade union

strategy is as an attempt to force the hand of the Jewish employer by taking up the cause of the Jewish worker. Buoyed up by this support the Ancoats cabinet-makers pressed the strike to a successful conclusion, first by picking off the more vulnerable employers and finally by the threat of establishing workers' co-operatives.[109] On 12 June, the employers accepted 'what is practically the new price list of the men'.[110]

V

Within a month Isidore Sugar had brought the waterproofers to the brink of strike action. For over a year, since the foundation of the Waterproof Garment Makers' Union (WGMU), he had been campaigning as delegate to the Trades Council for improved conditions, and in particular for the organisation of women workers and the restriction of 'apprentices' entering the trade.

The apprenticeship system in waterproofing had become little more than a device used by employers to maintain a cheap force of child, female and alien 'greener' labour. Boys, girls and 'greeners' were taken on for periods of up to five years to 'learn the trade', only to be absorbed into the main workforce after a few months with only such minimal skills as would keep them tied indefinitely to low piece-work rates. At the end of five years, many knew no more than after the first month. 'The great number of apprentices as compared with adult workers' both had the same depressing effect as the women workforce on the pay of skilled male Jewish workers, and acted as an effective brake on the organisation of women workers.[111] The answer for the male Jewish workforce lay in the elimination of all but bona fide apprentices, the levelling-up of women's rates and the unionisation of women workers.

With the encouragement of the Trades Council the water-proofers formulated a series of demands at a lively public

284

meeting at the Cotton Waste Exchange on 2 August 1890. The
main speakers were Remond (providing a direct link with the
cabinet-makers' victory), Arrandale, Kelley (who was 'received
with much cheering' as the champion of the sweated workers)
and John Jenkins, secretary of the Operative Bakers, who were
themselves in the process of formulating a wage-demand.[112]
Again, the waterproofers' claims were modest enough against a
background of the eight-hour day agitation: a maximum week of
fifty-nine hours, no more than ten hours overtime in any one
week, a limited advance of between 1d and 3d on different
classes of garment, and a moratorium on apprenticeships for
twelve months during which time employers and employed would
come to some agreement on the admission of new workers to the
trade.[113] When these claims were peremptorily rejected by
the master-waterproofers, the WGMU called for an immediate
strike, which began on 12 August.[114]

The Jewish workers in the garment trades (and their English
trade union supporters) saw themselves as fighting different
campaigns in the same war on sweating. A procession of 500
waterproofers and 850 tailors and pressers marched together to
Belle Vue for a meeting under Kelley's chairmanship at which
the tailors approved the steps taken by the WGMU and the two
bodies of workers expressed satisfaction at the 'friendship and
amity' which existed between them.[115] The waterproofers' battle
was, however, particularly severe. When the WGMU had been formed,
Isidore Frankenburg, whose Greengate Rubber Works was the major
employer of waterproofers, had written to Sugar that 'he would be
glad to support the union if carried on on sound principles'.[116]
A little later Frankenburg had become the workers' friend as
mediator in the tailoring dispute,[117] Now he and Sugar became
locked in a battle of words in which personal animosity overlapped
with conflicting interests. Frankenburg found it difficult to
accept a change of role from workers' friend, father of the
Jewish poor (as vice-president of the Jewish Board of Guardians)

295

and chief representative of the Jewish community in the non-Jewish world (as a Salford City Councillor) to villainous exploiter of sweated labour.

For his part, Sugar was particularly stung by Frankenburg's accusation that in attempting to limit apprenticeships he was trying to drive English girls out of the trade.[118] Sugar replied that the suggestion had 'not the slightest foundation': on the contrary

> Jews and Christians have worked together in many establishments for years in amity and friendship, and there never has been a case where one class of worker have (sic) shown the slightest animosity towards the other. The only harm that the Jewish waterproofers wish to English girls in Mr Frankenburg's employ is that Mr Frankenburg would raise their piece-work rates to those paid to the men...Then one class of worker will cease to have to compete with the other. [119]

The fact that women workers were not on strike was a reflection of their weaker bargaining position rather than any conflict of interests with the Jewish labour force.[120]

Resolution of the dispute was delayed by personal wrangling. The masters refused to negotiate with any workers' committee which included Sugar until he published an apology for an inaccurate account of the weekly earnings of workers at Frankenburg's factory,[121] or to consider any agreement until the men had returned to work and worked out a fortnight's notice: the 'most important grievance' of the masters, according to Frankenburg, was the men's departure from work without the customary notice.[122] The masters promised that if the men returned to work they would submit a new log within fourteen days 'on a scale to enable any ordinary workman to earn 35/- to 40/- a week';[123] the men insisted that the log should be submitted and agreed before their return.[124] Finally, the strike ended on 25 August when, on Kelley's advice, the men agreed to work out their notice.[125]   The new log was ready by 9 September, when it was accepted by the men with only minor amendments; it was, according to Sugar, 'on the whole satisfactory'.[126]

VI

Meantime, towards the end of August, Jewish workers in a fifth trade had come out on strike.[127]   Until the late 1870s the Manchester boot and shoe industry was entirely in the hands of English workers.   But the gradual replacement of hand-stitching by the less skilled technique of rivetting during the 1880s opened the way to the entry of unskilled workers, particularly in the manufacture of loose shoes and slippers.   'The refugee Jew stepped in' and worked for 'the barest living'.[128]   By 1890 the cheaper class of boot and shoe making in Manchester was 'like that of ready-made clothing, very largely in the hands of Jews'.[129]   Of the 600 men affiliated in 1890 to the Manchester branch of the National Union of Boot and Shoe Operatives 'fully one half are Jews, principally Polish and Lithuanian'.[130]

As in cabinet-making, the aim of the strike was not an increase in wages so much as a 'levelling-up' which would eliminate sweating, check declining rates of pay and create a uniform platform for future progress.   The aim of a new log proposed by the men was 'to create a uniform price list and so do away with the "sweating" class of work which is under-taken by some of these newcomers to the trade'.[131]   If the new log were to be accepted, forty of the men employed in the better class of work would be faced with slight reductions, but the rest would obtain an increase of from 4/- to 7/- a week.[132]   It was not the case only that English workers sought to defend themselves against the competition of sweated

287

alien labour; the Jewish workers were equally alive to the
injustices of their position, Writing of the boot and shoe
trade, the Manchester Guardian commented: 'Today the Jew is
as ardent a trade unionist as any Englishman, and often far
more voluble'.[133]

As in tailoring, waterproofing and cabinet-making, the
men had chosen to strike at a time of optimum employment and
maximum consumer-demand. Like cabinet-makers, they were
able to pick off individual employers who gave way as the
pressure of the market increased;[134] finally, on 17 September,
the masters accepted a new log which gave poorer-paid workers
pay increases of from 10 to 20 per cent.[135]

VII

It is against the background of the five Manchester strikes of
1889-90 that Gartner's analysis appears most insubstantial.
It becomes perfectly plain that in its beginnings Jewish trade
unionism in Manchester was neither a specifically Jewish nor a
structurally independent movement. In four of the strikes,
Jewish workers were integrated from the very beginning in
English unions. In the case of the fifth - tailoring - the
separation of Jewish unionists was essentially the product not
of cultural separation, hostility, uneasiness or the watertight
compartmentalisation of the English and Jewish sectors of the
trade, but of English trade union strategy, There are no
signs of hostility to Jewish workers amongst English trade
unionists during 1889-90: on the contrary, it was in the
interests of the English labour movement to support Jewish
workers in a 'levelling-up' of conditions in the workshop
trades. This strategy was determined only circumstantially
by public evidence of sweating; more fundamentally it was the
outcome of the general state of trade union development in
England. In a particularly favourable year of full employment

288

and spurred on by the early successes of the 'new unionism',
the organised trade union movement sought to check the decline
of wages which had set in during the adverse trading conditions
of the 1870s and 80s, and to prepare the way for a fresh
advance.   In trades with immigrant employees, it was necessary
to carry the Jewish workforce with them.

Although the details are lost, the Socialist League had
almost certainly played an important role in pressing these
policies on the Trades Council, even while snapping at the
heels of 'the official clique' who ran it.   Kelley, the
Council's secretary, was a craft unionist and a Liberal in
politics, deeply suspicious of the political leanings of the
'new unionism.'[136]   But he had been persuaded that the well-
being of English skilled workers demanded the unionisation of
Jewish workers, and in the long run he emerged as their most
effective supporter.   It is possible that early socialist
effort persuaded him to take command of the situation before
it ran out of control.   The impact of Jewish anarchism is
less evident.   Wess and Diemschitz were certainly active
during 1889-90, at least amongst the tailors.   The Manchester
International Working Men's Club was clearly a local satellite
of Berner Street.   A meeting at the club in November 1889 to
commemorate the Chicago Martyrs ended with speeches in Yiddish
and revolutionary songs.[137]   But such manifestations in no
way justify Gartner's identification of European socialism as
the root or mainstay of Jewish trade unionism in England.   The
International Working Men's Club was pitifully small and
unstable.[138]   By the end of 1892 it had disappeared, leaving
as an alternative only the Jewish Working Men's Club, an
association formed earlier by the Anglo-Jewish elite to promote
the anglicisation, respectability and depoliticisation of
immigrant workers.[139]   There is no hint in the speeches of
Jewish strike leaders of the millenarian hopes of Jewish
anarchism; on the contrary, they were every bit as pragmatic
in their approach as their English allies.

English trade unionists were not concerned with Jewish workers alone. Their concern was for the poorly paid in every trade. Attempts to unionise Jewish workers and to help improve their conditions of work coincided with efforts to unionise other trades and to improve the lot of non-Jewish workers. It coincided also with a renewed attempt to unionise women workers. In October 1890 the Trades Council decided to back Lady Dilke's missionary efforts: the Manchester Guardian commented: 'It is beginning to be realised by working men that their own wages will never be safe against reduction if women are allowed to remain as rivals always ready to under-sell them.'[140] Self-interest as much as chivalry led organised male labour to take up the women's cause.[141] By the end of October, the Trades Council had 'fairly taken the matter up' and Lady Dilke was convinced that 'for the future...the working women of Manchester will not be left to themselves to carry on the struggle.'[142]

Moreover, attitudes towards trades in which women were involved differed in much the same way, and for much the same reasons, as attitudes towards different trades employing Jewish labour. Kelley commented: 'In some trades women are to be admitted as fellow-workers with the men; in others a separate union for women will be formed.'[143] The work of the Trades Council with immigrant workers during 1889-90 was, in fact, almost a tactical rehearsal for the drive amongst women workers in the autumn. Again Kelley spoke of the need to counteract 'the tendency to drag down the wages of the men'.[144] For this purpose, the Trades Council 'would help women in the formation of unions, they would teach them how to conduct their affairs on a good basis, and they would give them meeting rooms'.[145] Unlike the restrictionists, the English trade unionist saw Jewish workers as a practical problem in the context of the whole body of sweated workers, the improvement of whose conditions he saw as a pre-requisite for a more general and permanent improvement of working conditions. The offer of help to Jewish workers was part of a general reaching out to the more vulnerable sectors of the English workforce.

But Jews were not only the passive recipients of English trade union encouragement. Jewish workers (many of them settled in England for several years) were equally carried along by the new currents of trade union optimism and militance; again, the notoriety of sweating was only the circumstantial catalyst. This is clearest, perhaps, in waterproofing, in which it was the Jewish worker who needed to weigh the anchor of native labour. It is clear too in Isidore Sugar's efforts on behalf of male non-Jewish workers in other trades (such, for example, as the spreaders and mixers in the India-rubber goods industry)[146] and women workers in all trades. It was Sugar who seconded the vote of thanks to Lady Dilke after the mass meeting in Peter Street to promote the formation of women's trade unions.[147]

Sugar's most remarkable intervention in the development of the Manchester labour movement during 1890 took the form of a motion he put before a special meeting of the Trades Council in November. This proposed the setting up of a sub-committee, '(1) to make enquiries as to what trades in Manchester and district are as yet unorganised and to promote and assist them in the formation and organisation of such trades', and '(2) to enquire into those branches of industry in which unskilled workers were employed', to 'promote the organisation of such unskilled workers, and to recommend their affiliation to the Trades Council'. This was too much for the politically conservative, cautious and craft-oriented Council. The motion, the Council decided, was 'a new departure in (sic) the methods employed by the Council in the past'. Sugar was given permission to withdraw it and to return with it in an amended form at some future date.[148]

While the focus on 1890 highlights the militance of some
Jewish workers, subsequent events suggest the fragile nature
of some Jewish unions. Within a month of the successful
conclusion of the tailor's strike, some of the men were
claiming that the employers were failing to honour their
undertakings.[149] Following the end of the busy season at
Whitsun, some employers were said to have told their workers
that they would be retained only on the pre-strike terms,[150]
Moreover, the union itself was showing signs of breaking up.
Some men had seceded as soon as better terms had been achieved,
and some employers had taken the opportunity to revert to the
old conditions.[151] In September it was again reported that
Jewish employers were lengthening hours and reducing prices.
The fluidity of union membership was again emphasised:
'there were frequent additions to the roll of members but
contributions were decreasing'.[152] By May 1891 Jewish workers
in tailoring workshops were again doing the same class of work
as their native equivalent at some 4 - 5/- a week less.[153]
The failure of the workers to prevent this was attributed to
lack of 'organisation and sound trade union feeling'; their
union was 'wretchedly weak', and if they didn't strengthen it
'they would in the end go to the wall'.[154]

These indications of weakness were greeted by English
trade unionists with a growing sense of exasperation. In May
1890 Kelley told the Jewish tailors bluntly that if they fell
away from their own union 'they would show themselves unworthy
of sympathy and assistance'.[155] By September Kelley's
impatience was tinged with anti-semitism.[156] Six months later,
attitudes within the Trades Council had hardened still further.
John Jenkins commented: 'The English trade unionist had worked
hard to improve his own condition...Neither had he up to the

present complained of the Jewish workman coming in and working side by side with the Gentile'. But it was now 'absolutely necessary' for the English worker

> to tell the Jew that he must not rest
> satisfied with his present condition.
> The English trade unionists had no
> objection to any class of men coming
> to live amongst them so long as there
> was room for that class to live and
> work, but they would insist that if
> the Jews came away then they must make
> some effort to improve such a condition
> as they were now under. Otherwise the
> feeling produced would become a real
> danger to the state. 157

It is easy to see how such attitudes spilled over into restrictionism, particularly as the pace of immigration increased and anti-alienism took hold, for other reasons, on local sectors of urban society. It seemed that the strategy of drawing Jewish workers into the trade union movement had failed; the apparent alternative was restriction. By the end of 1892 the Trades Council had come to regard the immigration of 'destitute foreigners' as a matter 'of great importance...The labour of our countrymen is being undersold by foreigners coming into this country ready to accept any wages that may be offered to them and willing to work any number of hours'. The Trades Council had no objection to Britain receiving political exiles: but

> when the foreign workman is induced to
> come over here by some of his wealthy
> countrymen or co-religionists so that
> he may be worked or sweated to the
> detriment of our own people, and for
> the purpose of putting extra money
> into the pockets of the employer or
> sweater,

then it was time the workers 'rose in arms and protested with firmness and determination against the continuance of this curse.'[158]   A deputation was appointed to wait on the Home Secretary and urge the need for legislation.[159]   During the elections of 1892 Manchester's parliamentary candidates were asked by the Trades Council whether or not they favoured 'A Law to prohibit the Importation of Foreign Workmen'.[160]

Is the weakness of Jewish trade unionism, which helped to produce this reaction, to be interpreted, in line with Gartner's analysis, as a peculiarly Jewish phenomenon, arising out of the special nature of the Jewish trades and the special character of the Jewish immigrant?   It is certainly the case that the structure of the trades in which Jewish immigrants found employment made the workers particularly vulnerable. Opportunities for employment were seasonal and sporadic. Many of the smaller workshops lacked stability and continuity; bankruptcy was endemic.   The workshop trades could also draw upon a vast pool of unskilled male and female labour, of which Jewish immigrants formed only a small part.   Moreover, the constant arrival of new waves of 'greeners' both provided an alternative pool of cheap and gullible labour within the Jewish community itself[161] and produced a socially laminated immigrant society given to perennial factionalism.

But Gartner's analysis is none the less open to challenge. His comment that small units of production sapped the collective strength of the Jewish workforce is at least open to doubt in view (for example) of the success of Remond's cabinet-makers, grouped in workshops of between three and twenty-five persons,[162] or of the Manchester bakers, working mostly in units of two or three men, who conducted a successful strike and secured permanent gains during September 1890.[163]   Nor is it certain that the 'entrepreneurial ambition' of the Jewish worker and the economic weakness of the Jewish master blurred the distinction between them.   The entrepreneurial ambitions of a few have masked the economic weakness and chronic exploitation

294

of the majority. Nor should the transience of Jewish unions
be exaggerated. The Jewish tailors' union, whatever its
limitations, was affiliated to the Trades Council during 1892
and survived until such time as a levelling-up (or was it
down?) of working conditions warranted its permanent integration
as a branch of the AST in 1906.[164] If the foregoing analysis
is correct, 1889-90 was significant as the point of entry of
Jewish workers into English trade unionism. Teething troubles
are hardly surprising;[165] over a longer period, the loyalty
and determination of the Jewish trade unionist is more
impressive than his weakness.[166] In 1903 Kelley characterised
the Jewish worker as 'sober, regular in his employment, punctual
in the payment of his contribution and loyal to his union';
the Jewish tailors' union might be 'taken as an object lesson
by a good many British societies'.[167]

But the central error of Gartner's analysis is again to
treat the Jewish workers as a special case. During 1889-90
English trade unionism as a whole was emerging from a period
of relative dormance. Gains were hard to achieve and difficult
to defend, even by the longer-established craft unions. The
Manchester branch of the AST had as much trouble with non-
Jewish masters during 1890-1 as the JMTPTU had with the Jewish.
An attempt to fight reductions in one workshop had led to
Quinn's successful prosecution for libel by the president of
the Master Tailors' Association.[168] The newly organising
unskilled workers faced correspondingly greater difficulties.[169]
In the sweated industries these difficulties were for most
workers insuperable.[170] The fact that of all sweated workers
Jewish immigrants were the most militant, the best organised
and the most successful hardly supports the view that their
trades, background and temperament constituted special barriers
to effective trade unionism. On the contrary, they learnt
the lessons of collective bargaining early and well.[171] What
limited their achievement was not lack of courage or commitment

295

but their chronically weak position in the labour market. The events of 1889-90 suggest what was possible in spite of this weakness. Thereafter, Manchester Jewish workers not only remained loyal and militant trade unionists but played a crucial role in the history of the whole labour movement in the city.[172]

The contrasting case of women workers is especially striking. The same report of the Trades Council which attacked the destitute immigrant for under-selling native labour commented equally forcefully on the failure of women workers to organise effectively. The efforts of the Trades Council to organise female labour - including the appointment of a full-time organiser and the circulation of thousands of leaflets - had 'not met with the success that was hoped for': from 'either apathy or fear', meetings of women workers had been poorly attended.[173] Perhaps they too should be sent home? In fact, the Council did not meet this problem with legislation to ban the employment of women. Kelley wrote: (the Trades Council) 'will not be dismayed, but will try again, and make yet another effort to rouse them to a sense of protecting themselves.'[174] Once the brief wave of restrictionist hysteria had passed, and the Trades Council had itself again identified the problem as the vulnerability of the unskilled labour force as a whole rather than the presence of Jewish immigrants within it, Kelley and his colleagues returned to a similarly constructive and flexible approach to Jewish workers. The restrictionist motion of 1892 was never repeated, even in the years immediately preceeding the Aliens Act; on the contrary, in 1904 the Trades Council associated itself with the JMTPTU in planning a public protest against restrictionist legislation.[175]

This is not to suggest that English trade unionists were either especially tolerant or particularly altruistic. The argument in this paper is that the Manchester trade union

leadership drawn chiefly from the skilled labour aristocracy
of the older craft unions, was essentially pragmatic. In
the 1880s in the garment trades and cabinet-making, it faced
new techniques of production which reduced skills and introduced new groups of workers - women and semi-skilled and
unskilled male workers as well as immigrants. At first the
leadership was reluctant to recognise the rights of the newcomers. But by 1888- 9 it was clear that it faced an
irreversible process which could well undermine the wage
levels of skilled workers if it were not brought under control.
It also began to seem likely that unless the craft leadership
took the initiative, the new groups of workers would organise
themselves and in ways which would not necessarily promote
the fortunes of the skilled workforce. In the process, it
was possible that they would fall under the radical influence
of socialist agitators. The Socialist League itself urged
on the Trades Council the need to organise the city's unskilled
workers, including the Jewish immigrants, and encouraged Jewish
workers to join hands with the English trades union movement.
In these circumstances trade union leaders in Manchester
attempted in 1889-90 to orchestrate the unionisation of
immigrants and women workers. In spite of a hard restrictionist
response in 1891 to the apparent pliability and lack of determination of the Jewish workforce, in the long run they held to
the more realistic policy of winning their Jewish co-workers
over to the tactic of collective bargaining.

The object of this paper has been to locate the beginning
of Jewish trade union activity in English labour history. I
have argued that its origins formed part of the general
reawakening of trade union aspirations and socialist hopes in
the late 1880s, that English trade union attitudes towards it
reflected the preoccupation of the English trade union movement with the need to advance the cause of the poorer-paid
workers, that its weakness was essentially a function of the

place of the Jewish immigrant worker as part of a more general overstocked pool of cheap, semi-skilled, unskilled and female labour. Whatever the historian has said, Jewish workers identified themselves with the mass of English workers seeking better conditions from the 1880s; with rare exceptions, the Manchester trade unionist treated them in this light. More broadly, I have tried to suggest the limitations of relying on real or supposed ethnic characteristics to interpret the labour history of minority groups or to explain external attitudes towards them. The 'Jewishness' of the immigrant workers of the 1880s was only one, and not necessarily the most important, of the determinants of English trade union responses. Equally important were the general state of trade unionism in England, the particular ambitions and ideas of trade union activists, the structure of the workshop trades and the place of unskilled workers (and not only immigrant workers) within them, and a massive swing of popular feeling against the sweated industries. It was the context in which Jewish immigrants arrived as much as their role as Jews or immigrants which shaped the attitudes towards them.

NOTES

JC   Jewish Chronicle

MCN   Manchester City News

MG   Manchester Guardian

1. In 1891 the Manchester Jewish community totalled some 15,000 persons, of whom at least two-thirds belonged to families of immigrant workers from Russia and Poland. The institutions of the community, on the other hand, were dominated by an elite of Anglo-Jewish families, some of whom had resided in the city for over a century, or by a nouveau riche of immigrant shopkeepers and workshop entrepreneurs. Immigrant workers were at a double disadvantage, since their bosses also controlled the educational, welfare, social and religious agencies of a tightly knit community.

2.   C. Russell and H.S. Lewis, The Jew in London : A Study
of Racial Character and Present Day Conditions (1901), pp.
192-3.

3.   For a similar criticism of Jewish history generally:
Werner Cahman's introduction to Mark Wischnitzer, A History
of Jewish Crafts and Guilds (New York, 1965), pp. xviii - xx,
and Ezra Mendelson, Class Struggle in the Pale: the Formative
Years of the Jewish Workers Movement in Tsarist Russia
(Cambridge, 1970), p. 98.

4.   e.g. B.A. Kosmin, M. Bauer and Nigel Grizzard, Steel City
Jews (1976), pp. 24-8.

5.   This is one major theme in Bill Williams, The Making of
Manchester Jewry, 1740-1875 (Manchester, 1976), particularly
Ch. 12, 'A Pattern of Synagogues'.

6.   Lloyd Gartner, The Jewish Immigrant in England 1870-1914
(2nd ed., 1973), p. 100.

7.   Gartner, Jewish Immigrant p. 102.   A similar view is
found in John Garrard, The English and Immigration (1971),
p. 179.

8.   Bernard Gainer, The Alien Invasion: The Origins of the
Aliens Act of 1905 (1972), p. 30.

9.   Gainer, Alien Invasion p. 30.

10. Ibid.

11. Gartner, Jewish Immigrant p. 120.

12. Gainer, Alien Invasion p. 30.

13. Ibid.; cf. Gartner, Jewish Immigrant p. 119.

14. Gartner, Jewish Immigrant p. 119.

15. Ibid., p. 126.

16. Ibid., p. 129.

17. Ibid., p. 101.

18. Ibid., p. 102.

19. Ibid., p. 118.   Garrard puts forward the theoretical
'continental' socialism of the immigrants as one explanation
of strife within Jewish unions, of the impatience of Jewish

workers with the slow procedures of English trade unionists
and of the supposed indifference of the Jewish workers towards
the TUC and Trades Councils (pp. 170-1).

20. Gartner, Jewish Immigrant pp. 38-44.

21. For Manchester: Williams, The Making Appendix B.

22. Of the Manchester Jewish strike leaders of 1889-90 whose
names are known, none had been in England for less than 8
years. Michael Frenchman, secretary of the Manchester
tailors' union in 1891, had then resided in England since
1869 (MG, 4 May 1891). Lewis Lyons, leader of the London
Jewish tailors in 1889, was born in England.

23. MCN, 2 March 1889; The Commonweal, 2 March 1889:
according to this report, most of the Jewish workers were
women.

24. The Commonweal, 2 March 1889.

25. MCN, 2 March 1889.

26. JC, 22 Feb. 1889.

27. MCN, 2 March 1889.

28. JC, 22 Feb. 1889.

29. The outcome of the strike is not recorded, but The
Commonweal was pessimistic about the chances of success.

30. MCN, leader, 26 November 1887.

31. MCN, 10 December 1887; Minutes of the Manchester Jewish
Board of Guardians, 7 December 1887.

32. MCN, 17 March 1888.

33. The Lancet, 14 and 21 April 1888.

34. MCN, 28 April 1888.

35. Ibid.

36. MCN, 5 May 1888.

37. MCN, 5 and 12 May 1888.

38. MCN, 28 April 1888.

39. MCN, 12 May 1888.

40. Report of the House of Lords Select Committee on the Sweating System, III, Minutes 28747-50, 29790.

41. MCN, 28 April 1888.

42. Ibid.

43. MCN, 20 April 1889. Remond was speaking to a monthly meeting of the Trades Council. Since the minutes of the Council have been lost, a reconstruction of its activities and policies is based on surviving annual reports and accounts of monthly and other meetings in MCN and MG.

44. MCN, 12 May 1888.

45. Report of the House of Lords Select Committee on the Sweating System, III, Minutes 29808, 29819, 19834.

46. MCN, 2 February 1889.

47. Report of the House of Lords Select Committee, III, Minute 29839-42.

48. MCN, 9 March 1889; cf. Eddie and Ruth Frow, To Make That Future - Now!, ch. 4.

49. Report of the House of Lords Select Committee, III, Minutes 29834-42.

50. Ibid., Minutes 29780-1. Quinn attributed a reduction in wage rates since 1861 to foreign labour, non-unionised outworkers and an increase of women workers.

51. MCN, 28 April 1888, quoting a spokesman for the AST. The danger was particularly great since English masters had begun to employ foreign Jewish labour (Report of the House of Lords Select Committee, III, Minute 29774).

52. There is a parallel between this form of 'levelling-up' and attempts by craft unionists in industries not affected by immigration to improve the condition of their less skilled co-workmen: the object, too, was the same.

53. MCN, 16 January 1888.

54. MCN, 20 April 1889.

55. MCN, 19 May 1888.

56. MCN, 13 July 1889.

57. Ibid.; MG 16 May 1890.

58. MG, 15 April 1890,

59. MG, 2 May 1890.

60. MG, 16 May 1890.

61. MG, 20 June 1890.

62. The Commonweal, 19 January 1889.

63. Ibid.

64. The Commonweal, 10 August 1889.

65. The Commonweal, 21 Sept. 1889,

66. The Commonweal, 9 Nov. 1889.

67. MG, 10 Dec. 1889; MCN 14 Dec, 1889.

68. The claims of Gartner and Gainer that the success of
Anglo-Jewish trade unionism depended upon the London
experience are also open to challenge. There is no reason
to suppose that provincial Jewish effort depended on London
Jewish success in trade unionism any more than it did in
other spheres of Anglo-Jewish life. Local factors were
crucially important; for example in determining English
trade union attitudes. In London, as a port of entry for
immigrants which lacked Manchester's strong radical-liberal
tradition, attitudes towards Jewish workers were perhaps
less tolerant. In the provinces too, Jewish trade unionists
were less overawed by the Anglo-Jewish plutocracy.

69. MG, 10 Dec. 1889.

70. Ibid.

71. MG, 17 April 1890,

72. MG, 10 Dec. 1889.

73. MG, 14 April 1890; JC, 18 April 1890 has 1,000 workers.

74. MG, 15 April 1890.

75. Ibid. The strike was timed to coincide with the high
demand prior to Whit week; there was some hope that masters
would give way under pressure from wholesalers and retailers
(MG, 19 April 1890).

76. MG, 15 April 1890.

77. MG, 15 and 16 April 1890.

78. MG, 16 April 1890.

79. Ibid.

80. MG, 7 July 1890.

81. MG, 16 April 1890; the Trades Council also raised
money for the Jewish strike fund (MG, 2 May 1890).

82. MG, 16 April 1890. Almost certainly, Marshall's role
was to convey the Trades Council's advice and guidance at
ground level.

83. MG, 21 April 1890.

84. MG, 17 April 1890.

85. MG, 21-23 April 1890.

86. MG, 23 April 1890.

87. MG, 21 and 26 April, 14 May 1890.

88. MG, 18 April 1890.

89. MG, 7 July 1890.

90. 23rd Annual Report, Manchester Jewish Board of Guardians,
pp. 5-6.

91. MG, 21 April 1890.

92. Ibid.

93. MG, 27 May 1890.

94. MG, 14 May 1890.

95. MG, 29 April 1890.

96. Ibid.

97. MG, 12 May 1890.

98. MG, 29 April 1890.

99. MG, 6 May 1890. They were 'worse off...than the
unskilled worker', according to one of them (MG, 12 May
1890).

100. MG, 12 May 1890.

101. MG, 14-15 May 1890.

102. MG, 14 May 1890.

103. MG, 15 May 1890.

104. MG, 10 June 1890.

105. MG, 19 May 1890.

106. MG, 15 May 1890.

107. MG, 14 May 1890.

108. MG, 22 May 1890.

109. MG, 22 May, 10 June 1890.

110. MG, 13 June 1890.

111. MG, 16 May 1890. A subsidiary grievance was the form
of agreement developed by the masters: employers guaranteed
a low steady wage during the slack season and during the
busy season undertook to supply men with as much piece-work
as they could do.   The workers claimed that the wage in the
slack season was too low, the amount of work during the busy
season too uncertain (MG, 20 Aug. 1890).

112. MG, 4 Aug. 1890.

113. Ibid.

114. MG, 13 Aug. 1890.

115. MG, 11 Aug. 1890.

116. MG, 15 April 1890.

117. MG, 17 April 1890.

118. MG, 16 Aug. 1890. Frankenburg based his accusation
on the supposition that the real reason for apprenticeships
was to replace a 20-25% annual drop-out of women workers.

119. MG, 18 Aug. 1890.

120. MG, 20 Aug. 1890.

121. Ibid.

122. MG, 20 and 25 Aug. 1890.

123. MG, 25 Aug. 1890.

124. Ibid.

125. MG, 26-27 Aug. 1890.

126. MG, 10 and 18 Sept. 1890.

127. MG, 12 Sept. 1890.

128. MG, 17 Sept. 1890.

129. Ibid.

130. Ibid.

131. Ibid.

132. Ibid.

133. Ibid.

134. Ibid.

135. MG, 18 Sept. 1890.

136. Eddie and Ruth Frow, To Make That Future p. 31;
Manchester Faces and Places, 10 March 1891, pp. 92-5.

137. The Commonweal, 16 Nov. 1889.

138. Gartner, Jewish Immigrant p. 112.

139. Established in 1886. MG, 19 April 1890 includes a
letter from the club's secretary inviting the strikers to
take advantage of its 'healthy recreations'. At the
opening of the club's new premises in Exchange Street in
1891 the Mayor and 'leading Jewish families' on the platform
were backed by a banner with a portrait of the Queen and the
motto 'God Bless England, Land of Freedom'; in describing
the club's activities, the president noted: 'The only
subject excluded was politics' (MCN, 7 Feb. 1891).

140. MG, 27 Oct. 1890.

141. Ibid.

142. MG, 20 Oct. 1890.

143. MG, 28 Oct. 1890.

144. Ibid.

145. Ibid.

146. MG, 26 May 1890.

147. MG, 28 Oct. 1890.

148. MG, 14 Nov. 1890.

149. MG, 26 May 1890.

150. Ibid.

151. Ibid.

152. MG, 8 Sept. 1890.

153. 4 May 1891.

154. Ibid. Following Sugar's partial victory, the waterproofers' union also went into a decline from which it did
not emerge fully until 1907 (The Waterproofer, vol. I, no. 3
(July 1935), p. 4: 'A Short History of the Union'). The
probable reason was the vulnerability of the women workforce,
which remained ununionised, in spite of Sugar's efforts.

155. MG, 26 May 1890.

156. MG, 8 Sept. 1890, particularly the reference to 'love
of money'.

157. MG, 4 May 1891.

158. 26th Annual Report (1892), Manchester and Salford
Trades Council, p. 6. No annual reports survive from before
1892. The minute books of the Council have also been lost.

159. Ibid., p. 6.

160. Ibid., p. 7.

161. This was as much a threat to long-established Jewish
workers as to English trade unionists. In May 1891 Michael
Frenchman, then secretary of the JMTPTU, protested at the
importation of cheap Russian and Polish workers by the Jewish
masters - an indication of the way in which Jewish workers
could be won over to restrictionism (MG, 4 May 1891).

162. MG, 1 May 1890.

163. MG, 15 Sept. 1890.

164. 40th Annual Report, Manchester and Salford Trades
Council: list of affiliated unions and delegates.

165. One source of weakness which new Jewish unions shared
with new unskilled unions was the formation of Masters'
Associations. During 1889-90 such Associations were
formed in tailoring, waterproofing and cabinet-making.

166. In spite of the setbacks of 1891, Jewish workers were
prominent in the May Day Demonstrations and processions of
1892 and 1893 (The Clarion, 30 April 1892, 6 May 1893).

167. Manchester Evening News, 28 Jan. 1903.

168. MG, 2 Dec. 1890.

169. Of the six 'new unions' which existed in 1890 two had
disappeared by 1894 and the rest had suffered serious falls
in membership. In the depression of the early 1890s, all
unions were on the defensive.

170. Duncan Bythell, The Sweated Trades : Outworkers in
19th Century Britain (1978), pp. 204-5.

171. The 'independent tone', trade union loyalty and
militance of Jewish workers impressed even the anti-semitic
author of 'The Foreign Invasion of a City Suburb' (MCN, 24
Jan. 1891), suggesting the major contribution of Jewish
workers to the fight against anti-alienism.

172. Which has still to be written. The contribution of
Jewish sweated workers, especially in the waterproofing
industry, to early Communist organisations in Manchester,
to the labour struggles of the 1930s and to the war in Spain
is documented in taped interviews with many former workers,
including Ben Ainley, Benny Segal, Jack Cohen, Phil Glantz,
Martin Bobker, Mick Jenkins, Juddy Clyne.

173. 26th Annual Report, Manchester and Salford Trades
Council, p. 8.

174. Ibid.

175. JC, 10 June 1904. For a discussion of other possible
reasons for the retreat of English trade unions from
restrictionism: Garrard, The English pp. 174-7. The Manchester Trades Council concentrated much of their subsequent
anti-sweating propaganda on a fight for 'fair contracts'
(29th Annual Report, pp. 5-6, 9; 31st Annual Report, p. 9).

11

Reactions to Lithuanian and Polish Immigrants in the Lanarkshire Coalfield, 1880–1914

KENNETH LUNN

Immigration into Britain in the late nineteenth and early twentieth centuries has received a good deal of attention in recent years and yet, as a new book has suggested, many significant questions still remain unanswered (and some unasked).[1]   Most studies have concentrated on the movements of Jews and identify the fear of being labelled 'anti-semitic' as a moderating factor in the host community's reaction towards such immigration.[2]   More specifically, on trade union attitudes, Garrard has proposed that a policy of restriction or exclusion clashed with the ideas of 'international brother-hood, labour mobility, and free trade, and their strong attachment to the tradition of political asylum.'[3]   He maintains that institutionalised protest against immigrants ceased after 1895.[4]

Studies like Garrard's and that of Bernard Gainer,[5] concentrating on the historical synonymity of the terms 'Jew' and 'immigrant', have tended to dismiss non-Jewish immigration because of its relative numerical insignificance.[6]   However, the influx of mainly Lithuanian Catholics into Lanarkshire constituted the kind of concentration to be found in other 'immigrant' areas of the time, and the native population, particularly those involved in mining, perceived a distinct

threat to their way of life.   The situation is, therefore,
well worthy of detailed investigation.   It poses the question
of whether opposition to non-Jewish immigrants was more
'legitimate', since it escaped the anti-semitic label.   In
addition, the impression conveyed by Garrard of the cessation
of institutionalised protest will be challenged.   Much of his
case rests on the presumption that no anti-alien resolutions
were received by the TUC after 1895.   But, as this study will
show, there was a programme of opposition to alien labour in
the Scottish coal industry;   a campaign which continued into
the twentieth century and which resulted in official resolutions
to the TUC.   In addition, the details here will indicate that
the reactions towards the aliens in this period were rather
more complex than any simple over-view or brief impressions can
suggest and, therefore, that current generalisations about
immigration in these years should be approached with some caution.

In considering the immigration and employment of 'Polish'
miners in Lanarkshire, the first point of importance is their
origin and nationality.   Although the term 'Poles' was commonly
used at the time to describe these immigrants, it is clear from
many statements that the majority were Lithuanians.   Hence, in
this article, my references will be to 'Lithuanians';   'Poles'
is the descriptive term used by contemporaries.

From 1385, there existed a double kingdom of both Lithuanian
and Polish states, although the name 'Poland' was commonly used
in the eighteenth century to describe the entire republic.[7]
With the partitioning of the republic at the end of the century,
the Lithuanian state, together with certain parts of Poland,
became part of the Russian Empire, a domination which was to
last until the First World War.   A fairly intensive process of
Russification and colonisation took place, and attempts to
obliterate Lithuanian culture, even to the extent of banning
the publication of material in the Lithuanian language, were
put into practice.   As well as political and religious repression,

there were economic pressures, particularly on land. The
emancipation of serfs in 1865 had created a large landless
proletariat and an increasing population added to the problem.
In the period 1870-1914, about one and a quarter million people
left Russian Poland, the majority heading for the Americas,
and most of those who left were peasants or agricultural
labourers.[8]   Those Lithuanians and Poles who came to work in
the Lanarkshire coalfields were mainly from such a background
and the claims by the union that most had never seen a mine
before appear to have been correct.   It is important to stress
this point, since it was the focus of much of the union's
opposition.   The recent study of Scottish population history
states that the Polish and Russian immigrants of the period
came with industrial skills and hence the transition to mining
(and to the iron and steel industry) was a simple one.[9]   This
is clearly not the case.

INITIAL EMPLOYMENT

It seems most likely that Lithuanians found employment in the
Lanarkshire coalmines in the 1890s.   The first written evidence,
from the returns of employers and unions to the Royal Commission
on Labour, which began its hearings in 1892, states that
foreigners were beginning to be introduced 'to the detriment of
native labour and the safety of mines'.[10]   Indications are that
many came to mining through labouring work in iron and steel.
For example, at Glengarnock in Ayrshire, Lithuanians began work
in 1884 as 'spare furnacemen'[11] and some then went into the
mining industry in that area.[12]   Indeed, it was frequently
alleged that their employment at Glengarnock was the beginning
of the 'invasion', although there is a suggestion that Merry
and Cunningham, the employers there, had introduced some
Lithuanian labour into their Carnbroe, Lanarkshire, works in
1880.[13]

   Initial reaction to the fact that foreigners were being

employed at Glengarnock seems to have been muted and it was only in 1887 that publicity was given to the fact. Keir Hardie saw their employment as a possible threat to the new Ayrshire Miners' Union and, as a recent biography shows, conducted a campaign of hostility against the Lithuanians.[14] The Lanarkshire miners were clearly troubled by the news. At a meeting of miners in Irvine, Ayrshire, addressed by Robert Smillie, president of the Lanarkshire organisation, a resolution calling for the removal of the 'Poles' was passed unanimously.[15] Objections to the employment of Lithuanians at Glengarnock were based on the premise that they were used as cheap labour to keep wages down. Hardie, having talked to some of the workforce at Glengarnock, claimed that the immigrants were introduced to allow a reduction of wages to be put into force and that the threat of more foreigners was used by the employers to keep wages at a low level.[16] There was also a xenophobic reaction to the newcomers and claims that 'their presence is a menace to the health and morality' of the district.[17] It so happened that there was an outbreak of typhoid in the adjoining village of Kilbirnie at the time of the publicity about the immigrants, and at least one newspaper, the North British Mail, made a causal link.[18] Other journals, however, like the Ardrossan and Saltcoats Herald, simply discussed the outbreak in terms of poor living conditions, without any reference to the Lithuanians, who, after all, had been in the area for some time before the outbreak. There was also a suggestion that the Russian Consul had played some part in sending these 'Russian Poles' to Glengarnock, a claim repeated by Hardie in his evidence to the Select Committee on Emigration and Immigration (Foreigners) in 1889.[19] However, Merry and Cunningham denied that there was any organised basis to the employment of foreign labour:

> Some of them come to us from the sugar
> works at Liverpool, and the salt works
> in Cheshire, and those who come

> direct have in many cases, we believe, fled
> from the Army.   Long before we had any of
> them they were employed in railways work by
> Mr McDonald, the contractor for the Fairlie
> Tunnel on the Glasgow and South Western
> Railway near Largs, and now they are to be
> found at most of the iron works around
> Coatbridge.   20

It has already been suggested that Lithuanians were employed in the Lanarkshire iron and steel industry from about 1880.   More definite evidence of their presence comes in the report of the Royal Commission on Labour.   Charles Vickers, Scottish agent of the National Association of Blast-Furnacemen, drew attention to about 200 Poles who were working at furnaces in Lanarkshire and Ayrshire, claiming that the employers had introduced more foreigners during the 1891-2 dispute, which lasted over five months.[21]

The 1891 census returns for Scotland show a total of 323 male Russian Poles (foreign born) and sixty-three naturalised British male subjects born in Russian Poland.   Taking the first figure as a more likely indicator of recent immigration, we find only eight recorded as employed in coalmining, thirty-six in iron manufacturing and two in steel.[22]   The pattern of settlement was already becoming established - of the 323 males, 198 (61 per cent) were in Lanarkshire.   Of the 153 females of Russian Polish birth, seventy three (48 per cent) lived in the country.[23]

However, if these returns show little apparent threat to the employment of native labour in the traditional industries of the country, then they also give no hint of the growth of immigration in subsequent years.   Vickers suggested an influx soon after the census data had been collected and we find an indication of the perceived problem for the Lanarkshire miners at the MFGB conference in 1897.   David Gilmour, for the Scottish miners, speaking on a motion about the employment of unskilled labour, referred to the specific difficulty experienced in his area.

> In Scotland, 25 per cent of the working
> miners are Russian Poles who had never
> seen a coal mine in their lives until
> they arrived in Scotland.   These men
> have been allowed to work two, three and
> four together at the coal face, who have
> never been working in a mine before, and
> they are endangering all the lives at
> the colliery.   24

25 per cent was clearly an exaggeration on Gilmour's part and
there was a general tendency in the following years to overestimate the number of Lithuanian miners.   The 1901 census
of Scotland gives the total male population of Russian birth
(which category would include Lithuanians and Poles) of 4,929.
1,135 of these were recorded as working in coal mining and
624 in iron and steel, the bulk of these based in Lanarkshire.
Since there were 52,682 recorded miners in Lanarkshire,[25] the
overall proportion of Russian born was very small, even
allowing for inaccuracy of census data.   More important, however,
was the question of concentration and later evidence will show
that certain pits were worked with a much higher percentage of
immigrants, which helps to explain the apparently exaggerated
and alarmist claims expressed by Gilmour and others.

For the next ten years or so, the question of unskilled
foreign labour was one of the major concerns of the Scottish
miners, and in particular of the numerically-strong Lanarkshire
union.   From 1900 to 1906 inclusive, motions calling for either
the banning or the regulation of foreign unskilled labour in
mining were passed at MFGB conferences, usually on the initiative
of the Scottish Miners' Federation.   The 1904 TUC accepted
nem. con. Smillie's motion urging the government to take such
steps as should prevent the influx of foreign and unskilled
labour from entering the mines of the country.[26]   These examples,
whilst not destroying Garrard's somewhat narrow analysis of the

immigrant 'lobby' referred to earlier, indicate a more complex
and long-lasting campaign than his commentary suggests.   The
Royal Commission on Mines, of which Smillie was a member,
heard evidence throughout 1907 on the growing number of immigrant
miners in Scotland and, in 1910, the Lanarkshire union was still
concerned with the problem of Polish miners being employed at
cheaper rates than native workmen.   The recorded number of
Poles and Russians employed in mining had more than doubled by
1911, according to the official figures - 2,611 coal miners
were recorded in the census[27] - and the increasing concentration
would have heightened the concern of those unhappy with the
results of the immigration.   It can be seen that the presence
of immigrant labour led to fairly constant discussion, particularly at local level, throughout these years.   In order
to produce a more meaningful analysis, however, it is necessary
to examine the bases of the arguments and the course of the
debate.

THE NATURE OF COMPLAINTS AGAINST THE IMMIGRANTS

Much of the general reaction to the Lithuanians was of a mildly
curious and ethnocentric nature, a fairly general attitude
exhibited to foreigners of any description.   Thus, 'another
batch of Poles arrived in Motherwell on Monday, and as they
wended their way up Brandon Street in search of their destination
they attracted considerable attention.'[28]   Similarly, there
was a certain degree of amusement to be obtained from the
language difficulties involved in communication, particularly
at court appearances.   In one case, a Lithuanian witness was
never called because no-one could pronounce his name and two
attempts had brought in the wrong men, a fact which the local
paper recorded occasioned great bursts of laughter.[29]

At certain times, there arose a fairly intense outcry
against the alleged moral weaknesses of the immigrants.   The
publicity, as seen for example in the local press, contained

elements of racist assumption or at least ethnocentric short-sightedness. The most frequent targets were the Lithuanians' drinking and fighting and their living conditions. Incidents involving the immigrants were stressed as such, the implication being that they were due to an inherent characteristic of the race. Thus, reports of Saturday night fighting appeared under the headlines 'Those Troublesome Poles', ignoring the far more numerous incidents involving Scots.[30] Since many of the immigrants had Scottish names it was felt necessary to identify them as foreigners, e.g. 'Alex Brown, a Pole'. Most reports went under eye-catching headlines: three, all from the same edition were, 'Peter the Pole', 'A Pole Assaults a Female' and 'A Filthy-Tongued Pole'.[31]

It was also asserted that fighting between Lithuanians involved an additional danger, because of the use of weapons.[32] Thus a stabbing incident was described as '...the usual drunken and dangerous kind among these foreigners, the knife having been used with great freedom and effect'.[33] During the trial it was stated 'That the Poles as a rule carried knives and were responsible for many disturbances in the district'.[34] No purpose is served in denying that Lithuanians were involved in such incidents but it is difficult to justify such generalised statements, particularly since similar violence at this time involving Scots or Irish did not produce the same kind of racial judgements. Similarly, the claim by James White that the 'evidence of moral and physical degradation, of drinking, gambling, and all manner of hooliganism' was 'remarkable even in comparison with local standards of the time'[35] needs much closer and detailed statistical investigation before it can be accepted.

On the question of environmental conditions, again there were detailed accounts of any prosecutions of the foreigners for over-crowding or insanitary living, and an ignorance of the context of such occurrences. The prosecution of fourteen 'Polish' miners at Motherwell Police Court for over-crowding

despite the warning of the sanitary inspector produced a
grave warning from the Lanarkshire Examiner. 'The evidence
led showed a very serious state of matters, and the danger
to the community from the insanitary habits of these
foreigners.'[36]   In fact, there is evidence that discrimination
created pressure on housing for immigrants - during a strike
at the Carnbroe iron-works, when there were attempts to eject
strikers from company houses, it was claimed that the reason
why many of the 'Poles' refused to comply with the ejection
order was because of the difficulty finding alternative
accommodation: '...they had no reputation in this country
and landlords as a rule were not willing to give them houses'.[37]
As suggested earlier in relation to the Ayrshire hostility, to
see the immigrants as the threat to housing and living standards
ignores the generally poor conditions existing in mining areas.[38]
The information produced by the long-overdue Royal Commission
on Housing in Scotland (1918)[39] gives some indication of the
problem.

> The last census showed that thousands of
> one-room houses continued to be occupied
> by families: that overcrowding reckoned
> even by the most moderate standard is
> practically universal in the one- and two-
> room houses: that, in spite of protest
> and administrative superintendance,
> domestic overcrowding of houses and over-
> building of areas have not been prevented. 40

    Behind the local press coverage lies an element of middle-
class unease and perhaps slight hysteria. During the 1903
publicity, there were general complaints, not specifically
aimed at the immigrants, that drunken miners were blocking the
streets on a Saturday night and preventing decent citizens
from taking the air.   It is more difficult to discover what
the native working-class reaction was to the Lithuanians,

other than at the place of work. Most witnesses before the
various parliamentary investigations referred to the lack of
contact between immigrants and native communities and the
little general opinion expressed about the Lithuanians is
clearly only a crude summary. Keir Hardie, in 1889, in
evidence based on his discussions with Ayrshire iron and steel
workers, stated that the Lithuanians were thrifty but lived
in filthy conditions.[41] Peter Muir, Secretary of the Ayrshire
Miners Union in 1907 said that his members regarded the Poles
as 'rather inferior men it is not desirable to have...I think
that obtains generally amongst the Poles'.[42] Before the same
Royal Commission, Robert Brown, Secretary of the SMF, citing
his experience of the Lothians coalfield, felt that there were
two classes of immigrant. The first were generally reasonable
men but the second were not respectable, many being taken to
court for brawling. 'They seem to have a great regard for
Scotch after they come here.'[43] However, the main clash
between immigrant and native labour was in the area of
employment and it is in this context that most evidence is to
be found.

TRADE UNION REACTION

As has already been indicated, one of the major objections
raised by the Lanarkshire union was that the Lithuanian
immigrants were unskilled and therefore a danger to their
fellow workers. This attitude fitted into a more general
and long-term opposition towards unskilled labour,[44] a problem
which was growing as the number of men employed in the industry
increased. In such a situation, the concept of the 'independent
collier' was clearly still in operation. As Campbell and
Reid suggest: 'Pride in his skill and resentment of interlopers
were, then, as much important parts of the value-system of the
independent collier as of the independent artisan.'[45] In 1873.
Alexander MacDonald, the miners' leader who perhaps typified

317

such an outlook, had argued that 'the time has now come when
we think that miners generally should demand that only skilled
labour should be allowed. The unskilled destroy themselves
and others as well.'[46] And the sentiments against dilution
of what was felt to be (with some justification) still a
skilled trade continued to be a constant feature of mining
union conferences, speeches, discussion and other forms of
publicity in the years under consideration here. At the
1897 MFGB conference where Gilmour first raised the specific
issue of the Lithuanians, Ben Pickard's presidential address
had laid great emphasis on the need to limit the influx of
men into the industry. The aim was to prevent the build-up
of unskilled labour, and to avoid over-crowding and 'sweating',[47]
and it seems that a double threat was perceived; first, to
the employment of traditional mining stock and second, to the
safety of all miners, because of the dangers involved in
employing unskilled workers, unfamiliar with the mining
environment.

Undoubtedly, the Lanarkshire miners saw the employment
of Lithuanians as a direct threat, sometimes implemented, to
their own jobs. Smillie's evidence to the Royal Commission
on Alien Immigration noted that about 1,000 native miners in
the county were unemployed and that many were leaving for the
USA and Canada. He argued that native labour ought to have
precedence[48] and at the next meeting of the council of the
Lanarkshire union, it was agreed that a representative be
sent to the International Miners Congress in Berlin, warning

> ...Lithuanian and other miners on the
> Continent against leaving their own
> country to work in coal mines particularly
> in the West of Scotland, as the majority
> of the pits were overcrowded with no hopes
> of full employment being obtained for men
> presently here.   49

The following year, Smillie claimed that, whilst 1,500 of his

own men were out of work, only fifty foreigners were walking
the streets. 'They have preference of employment because
they are more docile, because they are prepared to do things
which our people would not do.'[50] However, these were
responses to particularly difficult times in Scotland's
mining industry and were linked to the obvious attempts of
employers to reduce costs in any possible way, hence the
employment of the Lithuanians, usually at lower rates.
Although there were claims that Lithuanians were brought in
by employers, the Lanarkshire union maintained that there was
no attempt to do so directly to break a strike, although
Smillie, in his autobiography, gives an example during the
1909 strike of an offer to the mine-owners of an 'unlimited
number' of Polish workers, made by an Austrian 'labour
contractor'.[51] It might be argued that it was the publicly
expressed attitude of certain employers towards the immigrant
workforce, stressing hard work, reliability etc. and of
Ronaldson, the mining inspector for the district, who saw the
Lithuanians as more amenable to discipline, which helped
produce the initial union hostility towards their employment.

A general problem of unskilled labour in the industry
was the danger posed by the employment of inexperienced men
and the Lanarkshire union based many of its attempts to
regulate the immigration on this factor. The situation was
compounded, it was claimed, by the language barrier, since
few of the immigrants spoke English. It was largely due to
SMF pressure that the series of resolutions passed by the
MFGB talked about the limitation or control of 'foreign' and
'unskilled' labour. In the main, Scottish contributors
stressed the particular problems associated with foreigners,
whilst other area representatives sought to broaden the issue
to all unskilled labour.[52]

Little hard evidence that the Lithuanians constituted
a particular danger within the mine and that they were

disproportionately involved in accidents can be found, as the miners' union also discovered.[53]   In part, this was due to the problem of names.   As Gilmour pointed out,

> when the foreigners came there, they
> assumed in many instances the name of
> the checkweighman and there were nearly
> every common name found on the colliery
> books and it was proved conclusively
> before the colliery manager, he did not
> know who were foreigners and who were
> not.   54

Thus, it was difficult to ascertain just what proportion of foreign workmen was involved in accidents.   James Murdoch, agent for the Lanarkshire union claimed in 1904 that the largest proportion of men receiving money from the accident fund were Poles.[55]   Amplifying his statement two years later, he claimed that his branch was 10 per cent Polish but there were always equal numbers of foreigners and native workmen on the accident fund.   He also stated that there was a higher mortality rate amongst Poles than his own men.[56]

Union officials cited instances of unskilled immigrants being involved in accidents; a gruesome 'hardy annual' concerned a Lithuanian who, on being told by the engineman to keep his head in as the cage descended the shaft, leaned out and was decapitated.[57]   Gilmour told of a Pole who, warned off his usual working place by the fireman because of gas, made repeated attempts to return because the face there was easier to work than his alternative one.[58]   Similarly, Murdoch claimed that some immigrants removed the glass from their safety lamps because the light was then better.[59]

However, in spite of these incidents and the alleged statistics of the accident fund, the union seems to have had difficulty proving the main grounds for their objection to the Lithuanians, the language problem.   The dangers of any

unskilled worker, whatever nationality, were, in theory,
dealt with by Rule 39 of the 1887 Mines Act and the particular
case of the immigrants had to be based on the additional
hazard of lack of English. In this, the union ran up against
the double barrier of employer and government inspector.
Hardly surprisingly, employers who gave evidence to the RC
on Mines claimed that the Poles constituted no extra danger
and provided statistics to 'prove' this fact.[60] Some owners
maintained that they had the Special Rules printed in the
immigrants' own language,[61] whilst others said the experienced
Lithuanians made the new arrivals aware of the regulations.
This view was reinforced by the evidence of John Ronaldson,
the inspector for the West of Scotland, who had a somewhat
jaundiced view of the Scottish miner, particularly in the
matter of pit safety and discipline. Thus, he felt the
foreign miners were a positive benefit to the industry.

> ...I have watched for years the conduct
> of those men; they are far more amenable
> to discipline than our own men. It is
> the universal testimony of the managers
> that these men are much more amenable to
> discipline, and that they will do what
> they are told. If they know that they
> are obliged to do a thing they will do it,
> and they are a striking contrast to a
> good many of our own workmen in that
> respect. I have only so far come across
> one case of a trifling accident, apparently,
> where one of those foreign workmen was the
> cause of another man meeting with an injury. 62

In the face of such attitudes, it is hardly surprising
that questions on the subject to the Home Office met with a
similar response. Following a fatal accident to a Russian
Pole at Glen Clelland Colliery in August 1899, the then Home
Secretary, Sir M. White Ridley, denied that, although the
inquest jury had determined that the deceased spoke no English

and declared that the employment of such unskilled men was too
dangerous, these were relevant factors in this particular case.
The information from the inspector of mines was that no accident
caused by ignorance of the language had come to his knowledge.[63]
When Arthur Markham, in 1904, raised in Parliament the possibility
of preventing the employment of aliens in British coal mines,
Akers-Douglas, the Home Secretary, replied that there was no
evidence that foreigners were a danger to the other men employed
in the same mines. 'I have satisfied myself that adequate
steps are taken at the mines where they are employed, to instruct
them in their duties.'[64]

The MFGB wrote less than two months later asking for a
meeting with the Home Secretary to discuss further the question
but his secretary was instructed to reply that

> ...no evidence has so far been laid before
> him showing that danger or accident has
> actually been caused by the employment of
> foreigners: and careful and repeated
> inquiry in Scotland, where the majority
> of the foreigners are employed, has failed
> to elicit any case in which ignorance of
> the language or regulations on the part of
> the foreigners has been the cause of
> accident to others employed in the same
> mine.

Unless written evidence to the contrary was provided, it was
felt that there were no grounds for a meeting.[65] The evidence
of employers and inspectors before the 1907 Royal Commission
indicates that the 'official' view had not changed. Thus, in
spite of the fact that many Lithuanians were involved in
accidents at work, and impressionistic reading of local newspapers suggests at a disproportionate level, the case against
the use of unskilled foreign labour for this reason would seem
to have been 'not proven'.

Other problems which the union faced in these years were

322

the constant pressure on wage rates and the use of blacklegs during strikes. Indeed, the two issues often merged into one, where a strike over the rate for work in a particular place would be undermined by the employment of non-union labour at a lower rate than that asked for by the union. The evidence is that immigrant labour in Lanarkshire was used both in under-cutting rates and as blacklegs.

The question of under-cutting was a persistent theme of critics of the immigration of this period[66] and it is undoubtedly the case that employers took advantage of the immigrants' poor economic bargaining status to help reduce costs.[67] In the Lanarkshire coalfield, where there were continual disputes over the rate for the job throughout the period, employers did use the Lithuanian workers to keep down wages. At Thankerton Colliery, in 1902, it was alleged that Polish miners were being employed to replace British workmen, and that this move was accompanied by a reduction of 4d a ton.[68] That same year, Smillie reported the actions of the manager at Neilsland Main Coal, in trying to reduce two places ½d per ton below the common rates. A deputation, led by James Murdoch, had examined the places and a decision had been taken to block them, whereupon the manager tried to fill them at the reduced rate with Poles.[69] A few similar incidents are noted here and there in the union minutes,[70] the last recorded being in 1909, when it was reported that some Poles had been started at Watson's, Motherwell, at rates under standard in two places.[71] The most publicised occurrence, however, was at Tannochside in 1903, and a brief study of the dispute indicates the use of the immigrant work-force by the employer against the union.

The dispute began in early April, when twenty or thirty Poles were introduced to work on the Drumgray seam of one of the pits at Tannochside. The rates they were paid were 5d a ton less than the British miners, a fact which alarmed the Lanarkshire union. A meeting between Murdoch and the manager

produced a statement that the Poles were quite content with
the reduced rate. The matter was remitted to the SMF, who
resolved to bring out all the men employed at Russell's
collieries (c. 4,000) if the firm persisted in employing
foreigners at less than the county rate of 5/9d a day. They
sought the support of the MFGB in this. A meeting with the
general manager, Mr Salmond, indicated the reasoning behind
the reduction. He began by claiming that some miners on the
Drumgray seam had been getting seven or eight shillings a day,
way above the county rate, and then announced that the management was now giving early notice of a partial reduction to
bring the wages of these men nearer the standard rate. Salmond
also insisted on the firm's right to employ as many foreign
workmen as it liked. On 2 May, many of the men received
notice of reductions of between four and seven pence a ton,
rates which they claimed would leave them below the county
standard.

After long drawn out negotiations, the dispute was
eventually settled. A general reduction of 2d a ton, instead
of 6d, was accepted on the recommendation of the union's
Executive Committee, with the exception of the Drumgray seam,
where the rates were lower, and further talks were required
to settle this particular exception. Thus, the management
had been partially successful in its reductions, a move begun
by the introduction of immigrant labour.[72]

Certain Poles were also used directly as strikebreakers -
instances are recorded at Eddlewood, Kenmure Colliery, Tollcross,
Baljaffray Colliery, Maryhill and Watson's, Motherwell.[73] Such
incidents were seen as direct attempts by employers to break the
union; in the dispute at Bothwell Castle, where rates were
reduced and foreign labour introduced, it was claimed, to
threaten the men into submission, the union was in no doubt
as to this. 'The Executive unanimously expressed the opinion
that vigorous action should be taken by the Association to

324

defeat the management in their efforts to supplant our members
by the introduction of Poles, and thereby smash the union at
the pits.'[74]   Union officials frequently related the use of
immigrant labour to the growing strength of the union and the
expressed views of employers about the submissiveness and
suitability of the Lithuanians would seem to justify such a
causal analysis.

However, wage-cutting and blacklegging by immigrants was
only one side of a complicated process of adaptation to rapidly-
changing economic circumstances and it would be wrong to
suggest that the Lithuanians were only involved in activity
against the union.   For example, at Kenmure, the 'Polish'
blacklegs were quickly discouraged from working by some of
their fellow countrymen who were on strike.[75]   In 1905 at
Loganlea, a pit with a considerable number of immigrant workers,
a strike against low rates was successful because of the
solidarity of the men.   In its half-yearly report, the union
was full of praise for the immigrants.   'This is the first
dispute in the County in which we have had such a majority of
Polish miners engaged, and it is satisfactory to find that
those workmen are quite as determined fighters for justice as
the British themselves.'[76]   Indeed, in attempts to break the
strike of the immigrants, Scottish blacklegs were brought in
from Denny, in Stirlingshire![77]   Thus, the situation of 1903,
when John Brady, a miner from Carfin, could complain of the
threat that immigrants posed to wages ('If the Poles would join
the County Union, they would find it to their benefit...'),[78]
had clearly been remedied.[79]

In fact, it could be suggested that the problems encountered by 'Poles' working for lower rates was simply a
wider question of non-union labour.   There were, in spite of
Brady's protest, few union complaints about immigrant membership.
At the 1903 MFGB conference, Gilmour stated that Poles were not
banned from the union;   on the contrary some had served on union

325

committees for ten years.   There was said to be little
difficulty in getting them to join the union and in a strike,
they would fight with the rest,[80] and this was clearly shown
at Loganlea in 1905.

The Lanarkshire union did offer some positive incentives
to encourage immigrant membership.   After some initial hesitation, it was agreed that the union rules should be printed
in the Lithuanian or Polish language.[81]   The union also stood
by the strikers at Loganlea.

> The Secretary gave a report of the trial
> in which a number of Lithuanians had been
> fined for assault in connection with
> picketing during the pending strike at
> that colliery.
> After discussion, it was decided to pay
> the fines.   82

As members of the union, the immigrants were deemed entitled
to full benefits, even the inclusion of families still in their
country of origin.   Thus, in 1909, the executive agreed that
funeral benefit be paid for the death of children of Polish
members, provided they bore the cost of translating the death
certificate.[83]

Clearly, then, there was a growing commitment by the
immigrant workforce to the ideas and organisation of the union,
a fact recognised and welcomed by the union itself.   In part,
this can be seen as a 'natural' development as the workforce
became more integrated but I would suggest that the process
was rather more involved.   Consideration needs to be given to
the changing nature of the union organisation in Lanarkshire;
the shift from 'labour aristocratic' to 'industrial unionist
form'[84] and the more unified and socialist approach of much of
the membership.   But, perhaps even more important, we need to
look at the attitudes of the Lithuanian immigrants themselves.[85]
It is clear that, from the early days of their settlement, there

developed a range of community institutions, including a newspaper, which was published in Glasgow in 1899 and lasted for
five issues. In this, there were comments on the strike-
breaking, through lack of class consciousness, by certain
immigrants and pleas for workers to join trade unions and to
learn English in order to overcome the barriers which prevented
solidarity against the employers.[86] Later, in 1903, a branch
of the Lithuanian Social Democratic Party was formed in Bellshill and the 1905 Revolution 'gave a considerable impetus to
the spread of Socialism among Lithuanians in Britain'. The
movement grew in strength and influence in the Lithuanian
community and from 1907 onwards, a weekly socialist paper
appeared, published in Bellshill.[87]

What can be seen in the early years of the twentieth
century is thus a growing commitment to socialist principles
from both the native workforce and the Lithuanian immigrants,[88]
a commitment which brought increasing strength and solidarity
to the mining union. The mutual involvement became particularly
apparent during the 1912 strike. The dispute over the minimum
wage came to a head in February 1912 and on 1 March, a complete
stoppage resulted. The strike in Scotland, however, was not
as solid as Arnot suggests,[89] and there were several instances
of pits continuing work, which produced picketing and angry
demonstrations. From various reports, it is obvious that many
Lithuanians were to the fore in these incidents. Tarbrax
Colliery, near West Calder, which had continued working, was
burnt to the ground by striking miners, led by immigrants,
according to the newspaper reports.[90] Three out of eight men
tried for offences arising from the attack were 'Poles'.[91]
During picketing, immigrants were also arrested on charges of
breach of the peace and assault on the police. In certain
cases, on being found guilty, deportation was recommended.
A total of eight 'Poles' suffered such a sentence for offences
during the strike, five during picketing and three as a result of

the disturbances in Bellshill, which were directed against
the return to work by non-union men at Rosehall. The three
involved in the Bellshill disturbances were deported, on
completion of their sentences, despite the intervention of
the union, through J.D. Millar, Labour MP for North-East
Lanarkshire, and questions in the House of Commons by Ramsay
MacDonald.[92] McKenna, the Home Secretary, made it clear that
the previous convictions of these miners, although 'not of a
very serious character', had convinced him that it would not
be right to overrule the magistrate's suggestion. The other
five, arrested during picketing at Hamilton Palace Colliery
and Rosehall, were also supported by the union[93] and by Millar.
In this case, some small measure of success was achieved.
The Home Office agreed that the cases deserved separate consideration. The two sentenced for the Rosehall disturbance,
Dross and Prenytis, had previous convictions for offences like
breach of the peace (Prenytis had six) and deportation was
confirmed in their case. The other three, Wilson, Stangle,
and Braski, had no record and McKenna had decided, 'with some
hesitation', to give them another chance. However, it was
clearly stated that this did not imply a total amnesty for
all 'first offenders'.[94]

There is some circumstantial evidence which indicates
that the immigrants were singled out during the disturbances.
In the Tarbrax case, the defence claimed just that - 'The Poles
were the unfortunate victims of their race'.[95] Gilmour,
speaking at the STUC, claimed that the foreigners were treated
unfairly during the strike, receiving harsher sentences than
those imposed on native miners.[96] Whether this indicates a
particular attempt to quell Lithuanian involvement in the
strike by the local magistracy and police force is difficult
to say. Deportations were used in other assault cases, without
the context of the dispute, the grounds being previous convictions for similar offences.[97] The claims of persecution

328

probably merely reflect the general union pleasure at the extent of participation by the immigrant workforce and, indeed, the strength generated by mass involvement.[98] Speaking at Bellshill on 1 April, John Robertson, vice-president of the SMF, referred to the 1894 strike, when the union had been 'crucified between racial and religious prejudices', an obvious reference to the Protestant/Catholic, Scots/Irish split in the workforce which William Small, secretary of the union, had brought to the attention of the Royal Commission on Labour.[99] Now Robertson, who identified himself as a Protestant and a Scotsman, felt that the experience of the strike had welded together the miners, irrespective of 'nationality and creed'[100] and this view seems to have included the Lithuanians, as well as Irish and Scots. This statement provides further evidence that Lithuanian involvement had gone beyond the mere participation in a strike or disturbance and had begun to contribute to the organisation of a stable and enduring union, a factor often missing in the period of early Irish immigration in the previous century.[101]

SOME COMPARATIVE SUGGESTIONS

Within the confines of this article, a comprehensive comparative study is not possible. However, two situations of some interest can be identified. The first is that of the mining industry in the USA, which attracted many of the Lithuanian immigrants arriving in that country, sometimes _via_ the Scottish coalfields.[102] In this setting, there are similar examples of gradual involvement in union organisation and strikes. In the 1902 anthracite strike, which won acceptance of the collective bargaining system for the United Mineworkers, it was the Slav nationalities who contributed most to the success. 'Poles and Lithuanians, Slovaks and Ruthenians, put aside their mutual grudges and responded to a man to the strike call.'[103]

Nor were the Lithuanians the first immigrant group with

which the Scottish mining industry's workforce had to deal.
The mining community at the turn of the century contained a
large number of Irish-born and the descendants of Irish
immigrants. The 1911 census records 175,000 Irish-born in
Scotland, a figure to which second and successive generation
Irish would add considerably, and of this total, nearly
12,000 were employed in mining. In the earlier years of the
century, there were protests against the employment of Irish
in mining, couched in very similar terms to the objections
against the Lithuanians;[104] wage-cutting, blacklegging,
drinking to excess and creating bad living conditions.[105]
Even the attitude of certain employers towards the Irish
labour force bears a strong resemblance to later comments on
the Lithuanians.

> The Irish in the coal mines with us bear
> a good character; we have nothing to
> complain of them on that score; they are
> fully more obedient and tractable than
> the native, and are not so much given to
> combine; they are lively, and sometimes,
> when they get drink among them, they are
> a little excited, but not to any extent
> worth speaking of...We find them very
> useful labourers, and their services are
> of considerable importance to us; at
> present we could not do without them. 106

Substitute 'Lithuanian' for 'Irish' and we have the views put
before the Royal Commission on Alien Immigration and on Mines,
as referred to above.

    It has frequently been suggested that the presence of
this Irish element was a barrier to union development in the
nineteenth century. Whilst accepting that the general
mobility of all labour, and the resultant unsettling effect
upon the mining community was more likely to have been the
fundamental weakness,[107] Alan Campbell's recent work on the
Lanarkshire coalfields in the nineteenth century has pointed

to the particular problems that Irish immigration posed for union organisation.[108]   He suggests two main factors: the 'cultural exclusion of the Irish from the whole tradition of the independent Scots collier, which sustained many of the union activists' and the greater geographical mobility of the Irish.[109]   Campbell also records the element of religious friction,[110] a problem which Robertson's speech, quoted above, suggests was still a weakening force in 1894.[111]   Clearly, many of the issues thrown up by the Lithuanian immigration were by no means new to the Lanarkshire mining industry.

CONCLUSION

What, then, was the significance of the union attitude towards the Lithuanian influx?   First, it established a view about the dangers of employing underground workers who did not speak English, which, although rejected by owners, inspectors and the Home Office at the time, was to be accepted shortly thereafter.   During the First World War, certain Belgian miners were employed temporarily in the British industry. The Home Secretary issued instructions that they should only be allowed to work under strict supervision, despite the fact that they were skilled men, and that an interpreter, travelling with the fireman, should be present if there were any language difficulties.[112]   In a similar situation, the employment of European Volunteer Workers after 1945, again the particular danger of language barriers in mining were recognised.   'Steps were therefore taken, in this industry alone, to set up several English Teaching Centres where the recruits were given ten weeks' instruction in English before proceeding to a Coalmining Training Centre for a further three weeks.'[113]

Secondly, it raises a general question about the nature of union opposition to immigration in this period.   Garrard has suggested that the force of the general anti-Jewish opposition was moderated by certain moral sanctions, e.g. the

contradiction of a demand for restriction with the principles
of socialism and the stigma of being labelled 'anti-semitic'.[114]
In the case of the Lanarkshire miners, can we suggest that
their cries about danger in the mines were simply a cover for
racial antipathy? In the light of the Protestant/Catholic
conflict, which has been briefly described, and which at times
exhibited an obviously racist dimension directed against the
Irish, this seems a relevant question to pose.

Elements of xenophobia can be detected in remarks about
'strange habits' and the earlier references to press comment
on the Lithuanians' affinity for drink and crime which
suggested a genetic weakness could be construed as racist.
However, the local newspapers appear to represent petit
bourgeois viewpoints rather than those of the miners; the
coverage of strikes and picketing reinforces this feeling.
The response of the labour movement was, it must be said,
not itself always free from hostility verging on racism.
For example, an editorial in the Labour Leader in 1901, in
reply to the charge that opposition to the Lithuanians was
inhospitable, remarked 'Is it inhospitable to keep out a
plague, though it comes with the highest recommendations?'[115]
Individuals such as Smillie were condemned for exploiting
'the sentiment of race-hatred' against the Polish miners in
an attempt to gain electoral support, although such charges
clearly owe something to the factionalism of the left in
Britain at the time, as well as to Smillie's approach to the
immigrant question.[116] The response of the miners or, more
accurately, the union,[117] was part of a much longer-term
reaction against unskilled labour which had begun much earlier
in the nineteenth century.[118] In the period under consideration,
the situation took on a particular dimension and involved the
additional problem of a language barrier, alleged to compound
the dangers. Union officials were clearly aware of the
delicate nature of any campaign against the immigrants and the

332

possibilities of opposition being based on racial lines,
Their continual denials of any racial bias may be seen as
part of the general syndrome Garrard has described. The oft-
quoted fact that the union made no complaint against the
employment of skilled German miners, who had sufficient English,
as evidence of lack of prejudice,[119] is also rather undermined
by the numerical insignificance of this particular group
(ninety-one in Scotland, 1911 census). And yet it seems too
easy a judgement to look at the attitudes expressed in the
public speeches of union officials and denounce them as a
disguise for prejudice. The positive actions of the Lanarkshire union towards the immigrants, as referred to above,
were in marked contrast to those of some other mining unions.
According to their delegate at the MFGB conference, the South
Wales miners had branch resolutions that no-one should join
the Miners' Federation unless he spoke the language of the
people.[120] There was no similar ban on Lithuanian recruitment
to the Lanarkshire union and it has been shown that other
positive incentives were offered, with suitable responses from
the immigrants.

Without much more thorough research, it would be unwise
to claim that the response of the Lanarkshire workforce to the
immigrants did not involve elements of racist thinking. What
can be said is that racial antipathy was not the central
element in the programme of opposition embarked upon by the
union. Evidence for the lack of any deep-seated hostility
is the parallel political development of both native and
immigrant which led to rapid acceptance by the union of the
Lithuanians when a commonality of interests had been shown.
This was epitomised by the solidarity achieved in 1912,

NOTES

I wish to acknowledge the financial assistance of the Twenty-
Seven Foundation in the preparation of this article, which is
a revised version of the paper delivered at the 1978 conference
of the Society for the Study of Labour History.

1.   See Colin Holmes, 'Introduction: Immigrants and
Minorities in Britain', in Holmes (ed.), Immigrants and
Minorities in British Society (1978), p. 20.

2.   See, for example, John Garrard, The English and Immigration (1971), passim; Catherine Jones, Immigration and
Social Policy in Britain (1977), p. 72.

3.   Garrard, The English and Immigration p. 176.

4.   Ibid., p. 174.

5.   Bernard Gainer, The Alien Invasion (1972).

6.   For example, Gainer limits his comments on the topic to
one footnote (pp. 217-18).

7.   Simas Suziedelis, 'Lithuania from Medieval to Modern
Times: A Historical Outline', in V. Stanley Vardys (ed.),
Lithuania under the Soviets (New York, 1965), p. 6.

8.   This account is based on material from Suziedelis,
'Lithuania', pp. 3-7; Stanley Page, The Formation of the
Baltic States (New York, 1970), pp. 1-10; E.J. Harrison,
Lithuania, Past and Present (1922), passim; Jerzy Zubrzyvki,
Polish Immigrants in Britain (The Hague, 1956), pp. 10-47.
Harrison, p. 124 claims that over 90% of the Lithuanian
population in these years lived in rural areas.   For two
examples, see the evidence of William Yorksin and Joe
Yimities, Minutes of Evidence before Royal Commission on
Mines, volume 3, Cd 4349 (1908), particularly Q22911-22927
(hereafter RC on Mines).

9.   See Michael Flinn (ed.), Scottish Population History
from the 17th Century to the 1930s (1977), p. 458.

10.   Royal Commission on Labour, Answers to Schedules on
Questions, Group 'A', C-6795-VII (1892) (hereafter RC on
Labour), return of Blantyre Miners' Association.
Note the contradictory evidence, both in the written return
from the Lanarkshire Coal Masters Association, who claimed
no foreigners were employed, and the verbal evidence of
Robert Smillie, president of the Blantyre Miners' Association,
who made a similar statement.   However, the union secretary,
William Small, referred to a small influx of foreigners (RC
on Labour, Minutes of Evidence Taken Before Group 'A', vol.
II, C-6795-IV (1892), Q10279.

11.   Minutes of Evidence from Select Committee on Emigration
and Immigration (Foreigners), 311 (1889) (hereafter SC on
Emigration), Appendix 8, letter from Merry and Cunningham,
Iron and Coal Masters and Steel Manufacturers, 29 July 1889.

12. SC on Emigration, 311 (1889), evidence of Keir Hardie, Q1565.

13. See Ardrossan and Saltcoats Herald, 18 Nov. 1887.

14. See the details in Fred Reid, Keir Hardie: The Making of a Socialist (1978), p. 122. Note, however, the slight discrepancies between Reid's account and the wider range of views presented in this article.

15. See Commonweal, 26 Nov. 1887.

16. SC on Emigration, 311 (1884), Q1419.

17. Commonweal, 26 Nov. 1887. See also Reid, Keir Hardie p. 122. For details of the anti-alien resolution to Glasgow Trades Council, see Commonweal, 3 Dec. 1887.

18. See 11 Nov. 1887 edition, quoted in Commonweal, 19 Nov. 1887.

19. SC on Emigration, 311 (1889), Q1482.

20. Ibid., Appendix 8. For details of employment at the Cheshire Salt Works, see ibid., 305 (1888), passim.

21. RC on Labour, Minutes of Evidence (Group 'A'), vol. II, Q14455-7.

22. Tenth Decennial Census of Population of Scotland, 1891, vol. II - part 1, C-6937, (1893), Abstracts, Section XIV.

23. Note that the census figures do not distinguish between the Catholic Lithuanians and Poles and those of the Jewish religion. There is some evidence that many of these immigrants were Jewish (see Tova Benski, 'Glasgow', in Provincial Jewry in Victorian Britain, papers for a conference of the Jewish Historical Society of England, July 1975, p. 6).

24. Annual conference, 5 Jan. 1896, MFGB Minutes 1897.

25. Eleventh Decennial Census of Population of Scotland, 1901, vol. III, Cd 1798 (1903), Section XII, Table XVII.

26. The Times, 9 Sept. 1904.

27. Twelfth Decennial Census of Population of Scotland, 1911, vol. 3, Cd 7163 (1913), Report, p. ix.

28. Motherwell Times, 20 March 1903.

29. Ibid., 11 Sept. 1903.

30. See, for example, Lanarkshire Examiner, 9 May 1903, for an illustration of this.

31. Ibid., 20 June 1903.

32. See statement of Robert Brown, President of the Scottish Miners' Federation, RC on Mines, Minutes of Evidence, vol. II, Cd 3873 (1908), Q22327.

33. Bellshill Speaker, 6 March 1903.

34. Lanarkshire Examiner, 2 May 1903.

35. James D. White, 'Scottish Lithuanians and the Russian Revolution', Journal of Baltic Studies, vol. 6, no. 1 (1975), p. 2.

36. Ibid., 9 May 1903.

37. Ibid., 25 July 1903.

38. See the survey of conditions in a Scottish mining village in Glasgow Observer and Catholic Herald (hereafter Catholic Herald), 15 Aug. 1903, for some background details.

39. See R. Page Arnot, A History of the Scottish Miners (1955), p. 134.

40. Quoted in ibid., pp. 136-7.

41. SC on Emigration, 305 (1888), Q1426.

42. RC on Mines, vol. III, Cd 4349 (1908), Q21976-7.

43. Ibid., Q22325.

44. A skilled miner was defined as someone employed in the industry from leaving school. 'We call a skilled Scotch miner a person who has been brought up at the colliery from 13 or 14 years of age? - That is how it is looked upon.' Smillie questioning John Weir, Secretary of Fife and Kinross Miners Association, RC on Mines, vol. III, Cd 4349 (1908), Q20895.

45. Alan Campbell and Fred Reid, 'The Independent Collier in Scotland', in Royden Harrison (ed.), Independent Collier: The Coal Miner as Archetypal Proletarian Reconsidered (Hassocks, Sussex, 1978), p. 60.

46. Glasgow Sentinel, 27 Dec. 1873, cited in Alan Campbell,

'Honourable men and degraded slaves: a social history of
trade unionism among the Lanarkshire miners 1775-1875, with
particular reference to the Coatbridge and Larkhall districts'
(unpub. Ph.D. thesis, Warwick University, 1977), p. 259.

47. See conference reports, MFGB Minutes, 1897.

48. Royal Commission on Alien Immigration (hereafter RC on
Alien Immigration), Minutes of Evidence, vol. II, Cd 1742 (1903),
Q22954.

49. Quotation from Glasgow Herald, 29 May 1903. See
minutes of council of Lanarkshire Miners' County Union
(hereafter LMU council minutes), 28 May 1903, Dep 227, 26,
National Library of Scotland.

50. Special conference, 11 March 1904, MFGB Minutes, 1904.

51. Robert Smillie, My Life for Labour (1924), pp. 136- 40.

52. The actual terms of the resolutions varied only slightly -
the one passed in 1906 is a reasonable general example.
'That, seeing the employment of unskilled labour in mines,
and especially of foreign workmen, is a source of great danger
to themselves and other workmen, this Conference urges upon
the Government the necessity of adopting such precautions,
by legislation or otherwise, as will bring it to an end.'

53. See evidence of Gilmour, RC on Mines, vol. III, Q21459.

54. Annual conference, 1903, MFGB Minutes, 1903. For
confirmation, see Smillie's speech at 1901 annual conference,
MFGB Minutes, 1901; Gilmour, RC on Mines, vol. III, Q21262-3.

55. Annual conference, 1904, MFGB Minutes, 1904. See
similar claim put forward by Robert Brown, RC on Mines, vol.
III, Q22322.

56. Annual conference, 1906, MFGB Minutes, 1906.

57. See RC on Mines, vol. IV, Cd 4667 (1908), Q44633-5.

58. Special conference, 11 March 1904, MFGB Minutes, 1904 -
repeated to RC on Mines, vol. III, Q21275 by Gilmour.

59. Annual conference, 1904, MFGB Minutes, 1904.

60. See evidence of Richard McPhee, manager of Bothwell
Park Colliery, vol. III, Q22863A, 22876; James Forgie,
partner and director of William Baird and Co., vol. IV,
Q43874-6; David Mowat, General Manager of Iron Works and
Collieries of Summerlee Iron Works, vol. IV, Q44163-4.

61. This produced two very relevant questions from the union: (a) were the immigrants literate and (b) were the rules printed in the correct language?

(a) A good deal of evidence indicated that there was a fair degree of illiteracy which, given the immigrants' rural background, seems unexceptional. However, more work needs to be done on this area.

(b) Indications are that the Rules were often printed in Russian, since the Russian Consulate took some interest in its subject peoples in Britain and the country of origin was deemed to be Russia, but as the union continually stressed, this was a foreign language to Poles and Lithuanians. The problems encountered in certain court appearances by Lithuanians, even when aided by Russian Consulate officials, is a measure of the language difficulties the immigrants had to face.

In a comparative context, note that the United States Immigration Commission found that, in 1909, of its sample study of some 4500 Lithuanian immigrants, 50% spoke English, i.e. were able to 'carry on conversation' and nearly 80% were literate (able to read), although the basis for this assessment was very vague.

See Robert Higgs, 'Race, Skill and Earnings: American Immigrants in 1909', Journal of Economic History, 31 (1971), p. 424.

62. First Report of RC on Mines, Cd 3548 (1907), Q5022.

63. Hansard, 4th series, vol. 78, cols. 1368-9 (13 Feb. 1900).

64. Ibid., vol. 130, col. 446 (19 Feb. 1904).

65. Letter of 14 April 1904, reproduced in Minutes of MFGB Executive Committee meeting, 21/22 April 1904, MFGB Minutes, 1904.

66. See Garrard, The English and Immigration p. 162; Jones, Immigration and Social Policy pp. 78-80.

67. For an interesting theoretical economic discussion of the weakness of the immigrant bargaining position, see Higgs, JEcH 31, pp. 420-8.

68. LMU council minutes, 24 March 1902, Dep 227, 25.

69. Ibid., 29 April 1902.

70. See, for example, minutes of executive committee of Lanarkshire Miners' County Union (hereafter LMU exec. comm. minutes), 16 March 1904, 19 April 1904, Dep 227, 48.

71. Ibid., 17 April, 1909, Dep 227, 52.

72. This account is based on LMU council minutes, 13 April
1903, Dep 227, 26; minutes, Scottish Miners' Federation,
20 April 1903, Acc 4312, 20, National Library of Scotland;
Lanarkshire Examiner, 2-30 May 1903; Labour Leader, 2 and 3
May 1903; Catholic Herald, 18 April - 30 May 1903; evidence
of Smillie, Gilmour, Ronaldson and Robert Baird, Secretary
of Lanarkshire Coal Masters Association, RC on Alien
Immigration, Minutes of Evidence, vol. II.

73. See Catholic Herald, 8 Aug. 1903; 19 Dec. 1903;
report of LMU for six months ending 30/6/1904, LMU council
minutes, Dep 227, 31; LMU exec. comm. minutes. 16 March,
1904, Dep 227, 48.

74. LMU exec. comm. minutes, 16 March, 1904, Dep 227, 48.

75. Catholic Herald, 8 Feb. 1903.

76. Report of LMU for six months ending 30/6/1905, LMU
council minutes, Dep 227, 28.

77. LMU exec. comm. minutes, 11 and 18 Oct. 1905, Dep 227,
49.

78. Letter in Catholic Herald, 9 May 1903.

79. It is recorded that a union branch was formed at
Loganlea in October 1904. LMU exec. comm. minutes, 22 Oct.
1904, Dep 227, 48.

80. Annual conference, 1903, MFGB Minutes, 1903.

81. See LMU council minutes, 29 April 1907, motion to this
effect from Bellshill branch passed 38 to 17. This action
was confirmed by Smillie, RC on Mines, Q22897. Note,
however, an executive committee decision, 15 August 1905,
not to print the union's rules in Lithuanian - presumably
it was felt that since the campaign was based on the dangers
of the language barrier, the immigrants ought to be encouraged to learn English.

82. LMU exec. comm. minutes, 4 Oct. 1905.

83. Ibid., 17 Feb. 1909.

84. Fred Reid, 'Alexander MacDonald and the crisis of the
independent collier', in Harrison (ed.), Independent Collier
p. 164.

85. Little work has been done on the lives of the Lithuanian

immigrants and the research of Murdoch Rodgers, a post-
graduate student at Edinburgh University, is awaited with
interest.   I am grateful to Mr Rodgers for some of the
detail contained in this article and have benefitted greatly
from our correspondence.

86. For details, see White, Journal of Baltic Studies 6,
pp. 2-3.

87. For details, see ibid., pp. 4-5.

88. Thus we ought to revise the judgement of a traditional
study of 'labour' on Clydeside, which, in looking at the
weakness of socialism before 1914, identifies immigration,
particularly from the Highlands and Ireland as a major
factor.
'Other racial groups, even less responsive to the Socialist
message, were the Poles and Lithuanians, brought in to break
miners' strikes, who lived in small tightly-knit colonies...'
R.K. Middlemass, The Clydesiders: A Left Wing Struggle for
Parliamentary Power (1965), p. 29.
Such an approach clearly needs a good deal of qualification.

89. Arnot, Scottish Miners pp. 125-6.

90. See, for example, Bellshill Speaker, 8 March 1912.

91. Ibid., 10 May 1912.

92. Hansard, 5th series, vol. 38, cols. 778-9 (13 May 1912).

93. See receipt by Home Office of petition on behalf of
Stangle, Braski and Wilson from Bothwell Park Miners Union,
3 May 1912, HO 46/169.

94. See letter to Millar, copy sent to union, reproduced
in Lanarkshire Examiner, 25 May 1912.

95. Quoted in Bellshill Speaker, 10 May 1912.

96. Ibid., 3 May 1912.

97. See ibid., 19 Jan. 1912; Lanarkshire Examiner, 23
March 1912.

98. See Arnot, Scottish Miners p. 133.

99. RC on Labour, vol. II, Q10279.   This was a view
commonly held by union officials in the 1890s.   See, for
example, Alan Campbell, 'Honourable Men and Degraded Slaves',
in Harrison (ed.), Independent Collier p. 102.

100. Bellshill Speaker, 5 April 1912.

101. See Campbell, thesis, p. 291.

102. For some details, see SC on Emigration, 305 (1888),
Appendix 6, 11, extract from report of Bureau of Industrial
Statistics (USA); RC on Labour, Foreign Reports, vol. X
(Russis), C-7063-XIV (1894).

103. Maldwyn Jones, Destination America (1976), p. 149.

104. For a general survey, see J.E. Handley, The Irish in
Scotland, 1790-1845 (Cork, 1943).

105. See A. Slaven, 'Coal Mining in the West of Scotland in
the Nineteenth Century; the Dixon Enterprises' (unpub.
B.Litt. thesis, Glasgow University, 1967), p. 93; A.J. Youngson Brown, 'The Scots Coal Industry, 1854-1886' (unpub. B.Litt.
thesis, Aberdeen University, 1953), p. 200.

106. Evidence of William Dixon to Select Committee on the
State of the Irish Poor in Great Britain, 1836, quoted in
R.H. Campbell and J.B.S. Dow, Source Book of Scottish Economic
and Social History (Oxford, 1968), p. 8.   For some harsh
judgements on the Irish miner in the late nineteenth century,
see R. Haddow, 'The Miners of Scotland', The Nineteenth Century,
CXXXIX (1888), pp. 360-71.

107. See Youngson Brown, thesis, p. 200.

108. See Campbell, thesis, pp. 290-303.

109. See precis of paper to 1973 conference, Bulletin of the
Society for the Study of Labour History, 28 (Spring 1974),
p. 10.

110. Campbell, thesis, pp. 267-81 and passim.

111. There is evidence to suggest it was still a weakening
force in the twentieth century.   See Abe Moffat, My Life with
the Miners (1965), p. 60, on the 1930 Shotts strike and the
religious difficulties which had to be overcome.

112. Report of Departmental Committee into Conditions Pre-
vailing in the Coal Mining Industry Due to the War, Part II -
Minutes of Evidence, Cd 8009 (1915), Q430, 852.

113. J.A. Tannahill, European Volunteer Workers in Britain
(Manchester, 1958), p. 63.

114. Garrard, The English and Immigration pp. 176-7.

115. _Labour Leader_, 12 Oct. 1901,   It seems likely that this editorial was written by Keir Hardie.

116. See _Socialist Monthly_, June 1903.

117. The available sources give little indication of the attitudes of the general workforce, except as conveyed by union officials.   One clue may be an article by Francis McLaughlan, a miner sent to Ruskin College by the Lanarkshire union, who wrote of the grievances against the immigrants by the native workforce.   (See '"Polish Labour" in the Scottish Mines.   From the Miner's Point of View', _Economic Journal_, vol. 17, no. 66 (June 1907), pp, 287-9.)

118. Youngson Brown, thesis, pp. 195-211.

119. See, for example, speech of Gilmour, annual conference, MFGB Minutes, 1903.

120. Speech of Davies of South Wales, annual conference, MFGB Minutes, 1902.

12

The British and American Labour Movements and the Problem of Immigration, 1890–1914

A. T. LANE

High claims have been made for comparative history. We are told that it compels us to see our past in a new light, that it makes us 'revise complacent assumptions of national exclusiveness, uniqueness or excellence'. It has methodological advantages too, for it helps us, as Genovese remarks, 'to shed false generalizations by providing much better controls than insulated studies can' and hence to form richer hypotheses.[1] Such assertions invite us to compare the response of British and American labouring men to the challenge of immigration in the two decades before the First World War.

Such a comparison is not inappropriate. By the beginning of the twentieth century both the United States and Great Britain were developed, largely urban-industrial societies. Great Britain was second only to the United States as a Mecca for migrants from Eastern Europe,[2] both countries prided themselves on their humanitarianism in offering asylum to refugees from oppression, and in both there had emerged labour movements of some size and potential with an awareness of common problems. Among the latter was the need to come to terms with a substantial inflow of impoverished, mainly unskilled and ethnically distinct immigrants from Eastern Europe. In the face of this common challenge, the response of American labour was more

restrictive and discriminatory. How significant was this
difference in attitude and how can it be explained? Are we
able, by undertaking a comparison with the American experience,
to strengthen our generalisations about attitudes to immigration
in the British labour movement?

Organised labour's attitude towards immigration in the
United States in the three decades before the First World War
was expressed by the Knights of Labor and then the American
Federation of Labor which supported the various restrictive
measures passed by the Federal Government in the 1880s and
1890s. These excluded, among others, the Chinese, paupers,
criminals, the mentally ill, those suffering from contagious
diseases, and contract labourers. In the decade after the
passage of the Contract Labor Law in 1885 most labour representatives tried to distinguish between immigrants who had been
induced to leave their homelands by American employers, labour
agencies, steamship companies and the like, and those who settled
'voluntarily' in the United States. It was assumed that anyone
who had made a voluntary, individual decision to pull up his
roots in Europe, having first assessed the advantages offered
by the United States, would make a good American citizen and
soon learn to demand American wage levels and working conditions.[3]
When workers went to the United States voluntarily, said William
Weihe of the Iron and Steel Workers, they quickly became identified
with the country.[4] There could be little objection to such
newcomers since most native-born and first-generation Americans
placed their own families or themselves in this class of worthy
voluntary immigrants. Instead, the weight of criticism was
borne by the so-called imported immigrants, and especially by
the employers and agents who induced them to go to the United
States.[5] It was fervently hoped and mistakenly assumed that
the Contract Labor Law would exclude this type of immigrant.
When it became clear that it was failing to do so to any
satisfactory extent, most labouring men and their spokesmen

344

stressed the need for a more effective administration of the
act and a closing of loopholes.   By the mid-1890s, however,
it was widely recognised that the act had been adequately
tightened and that it was being competently administered.   Yet
undesirable immigrants continued to pour in.   This threw the
labour world into confusion.   Whilst some unwelcome immigrants
were being brought over by agencies of various kinds, others
had merely responded to family invitations or had made individual
decisions to leave for the United States.   Yet these could only
be classed as voluntary immigrants whom it had hitherto been
deemed wrong to debar.   If they were to be excluded, a powerful
case would have to be made to overcome traditional American
notions of fraternity, hospitality and asylum for the oppressed
of Europe.   The debate had only just begun when, in 1897, the
AFL cast an overwhelming vote in support of a new measure of
restriction, the literacy test, already approved by Congress
though vetoed by President Cleveland.[6]   This test would have
had the effect of excluding all illiterate immigrants whether
voluntary or induced, though it was assumed that it would
disproportionately affect induced immigrants.[7]

It would be a mistake to suppose that this AFL vote
accurately represented opinion within the ranks of organised
labour.   It was testimony to the manipulative skills of the
leadership rather than to the passionate conviction of the
rank and file.[8]   Nevertheless, there can be little doubt that
by 1906 the literacy test had become largely accepted by trade
union opinion as the most effective means of limiting the more
undesirable forms of immigration from Southern and Eastern
Europe.   What had occurred was of great significance, for
labour had had to make a choice between its national and its
international loyalties and it had chosen nationalism.   Or
rather, it had chosen a severely limited internationalism, and
the limits were determined by ethno-cultural criteria.   In
other words, it had become clear that labour's distinction

between voluntary (i.e. desirable) and induced (i.e. undesirable)
immigration was threadbare and could no longer be sustained.
If the literacy test were to be accepted by the labour movement, it would have to be shown that the groups to be discriminated against constituted a genuine threat to the well-
being and prosperity of American workers. On what grounds was
the case against the so-called new immigrants made?

In 1904 J.W. Sullivan of the Garmentworkers' Union out-
lined the consequences of a failure to tighten immigration
legislation. There would be, he said

> more rackrents for slum landlords, more
> dividends for foreign corporations
> subsidised by European governments, more
> rake-offs for contractors, padroni, and
> foreign agents of transportation (companies),
> more voting cattle for our political
> stockyards, more blood for real estate
> sharks, more non-unionists for manufacturing
> combines, more outlay for every charitable
> and penal institution...and incalculably
> more misery for America's wage earners. 9

Of all these adverse consequences, the threat to the wages,
employment prospects and working conditions of American
labouring men was paramount among the factors influencing
American labour to adopt the literacy test. This threat had
existed intermittently for much of the nineteenth century,
but the greatly increased volume of immigration in the 1880s,
together with the rising proportion from Southern and Eastern
Europe focussed attention on it, particularly since tehcno-
logicial changes in many industries were leading to the
displacement of many skilled artisans by machines manned by
unskilled immigrant workers. At first the major target of
criticism was the employers, because of their alleged
importation of helpless and ignorant immigrants to act as
cheap labour and strikebreakers.[10] But by the mid-1890s, not
a few labour organisations recognised the diminished role of

the employers and increasingly made direct criticism of cheap labour which was difficult to organise and weakened the bargaining power of labour organisations.[11]   Of course, the employer was still a villain, but the nature of his villany had changed; from attempting to create a labour surplus, he now merely utilised the surplus which existed.

From the 1890s until the First World War, and after, the most constant and sustained criticism of immigration from the ranks of labour focussed on its economic impact.   That is not to say, however, that opposition based on grounds of ethnicity, culture and morality was merely an embellishment of the economic conflict.[12]   It is true that Marx believed that social antagonisms of a non-economic kind were secondary and would wither away as economic class consciousness developed.   But as Ware argued, the history of the American labour movement has shown that the time scale for such withering away has had to be considerably extended, largely as the result of the continuous reinforcement of such antagonisms by the large volume of immigration from a multiplicity of ethno-cultural backgrounds.   Consequently we cannot dismiss as unimportant or 'vestigial' the other allegations made by American labour against recent immigrants.[13] On the contrary, they assumed greater importance and prominence in the anti-immigration case after the turn of the century.

Recent immigrants, it was alleged, constituted a threat to the existence of the American Republic.   Republican forms of government relied on the participation in civic affairs of an enlightened, well-informed, and patriotic citizenry.   In turn, such a citizenry could only be sustained on the basis of a reasonably high standard of life.   Pauperisation of the American wage-earner under the stress of immigrant job com-petition weakened democracy and prepared the way for servility and corruption.[14]   But, more importantly, the newcomers themselves made very poor material for transforming into

American citizens, coming as they did from the 'most utterly alien and ill-conditioned nationalities of the continent'. Their present 'poverty, ignorance, bigotry and degradation' made them unfit to participate in the government of the United States, whatever their 'natural capabilities'.[15] Most recent immigrants had been the subjects of despots and were wholly unused to self-government.[16] Yet, they had been thrust into the 'delicate fabric' of free political institutions, by a too lax naturalisation procedure devised and utilised by the urban political bosses for their own corrupt purposes.[17] In virtually every major city in the United States, the indictment continued, the naturalised foreign-born held the balance of political power, despite ignorance of the English language, of the political issues and of the fundamental principles of free government.[18] The perpetuation of the American Republic depended on the internalisation by the newcomers of American beliefs, values and modes of behaviour. It was doubtful if that could be achieved whilst ever more immigrants poured in and undermined whatever assimilation had taken place in a previous generation. Paradoxically, whilst there was resentment at immigrants becoming citizens too soon, there was strong condemnation of those newcomers whose sole intention was to remain in the United States long enough to accumulate sufficient savings to return home in relative affluence. They 'compete, save, pay no taxes, own no homes, spend little or nothing, support neither churches, schools nor public institutions...'[19] The common characteristic of both types was an incapacity or a refusal to identify in a meaningful way with the United States.

Another important anti-immigrant theme achieving greater prominence in the decade before the First World War was the alleged burden and danger to the United States of immigrant poverty, disease, criminality, vice, low sanitary standards, and bad housing. Immigrant poverty and criminality, it was charged, were disproportionately high and constituted a substantial financial cost to the host nation. Immigrant slums were a blot on the community, a 'festering sore', a breeding ground for diseases which then spread to the native-born population.[20] A wise host, one labour editor admonished his readers, does not open the door of his 'clean, warm, healthy, virtuous, frugal, and industrious home to the unclean, the vicious, the thriftless, the lazy, and the lawless'.[21]

There was no reference in that catalogue of undesirables to the racially inferior. It is clearly pertinent to consider whether labour spokesmen in this period opposed immigration on account of the immutable, indestructible racial characteristics of a proportion of the immigrants, which rendered assimilation impossible. How many took the view that a prerequisite of national greatness was a population of wholly Aryan stock? What proportion shared with the sociologist E.A. Ross, the conviction that the blood being injected into the veins of the American people was of a 'sub-common Caliban type', the possession of ox-like men whose soul burned 'with a dull smoky flame' and who clearly belonged in the skins and wattled huts at the close of the Great Ice Age.[22] Such sentiments were expressed extremely rarely by labouring men or their representatives. In his memoirs Samuel Gompers, President of the AFL at this time, pointed to the 1890s as a period 'before there was a general understanding of the principle that the maintenance of the nation depended upon the maintenance of racial purity and strength'.[23] Most labour spokesmen, to do them justice, believed that recent immigrants were capable of being assimilated and that their backwardness was the product of their culture rather than of a fixed genetic endowment. Gosset has remarked that frequently 'the temptation was irresistible...to note that the immigrant was often defective because of his race.'[24] That temptation was resisted far more strongly by organised labour than by the blue bloods of

the Immigration Restriction League and the academics who
ploughed the same furrow.

In retrospect, the two decades from 1890 to 1910 were
crucial in the evolution of American labour attitudes towards
immigrants, transforming an anxious hospitality into outright
hostility towards even 'voluntary' immigrants from Southern
and Eastern Europe. In Great Britain these two decades were
of comparable importance in the evolution of labour attitudes
to immigration, but here the tide of restrictionist sentiment
appeared to ebb after the mid-1890s and labour offered no
support for the 1905 Aliens Exclusion Act, the purpose of
which was to exclude not only criminals, the insane, and the
diseased, but also paupers, that is to say, those who could
not prove that they could secure the means of subsistence.
In considering immigration in the 1890s, the Trades Union
Congress started from a different base from the American
Federation of Labor, since there was no restrictionist
legislation on the statute book. There was, however, a quite
striking parallel between the campaigns of restrictionists in
the American and British labour movements in the 1880s and the
early 1890s. Both concentrated on the 'induced' nature of
much immigration; both tended to place primary responsibility
on employers; both regarded immigrants as instruments of a
capitalist class; both were particularly concerned by
immigrants from Southern and Eastern Europe, in the British
case mainly Russian Jews. Resolutions passed by the TUC at
annual conferences between 1888 and 1895 referred to 'the
importation of foreign pauper labour', to paupers being
'shipped' into the country, to employers contracting for the
hire of labour outside the United Kingdom, especially during
labour disputes. The intention of the resolutions passed at
the Bradford and Dundee conferences in 1888 and 1889 respectively,
was to cut out the landing or importing of foreign pauper
labour.[25] Keir Hardie spoke at Bradford along the lines of

his evidence to the Select Committee on Emigration and
Immigration in 1889, in which he referred to an ironworks in
Ayrshire recruiting Polish workers through the Russian consul
at Glasgow.[26]   So long as some mention was made in the
resolutions of the role of employers, delegates seemed happy
to pass them, and this they did at the 1890, 1892 and 1893
Congresses, without much debate.   By 1894 and 1895, the
question of immigration restriction assumed greater importance
and the attack on pauper immigrants was intensified under the
direction of delegates Inskip and Freak of the Boot and Shoe
Workers, a union particularly hard hit by Jewish immigration.
The resolution moved by Inskip at both Congresses deserves
quotation because it illustrates the nature of the anti-
immigration campaign within labour organisations.

> In view of the injury done to a large
> number of trades and trade unions by the
> wholesale importation of foreign destitute
> paupers, this Congress calls upon the
> Government... to prohibit the landing of
> all pauper aliens who have no visible
> means of subsistence.   [27]

If this resolution is considered in the context of previous
TUC debates, it may be interpreted as a move against employer-
stimulated immigration, but there was sufficient ambiguity in
it to permit those delegates who wished to interpret it as
opposing all pauper immigration, whether imported or 'voluntary'.
However, even if the latter had been the general interpretation,
so tiny was the majority and so large were the abstentions that
the vote could hardly have been regarded as firmly committing
the TUC to a policy of restricting voluntary immigration.[28]
Furthermore, there are compelling grounds for believing that
the resolution was generally understood to refer to 'imported'
aliens, hence the majority for the resolution.   When an
attempt was made at the 1892 Congress to exclude foreign

paupers without implying that they were the tools of employers, delegates bridled at the illiberality of the proposal and rejected it.[29]   In similar fashion, an 1894 move to prevent the immigration of any foreign worker belonging to a trade or industry in which unemployment in Great Britain was over 3 per cent was defeated.[30]   Additionally, some delegates were clearly unhappy with restriction of any kind, either because it would impede the development of international understanding or because it failed to attack the roots of the labour problem, which lay in the capitalist system itself.   Delegate Walker supported the 'Socialist tailor' James MacDonald in 1895 in opposing the restrictionist resolution, calling for the reform of the Land Laws, the organisation of all foreigners into trade unions and the establishment of a world-wide brotherhood to 'prevent the workmen from being robbed of their rights', themes which gained some support in the United States.[31]

In any full consideration of the context of the 1894 and 1895 resolutions, of the forthright opposition to restriction of voluntary immigration, and of the strand of sentiment totally opposed to restriction of any sort, it is difficult to conclude that British labour representatives had gone further along the restrictionist road than American labouring men had done in supporting the 1885 Contract Labor Law.   In any event, the Congress of 1895 was the last before the First World War at which a restrictive resolution was introduced. Not even the acrimonious debates in Parliament over the Aliens Bills in 1904 and 1905 bestirred the TUC to register a view. Silence should not necessarily be taken to mean opposition to the proposed legislation.   It could have been dictated as much by political expediency, or as Garrard suggests, 'paralyzing embarrassment' at the prospect of having to register support for a proposal which violated traditional ideals.[32]   Whatever the reason, after 1895 the TUC took no further steps along the restrictionist path.

The arguments advanced by restrictionists in labour's discussions on immigration only partially corresponded to those put forward in the United States. In the British debate, there was no parallel to American nativist arguments about the deleterious effects of recent immigrants on civic standards. The attention of labour representatives was concentrated on the effects of immigration on wage levels, on the outcome of strikes, on unemployment, and on union organisation. 'There is no feeling against foreigners, as foreigners', reported Charles Freak in 1888, 'only when they work against our interest by taking a reduced price...,'[33] Keir Hardie alleged that wage reductions had been brought about in the Glengarnock Iron Works in Ayrshire as a result of the recruitment of cheaper Polish labour and the threat of more.[34] Allegations of wage reductions resulting from cheap immigrant competition, and of displacement of British workers by foreigners, were commonplace in the labour press and in conference proceedings in the 1890s. But references to the costly and degrading impact on British life of immigrant poverty, vice, criminality, disease and mental illness, quite common in the United States, were conspicuous by their absence. Attention was sometimes drawn to the excessively low sanitary and general living standards of Jewish sweaters' dens and to the way in which infectious diseases could be spread through the sale of garments made up in these sweating establishments.[35] In general, though, such observations achieved little prominence within labour's ranks.

It is evident that in its restrictive proposals and the arguments advanced in their justification, the British labour movement showed itself far more moderate than its American counterpart. Why was this? More specifically, what caused American labour to demand that the traditional practice of free entry be jettisoned in favour of restrictive and dis-criminatory legislation against even voluntary immigrants from Europe whilst workers in Great Britain refused to take

unequivocal action against the immigration of cheap labour?
We perhaps need look no further than to the comparative volume
of immigration into the respective countries.   In the United
States Census of 1900 the number of foreign-born residents in
the United States (excluding Alaska and Hawaii) was stated to
be about 14 per cent of the total population.   Of the total
foreign-born, about 18 per cent were of Italian, Slavonic and
Hungarian birth and it was feared that this proportion would
increase if existing trends in immigration continued.[36]   By
contrast, the census returns for England and Wales for 1901
showed that the proportion of aliens in the total population
was just over 1 per cent, one-third of these being Russian and
Polish Jews.[37]   As in the United States, the proportion of
Jews would increase if existing trends in immigration continued.
However, the overall proportions of immigrants to total
population concealed what was happening within regions, cities
and industries.   For example, 73 per cent of the Italians,
Slavs and Hungarians in the United States in 1900 lived in
seven industrialised states of Massachusetts, Connecticut,
New Jersey, New York, Pennsylvania, Ohio and Illinois.   In
1900 the foreign-born constituted 25 per cent or more of the
population in eighteen of the twenty-eight largest American
cities.   New York, Chicago and San Francisco could each
point to the fact that more than 40 per cent of their population
was foreign-born.[38]   Great Britain could show a similar urban
concentration of the most recent Jewish immigrants but one
which was confined to fewer cities, notably London, Leeds and
Manchester.   But in further contrast to the United States,
the proportion of aliens in the total population of the large
British cities never reached comparable levels.   Only in one
or two boroughs of London's East End was comparability achieved.
In Whitechapel the proportion of aliens reached 32 per cent of
the population by 1900 but in the two northern cities of
Manchester and Leeds, which had the largest concentrations of

aliens outside London, only about 3 per cent of the inhabitants were foreign born.[39]   The aliens were also concentrated
in certain occupations in both the United States and Great
Britain.   From 1880 to 1910 the proportion of foreign-born
in 'manufacturing and mechanical' industries in the United
States averaged about 30 per cent of the total work force
with even higher proportions in some of the service trades.
The significant proportion of Southern and Eastern Europeans
among the foreign-born employees in particular industries is
shown by figures for 1905 in Pennsylvania where 41 per cent
of all employees in the anthracite and bituminous coal, pig
iron and iron and steel industries were Italians, Slavs and
Hungarians.   Large concentrations of 'new immigrants' were
also found in the garment, textile and public utilities
industries.[40]   In Great Britain, the recent Jewish immigrants,
like their co-religionists in the United States, concentrated
in a much narrower range of industries than the 'new immigrants'
across the Atlantic.   Roughly 40 per cent of all immigrants
gainfully employed in 1901 were in the tailoring trade (about
14 per cent of the labour force), most of the rest being
employed in boots and shoes, capmaking, cabinet making, and
furs.[41]   Because of this narrower concentration, protest
against immigration in Great Britain had a more limited base.
However, levels of protest were related, not to the real
dimensions of immigration, but to imagined ones.   In Great
Britain there was considerable misapprehension about the
volume of immigration, arising in part out of the inadequate
statistics published by the Board of Trade.   The statistics
divided immigrants up into those en route to other countries
and 'those not stated to be en route'.   The latter were in
fact those who did not possess a through steamer ticket;   a
stated intention to travel on to the United States in due
course did not qualify an immigrant as a transient.[42]   As a
result propagandists could claim with some degree of

355

plausibility that upwards of ten times the actual number of
permanent immigrants were arriving in British ports. Even
so, if nine-tenths of the immigrants were admitted to be
transmigrants, they still had to find shelter and employment
for the duration of their stay. To a British resident in
the East End of London whether an immigrant was permanent or
temporary was immaterial - the practical consequences were
the same.[43]

We may ask whether these comparative figures were, by
themselves, able to account for the differential response of
British and American labour to immigration. Although new
immigrants in the United States constituted a markedly higher
proportion of the total population in 1900 than Russian Jews
in Great Britain, perhaps the major differences between the
two migrations lay in the greater number of regions, cities
and industries affected in the United States. Additionally,
there was a more intense psychological pressure: restrictionists tended to anticipate the worst. The untold millions
of potential immigrants from Southern and Eastern Europe were
more alarming to American restrictionists than the more limited
numbers of Russian Jews to the British. Nevertheless, implicit
in any explanation of restriction which relies solely on the
intensity and extent of the challenge is the belief that response
was roughly proportionate to stimulus. This omits the
possibility of higher levels of toleration in one community
than another either because of different traditions, beliefs,
and circumstances or because the culture, ethnicity and levels
of income and skill of different immigrant groups differed
substantially.

In view of this possibility, we will examine five factors
which may have contributed to the development of a different
response within the organised labour movement in Great Britain.
These were socialist ideology, the relative weakness of racial
and nativist thought, the free trade tradition, the character

of the immigration, and the contemporary political configuration.

Historians have argued that the exceptionalism of American
labour history has been in the relative weakness of the socialist
movement. The ideal of international solidarity of the working
class had relatively little influence and this fact may have
played an important part in the formulation of attitudes to
immigration. Admittedly there is plausibility in such a view.
It is arguable that the alienation of many trade union members
from socialism as a result of De Leon's activities after 1894
sufficiently weakened the influence of internationalist thinking
to permit the passage of the literacy test resolutions at the
AFL in 1897. Though the Socialist Party began to gain strength
in the first decade of this century, there was a substantial
body of opinion within it which saw major advance as conditional
on converting trade unionists. Hence the need to accommodate
its policies, where possible, to those of the AFL. So far as
immigration was concerned, the AFL now had a firm policy; and
the socialists, if they wished to increase their influence, had
to reconcile their commitment to internationalism with the
unions' obvious desire for protection from cheap foreign labour.
The unhappiness of many socialists in this position was reflected
in the debate on immigration at the two national congresses of
the Socialist Party in 1908 and 1910, when 'to get out of their
trouble', to use Robert Hunter's phrase, delegates hid behind
an evasive resolution from Morris Hillquit.[44] By defining the
unwelcome immigrant as a strikebreaker 'imported by the capitalist
class to break the organisation of the working class', restrictionist delegates were able to disguise their racial animus
against Asiatics, and internationalists could rationalise that
barring strikebreakers was consistent with resolutions passed
at international socialist conferences. Under pressure to
make converts for socialism within the restrictionist ranks
of the AFL and in face of increasing numbers of restrictionists
within their own party, socialists were unable to stand out for

free immigration. Nevertheless their decision to shelter behind Hillquit's resolution clearly revealed that their internationalism had not been totally eroded. They were not yet ready to face the unpalatable fact, which Victor Berger insisted on pointing out to them, that a Chinese coolie (and possibly next year a Sicilian peasant) was just as dangerous to American labour whether he came under contract or not.[45]

By contrast the growing strength of socialism in trade unions in Great Britain in these decades may have contributed to keeping restrictionist sentiment among labour organisations at an unimpressive level. Keir Hardie's comment that the majority of the delegates to the 1898 Trade Union Congress had socialist sympathies may not have been an exaggeration.[46] Most socialists were anti-restrictionists. Of course, they were strongly opposed to alien strike-breakers entering the country and intolerant of immigrants imported by capitalists to force down the wages of British workers. Hardie's denunciation of imported Polish labourers in Ayrshire iron-works was reminiscent of T.V. Powderly's earlier strictures against Poles and Hungarians in the mining and steel industries of Pennsylvania.[47] Hardie and his labour colleagues in the House of Commons tried to amend the Aliens Bill in 1905 in order to exclude strikebreakers. However, they were keen opponents of the main provisions of the bill, as had been the Independent Labour Party and the Social Democratic Federation. They showed considerable sympathy for 'voluntary' immigrants attempting to escape from economic distress, oppression and political and religious persecution. Nonetheless, Hardie's comment that the 'problem of the foreign worker is not the least perplexing of the many-sided Labour question' revealed ideological doubts and the consciousness that working-class opinion was suspicious of impoverished aliens.[48]

How much weight therefore should be placed on socialist internationalism in explaining the differential response to

immigration?   Was its growth robust enough to withstand the
fierce blasts of discontent which would undoubtedly arise from
a labour movement under severe siege?   This seems doubtful.
Already that most popular of socialist papers, The Clarion,
had voiced concern in the 1890s about the economic competition
which poor Jews offered, their Smilesian qualities, their
apparent rejection of socialism, the 'unclean' habits of the
'poor unshorn and unsavoury children of the Ghetto' and, in
the words of the Webbs, their 'constant influence for
degradation' on the British national character.[49]   For those
who condemned such thinking as incompatible with socialism,
the reply came that there was no right course but only 'a
choice between greater or lesser degrees of wrongdoing'.[50]
To socialist internationalist arguments about brotherhood,
equality and the irrelevance of anti-alien measures to
solving the problems of capitalism, socialist 'heretics'
like Blatchford and Hall responded that brotherhood began at
home.   Whilst he might rejoice that the 'thief on the cross,
the Magdalen at the well are our brother and sister, bone of
our bone, flesh of our flesh' Blatchford's juxtaposition of
a stirring passage from Milton lauding the character of the
English nation showed that the thief's chances of brotherly
recognition were greater if he had the good fortune to be
born in England.   Blatchford claimed that he sought the
social elevation of the people of England.   It would, therefore, be criminal lunacy 'to allow such improvements as had
been made' to be threatened by the flow of 'unhappy, hopeless,
benighted creatures' to England 'to fight the battle of the
capitalist and the sweater'.   All reform measures espoused
by socialists were palliatives and true socialism consisted
in defending the gains made by the workers, not allowing them
to be destroyed in the interests of capitalists, a theme which
found echo among such American socialists as Berger, Untermann
and Hunter.[51]   Is it not realistic to suppose that such

arguments would be heard increasingly in Great Britain if
more cities and more industries began to feel the increasing
burden of immigrants? And was it not, as one Clarion
correspondent put it, the 'veriest commonplace cant' for
Hardie to try to amend the Aliens Act to exclude imported
strike-breakers when 'voluntary' immigrants, to whom he was
not opposed, could break strikes with impunity, once in the
country?[52] This, it could be argued, was just the evasion
which trans-Atlantic socialists were to engage in. These
evasions arose out of guilt at what seemed a betrayal of
socialist faith and from a failure to see socialism as the
product of the particular historical circumstances of the
second third of the nineteenth century. The rise of
nationalism and the increasing acceptance among socialists
of gradualism and its benefits were weakening adherence to
internationalism both in Europe and the United States. The
pressures of events and the dictates of expediency could be
expected to modify it further in the course of time. Jewish
and other immigrants to Great Britain were protected at that
time by socialist ideology but they would have been unwise
to place great reliance on it for the future. Hence, greater
numbers of socialists within the AFL would not necessarily
have reduced the commitment to restrictionism. Whether on
the inside or the outside of the organised labour movement,
socialists sooner or later had to come to terms with the
growing weight of restrictionist sentiment among the trade
unions. A compromise of their internationalism was the
result.

If, secondly, we attribute to ethno-cultural differences
a diminished confidence in the assimilative power of American
society and regard this as a major factor in converting American
labour opinion to discriminatory restriction, are we justified
in arguing that British labour's more limited restrictionism
stemmed from a greater tolerance of such differences? It is

360

undoubtedly true that ethnic prejudice and racist thinking
were present in Great Britain. J. Bruce Glazier of the ILP
perceived that anti-alienism was derived partly from race
aversion, based on instinct or prejudice.[53] This aversion
was no doubt reinforced by Social Darwinist ideas, by Anglo-
Saxonism, and by eugenics. These ideas became 'elements in
the (general) climate of opinion', usable tools in case of
need. Labour was affected by these ideas and prejudice to
some extent. TUC and Labour opposition to Chinese labour
in South Africa, compounded of several factors, was founded
in part on racial hostility to the Chinese. The 'heathen
Chinee' was a familiar enough stereotype in sections of the
labour press in the 1890s. The TUC fraternal delegates to
the AFL in 1898 returned full of praise for the AFL's
opposition to Chinese immigration. It represented, they
claimed, a defence of white labour.[54] Yet there may be
justifiable doubt that racist ideas present in anti-Chinese
feeling were widely extended to Jewish immigrants. Too many
pressures were against it. The Jews' status as refugees and
the fear of accusations of anti-semitism prevented the full
invocation of racist ideas latent, though deeply-rooted, in
British society. In addition, Great Britain lacked a strong
nativist tradition, a concern with national identification
which resisted tendencies threatening to weaken it. There
was little disposition to regard immigration as a menace to
some ill-defined concept of Britishness. Labour in Great
Britain was, by the 1890s generally forward-looking, anxious
to cast off the bonds of unlamented past and to reshape
British society. American labour, in its anti-immigration
sentiments, shared the general tenderness towards a pure,
uncorrupted American past and voiced a concern that immigration
was one of the factors threatening to undermine Americanism,
through being identified with damaging and disconcerting
change.[55] The inability in Great Britain to see immigrants

361

in a nativist context combined with still more powerful
forces among the ranks of labour to weaken restrictionism.

One of the strongest defences of immigrants to Great
Britain in the 1890s and 1900s was that they were overwhelmingly
poor Jews. They were depicted with complete conviction as
refugees from economic, political and religious oppression.
As such, they were protected by British liberal traditions of
offering asylum to the persecuted. In this context, attacks
on Jewish immigrants were condemned as anti-semitic and hence
disreputable. There was, indeed, similar sympathy for Jews
in the United States; but since they constituted only a
relatively small proportion of immigration from Southern and
Eastern Europe, the restrictionist attempts were maintained
without drawing the full fire of charges of anti-semitism and
of infringing traditions of hospitality for victims of religious
and political persecution. And because of higher levels of
literacy among the Jewish immigrants it was quickly realised
that operationally the literacy test would have less impact
on them than on other 'new' immigrants.[56]

Again, the strength and persistence of the Free Trade
doctrines in Great Britain assisted the anti-restrictionist
cause, whereas the strong protectionism in the United States
gave a hostage to restrictionists who frequently dwelt on the
inconsistency of protecting employers but not workers. If
protection, as often claimed, was beneficial to the workers
as well as to the employers in safeguarding wages and conditions, it was nonsensical to threaten these wages and
conditions by refusing to apply the same restrictions on
entry to cheap workers as to cheap goods. By contrast, in
Great Britain attacks on Free Trade were resisted not only by
Cobdenite Liberals but also, with few exceptions, by members
of the trade unions and the various socialist parties. In
adhering to Free Trade while supporting increased state
intervention and collectivism in domestic economic and social

policy, trade unions were re-affirming labour's long-standing commitment to cheap food. Free Trade and free immigration were logically connected. A refusal to protect British goods from foreign competition was irreconcilable with a determination to protect the labour which produced these goods. If immigration restriction were adopted, however, protection would logically follow. The influx of cheap goods would constitute as severe an attack on wages and hours of work as the competition of cheap alien labour and other interested groups could rightly demand similar protection.[57]

Finally we may note that because trade unionists saw the Liberal Party after 1900 as their major ally in the campaign to reform trade union law to prevent any more cases like Taff Vale, they felt constrained not to oppose policies, for example free and unrestricted immigration, to which there was strong Liberal commitment. In order to obtain reform of trade union law, labour was prepared to subordinate such restrictionist leanings as it had to the greater goal. This interpretation is surely strengthened by the simultaneous refusal of the 1905 Trade Union Congress either to accept the invitation of their President to condemn the Aliens Bill or to produce a resolution in support of it.[58] This was an embarrassment caused by an awareness of two inconsistencies; firstly between restrictionism and internationalism; secondly, between restrictionism and the necessities of political alliance. By contrast, American labour did not find itself in a comparable position, where one of the two major parties could persuade it to drop its immigration restrictionism in return for other, more coveted political gains.

One conclusion we can draw from this comparative study is that immigration restrictionism within organised labour in Great Britain was paralleled by similar, though more powerful and varied responses in the labour movement in the United States. This attempt to explain why the response to

the challenge of immigration was more inhibited in Great
Britain has focussed, not only on the different magnitude
of the challenge, but also on a combination of the differing
circumstances, political, social, and economic, under which
organised labour in two countries was forced to conduct its
activities and to establish policies for the protection of
its members. In fact, this comparison leaves open to doubt
whether, in Great Britain, socialism, the free trade tradition
and immediate political circumstances could have continued to
restrain restrictionist demands within the labour movement
under the impact of a volume and type of immigration comparable
to that in the United States. In consequence we may need to
revise any assumptions we may have had about the exceptionalism
of the American response to immigration. What was exceptional
in United States' immigration was its volume and heterogeneity.
Given analogous circumstances in Great Britain, can we seriously
doubt that British workers and their representatives would have
responded differently from their American cousins?

NOTES

1. C. Vann Woodward (ed.), The Comparative Approach to
American History (New York, 1968), p. xi; Eugene Genovese,
In Red and Black: Marxian Explorations in Southern and
Afro-American History (New York, 1968), p. 378.

2. Bernard Gainer, The Alien Invasion: The Origins of the
Aliens Act of 1905 (1972), p. 2.

3. The Craftsman, 13 Sept. 1884.

4. Report of the Senate Committee on Labor and Capital, II
(1885), p. 5.

5. Advance Advocate, March 1905, July 1905.

6. Report of the Proceedings of the Seventeenth Annual
Convention of the American Federation of Labor, 1897, pp.
91 and 94 (hereafter AFL Proceedings).

7.   Report of the Committee on Immigration (54 Cong. 1 Sess. Senate Report No. 290), II, p. 1.

8.   A.T. Lane, 'American Labour and European Immigrants in the Late Nineteenth Century', Journal of American Studies, XI (1977), pp. 257-60.

9.   The Garment Worker, 23 June 1905.

10. Locomotive Engineers' Journal, 23 Sept. 1889.

11. AFL Proceedings, 1897, p. 56.

12. Wisconsin State Historical Society Saposs Papers (unprocessed) unpublished MSS.   'The Newcomers in Industry'.

13. Norman J. Ware, Labor in Modern Industrial Society (New York, 1935), p. 33.

14. John Swinton's Paper, 10 July 1887.

15. Locomotive Engineers' Journal, May 1890.

16. Amalgamated Journal, 14 May 1903.

17. John R. Commons, Races and Immigrants in America (repr. New York, 1967), p. 5.

18. The Railroad Trainman, Aug. 1905.

19. The Typographical Journal, Jan. 1904.

20. Monthly Journal of the International Association of Machinists, Sept. 1904; Iron Molders' Journal, April 1906; The Typographical Journal, May 1912.

21. Locomotive Engineers' Journal, March 1891.

22. E.A. Ross, The Old World in the New (1914), pp. 285-6.

23. Samuel Gompers, Seventy Years of Life and Labour (1925) p. 160.

24. Thomas F. Gossett, Race: The History of an Idea in America (repr. New York, 1969), p. 292.

25. Report of the Twenty-Second Annual Trades Union Congress, 1888 p. 41 (Hereafter TUC Report).

26. TUC Report, 1888 p. 50.

27. TUC Report, 1894, p. 59.

28. TUC Report, 1895, p. 46,

29. TUC Report, 1892, pp. 53-4.

30. TUC Report, 1894, pp. 59-60.

31. TUC Report, 1895, p. 46.

32. J.A. Garrard, The English and Immigration 1880-1910 (1971), p. 175.

33. Select Committee on Emigration and Immigration Parliamentary Papers 1888, XI, Q. 2661.

34. SC on Emigration and Immigration P.P. 1889, X, Q. 1419.

35. J. Buckman, 'The Economic and Social History of Alien Immigrants to Leeds, 1880-1914' (unpublished Ph.D. thesis, Strathclyde University 1968).

36. E.P. Hutchinson, Immigrants and their Children 1850-1950 (1956), p. 2; Frank J. Sheridan, 'Italian, Slavic, and Hungarian Unskilled Immigrant Laborers in the United States', Bulletin of the Bureau of Labor, no. 72 (Washington, 1907), p. 404.

37. Gainer, Alien Invasion pp. 2-3.

38. Sheridan, Bull. Bureau of Labor, no. 72, p. 409; US Industrial Commission, Report of the Industrial Commission, XV, p. xx.

39. Gainer, Alien Invasion pp. 3-4; B.R. Mitchell with Phylis Deane, Abstract of British Historical Statistics (Cambridge, 1962), pp. 24-7; Garrard, The English and Immigration p. 213.

40. Grace Abbott, The Immigrant and the Community (New York, 1917), p. 200; US Ind. Comm. XV, p. 299; Sheridan, Bull. Bureau of Labor, no. 72, p. 414.

41. Gainer, Alien Invasion pp. 17-19.

42. Gainer, Alien Invasion p. 10,

43. Garrard, The English and Immigration pp. 213-4.

44. Proceedings of the National Convention of the Socialist Party, 1910, p. 117.

45. Ibid., p. 120.

46. H.A. Clegg, Alan Fox and A.F. Thompson, A History of British Trade Unions since 1889 (1964), I, p. 262.

47. TUC Report, 1888, p. 50; Proceedings of the Eighth Regular Session of the General Assembly of the Knights of Labor, 1884 (Address of the General Master Workman).

48. Garrard, The English and Immigration p. 188.

49. The Clarion, 22 Oct. 1892; Edmund Silberner, 'British Socialism and the Jews', Historia Judaica, XIV (1952), pp. 37-40.

50. Garrard, The English and Immigration p. 198; The Clarion, 12 Oct. 1895.

51. The Clarion, 15 Oct. 1892, 17 Nov. 1894, 12 Oct. 1895.

52. The Clarion, 28 July 1905.

53. Garrard, The English and Immigration p. 195.

54. B.C. Roberts, The Trades Union Congress 1868-1921 (1958), p. 181; The Clarion, 20 Feb. 1892; TUC Report, 1900, p. 54.

55. See e.g. Granite Cutters' Journal, Oct. 1897.

56. US Immigration Commission, Abstracts of Reports of the Immigration Commission, I, p. 99; Garrard, The English and Immigration p. 184.

57. Gainer, Alien Invasion pp. 141-2; Garrard, The English and Immigration pp. 90-1; Trades Union Congress Parliamentary Committee Minutes, 17 June 1903; Frank Bealey and Henry Pelling, Labour and Politics 1900-1906 (1958), p. 202; Roberts, Trades Union Congress p. 180.

58. TUC Report, 1905, p. 48.

Index

Waterproof Garment Makers
Union, 274-5, 284, 285
waterproof garment trade,
274-5, 284, 291
Watson, J.L., 16
Weber, Max, 28
Webster, Martin, 45, 56
Webster, Nesta, 41, 43, 44,
46
Weihe, William, 344
Weiss, William, 276, 289
West Indian immigrants, 29,
32-4, 35, 37n9
West Indian immigration, 22,
24
Wheatley, John, 169-95
Wheatley Act 1924, 170

White, Arnold, 119
White, James, 315
Whitechapel, 354
Wigan, 76
women workers
role in sweating, 270, 272,
290
unionisation, 284, 290, 291,
296
Workers' Friend, 225, 226-7,
230, 234

Yorkshire Post, 231, 251